中文注释版

邂逅莎翁

莎士比亚阅读入门

莎士比亚戏剧故事

Tales from Shakespeare

Shakespeare

策　划　卞学华　刘慧敏　印　娜
主　编　居正华　强友芳　印　娜
副主编　王　芸　冯青韵　许光辉
编　委　颜颖群　范永梅　陈书军　金艳秋　王文雪
　　　　唐　淼　袁大梦　张　莎　董佳琪　朱学丽

華東理工大學出版社
EAST CHINA UNIVERSITY OF SCIENCE AND TECHNOLOGY PRESS
·上海·

图书在版编目(CIP)数据

邂逅莎翁 ：莎士比亚阅读入门 ：莎士比亚戏剧故事 ：中文注释版 ：英文、中文 / 居正华，强友芳，印娜主编. 上海 ：华东理工大学出版社，2025. 1. -- ISBN 978-7-5628-7588-8

Ⅰ. H319.4

中国国家版本馆 CIP 数据核字第 2024ME4375 号

策划编辑 / 舒欣如
责任编辑 / 刘　溱
责任校对 / 金美玉
装帧设计 / 徐　蓉
出版发行 / 华东理工大学出版社有限公司
地址：上海市梅陇路 130 号，200237
电话：021－64250306
网址：www.ecustpress.cn
邮箱：zongbianban@ecustpress.cn
印　　刷 / 上海展强印刷有限公司
开　　本 / 787mm×1092mm　1/16
印　　张 / 15.25
字　　数 / 385 千字
版　　次 / 2025 年 1 月第 1 版
印　　次 / 2025 年 1 月第 1 次
定　　价 / 60.00 元

名家寄语

莎士比亚是一位使人类永久又惊又喜的巨人!

——曹禺(1910—1996,原名万家宝,中国杰出的现代剧作家)

许多人是通过这个译本[①]首先接触到莎士比亚的艺术的,而且长远保持了深刻印象。

——王佐良(1916—1995,诗人、翻译家、教授、英国文学研究专家)

Lamb 的 *Tales from Shakespeare*,林琴南译为《英国诗人吟边燕语》,也使我感受着无上的兴趣。它无形之间给了我很大的影响。后来我虽然也读过[The] *Tempest*、*Hamlet*、*Romeo and Juliet* 等莎氏的原作,但总觉得没有小时所读的那种童话式的译述来得更亲切了。

——郭沫若(1892—1978,中国现代作家、历史学家、考古学家)

上高中以后,大家就开始看点英文的课外读物了。起初看些简单的,比如 *Tales from Shakespeare*(《莎士比亚故事集》),当时译成《莎氏乐府本事》,作者是 19 世纪初年英国文学家 Charles Lamb,他把莎士比亚的剧本编成故事,等于是剧情的说明,写给一般读者看。

——何兆武(1921—2021,历史学家、翻译家、清华大学教授)

读文学作品要有耐性,要看下去,直到看出味道。……四个月读书,最得益的,还是养成了自学英语的习惯。读的是周越然注的《莎氏乐府本事》。

——许国璋(1915—1994,英语教育家、语言学家)

在中学时,英文列入正式课程。在我两年半的初中阶段,英文课是怎样进行的,我已经忘了。我只记得课本是《泰西五十轶事》、《天方夜谭》、《莎氏乐府本事》(*Tales from Shakespeare*)、Washington Irving 的《拊掌录》(*Sketch Book*),好像还念过 Macaulay 的文章。

——季羡林(1911—2009,语言学家、文学家、翻译家、东方学家、古文字学家、佛学家)

---

① 指林纾、魏易翻译的《英国诗人吟边燕语》(*Tales from Shakespeare*)。——编者注

编者寄语

460 年前的今天，1564 年 4 月 23 日，威廉·莎士比亚（William Shakespeare）出生于英国沃里克郡斯特拉福镇，埃文河从城南流过，两岸绿树成荫，风景秀丽，鸟语花香。皇家莎士比亚剧院就坐落于此，如今，来自世界各地的人们都来此“朝圣”，正如莎士比亚在《威尼斯商人》中描述的那样：

From the four corners of the earth they come,
To kiss this shrine, this mortal — breathing saint
（他们从地球的四角迢迢而来，
顶礼这位尘世的仙真）

1616 年 4 月 23 日，莎士比亚去世，与他的生日是同一天，享年 53 岁。莎士比亚创作的作品当中流传下来的有 38 部剧本、两首长诗、154 首十四行诗，以及若干首不同题材的短诗。研究者根据创作类型、思想倾向和风格等因素把莎士比亚戏剧创作生涯分为三个时期：第一个时期，从 1590 年至 1600 年，主要创作的是历史剧和喜剧；第二个时期，从 1601 年至 1607 年，主要创作的是悲剧；第三个时期，从 1608 年至 1612 年，主要创作的是传奇剧。

莎士比亚的喜剧作品以其丰富的情节、生动的人物刻画和深刻的社会洞察而著称。莎士比亚的喜剧作品不仅在当时广受欢迎，而且对后世的文学和戏剧创作产生了深远的影响。莎士比亚的著名喜剧作品包括《仲夏夜之梦》《威尼斯商人》《皆大欢喜》和《第十二夜》等。这些作品不仅展示了莎士比亚对人性深刻的洞察，也反映了他对爱情、友谊、婚姻以及社会问题的看法。《仲夏夜之梦》是一部富有浪漫色彩的喜剧，讲述了一个有情人终成眷属的爱情故事，充满了幻想和抒情。《威尼斯商人》是一部具有讽刺性的喜剧，通过三条线索展开剧情，歌颂了仁爱、友谊和爱情，同时也反映了资本主义早期商业资产阶级与高利贷者之间的矛盾。《皆大欢喜》描绘了一个远离尘世喧嚣的乌托邦世界，充满了对人性美好的歌颂。《第十二夜》讲述了孪生兄妹在海上遇险后各自流落异国他乡，最终找到各自幸福的故事。

莎士比亚的悲剧作品表现了主人公因客观条件、恶势力的迫害及自身过错而陷入失败和毁灭的境地，集中体现了其人生智慧，反映了善与恶的伦理范畴中各种人性的矛盾和冲突，启发了人类对自身及所处社会的深刻思考。莎士比亚著名的悲剧作品包括《罗密欧与朱丽叶》和四大悲剧《哈姆莱特》《奥瑟罗》《李尔王》《麦克白》等。《罗密欧与朱丽叶》讲述了青年罗密欧与朱丽叶倾心相爱，却因两个有着世仇的贵族家庭的阻挠而以身殉情。《哈姆莱特》讲述了丹麦王子哈姆莱特对谋杀其父、骗娶其母并篡夺了王位的叔父进行复仇的故事。剧本塑造了一个与现实有着不可调和矛盾的、孤军作战的、在复仇过程中犹豫彷徨的、最后以悲剧结局的典型形象——哈姆莱特。

莎士比亚在 1608 年到 1612 年间创作的带有相同特征的四部戏剧——《泰尔亲王配力克里斯》《辛白林》《冬天的故事》《暴风雨》，被称为传奇剧。《暴风雨》是莎士比亚的最后一部完整的杰作，歌颂了纯真的爱情、友谊和人与人之间的亲善关系，全剧充满诗意与平和宁静的气息。

19 世纪英国作家查尔斯·兰姆（Charles Lamb）与其姐姐玛丽·兰姆（Mary Lamb）合著的《莎士比亚戏剧故事集》（*Tales from Shakespeare*）是莎士比亚戏剧改编史上的重要里程碑。这部作品几乎可以说是独一无二的，任何其他改编作品都无法望其项背。兰姆姐弟将莎士比亚的戏剧语言改编成通俗易懂的叙事散文，同时努力保持原著的“原汁原味”。兰姆姐弟坚信，“这些故事足以丰富年轻读者的想象，提高他们的品质，帮助他们抛弃一切自私自利、唯利是图的想法；同时也教给他们一切美好而高贵的思想和行为，让他们变得有礼貌、仁慈、慷慨和富有同情心”。

《莎士比亚戏剧故事集》早期在中国的译名是《莎氏乐府本事》。在早期的中国英语教学中，无论是教会学校的英语教学，还是普通初高级中学的英语教学，一般都把《莎氏乐府本事》选入教科书或阅读材料之中。可以说，这本书在中国的英语教育史中占有重要的地位，影响了无数的英语学习者。

文学翻译领域的国际最高奖项之一“北极光”杰出文学翻译奖获得者许渊冲在中学时代曾一度非常厌恶英语，英语成绩在班里也只是中下游水平。高二的时候，他将教材《英文短篇背诵选》中的30篇文章全背下来，其中包括莎士比亚《裘力斯·凯撒》中的演说词。背诵这些文章，不仅使他的英语成绩显著提升，更引起了他对英语的兴趣。后来，在大学统一招生考试中，许渊冲在英文科目中取得了85分的高分，如愿考进了国立西南联合大学外文系。

著名美学家朱光潜先生曾说：“我觉得初学者与其费那么大劲去死记单词，作那些支离破碎的语法练习，倒不如精选精读几篇经得起仔细推敲的散文作品或诗歌，把它们懂透背熟，真正消化成为自己的精神营养，这样就会培养成敏锐的语言感，也就会明白语言和文学不能分门别户，各自独立。”无独有偶，著名翻译家梁实秋在建议学生如何学英语时曾经说过：“先背诵莎士比亚的戏剧，再谈如何学习英语。”

英国诗人弥尔顿曾为莎士比亚写下这样的诗句——

他善于用神圣的火焰
把我们重新塑造得更好。

无经典不英语，无莎翁不经典。邂逅莎翁，遇见更好的自己。

编 者

2024年4月23日

乐学亭·安定书院·泰州

To the Reader
致读者

This Figure, that thou here seest put,	这里印着,你看到的人像,
It was for gentle Shakespeare cut;	是为高贵的莎士比亚所镌刻;
Wherein the graver had a strife	在这里镌刻者同自然进行斗争,
With nature to outdo the life.	想做到胜过活着的本人;
O, could he but have drawn his wit	啊,倘若他能够在铜板上
As well in brasse as he hath hit	刻画出他机智的文才
His face, the print would then surpass	像他的面貌那样真,那这幅版画
All that was ever writ in brasse!	将超过以往一切铜刻的铭图。
But since he cannot, reader, look	但他既然做不到,请读者
Not on his picture, but his book	把目光从画像转向他的书。

——本·琼森(Ben Jonson,1572—1637)

目录
Contents

COMEDY 喜剧

皆大欢喜
As You Like It

All the world's a stage，
And all the men and women merely players：
They have their exits and their entrances；
And one man in his time plays many parts

全世界是一个舞台，
所有的男男女女不过是一些演员；
他们都有下场的时候，也都有上场的时候。
一个人一生中扮演着好几个角色

当我读到他(莎士比亚)的第一页,就使我这一生都属于他了!

读完第一部,我就像一个生下来的盲人,一只奇异的手在瞬间使我的双眼看到了光明……感谢赐我智慧的神灵。

——歌德

莎士比亚——这位神圣而崇高的莎士比亚——对地狱、人间和天堂全都了解。他是自然的主宰……通过他的灵感的天眼,看到了宇宙脉搏的跃动。他的每一个剧本都是一个世界的缩影,包含着整个现在、过去及未来。

——别林斯基

《皆大欢喜》是莎士比亚全部喜剧中最甜美、最愉快的一部。当莎士比亚写这部田园戏剧时,他正生活在亚登森林。他已经实现了一个伟大雄心——完成了历史剧的创作,但还没有开始他的悲剧。《皆大欢喜》正是一个暂停休息之处。他把他的想象力伸展到了森林里来寻求安息。

——爱德华·道登

主要人物

Duke Senior　老公爵　放逐在亚登森林

Jaques　杰奎斯　随侍公爵之贵族

Frederick　弗莱德里克　公爵之弟,篡位者

Rosalind　罗瑟琳　老公爵的女儿

Celia　西莉娅　弗莱德里克的女儿

Orlando　奥兰多　罗兰·德·鲍埃爵士(Sir Rowland de Boys)的儿子

Oliver　奥列佛　罗兰·德·鲍埃爵士(Sir Rowland de Boys)的儿子

Touchstone　试金石　小丑

地点　奥列佛宅旁庭园;篡位者的宫廷;亚登森林

As You Like It

During the time that France was divided into provinces (or dukedoms[1] as they were called) there reigned[2] in one of these provinces an usurper[3], who had deposed[4] and banished[5] his elder brother, the lawful duke.

The Duke, who was thus driven from his dominions[6], retired with a few faithful followers to the forest of Arden; and here the good duke lived with his loving friends, who had put themselves into a voluntary exile[7] for his sake, while their land and revenues[8] enriched the false usurper; and * custom soon made the life of careless ease they led here more sweet to them than the pomp[9] and uneasy splendour[10] of a courtier's[11] life.[i] Here they lived like the old Robin Hood[12] of England, and to this forest many noble youths daily resorted[13] from the court, and did fleet the time[14] carelessly, as they did who lived in the golden age. In the summer they lay along under the fine shade of the large forest trees, marking[15] the playful sports of the wild deer; and * so fond were they of these poor dappled[16] fools, who seemed to be the native inhabitants of the forest, that it grieved[17] them to be forced to kill them to supply

---

① dukedom [ˈdjuːkdəm] *n*. 公爵的领地
② reign [reɪn] *v*. 当政,统治 rule, govern, administer, be in power
③ usurper [juːˈzɜːpə(r)] *n*. 篡位者
④ depose [dɪˈpəʊz] *v*. 废黜 oust, dismiss, displace, demote
⑤ banish [ˈbænɪʃ] *v*. 驱逐 exclude, expel, deport, drive away
⑥ dominion [dəˈmɪnjən] *n*. 领土 kingdom, territory, domain
⑦ exile [ˈeksaɪl] *n*. 流放 banishment, expulsion, deportation
⑧ revenue [ˈrevənjuː] *n*. 收入 income, interest, returns, profits
⑨ pomp [pɒmp] *n*. 排场;盛况 ceremony, grandeur, splendour
⑩ splendour [ˈsplendə(r)] *n*. 壮丽 magnificence, glory, grandeur
⑪ courtier [ˈkɔːtiə(r)] *n*. 侍臣 attendant, follower, liegeman, lackey
⑫ Robin Hood 罗宾汉;绿林好汉;劫富济贫者
⑬ resort [rɪˈzɔːt] *v*. 常去 go, visit, haunt, frequent, head for
⑭ fleet the time 消磨时光 kill time
⑮ mark [mɑːk] *v*. 观看 look at, watch, observe, regard, remark
⑯ dappled [ˈdæpld] *adj*. 斑驳的;有斑点的 mottled, spotted, speckled, pied
⑰ grieve [griːv] *v*. 使悲伤 sadden, distress, dismay, agonize

themselves with venison① for their food.[ii] When the cold winds of winter made the duke feel the change of his adverse fortune, he would endure② it patiently, and say: "These chilling③ winds which blow upon my body are true counsellors④; they do not flatter⑤, but represent⑥ truly to me my condition; and though they bite sharply, their tooth is nothing like so keen⑦ as that of unkindness and ingratitude⑧. *I find that howsoever⑨ men speak against adversity⑩, yet some sweet uses are to be extracted⑪ from it; like the jewel, precious for medicine, which is taken from the head of the venomous⑫ and despised toad.[iii]" *In this manner did the patient duke draw a useful moral⑬ from everything that he saw; and by the help of this moralizing⑭ turn, in that life of his, remote from public haunts⑮, he could find tongues in trees, books in the running brooks, sermons⑯ in stones, and good in everything.[iv]

The banished duke had an only daughter, named Rosalind, whom the usurper, duke Frederick, when he banished her father, still retained⑰ in his court as a companion for his own daughter Celia. *A strict friendship subsisted⑱ between these ladies, which the disagreement between their fathers did not in the least interrupt, Celia striving⑲ by every kindness in her power to make amends⑳ to Rosalind for the injustice㉑ of her own father in deposing the father of Rosalind;[v] and whenever the thoughts of her father's banishment㉒, and her own dependence on the false usurper, made Rosalind melancholy㉓, Celia's whole care was to comfort and console㉔ her.

One day, when Celia was talking in her usual kind manner to Rosalind, saying: "I pray you, Rosalind, my sweet cousin, be merry," a messenger entered from the duke, to tell them that if

---

① venison ['venɪsn] *n*. 鹿肉
② endure [ɪn'djʊə(r)] *v*. 忍耐 stand, bear, tolerate, put up with
③ chilling ['tʃɪlɪŋ] *adj*. 寒冷的 chilly, cold, freezing, frigid, biting
④ counsellor ['kaʊnsələ(r)] *n*. 顾问 adviser, consultant, solicitor
⑤ flatter ['flætə(r)] *v*. 奉承 praise, compliment, court, butter up
⑥ represent [ˌreprɪ'zent] *v*. 描绘 depict, describe, outline
⑦ keen [kiːn] *adj*. 锐利的,敏锐的 sharp, pointed, edged, cutting, biting
⑧ ingratitude [ɪn'grætɪtjuːd] *n*. 忘恩负义 ungratefulness, thanklessnesss
⑨ howsoever [ˌhaʊsəʊ'evə(r)] *adv*. 不管怎样 nevertheless, nonetheless
⑩ adversity [əd'vɜːsəti] *n*. 困境 hardship, distress, misfortune
⑪ extract [ɪk'strækt] *v*. 提取 obtain, withdraw, draw out
⑫ venomous ['venəməs] *adj*. 有毒的 poisonous, toxic, virulent
⑬ moral ['mɒrəl] *n*. 寓意 lesson, meaning, point, message
⑭ moralize ['mɒrəlaɪz] *v*. 教化,说教 preach, teach, lecture
⑮ haunt [hɔːnt] *n*. 常去的地方 meeting place, resort, rendezvous
⑯ sermon ['sɜːmən] *n*.说教 homily, preaching, lesson, lecture
⑰ retain [rɪ'teɪn] *v*. 保留 keep, preserve, conserve, hold onto
⑱ subsist [səb'sɪst] *v*. 存在 live, last, continue, exist, be present
⑲ strive [straɪv] *v*. 努力 try, endeavour, make every effort
⑳ amend [ə'mend] *n*. 赔偿 reparation, compensation, recompense
㉑ injustice [ɪn'dʒʌstɪs] *n*. 不公平 unfairness, unjustness, inequity
㉒ banishment ['bænɪʃmənt] *n*. 放逐 expulsion, exile, dismissal
㉓ melancholy ['melənkəli] *adj*. 忧郁的 sad, low, blue, depressed
㉔ console [kən'səʊl] *v*. 安慰 comfort, relieve, soothe, solace

they wished to see a wrestling match, which was just going to begin, they must come instantly to the court before the palace; and Celia, thinking it would amuse Rosalind, agreed to go and see it.

In those times wrestling, which is only practised now by country clowns①, was a favourite sport even in the courts of princes, and before fair ladies and princesses. To this wrestling match, therefore, Celia and Rosalind went. They found that it was likely to prove a very tragical② sight; for a large and powerful man, who had been long practised in the art of wrestling, and had slain③ many men in contests④ of this kind, was just going to wrestle with a very young man, who, from his extreme youth and inexperience in the art, the beholders⑤ all thought would certainly be killed.

When the duke saw Celia and Rosalind, he said: "How now, daughter and niece, are you crept⑥ hither⑦ to see the wrestling? * You will take little delight in it; there is such odds⑧ in the men: in pity to this young man, I would wish to persuade him from wrestling.[vi] Speak to him, ladies, and see if you can move him."

The ladies were well pleased to perform this humane⑨ office, and first Celia entreated⑩ the young stranger that he would desist⑪ from the attempt; and then * Rosalind spoke so kindly to him, and with such feeling consideration for the danger he was about to undergo⑫, that instead of being persuaded by her gentle words to forgo⑬ his purpose, all his thoughts were bent⑭ to distinguish himself⑮ by his courage in this lovely lady's eyes.[vii] He refused the request of Celia and Rosalind in such graceful and modest words, that they felt still more concern for him; he concluded his refusal with saying: "I am sorry to deny such fair and excellent ladies anything. * But let your fair eyes and gentle wishes go with me to my trial, wherein if I be conquered⑯ there is one shamed that was never gracious⑰; if I am killed, there is one dead that is willing to die;[viii] * I shall do my friends no wrong, for I have none to lament⑱ me; the world no injury, for in it I have nothing; for I only fill up a place in the world which may be

---

① clown [klaʊn] *n*. 乡下人;粗鲁笨拙的人 peasant, boor
② tragical ['trædʒɪkəl] *adj*. 悲惨的 tragic, miserable, unfortunate
③ slay [sleɪ] *v*. (slew, slain) 杀死 kill, slaughter
④ contest ['kɒntest] *n*. 比赛 fight, game, match, competition
⑤ beholder [bɪ'həʊldə(r)] *n*. 观看者,旁观者 observer, onlooker, spectator
⑥ creep [kriːp] *v*. (crept) 爬行 crawl, worm, wriggle, squirm
⑦ hither ['hɪðə(r)] *adv*. 〈古〉向此处,到此处
⑧ odd [ɒd] *n*. 差别,不同 difference, disparity, dissimilarity
⑨ humane [hjuː'meɪn] *adj*. 仁慈的 kind, merciful, sympathetic
⑩ entreat [ɪn'triːt] *v*. 恳求,请求 beg, pray, petition, plead with
⑪ desist [dɪ'zɪst] *v*. 停止 stop, cease, end, discontinue
⑫ undergo [ˌʌndə'gəʊ] *v*. 经受 experience, suffer, go through
⑬ forgo [fɔː'gəʊ] *v*. 放弃 abandon, sacrifice, surrender, give up
⑭ bent [bent] *adj*. 下定决心的 determined, resolute, single-minded
⑮ distinguish oneself 使自己出众 excel oneself
⑯ conquer ['kɒŋkə(r)] *v*. 战胜 defeat, beat, triumph, prevail over
⑰ gracious ['greɪʃəs] *adj*. 慈悲的;尊贵的,仁慈的
⑱ lament [lə'ment] *adj*. 哀悼 bemoan, grieve, mourn, weep over

better supplied when I have made it empty.[ix]"

And now the wrestling match began. Celia wished the young stranger might not be hurt; but Rosalind felt most for him. The friendless state which he said he was in, and that he wished to die, made Rosalind think that he was like herself, unfortunate; and she pitied him so much, and so deep an interest she took in his danger while he was wrestling, that she might almost be said at that moment to have fallen in love with him.

The kindness shown this unknown youth by these fair and noble ladies gave him courage and strength, so that he performed wonders; and in the end completely conquered his antagonist①, who was so much hurt, that for a while he was unable to speak or move.

The duke Frederick was much pleased with the courage and skill shown by this young stranger; and desired to know his name and parentage②, meaning to take him under his protection.

The stranger said his name was Orlando, and that he was the youngest son of Sir Rowland de Boys.

Sir Rowland de Boys, the father of Orlando, had been dead some years; but when he was living, he had been a true subject③ and dear friend of the banished duke; therefore, when Frederick heard Orlando was the son of his banished brother's friend, all his liking for this brave young man was changed into displeasure, and he left the place in very ill humour④. Hating to hear the very name of any of his brother's friends, and yet still admiring the valour⑤ of the youth, he said, as he went out, that he wished Orlando had been the son of any other man.

Rosalind was delighted to hear that her new favourite was the son of her father's old friend; and she said to Celia: "My father loved Sir Rowland de Boys, and * if I had known this young man was his son, I would have added tears to my entreaties⑥ before he should have ventured⑦.[x]"

The ladies then went up to him; and seeing him abashed⑧ by the sudden displeasure shown by the duke, they spoke kind and encouraging words to him; and Rosalind, when they were going away, turned back to speak some more civil⑨ things to the brave young son of her father's old friend; and taking a chain from off her neck, she said: "Gentleman, wear this for me. * I am out of suits with fortune, or I would give you a more valuable present.[xi]"

When the ladies were alone, Rosalind's talk being still of Orlando, Celia began to perceive⑩ her cousin had fallen in love with the handsome young wrestler, and she said to Rosalind: "Is it possible you should fall in love so suddenly?" Rosalind replied: "The duke, my father, loved his father dearly⑪." "But," said Celia, "does it therefore follow that you should love his son dearly?

---

① antagonist [æn'tæɡənɪst] *n*. 对手 opponent, rival, adversary
② parentage ['peərəntɪdʒ] *n*. 出身 family, birth, origin, descent
③ subject ['sʌbdʒɪkt] *n*. 臣民
④ ill humour 坏心情 bad mood
⑤ valour ['vælə(r)] *n*. 英勇 bravery, courage, heroism, boldness
⑥ entreaty [ɪn'triːti] *n*. 恳求 plea, petition, prayer, appeal
⑦ venture ['ventʃə(r)] *v*. 冒险做 dare, risk, chance, stake
⑧ abashed [ə'bæʃt] *adj*. 窘迫的,不安的 embarrassed, ashamed
⑨ civil ['sɪvl] *adj*. 礼貌的 polite, civilized, courteous, considerate
⑩ perceive [pə'siːv] *v*. 察觉 see, notice, note, discover, observe
⑪ dearly ['dɪəli] *adv*. 深深地 greatly, deeply, extremely, profoundly

For then I ought to hate him, for my father hated his father; yet I do not hate Orlando."

Frederick being enraged① at the sight of Sir Rowland de Boys' son, which reminded him of the many friends the banished duke had among the nobility②, and having been for some time displeased with his niece, because the people praised her for her virtues, and pitied her for her good father's sake, his malice③ suddenly broke out against her; and while Celia and Rosalind were talking of Orlando, Frederick entered the room, and with looks full of anger ordered Rosalind instantly to leave the palace, and follow her father into banishment; telling Celia, who in vain pleaded④ for her, that he had only suffered⑤ Rosalind to stay upon her account. "I did not then," said Celia, "entreat⑥ you to let her stay, for I was too young at that time to value her; but now that I know her worth, and that we so long have slept together, rose⑦ at the same instant, learned, played, and eat together, I cannot live out of her company." Frederick replied: "*She is too subtle⑧ for you; her smoothness, her very silence, and her patience speak to the people, and they pity her.[xii] You are a fool to plead for her, for you will seem more bright and virtuous⑨ when she is gone; therefore open not your lips in her favour, for the doom⑩ which I have passed upon her is irrevocable⑪."

When Celia found she could not prevail upon⑫ her father to let Rosalind remain with her, she generously resolved⑬ to accompany her; and leaving her father's palace that night, she went along with her friend to seek Rosalind's father, the banished duke, in the forest of Arden.

Before they set out, Celia considered that it would be unsafe for two young ladies to travel in the rich clothes they then wore; she therefore proposed⑭ that they should disguise⑮ their rank⑯ by dressing themselves like country maids. Rosalind said it would be a still greater protection if one of them was to be dressed like a man; and so *it was quickly agreed on between them, that as Rosalind was the tallest, she should wear the dress of a young countryman, and Celia should be

---

① enrage [ɪn'reɪdʒ] *v*. 激怒 anger, provoke, irritate, infuriate
② nobility [nəʊ'bɪləti] *n*. 贵族 aristocracy, lords, elite, nobles
③ malice ['mælɪs] *n*. 恶意 spite, enmity, hatred, ill will
④ plead [pliːd] *v*. 恳求 appeal, beg, petition, solicit, beseech
⑤ suffer ['sʌfə(r)] *v*. 容忍 bear, stand, tolerate, brook, put up with
⑥ entreat [ɪn'triːt] *v*. 恳求 beg, appeal to, petition, plead with
⑦ rise [raɪz] *v*. (rose, risen) 起床;升起
⑧ subtle ['sʌtl] *adj*. 狡猾的 crafty, cunning, shrewd
⑨ virtuous ['vɜːtʃuəs] *adj*. 品行端正的 moral, upright, honourable
⑩ doom [duːm] *n*. 厄运,劫数
⑪ irrevocable [ɪ'revəkəbl] *adj*. 不可更改的 unchangeable, irreversible
⑫ prevail upon 说服 persuade, convince, win over
⑬ resolve [rɪ'zɒlv] *v*. 决定 decide, determine, make up sb.'s mind
⑭ propose [prə'pəʊz] *v*. 提议 suggest, advise, recommend
⑮ disguise [dɪs'gaɪz] *v*. 掩饰,伪装 hide, cover, conceal, keep secret
⑯ rank [ræŋk] *n*. 地位 status, level, position, standing

habited① like a country lass②, and that they should say they were brother and sister, and Rosalind said she would be called Ganymede, and Celia chose the name of Aliena.[xiii]

In this disguise, and taking their money and jewels to defray③ their expenses, these fair princesses set out on their long travel; for the forest of Arden was a long way off, beyond the boundaries④ of the duke's dominions.

The Lady Rosalind (or Ganymede as she must now be called) with her manly garb⑤ seemed to have put on a manly courage. The faithful friendship Celia had shown in accompanying Rosalind so many weary⑥ miles, made the new brother, in recompense⑦ for this true love, exert⑧ a cheerful spirit, as if he were indeed Ganymede, the rustic⑨ and stout-hearted⑩ brother of the gentle village maiden, Aliena.

When at last they came to the forest of Arden, they no longer found the convenient inns and good accommodations⑪ they had met with on the road; and being in want of food and rest, Ganymede, who had so merrily cheered his sister with pleasant speeches and happy remarks all the way, now owned to Aliena that * he was so weary, he could find in his heart to disgrace⑫ his man's apparel⑬, and cry like a woman;[xiv] and Aliena declared she could go no farther; and then again * Ganymede tried to recollect⑭ that it was a man's duty to comfort and console a woman, as the weaker vessel⑮;[xv] and to seem courageous⑯ to his new sister; he said: "Come, have a good heart⑰, my sister Aliena; we are now at the end of our travel, in the forest of Arden." But feigned⑱ manliness⑲ and forced courage would no longer support them; for though they were in the forest of Arden, they knew not where to find the duke: and here the travel of these weary ladies might have come to a sad conclusion, for they might have lost themselves, and perished⑳ for want of food; but providentially㉑, as they were sitting on the grass, almost dying with fatigue㉒ and hopeless of any relief㉓, a countryman chanced to pass that way, and Ganymede once more

---

① habit [ˈhæbɪt] *v*. 给……穿衣

② lass [læs] *n*. 少女 maiden, girl, maid, damsel, lassie

③ defray [dɪˈfreɪ] *v*. 支付 pay, cover, settle, discharge

④ boundary [ˈbaʊndri] *n*. 边界 limit, bound, confine, border

⑤ garb [gɑːb] *n*. 衣服,服装 garment, clothes, dress, costume, outfit

⑥ weary [ˈwɪəri] *adj*. 疲劳的 tiring, wearing, wearisome

⑦ recompense [ˈrekəmpens] *n*. 补偿 compensation, repayment

⑧ exert [ɪgˈzɜːt] *v*. 运用 use, apply, exercise, employ, put forth

⑨ rustic [ˈrʌstɪk] *adj*. 质朴的 simple, plain, unpolished, unrefined

⑩ stout-hearted [ˌstaʊt ˈhɑːtɪd] *adj*. 坚毅的 brave, bold, courageous

⑪ accommodation [əˌkɒməˈdeɪʃn] *n*. 住宿 board, lodging

⑫ disgrace [dɪsˈgreɪs] *v*. 使蒙受耻辱 shame, dishonor, humiliate

⑬ apparel [əˈpærəl] *n*. 衣服 garment, clothes, dress, costume

⑭ recollect [ˌrekəˈlekt] *v*. 想起,回忆 remember, recall, call to mind

⑮ vessel [ˈvesl] *n*. 容器;器皿 container, receptacle, bowl, tank

⑯ courageous [kəˈreɪdʒəs] *adj*. 勇敢的 brave, bold, heroic, fearless

⑰ have a good heart 有一颗善良的心

⑱ feign [feɪn] *v*. 假装 pretend, affect, put on, make a show of

⑲ manliness [ˈmænlinəs] *n*. 男子气概 masculinity, manhood

⑳ perish [ˈperɪʃ] *v*. 死亡 die, expire, decease, lose one's life

㉑ providentially [ˌprɒvɪˈdenʃəli] *adv*. 幸运地 luckily, fortunately

㉒ fatigue [fəˈtiːg] *n*. 疲劳 tiredness, weariness

㉓ relief [rɪˈliːf] *n*. 救济 aid, help, support, assistance, deliverance

tried to speak with a manly boldness[1], saying: "Shepherd[2], if love or gold can in this desert[3] place procure[4] us entertainment[5], I pray you bring us where we may rest ourselves; for this young

maid, my sister, is much fatigued with travelling, and faints[6] for want of food."

The man replied that he was only a servant to a shepherd, and that his master's house was just going to be sold, and therefore they would find but poor entertainment; but that if they would go with him, they should be welcome to what there was. They followed the man, the near prospect[7] of relief giving them fresh strength; and bought the house and sheep of the shepherd, and took the man who conducted them to the shepherd's house to wait on[8] them; and being by this means so fortunately provided with a neat cottage, and well supplied with provisions[9], they agreed to stay here till they could learn in what part of the forest the duke dwelt[10].

When they were rested after the fatigue of their journey, they began to like their new way of life, and almost fancied themselves the shepherd and shepherdess[11] they feigned to be; yet sometimes Ganymede remembered he had once been the same Lady Rosalind who had so dearly loved the brave Orlando, because he was the son of old Sir Rowland, her father's friend; and though Ganymede thought that Orlando was many miles distant, even so many weary miles as they had travelled, yet it soon appeared that Orlando was also in the forest of Arden: and in this manner this strange event came to pass[12].

Orlando was the youngest son of Sir Rowland de Boys, who, when he died, left him (Orlando being then very young) to the care of his eldest brother Oliver, [*] charging[13] Oliver on his blessing to give his brother a good education, and provide for him as became[14] the dignity[15] of their ancient house.[xvi] Oliver proved an unworthy[16] brother; and disregarding[17] the commands of his dying father, he never put his brother to school, but kept him at home untaught and entirely neglected[18].

---

① boldness [ˈbəuldnəs] *n*. 大胆 courage, nerve, fearlessness
② shepherd [ˈʃepəd] *n*. 牧羊人 herdsman, herder
③ desert [ˈdezət] *adj*. 荒凉的 barren, waste, wild, bare, desolate
④ procure [prəˈkjuə(r)] *v*. 取得 obtain, gain, secure, acquire
⑤ entertainment [ˌentəˈteɪnmənt] *n*. 招待,款待 accommodation
⑥ faint [feɪnt] *v*. 昏厥 pass out, swoon, lose consciousness
⑦ prospect [ˈprɒspekt] *n*. 希望 hope, promise, expectation
⑧ wait on 服侍 serve, tend/attend to, look after, take care of
⑨ provision [prəˈvɪʒn] *n*. 饮食供应 foodstuff, eatables
⑩ dwell [dwel] *v*. (dwelt) 居住 live, stay, reside, lodge, abide
⑪ shepherdess [ˌʃepəˈdes] *n*. 牧羊女 female shepherd
⑫ come to pass 发生 happen, occur, take place, spring up
⑬ charge [tʃɑːdʒ] *v*. 吩咐 command, order, demand, require, bid
⑭ become [bɪˈkʌm] *v*. (became, become)适合 suit, match, agree with, conform to
⑮ dignity [ˈdɪgnəti] *n*. 高贵 honour, standing, station, status
⑯ unworthy [ʌnˈwɜːði] *adj*. 不值得的 dishonourable, disgraceful
⑰ disregard [ˌdɪsrɪˈgɑːd] *v*. 不理会 ignore, overlook, neglect
⑱ neglect [nɪˈglekt] *v*. 忽视 ignore, overlook, turn sb's back on

* But in his nature and in the noble qualities of his mind Orlando so much resembled① his excellent father, that without any advantages of education he seemed like a youth who had been bred② with the utmost③ care; and Oliver so envied④ the fine person and dignified⑤ manners of his untutored⑥ brother, that at last he wished to destroy him; and to effect⑦ this he set on⑧ people to persuade him to wrestle with the famous wrestler, who, as has been before related⑨, had killed so many men.[xvii] Now, * it was this cruel brother's neglect⑩ of him which made Orlando say he wished to die, being so friendless.[xviii]

When, contrary to the wicked⑪ hopes he had formed, his brother proved victorious⑫, his envy and malice⑬ knew no bounds⑭, and he swore⑮ he would burn the chamber where Orlando slept. He was overheard⑯ making this vow⑰ by one that had been an old and faithful servant to their father, and that loved Orlando because he resembled Sir Rowland. This old man went out to meet him when he returned from the duke's palace, and when he saw Orlando, the peril⑱ his dear young master was in made him break out into these passionate⑲ exclamations⑳: "* O my gentle master, my sweet master, O you memory㉑ of old Sir Rowland![xix] Why are you virtuous? Why are you gentle, strong, and valiant㉒? And why would you be so fond㉓ to overcome the famous wrestler? * Your praise is come too swiftly home before you.[xx]" Orlando, wondering what all this meant, asked him what was the matter. And then the old man told him how his wicked brother, envying the love all people bore㉔ him, and now hearing the fame he had gained by his victory in the duke's palace, intended to destroy him, by setting fire to his chamber that night; and in conclusion, advised him to escape the danger he was in by instant flight; and knowing Orlando had no money, Adam (for that was the good old man's name) had brought out with him his own little

---

① resemble [rɪ'zembl] v. 相像 look like, be similar to, take after
② breed [briːd] v. (bred) 培养 rear, raise, nurture, nourish, bring up
③ utmost ['ʌtməʊst] adj. 最大的 greatest, highest, maximum
④ envy ['envi] v. 忌妒 resent, begrudge, be envious/jealous
⑤ dignified ['dɪgnɪfaɪd] adj. 高贵的 noble, distinguished, decorous
⑥ untutored [ˌʌn'tjuːtəd] adj. 未受教育的 uneducated, untaught
⑦ effect [ɪ'fekt] v. 实现 cause, effectuate, bring about, carry out
⑧ set on 唆使 urge, encourage, prompt, egg on, stir up
⑨ relate [rɪ'leɪt] v. 叙述 tell, recount, describe, express, narrate
⑩ neglect [nɪ'glekt] n. 忽略 negligence, inattention, unconcern
⑪ wicked ['wɪkɪd] adj. 邪恶的 bad, evil, vile, devilish, black-hearted
⑫ victorious [vɪk'tɔːriəs] adj. 胜利的 winning, successful, triumphant
⑬ malice ['mælɪs] n. 恶意 spite, animosity, enmity, bad blood
⑭ bound [baʊnd] n. 界限 limits, confines, boundary
⑮ swear [sweə(r)] v. (swore, sworn) 发誓 vow
⑯ overhear [ˌəʊvə'hɪə(r)] v. (overheard)偶然听到 listen in, eavesdrop, snoop
⑰ vow [vaʊ] n. 誓言 promise, commitment, pledge, oath
⑱ peril ['perəl] n. 危险 danger, risk, threat, hazard, jeopardy
⑲ passionate ['pæʃənət] adj. 狂热的 wild, excited, enthusiastic
⑳ exclamation [ˌekskləˈmeɪʃn] n. 惊叫 cry, shout, yell, utterance
㉑ memory ['meməri] v. 使想起 remind, call/bring to mind
㉒ valiant ['væliənt] adj. 英勇的 brave, heroic, courageous, fearless
㉓ fond [fɒnd] adj. 天真的,不切实际的 unrealistic, empty, foolish, absurd
㉔ bear [beə(r)] v. (bore, borne) 怀有 hold, maintain, entertain

hoard①, and he said: "*I have five hundred crowns②, the thrifty③ hire④ I saved under your father, and laid by to be provision⑤ for me when my old limbs⑥ should become unfit for service;[xxi] take that, and * he that doth the ravens⑦ feed be comfort to my age![xxii] Here is the gold; all this I give to you: let me be your servant; though I look old I will do the service of a younger man in all your business and necessities⑧." "O good old man!" said Orlando, "* how well appears in you the constant service of the old world![xxiii] You are not for the fashion of these times. * We will go along together, and before your youthful wages are spent, I shall light upon some means for both our maintenance⑨.[xxiv]"

Together then this faithful servant and his loved master set out; and Orlando and Adam travelled on, uncertain what course to pursue⑩, till they came to the forest of Arden, and there they found themselves in the same distress⑪ for want of food that Ganymede and Aliena had been. They wandered on, seeking some human habitation⑫, till they were almost spent⑬ with hunger and fatigue. Adam at last said: "O my dear master, I die for want of food. I can go no farther!" He then laid himself down, thinking to make that place his grave⑭, and bade his dear master farewell⑮. Orlando, seeing him in this weak state, took his old servant up in his arms, and carried him under the shelter of some pleasant trees; and he said to him: "Cheerly, old Adam, rest your weary limbs here awhile, and do not talk of dying!"

Orlando then searched about to find some food, and he happened to arrive at that part of the forest where the duke was; and he and his friends were just going to eat their dinner, this royal duke being seated on the grass, under no other canopy⑯ than the shady covert⑰ of some large trees.

Orlando, whom hunger had made desperate⑱, drew his sword, intending to take their meat by force, and said: "Forbear⑲ and eat no more; I must have your food!" * The duke asked him, if distress had made him so bold, or if he were a rude despiser of good manners.[xxv] On this Orlando said, he was dying with hunger; and then the duke told him he was welcome to sit down and eat

---

① hoard [hɔːd] *n*. 积蓄 store, fund, supply, reserve, accumulation
② crown [kraʊn] *n*. 克朗(英国旧币制的 5 先令硬币)
③ thrifty [ˈθrɪfti] *adj*. 节俭的 economical, frugal, saving, sparing
④ hire [ˈhaɪə(r)] *n*. 费用,工钱 charge, rental, price, cost, fee
⑤ provision [prəˈvɪʒn] *n*. 预备金 reserve fund, store, savings
⑥ limb [lɪm] *n*. 肢;臂;腿 part, arm, leg, extremity
⑦ raven [ˈreɪvn] *n*. 渡鸦
⑧ necessity [nəˈsesəti] *n*. 需要,必要
⑨ maintenance [ˈmeɪntənəns] *n*. 生活 subsistence, sustenance
⑩ pursue [pəˈsjuː] *v*. 致力于,从事 undertake, work at, engage in
⑪ distress [dɪˈstres] *n*. 危难 danger, risk, difficulty, peril, jeopardy
⑫ habitation [ˌhæbɪˈteɪʃn] *n*. 住处 residence, quarter, lodging
⑬ spend [spend] *v*. (spent) 耗尽 use up, exhaust, consume
⑭ grave [greɪv] *n*. 坟墓 tomb, sepulchre, last resting place
⑮ bid sb. farewell 同某人告别 say goodbye to sb.
⑯ canopy [ˈkænəpi] *n*. 顶篷,华盖;(顶篷似的)树荫 awning, covering, shade, shelter
⑰ covert [ˈkʌvət] *n*. 灌木林 thicket, bushes, underwood, coppice
⑱ desperate [ˈdespərət] *adj*. 绝望的 hopeless, despairing, in despair
⑲ forbear [fɔːˈbeə(r)] *v*. 克制 hold back, withhold, refrain, restrain

with them. Orlando hearing him speak so gently, put up his sword, and blushed① with shame at the rude manner in which he had demanded their food. "Pardon me, I pray you," said he. "* I thought that all things had been savage② here, and therefore I put on the countenance③ of stern④ command; but whatever men you are, that in this desert, under the shade of melancholy boughs⑤, lose and neglect the creeping hours of time;[xxvi] * if ever you have looked on better days; if ever you have been where bells have knolled⑥ to church; if you have ever sat at any good man's feast; if ever from your eyelids you have wiped a tear, and know what it is to pity or be pitied, may gentle speeches now move you to do me human courtesy⑦![xxvii]"

The duke replied: "True it is that we are men (as you say) who have seen better days, and though we have now our habitation in this wild forest, we have lived in towns and cities, and have with holy bell been knolled to church, have sat at good men's feasts, and from our eyes have wiped the drops which sacred⑧ pity has engendered⑨; therefore sit you down, and take of our refreshment⑩ as much as will minister⑪ to your wants."

"There is an old poor man," answered Orlando, "who has limped⑫ after me many a weary step in pure love, oppressed⑬ at once with two sad infirmities⑭, age and hunger; till he be satisfied, I must not touch a bit." "Go, find him out, and bring him hither," said the duke. "We will forbear to eat till you return." Then Orlando went like a doe⑮ to find its fawn and give it food; and presently returned, bringing Adam in his arms; and the duke said: "Set down your venerable⑯ burthen⑰; you are both welcome"; and they fed the old man, and cheered his heart, and he revived⑱, and recovered his health and strength again.

The duke inquired⑲ who Orlando was; and when he found that he was the son of his old friend Sir Rowland de Boys, he took him under his protection, and Orlando and his old servant lived with the duke in the forest.

Orlando arrived in the forest not many days after Ganymede and Aliena came there, and (as has been before related) bought the shepherd's cottage.

Ganymede and Aliena were strangely surprised to find the name of Rosalind carved on the

---

① blush [blʌʃ] *v*. 脸红 flush, glow, redden, turn red
② savage ['sævɪdʒ] *adj*. 野蛮的 wild, brutal, barbarous, uncivilized
③ countenance ['kaʊntənəns] *n*. 面容 face, feature
④ stern [stɜːn] *adj*. 严厉的 strict, hard, harsh, grim, rigid, rigorous
⑤ bough [baʊ] *n*. 大树枝
⑥ knoll [nəʊl] *v*. 敲钟 ring, sound, strike, chime, toll, clang, peal
⑦ courtesy ['kɜːtəsi] *n*. 恩惠 favor, help, aid, assistance, support
⑧ sacred ['seɪkrɪd] *adj*. 神圣的 holy, divine, blessed, consecrated
⑨ engender [ɪn'dʒendə(r)] *v*. 引起 produce, generate, bring about
⑩ refreshment [rɪ'freʃmənt] *n*. 茶点 food and drink, comestibles
⑪ minister ['mɪnɪstə(r)] *v*. 照料 tend/attend/cater/administer to
⑫ limp [lɪmp] *v*. 蹒跚 hobble, stagger, stumble, shuffle, totter
⑬ oppressed [ə'prest] *adj*. 被压迫的 burdened, distressed
⑭ infirmity [ɪn'fɜːməti] *n*. 疾病 frailty, ailment, malady, sickness
⑮ doe [dəʊ] *n*. 雌鹿
⑯ venerable ['venərəbl] *adj*. 令人尊重的 esteemed
⑰ burthen [bɜːrðən] *n*. 负担 burden, load, weight, charge
⑱ revive [rɪ'vaɪv] *v*. 恢复精神 revitalize, invigorate, reanimate
⑲ inquire [ɪn'kwaɪə(r)] *v*. 询问 ask, question, interrogate, look into

trees, and love-sonnets①, fastened② to them, all addressed③ to Rosalind; and while they were wondering how this could be, they met Orlando, and they perceived the chain which Rosalind had given him about his neck.

Orlando little thought that Ganymede was the fair princess Rosalind, who, by her noble condescension④ and favour, had so won his heart that he passed his whole time in carving her name upon the trees, and writing sonnets in praise of her beauty—but being much pleased with the graceful⑤ air⑥ of this pretty shepherd-youth, he entered into conversation with him, and * he thought he saw a likeness⑦ in Ganymede to his beloved Rosalind, but that he had none of the dignified⑧ deportment⑨ of that noble lady; for Ganymede assumed the forward⑩ manners often seen in youths when they are between boys and men, and with much archness⑪ and humour⑫ talked to Orlando of a certain lover, xxviii "who," said he, "haunts⑬ our forest, and spoils our young trees with carving Rosalind upon their barks; and he hangs odes⑭ upon hawthorns⑮, and elegies on brambles, all praising this same Rosalind. If I could find this love, I would give him some good counsel⑯ that would soon cure him of his love."

Orlando confessed⑰ that he was the fond lover⑱ of whom he spoke, and asked Ganymede to give him the good counsel he talked of. The remedy⑲ Ganymede proposed, and the counsel he gave him, was that Orlando should come every day to the cottage where he and his sister Aliena dwelt⑳: "And then," said Ganymede, "* I will feign㉑ myself to be Rosalind, and you shall feign

---

① love-sonnet 爱情十四行诗
② fasten [ˈfɑːsn] v. 系牢 tie, bind, lace, tie up, secure, lock, chain
③ address [əˈdres] v. 向……说话 talk/speak to, communicate with
④ condescension [ˌkɒndɪˈsenʃn] n. 屈尊
⑤ graceful [ˈgreɪsfl] adj. 优雅的 elegant, gracious, charming
⑥ air [eə] n. 神态 manner, style, appearance
⑦ likeness [ˈlaɪknəs] n. 相像 sameness, similarity, resemblance
⑧ dignified [ˈdɪgnɪfaɪd] adj. 高贵的 noble, distinguished
⑨ deportment[dɪˈpɔːtmənt] n. 风度 air, manner, bearing
⑩ forward [ˈfɔːwəd] adj. 莽撞的 disrespectful
⑪ archness [ˈɑːtʃnɪs] n. 淘气 playfulness, naughtiness, mischievousness
⑫ humour [ˈhjuːmə(r)] n. 玩笑 fun, joke, jest, kidding
⑬ haunt [hɔːnt] v. 经常出没 frequent, visit frequently, hang around
⑭ ode [əʊd] n. 颂诗;颂歌
⑮ hawthorn [ˈhɔːθɔːn] n. 山楂树
⑯ counsel [ˈkaʊnsl] n. 建议 advice, direction, suggestion
⑰ confess [kənˈfes] v. 坦白 admit, acknowledge, disclose
⑱ fond lover 痴情郎
⑲ remedy [ˈremədi] n. 疗法 solution, cure, treatment, therapy
⑳ dwell [dwel] v. (dwelt) 居住 live, reside, settle, lodge, abide
㉑ feign [feɪn] v. 假装 pretend, affect, assume, imitate, put on

to court① me in the same manner as you would do if I was Rosalind, and then I will imitate② the fantastic ways of whimsical③ ladies to their lovers, till I make you ashamed of your love; and this is the way I propose to cure you.[xxix]" Orlando had no great faith in the remedy, yet he agreed to come every day to Ganymede's cottage, and feign a playful courtship④; and every day Orlando visited Ganymede and Aliena, and Orlando called the shepherd Ganymede his Rosalind, and every day talked over all the fine words and flattering⑤ compliments⑥ which young men delight to use when they court their mistresses⑦. It does not appear, however, that Ganymede made any progress in curing Orlando of his love for Rosalind.

* Though Orlando thought all this was but a sportive⑧ play (not dreaming that Ganymede was his very Rosalind), yet the opportunity it gave him of saying all the fond things he had in his heart, pleased his fancy almost as well as it did Ganymede's, who enjoyed the secret jest in knowing these fine love-speeches were all addressed to the right person.[xxx]

In this manner many days passed pleasantly on with these young people; and the good-natured Aliena, seeing it made Ganymede happy, let him have his own way, and was diverted⑨ at the mock-courtship⑩, and did not care to remind Ganymede that the Lady Rosalind had not yet made herself known to the duke her father, whose place of resort in the forest they had learnt from Orlando. Ganymede met the duke one day, and had some talk with him, and the duke asked of what parentage⑪ he came. Ganymede answered that he came of as good parentage as he did, which made the duke smile, for he did not suspect the pretty shepherd-boy came of royal lineage⑫. Then seeing the duke look well and happy, Ganymede was content to put off all further explanation for a few days longer.

One morning, as Orlando was going to visit Ganymede, he saw a man lying asleep on the ground, and a large green snake had twisted⑬ itself about his neck. The snake, seeing Orlando approach, glided⑭ away among the bushes. Orlando went nearer, and then he discovered a lioness lie crouching⑮, with her head on the ground, with a cat-like watch, waiting until the sleeping man awaked (for it is said that lions will prey⑯ on nothing that is dead or sleeping). It seemed as if Orlando was sent by Providence⑰ to free the man from the danger of the snake and lioness; but

---

① court [kɔːt] *v*. 追求 woo, date, chase, pursue, make love to
② imitate [ˈɪmɪteɪt] *v*. 模仿 pretend, simulate, counterfeit
③ whimsical [ˈwɪmzɪkl] *adj*. 异想天开的 fanciful, fantastic, peculiar
④ courtship [ˈkɔːtʃɪp] *n*. 追求，求爱 wooing, courting, pursuit
⑤ flattering [ˈflætərɪŋ] *adj*. 恭维的，赞美的 laudatory, complimentary
⑥ compliment [ˈkɒmplɪmənt] *n*. 称赞 praise, admiration, flattery
⑦ mistress [ˈmɪstrəs] *n*. 心上人 sweetheart, dearest, beloved
⑧ sportive [ˈspɔːtɪv] *adj*. 嬉戏的 playful, joyous
⑨ divert [daɪˈvɜːt] *v*. 使娱乐 entertain, amuse, delight, recreate
⑩ mock-courtship 假装追求
⑪ parentage [ˈpeərəntɪdʒ] *n*. 出身 family, birth, origin, descent
⑫ lineage [ˈlɪniɪdʒ] *n*. 家系 descent, family, line, birth, ancestry
⑬ twist [twɪst] *v*. 缠绕 coil, curl, wind, wrap, twirl, intertwine
⑭ glide [glaɪd] *v*. 滑行 roll, slip, slide
⑮ crouch [kraʊtʃ] *v*. 蹲下，蹲伏 bend low/down, kneel, squat, stoop
⑯ prey [preɪ] *v*. 捕食 hunt, seize, devour, feed on, live off
⑰ Providence[ˈprɒvɪdəns] *n*. 天意 fate, fortune, destiny, God's will

when Orlando looked in the man's face, he perceived that the sleeper who was exposed to this double peril, was his own brother Oliver, who had so cruelly used① him, and had threatened to destroy him by fire; and he was almost tempted② to leave him a prey③ to the hungry lioness; but brotherly affection and the gentleness of his nature soon overcame his first anger against his brother; and he drew his sword, and attacked the lioness, and slew④ her, and thus preserved his brother's life both from the venomous⑤ snake and from the furious⑥ lioness; but before Orlando could conquer⑦ the lioness, she had torn one of his arms with her sharp claws.

While Orlando was engaged⑧ with the lioness, Oliver awaked, and perceiving that his brother Orlando, whom he had so cruelly treated, was saving him from the fury⑨ of a wild beast at the risk of his own life, shame and remorse⑩ at once seized him, and he repented⑪ of his unworthy conduct, and besought⑫ with many tears his brother's pardon for the injuries he had done him. Orlando rejoiced⑬ to see him so penitent⑭, and readily forgave him: they embraced⑮ each other; and from that hour Oliver loved Orlando with a true brotherly affection, though he had come to the forest bent on his destruction.

The wound in Orlando's arm having bled very much, he found himself too weak to go to visit Ganymede, and therefore he desired his brother to go and tell Ganymede, "whom," said Orlando, "I in sport⑯ do call my Rosalind," the accident which had befallen⑰ him.

Thither⑱ then Oliver went, and told to Ganymede and Aliena how Orlando had saved his life—and when he had finished the story of Orlando's bravery, and his own providential⑲ escape, he owned to them that he was Orlando's brother, who had so cruelly used him; and then he told them of their reconciliation⑳.

* The sincere sorrow that Oliver expressed for his offences㉑ made such a lively impression on the kind heart of Aliena, that she instantly fell in love with him; and Oliver observing how much she pitied the distress he told her he felt for his fault, he as suddenly fell in love with her.[xxxi] But

---

① use [juːz] *v*. 对待 treat, handle, deal with, act towards
② tempt [tempt] *v*. 引诱 attract, allure, entice, seduce, lead on
③ prey [preɪ] *n*. 猎物 quarry, game, kill
④ slay [sleɪ] *v*. (slew, slain) 杀死 kill, destroy, do away with
⑤ venomous ['venəməs] *adj*. 有毒的 poisonous, toxic, virulent
⑥ furious ['fjʊəriəs] *adj*. 狂怒的 mad, raging, enraged
⑦ conquer ['kɒŋkə(r)] *v*. 战胜 beat, defeat, overpower, triumph
⑧ engage [ɪn'geɪdʒ] *v*. 交战 fight, battle, combat, attack, take on
⑨ fury ['fjʊəri] *n*. 暴怒 anger, wrath, rage, irritation, indignation
⑩ remorse [rɪ'mɔːs] *n*. 懊悔 regret, shame, guilt, self-reproach
⑪ repent [rɪ'pent] *v*. 后悔 regret, lament, relent, feel remorse
⑫ beseech [bɪ'siːtʃ] *v*. (besought) 恳求 beg, pray, petition, solicit
⑬ rejoice [rɪ'dʒɔɪs] *v*. 感到开心,非常高兴 be overjoyed, delight, exult
⑭ penitent ['penɪtənt] *adj*. 忏悔的 regretful, apologetic, repentant
⑮ embrace[ɪm'breɪs] *v*. 拥抱 hug, cuddle, hold in one's arms
⑯ in sport 开玩笑地 jokingly, sportively
⑰ befall [bɪ'fɔːl] *v*. (befell, befallen) 降临到 happen to, fall upon
⑱ thither ['ðɪðə(r)] *adv*. 〈古〉向那边;在那个方向 there
⑲ providential [ˌprɒvɪ'denʃl] *adj*. 幸运的 lucky, fortunate
⑳ reconciliation [ˌrekənsɪlɪ'eɪʃn] *n*. 和解 reunion, reconcilement
㉑ offence [ə'fens] *n*. 过错,犯罪 crime, sin, wrongdoing, misdeed

while love was thus stealing① into the hearts of Aliena and Oliver, he was no less busy with Ganymede, who hearing of the danger Orlando had been in, and that he was wounded by the lioness, turned②; and * when he recovered, he pretended③ that he had counterfeited④ the swoon⑤ in the imaginary character of Rosalind, [xxxii] and Ganymede said to Oliver: "Tell your brother Orlando how well I counterfeited a swoon." But Oliver saw by the paleness of his complexion⑥ that he did really faint⑦, and much wondering at the weakness of the young man, he said: "* Well, if you did counterfeit, take a good heart, and counterfeit to be a man. [xxxiii]" * "So I do," replied Ganymede, truly, "but I should have been a woman by right." [xxxiv]

Oliver made this visit a very long one, and when at last he returned back to his brother, he had much news to tell him; for besides the account⑧ of Ganymede's fainting at the hearing that Orlando was wounded, Oliver told him how he had fallen in love with the fair shepherdess Aliena, and that she had lent a favourable ear to⑨ his suit⑩, even in this their first interview; and he talked to his brother, as of a thing almost settled, that he should marry Aliena, saying, that he so

well loved her, that he would live here as a shepherd, and settle his estate⑪ and house at home upon Orlando.

"You have my consent," said Orlando. "Let your wedding be to-morrow, and I will invite the duke and his friends. Go and persuade your shepherdess to this: she is now alone; for look, here comes her brother." Oliver went to Aliena; and Ganymede, whom Orlando had perceived approaching, came to inquire after⑫ the health of his wounded friend.

When Orlando and Ganymede began to talk over the sudden love which had taken place between Oliver and Aliena, Orlando said he had advised his brother to persuade his fair shepherdess to be married on the morrow⑬, and then he added how much he could wish to be married on the same day to his Rosalind.

Ganymede, who well approved of this arrangement said that if Orlando really loved Rosalind as well as he professed⑭ to do, he should have his wish; for on the morrow he would engage⑮ to

---

① steal [stiːl] v. 悄悄地移动 sneak, creep, slink
② turn [tɜːn] v. 昏厥 faint, swoon, pass out, lose consciousness
③ pretend [prɪˈtend] v. 自称 claim, insist, profess, maintain
④ counterfeit [ˈkaʊntəfɪt] v. 假装 pretend, feign, affect, imitate
⑤ swoon [swuːn] n. 昏厥 faint, coma, blackout, unconsciousness
⑥ complexion [kəmˈplekʃn] n. 面色 skin, colour, hue, skin tone
⑦ faint [feɪnt] n. 昏厥 swoon, pass out, black out
⑧ account [əˈkaʊnt] n. 叙述 description, report, explanation
⑨ lend a favourable ear to 乐于倾听 be willing to listen to
⑩ suit [suːt] n. 追求 courtship, courting, wooing, pursuit
⑪ estate [ɪˈsteɪt] n. 地产 land, property, holdings
⑫ inquire after 问候
⑬ morrow [ˈmɒrəʊ] n. 次日 tomorrow, the next/following day
⑭ profess [prəˈfes] v. 声称 claim, announce, declare, assert
⑮ engage [ɪnˈɡeɪdʒ] v. 承诺 promise, vow, guarantee, pledge

make Rosalind appear in her own person, and also that Rosalind should be willing to marry Orlando.

* This seemingly wonderful event, which, as Ganymede was the Lady Rosalind, he could so easily perform, he pretended he would bring to pass① by the aid of magic, which he said he had learnt of an uncle who was a famous magician.[xxxv]

The fond lover Orlando, half believing and half doubting what he heard, asked Ganymede if he spoke in sober② meaning. "By my life I do," said Ganymede, "therefore put on your best clothes, and bid the duke and your friends to your wedding; for if you desire to be married to-morrow to Rosalind, she shall be here."

The next morning, Oliver having obtained③ the consent of Aliena, they came into the presence of the duke, and with them also came Orlando.

They being all assembled④ to celebrate this double marriage, and as yet only one of the brides appearing, there was much of wondering and conjecture⑤, but they mostly thought that Ganymede was making a jest of Orlando.

The duke, hearing that it was his own daughter that was to be brought in this strange way, asked Orlando if he believed the shepherd-boy could really do what he had promised; and while Orlando was answering that he knew not what to think, Ganymede entered, and asked the duke, if he brought his daughter, whether he would consent to her marriage with Orlando. "* That I would," said the duke, "if I had kingdoms to give with her.[xxxvi]" Ganymede then said to Orlando: "And you say you will marry her if I bring her here." "* That I would," said Orlando, "if I were king of many kingdoms.[xxxvii]"

Ganymede and Aliena then went out together, and Ganymede throwing off his male attire⑥, and being once more dressed in woman's apparel⑦, quickly became Rosalind without the power of magic; and Aliena changing her country garb⑧ for her own rich clothes, was with as little trouble transformed into the lady Celia.

While they were gone, the duke said to Orlando, that he thought the shepherd Ganymede very like his daughter Rosalind; and Orlando said, he also had observed the resemblance⑨.

They had no time to wonder how all this would end, for Rosalind and Celia in their own clothes entered; and no longer pretending that it was by the power of magic that she came there, Rosalind threw herself on her knees before her father, and begged his blessing. * It seemed so wonderful to all present that she should so suddenly appear, that it might well have passed for⑩ magic;[xxxviii] but Rosalind would no longer trifle with⑪ her father, and told him the story of her

---

① bring to pass 使实现 bring about/off, cause to happen
② sober [ˈsəʊbə(r)] *adj*. 清醒的 cool, calm, serious, rational
③ obtain [əbˈteɪn] *v*. 获得 get, gain, acquire, attain, procure
④ assemble [əˈsembl] *v*. 聚集 gather, meet, come together
⑤ conjecture [kənˈdʒektʃə(r)] *n*. 猜测 guess, speculation
⑥ attire [əˈtaɪə(r)] *n*. 服装 clothes, clothing, outfit, costume
⑦ apparel [əˈpærəl] *n*. 衣服 clothes, garment, attire, garb
⑧ garb [ɡɑːb] *n*. 衣服 clothes, garment, dress
⑨ resemblance [rɪˈzembləns] *n*. 相似 similarity, parallel, likeness
⑩ pass for 被(误)认为 be taken for, be regarded as
⑪ trifle with 怠慢

banishment, and of her dwelling[1] in the forest as a shepherd-boy, her cousin Celia passing as[2] her sister.

The duke ratified[3] the consent he had already given to the marriage; and Orlando and Rosalind, Oliver and Celia, were married at the same time. * And though their wedding could not be celebrated in this wild forest with any of the parade[4] or splendour usual on such occasions, yet a happier wedding-day was never passed; [xxxix] and while they were eating their venison under the cool shade of the pleasant trees, as if nothing should be wanting[5] to complete the felicity[6] of this good duke and the true lovers, an unexpected messenger arrived to tell the duke the joyful news, that his dukedom was restored[7] to him.

The usurper, enraged[8] at the flight of his daughter Celia, and hearing that every day men of great worth resorted to[9] the forest of Arden to join the lawful duke in his exile, much envying that his brother should be so highly respected in his adversity[10], put himself at the head of a large force, and advanced towards the forest, intending to seize his brother, and put him with all his faithful followers to the sword[11]; but, by a wonderful interposition[12] of Providence, this bad brother was converted[13] from his evil intention; for just as he entered the skirts[14] of the wild forest, he was met by an old religious man, a hermit[15], with whom he had much talk, and who in the end completely turned his heart from his wicked design. Thenceforward[16] he became a true penitent[17], and resolved[18], relinquishing[19] his unjust dominion, to spend the remainder of his days in a religious house[20]. The first act of his newly conceived[21] penitence[22] was to send a messenger to his brother (as has been related) to offer to restore to him his dukedom, which he had usurped so long, and with it the lands and revenues of his friends, the faithful followers of his adversity.

* This joyful news, as unexpected as it was welcome, came opportunely[23] to heighten the

---

① dwelling ['dwelɪŋ] *n*. 住所 house, residence, abode, lodging
② pass as 被当作;假装成 pass for, pretend, feign, affect
③ ratify ['rætɪfaɪ] *v*. 批准 approve, confirm, sanction, authorize
④ parade [pə'reɪd] *n*. 游行 march, procession, pageant
⑤ wanting ['wɒntɪŋ] *adj*. 缺少的,缺乏的 lacking, missing, absent, needing
⑥ felicity [fə'lɪsəti] *n*. 喜悦,幸福 happiness, joy, ecstasy, bliss, mirth
⑦ restore [rɪ'stɔː(r)] *v*. 恢复 recover, re-establish, give/bring back
⑧ enraged [ɪn'reɪdʒd] *adj*. 被激怒的 furious, angry, angered, mad
⑨ resort to 去往 go, visit, head for, frequent
⑩ adversity [əd'vɜːsəti] *n*. 困境 hardship, catastrophe, calamity
⑪ put...to the sword 杀死 kill, murder, slaughter, put to death
⑫ interposition [ˌɪntəpə'zɪʃn] *n*. 干预
⑬ convert [kən'vɜːt] *v*. 改变 change, turn, transform, alter, adapt
⑭ skirt [skɜːt] *n*. 边缘 border, edge, margin, fringe, rim, outskirt
⑮ hermit ['hɜːmɪt] *n*. 隐士 recluse, monk, anchorite, eremite
⑯ thenceforward [ˌðens'fɔːwəd] *adv*. 从那以后 from then on
⑰ penitent ['penɪtənt] *n*. 忏悔者,悔罪者 confessor, repenter
⑱ resolved [rɪ'zɒlvd] *adj*. 下定决心的 determined, resolute
⑲ relinquish [rɪ'lɪŋkwɪʃ] *v*. 放弃 desert, abandon, let go, give up
⑳ religious house 修道院 cloister, monastery
㉑ conceive [kən'siːv] *v*. 设想 imagine, envisage, think up
㉒ penitence ['penɪtəns] *n*. 悔过 regret, repentance
㉓ opportunely ['ɒpətjuːnli] *adv*. 恰好 properly, appropriately

festivity① and rejoicings② at the wedding of the princesses.[xl] Celia complimented③ her cousin on this good fortune which had happened to the duke, Rosalind's father, and wished her joy very sincerely, though she herself was no longer heir to the dukedom, but by this restoration which her father had made, Rosalind was now the heir: so completely was the love of these two cousins unmixed with anything of jealousy④ or of envy.

The duke had now an opportunity of rewarding those true friends who had stayed with him in his banishment; and these worthy followers, though they had patiently shared his adverse⑤ fortune, were very well pleased to return in peace and prosperity⑥ to the palace of their lawful duke.

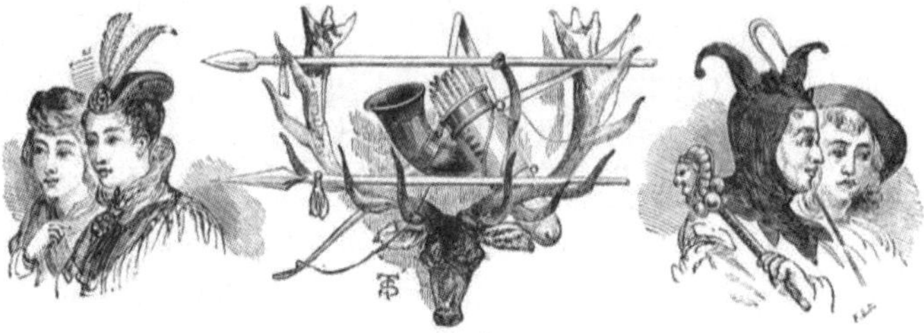

Jaques de Bois. Let me have audience for a word or two:
I am the second son of old Sir Roland,
That bring these tidings to this fair assembly
Act V. Scene IV.

① festivity [fe'stɪvəti] *n*. 欢庆 celebration, revelry
② rejoicing [rɪ'dʒɔɪsɪŋ] *n*. 喜庆 delight, joy, gaiety
③ compliment ['kɒmplɪmənt] *v*. 祝贺 praise, congratulate, laud
④ jealousy ['dʒeləsi] *n*. 忌妒 envy, resentment, enviousness
⑤ adverse ['ædvɜːs] *adj*. 不利的 unfavourable, disadvantageous
⑥ prosperity [prɒ'sperəti] *n*. 繁荣

i Custom soon made the life of careless ease they led here more sweet to them than the pomp and uneasy splendour of a courtier's life. 习惯很快使他们觉得在这儿过得自由自在的生活比宫廷里那种华丽而虚伪的排场可爱多了。(custom=experience;careless ease:自由自在)

ii So fond were they of these poor dappled fools, who seemed to be the native inhabitants of the forest, that it grieved them to be forced to kill them to supply themselves with venison for their food. 他们非常喜欢这些可怜的带斑纹的傻动物,它们好像是树林里的原住民,因此,当他们为了弄些鹿肉来充饥而不得不杀死它们的时候,他们心里总是觉得很难受。(so...that...:倒装结构;fools=innocent creatures:暗含亲昵的语气)

iii I find that howsoever men speak against adversity, yet some sweet uses are to be extracted from it; like the jewel, precious for medicine, which is taken from the head of the venomous and despised toad. 我发现,无论人们如何抱怨逆境,还是可以从中取得一些可喜的好处,就像那可以用来做贵重药材的宝石,却是从有毒的并且受人轻视的癞蛤蟆脑袋里面取出来的一样。(uses=profits;当时的人们认为癞蛤蟆有毒,但是它的脑袋里面有一块宝石,是珍贵的解毒剂)

iv In this manner did the patient duke draw a useful moral from everything that he saw; and by the help of this moralizing turn, in that life of his, remote from public haunts, he could find tongues in trees, books in the running brooks, sermons in stones, and good in everything. 这位有耐性的公爵就这样从他看到的每一件东西上得到有益的教训。虽然生活在这个不见人烟的地方,但靠着这种喜欢从事物上取得教训的性格,他也能够从树上找到言语,从潺潺的小河里找到书本,从岩石上找到教训,从一切事物上得到益处。(...did...draw...:倒装结构;moralizing turn:指喜欢从事物中取得教训的性格;public haunts=society)

v A strict friendship subsisted between these ladies, which the disagreement between their fathers did not in the least interrupt, Celia striving by every kindness in her power to make amends to Rosalind for the injustice of her own father in deposing the father of Rosalind. 这两位姑娘之间有一种密切的友谊,她们父亲的不睦一点儿也没有影响到她们的这种友谊。西莉娅竭力讨罗瑟琳的喜欢,来弥补她自己的父亲废黜罗瑟琳的父亲这种不公正的行为。(strict=close;Celia striving...:独立主格结构)

vi You will take little delight in it; there is such odds in the men: in pity to this young man, I would wish to persuade him from wrestling. 你们不会对决斗感兴趣的。这两个人的力量差得太远了,出于对这个年轻人的怜悯,我想劝他不要去决斗。

vii Rosalind spoke so kindly to him, and with such feeling consideration for the danger he was about to undergo, that instead of being persuaded by her gentle words to forgo his purpose, all his thoughts were bent to distinguish himself by his courage in this lovely lady's eyes. 罗瑟琳非常恳切地跟他谈,而且非常担心他就要承担的危险,结果这些温柔的话语不但没能劝动他放弃决斗,反而叫他更想凭自己的勇气在这个可爱的姑娘面前一显身手了。(so/such...that...结构)

viii But let your fair eyes and gentle wishes go with me to my trial, wherein if I be conquered there is one shamed that was never gracious; if I am killed, there is one dead that is willing to die. 让你们美丽的眼睛和温柔的心肠伴随我来参加这场比赛吧。在决斗中要是我输了,那不过是一个从未受过宠爱的人丢了脸;要是我死了,那也不过是死了一个心甘情愿去死的人。

ix I shall do my friends no wrong, for I have none to lament me; the world no injury, for in it

I have nothing; for I only fill up a place in the world which may be better supplied when I have made it empty. 我不会对不起我的朋友，因为我没有朋友来哀悼我；我也不会使世界受到任何损害，因为我在世上一无所有；我在世上占据的位置如果空出来，也许可以由更好的人来补充。

x If I had known this young man was his son, I would have added tears to my entreaties before he should have ventured. 假如我早知道这个年轻人是他的儿子的话，我本会流着泪求他不要冒这个险。（if I had known..., I would have added...：与过去事实相反的虚拟语气）

xi I am out of suits with fortune, or I would give you a more valuable present. 我的运气很不好，不然我会送你一件更贵重的礼物。（or＝or else, otherwise：否则；or I would...：含蓄条件句的虚拟语气）

xii She is too subtle for you; her smoothness, her very silence, and her patience speak to the people, and they pity her. 你捉摸不透她；她的圆滑、她的沉默和她的耐性都等于在向大家求情，他们可怜她。（speak to＝appeal to：对……有吸引力，向……求情）

xiii It was quickly agreed on between them, that as Rosalind was the tallest, she should wear the dress of a young countryman, and Celia should be habited like a country lass, and that they should say they were brother and sister, and Rosalind said she would be called Ganymede, and Celia chose the name of Aliena. 她们两人很快就达成共识：因为罗瑟琳个子高，所以她穿上年轻的乡下汉的衣裳，而西莉娅打扮成乡下妞儿的样子。她们要对人说两人是兄妹，罗瑟琳说她想化名叫盖尼米德，西莉娅就取了爱莲娜这个名字。（the tallest＝the taller; Ganymede：希腊神话中神的侍酒俊童；Aliena：拉丁文，意思是异国之女）

xiv He was so weary, he could find in his heart to disgrace his man's apparel, and cry like a woman. 他太累了，心里真想索性给他的男子打扮丢脸，像个女人一样大哭一场。（so...that...结构中省略了 that）

xv Ganymede tried to recollect that it was a man's duty to comfort and console a woman, as the weaker vessel. 盖尼米德试图记起男人有责任安慰、劝解生性软弱的女人。（the weaker vessel：更软弱的器皿，指女性。语出《新约·彼得前书》第三章第七节：你们做丈夫的，也要按情理和妻子同住，因她是软弱的器皿，与你一同承受生命之恩的，所以要敬重她。）

xvi Charging Oliver on his blessing to give his brother a good education, and provide for him as became the dignity of their ancient house. 在祝福当中，他嘱咐奥列佛要给弟弟良好的教育，把弟弟照顾得和他们古老门第的尊严相称。

xvii But in his nature and in the noble qualities of his mind Orlando so much resembled his excellent father, that without any advantages of education he seemed like a youth who had been bred with the utmost care; and Oliver so envied the fine person and dignified manners of his untutored brother, that at last he wished to destroy him; and to effect this he set on people to persuade him to wrestle with the famous wrestler, who, as has been before related, had killed so many men. 不过奥兰多的天性和高贵的品质非常像他卓绝的父亲，所以尽管他没有受到什么教育，他却像个极细心地培养出来的青年。奥列佛非常忌妒他这个没有受过教育的弟弟长得竟这样好，举止又这样落落大方，他终于想把他害死。为了达到这个目的，他叫人去劝他跟那个有名的拳师决斗——前面也说过，这个拳师打死过许多人。

xviii It was this cruel brother's neglect of him which made Orlando say he wished to die, being so friendless. 正因为这个残忍的哥哥对他的漠不关心，奥兰多才说出自己无朋无友、情愿去死

的话。(it was...which...：强调句，现代英语中不用 which 而用 that)

xix O my gentle master, my sweet master, O you memory of old Sir Rowland! 啊，我善良的主人，我的好主人，啊，您让人想起老罗兰爵爷！

xx Your praise is come too swiftly home before you. 您的名声传得太快，已经比您先到家了。(is come＝has come)

xxi I have five hundred crowns, the thrifty hire I saved under your father, and laid by to be provision for me when my old limbs should become unfit for service. 我有五百克朗，这是我在您父亲手下做事的时候从工钱里省下来的，本来是预备在我这副老骨头干不动活的时候花的。

xxii He that doth the ravens feed be comfort to my age! 上帝既然给乌鸦食物，我这一把年纪，就悉听他的慈悲吧！(he：指上帝；doth＝does)

xxiii How well appears in you the constant service of the old world! 从你身上可以多么清楚地看到古人的那种忠心耿耿啊！

xxiv We will go along together, and before your youthful wages are spent, I shall light upon some means for both our maintenance. 我们一起走吧，在把你年轻时赚的钱花光之前，我会有办法赚一点钱来维持我们俩的生活。(youthful wages：年轻时攒下的钱；spent＝exhausted：耗尽的)

xxv The duke asked him, if distress had made him so bold, or if he were a rude despiser of good manners. 公爵问他，是困境让他如此冒昧，还是他天生就是不知礼的莽汉。

xxvi I thought that all things had been savage here, and therefore I put on the countenance of stern command; but whatever men you are, that in this desert, under the shade of melancholy boughs, lose and neglect the creeping hours of time. 我还以为这里的一切都很野蛮呢，所以我才摆出一副粗暴地下命令的样子。可是无论你们是谁，在这片荒野里，躺在凄凉的树荫下，就会忘记时间的流逝。(the creeping hours of time：流逝的岁月)

xxvii If ever you have looked on better days; if ever you have been where bells have knolled to church; if you have ever sat at any good man's feast; if ever from your eyelids you have wiped a tear, and know what it is to pity or be pitied, may gentle speeches now move you to do me human courtesy! 只要你们曾经见过好日子，只要你们到过打钟召集礼拜的地方，只要你们参加过上流人的宴会，只要你们从眼皮上擦过泪水，懂得怜悯人和被人怜悯是怎么回事，那么现在就让这些温和的话语感动你们，用人间的礼貌来对待我吧！(排比修辞)

xxviii He thought he saw a likeness in Ganymede to his beloved Rosalind, but that he had none of the dignified deportment of that noble lady; for Ganymede assumed the forward manners often seen in youths when they are between boys and men, and with much archness and humour talked to Orlando of a certain lover. 他觉得盖尼米德有点儿像他心爱的罗瑟琳，只是他没有那位高贵小姐的庄严仪表。因为盖尼米德故意装出将要成年的小伙子常有的那种鲁莽样子。他非常调皮、诙谐地跟奥兰多谈起一个情人的事。

xxix I will feign myself to be Rosalind, and you shall feign to court me in the same manner as you would do if I was Rosalind, and then I will imitate the fantastic ways of whimsical ladies to their lovers, till I make you ashamed of your love; and this is the way I propose to cure you. 我装作罗瑟琳，你把我当作真是罗瑟琳一样，假装向我求爱。然后我就模仿起古怪善变的姑娘同她们的情人玩的种种奇怪花样，直到我叫你为你的痴情害起臊来。这就

是我提出的治你相思病的办法。(...would...if I was...:与现在或将来相反的虚拟语气,现代英语中一般不用was,只用were)

xxx Though Orlando thought all this was but a sportive play (not dreaming that Ganymede was his very Rosalind), yet the opportunity it gave him of saying all the fond things he had in his heart, pleased his fancy almost as well as it did Ganymede's, who enjoyed the secret jest in knowing these fine love-speeches were all addressed to the right person. 尽管奥兰多以为这不过是闹着玩(根本想不到盖尼米德就是他的罗瑟琳),可是这却给他机会把他心里一切温存的话都说出来。盖尼米德知道这些情话都是说给她自己的,她私下里感到一种快乐。而奥兰多的快乐几乎不比盖尼米德少。

xxxi The sincere sorrow that Oliver expressed for his offences made such a lively impression on the kind heart of Aliena, that she instantly fell in love with him; and Oliver observing how much she pitied the distress he told her he felt for his fault, he as suddenly fell in love with her. 奥列佛对自己所犯的过错诚恳地表示难过,这在爱莲娜仁慈的心里留下了强烈的印象,她立刻爱上了他。同时奥列佛也体会到爱莲娜听他说自己因犯错而感到苦恼的时候,有多么同情自己,于是他也立刻爱上了她。(such...that...结构;...distress (that)...:定语从句;he told her:插入语)

xxxii When he recovered, he pretended that he had counterfeited the swoon in the imaginary character of Rosalind. 当他清醒过来之后,他借口说他是为了模仿想象中的罗瑟琳的情态而假装晕厥过去的。

xxxiii Well, if you did counterfeit, take a good heart, and counterfeit to be a man. 好吧,假如你是假装的话,就振作起来,假装成一个男子汉吧。

xxxiv "So I do," replied Ganymede, truly, "but I should have been a woman by right." "我正在假装着呢,"盖尼米德老实地回答说,"可是凭良心说,我理应是个女人。"(by right = rightly, rightfully, with good reason:按理说)

xxxv This seemingly wonderful event, which, as Ganymede was the Lady Rosalind, he could so easily perform, he pretended he would bring to pass by the aid of magic, which he said he had learnt of an uncle who was a famous magician. 这件看起来很奇妙的事——因为盖尼米德就是罗瑟琳本人,他很容易就能做到——他假装是靠魔法的帮助实现的,而且说这魔法是从他叔叔,一名有名的魔法师那儿学来的。(pretended (that)..., which...who...:宾语从句中嵌套双重定语从句;he said:插入语;learn of = learn from)

xxxvi That I would, if I had kingdoms to give with her. 即使我要给她好几个王国作陪嫁,我也愿意。(虚拟语气)

xxxvii That I would, if I were king of many kingdoms. 即使我是统治许多王国的君王,我也愿意。(虚拟语气)

xxxviii It seemed so wonderful to all present that she should so suddenly appear, that it might well have passed for magic. 她出现得这么突然,在场的人都觉得十分奇怪,简直像是靠魔法的力量。(should:竟然)

xxxix And though their wedding could not be celebrated in this wild forest with any of the parade or splendour usual on such occasions, yet a happier wedding-day was never passed. 尽管婚礼是在这片荒凉的树林里举行的,不能有这种仪式应有的种种排场,可是这样快乐的结婚日子是从来也没有过的。

XI This joyful news, as unexpected as it was welcome, came opportunely to heighten the festivity and rejoicings at the wedding of the princesses. 这个可喜的、出人意料却又受人欢迎的消息来得很凑巧，大大增添了两位公主举行婚礼时的喜庆和快乐的气氛。

威尼斯商人
The Merchant of Venice

All that glitters is not gold; Often have you heard that told—
Many a man his life hath sold but my outside to behold—
Gilded tombs do worms enfold.

发闪光的不全是黄金，古人的说话没有骗人；
多少世人出卖了一生，不过看到了我的外形，
蛆虫占据着镀金的坟。

莎士比亚是人类最伟大的戏剧天才。

——马克思

他(莎士比亚)的作品是建立在广泛的生活基础上的,因此他笔底产生的每一样东西都使我们感到真实可信。

——恩格斯

《威尼斯商人》的重要价值,在于莎士比亚赋予了在原来的故事中表现得不明显的人物性格以应有的深度和严肃性,在于此剧结尾处那迷人月色中使人陶醉的优美歌曲……他的诗歌、他的整个存在,现在似乎全都献给了音乐,献给了和谐。

——勃兰兑斯

我在德瑞街剧院观看此剧的时候,在我的包厢后面立着一个面貌灰白而秀丽的不列颠人,到了第四幕临完之际,他竟痛哭起来,叹着气说了好几声:“那个可怜人是受冤抑了!”那个人的脸是有最高贵的希腊风度的,眼睛是大而黑。所以我永远忘记不了那一双为夏洛克而流泪的大黑眼睛!

——海涅

主要人物

Shylock　夏洛克　犹太富翁
Antonio　安东尼奥　威尼斯商人
Bassanio　巴萨尼奥　安东尼奥的朋友
Portia　鲍西娅　富家嗣女
Gratiano　葛莱西安诺　安东尼奥和巴萨尼奥的朋友
Nerissa　尼莉莎　鲍西娅的仆人
Jessica　杰西卡　夏洛克的女儿
Lorenzo　罗兰佐　杰西卡的恋人

地点　威尼斯;贝尔蒙特,鲍西娅邸宅所在地

The Merchant of Venice

Shylock, the Jew[1], lived at Venice: he was an usurer[2], who had amassed[3] an immense[4] fortune by lending money at great interest to Christian[5] merchants. Shylock, being a hard-hearted man, exacted[6] the payment of the money he lent with such severity[7] that he was much disliked by all good men, and particularly by Antonio, a young merchant of Venice; and Shylock as much hated Antonio, because he used to lend money to people in distress[8], and would never take any interest for the money he lent; therefore there was great enmity[9] between this covetous[10] Jew and the generous merchant Antonio. Whenever Antonio met Shylock on the Rialto (or Exchange), he used to reproach[11] him with his usuries[12] and hard dealings[13], which the Jew would bear with seeming patience, while he secretly meditated[14] revenge[15].

Antonio was the kindest man that lived, the best conditioned[16], and had the most unwearied[17] spirit in doing courtesies[18]; indeed, ‘he was one in whom the ancient Roman[19] honour more appeared than in any that drew breath in Italy.’ He was greatly beloved by all his fellow-citizens;

---

① Jew [dʒuː] *n*. 犹太人;犹太教徒
② usurer [ˈjuːʒərə(r)] *n*. 放高利贷者 moneylender, loan shark
③ amass [əˈmæs] *v*. 积累,积聚 collect, gather, assemble, accumulate
④ immense [ɪˈmens] *adj*. 巨大的 huge, massive, gigantic, enormous
⑤ Christian [ˈkrɪstʃən] *adj*. 基督教(徒)的
⑥ exact [ɪgˈzækt] *v*. 强求 demand, claim, extort, insist upon
⑦ severity [sɪˈverəti] *n*. 苛刻 strictness, seriousness, harshness, severeness
⑧ distress [dɪˈstres] *n*. 危难 danger, risk, difficulty, peril, jeopardy
⑨ enmity [ˈenməti] *n*. 敌意 hostility, hate, spite, hatred, ill will
⑩ covetous [ˈkʌvətəs] *adj*. 贪婪的 greedy, desirous, acquisitive, avid
⑪ reproach [rɪˈprəʊtʃ] *v*. 指责 blame, scold, abuse
⑫ usury [ˈjuːʒəri] *n*. 高利贷
⑬ hard dealing 刻薄的交易
⑭ meditate [ˈmedɪteɪt] *v*. 考虑 reflect, consider, deliberate
⑮ revenge [rɪˈvendʒ] *n*. 报复 retaliation, vengeance, retribution
⑯ the best conditioned 心地最为善良的
⑰ unwearied [ʌnˈwɪərid] *adj*. 不知疲倦的 untired, unweary, indefatigable
⑱ courtesy [ˈkɜːtəsi] *n*. 恩惠 favor, help, aid, assistance, support
⑲ Roman [ˈrəʊmən] *adj*. 罗马的

but the friend who was nearest and dearest to his heart was Bassanio, a noble Venetian①, who, having but a small patrimony②, had nearly exhausted his little fortune by living in too expensive a manner for his slender③ means④, as young men of high rank with small fortunes are too apt⑤ to do. Whenever Bassanio wanted money, Antonio assisted him; and it seemed as if they had but one heart and one purse between them.

One day Bassanio came to Antonio, and told him that he wished to repair his fortune by a wealthy marriage with a lady whom he dearly loved, whose father, that was lately dead, had left her sole⑥ heiress⑦ to a large estate⑧; and that * in her father's lifetime he used to visit at her house, when he thought he had observed this lady had sometimes from her eyes sent speechless messages, that seemed to say he would be no unwelcome suitor;[ii] but * not having money to furnish⑨ himself with an appearance befitting⑩ the lover of so rich an heiress, he besought⑪ Antonio to add to the many favours he had shown him, by lending him three thousand ducats⑫.[iii]

Antonio had no money by him at that time to lend his friend; but expecting soon to have some ships come home laden⑬ with merchandise⑭, he said he would go to Shylock, the rich money-lender and borrow the money upon the credit of those ships.

Antonio and Bassanio went together to Shylock, and Antonio asked the Jew to lend him three thousand ducats upon any interest he should require, to be paid out of the merchandise contained in his ships at sea. On this, Shylock thought within himself: "* If I can once catch him on the hip, I will feed fat the ancient grudge⑮ I bear him;[iv] he hates our Jewish⑯ nation; he lends out money gratis⑰, and among merchants he rails⑱ at me and my well-earned bargains, which he calls interest. * Cursed be my tribe if I forgive him![v]" Antonio finding he was musing⑲ within himself and did not answer, and being impatient for the money, said:

---

① Venetian [və'niːʃn] *n*. 威尼斯人
② patrimony ['pætrɪməni] *n*. 遗产 inheritance, heritage, legacy
③ slender ['slendə(r)] *adj*. 微薄的 little, small, meager, inadequate
④ means [miːnz] *n*. 钱财 money, funds, assets, wealth, fortune
⑤ apt [æpt] *adj*. 有……倾向的,易于……的 inclined, likely, disposed, prone, liable
⑥ sole [səʊl] *adj*. 唯一的 only, single, unique, exclusive
⑦ heiress [eə'res] *n*. 女继承人 female heir/successor/inheritor
⑧ estate [ɪ'steɪt] *n*. 庄园;地产 lands, property, domain, manor
⑨ furnish ['fɜːnɪʃ] *v*. 供应,提供
⑩ befit [bɪ'fɪt] *v*. 适合 suit, become, be fit/suitable/appropriate
⑪ beseech [bɪ'siːtʃ] *v*. (besought) 恳求 beg, petition, supplicate
⑫ ducat ['dʌkət] *n*. 达克特(旧时多个欧洲国家的通用金币)
⑬ laden ['leɪdn] *adj*. 满载的 loaded, burdened
⑭ merchandise ['mɜːtʃəndaɪz] *n*. 货物 goods, wares, commodities
⑮ grudge [grʌdʒ] *n*. 怨恨 resentment, malice, spite, animosity
⑯ Jewish ['dʒuːɪʃ] *adj*. 犹太人的;犹太教的
⑰ gratis ['grætɪs] *adv*. 免费地,无偿地 free, for free/nothing, free of charge
⑱ rail [reɪl] *v*. 责骂 attack, abuse, criticize, blame, scold, revile
⑲ muse [mjuːz] *v*. 沉思 consider, reflect, ponder, contemplate

"Shylock, do you hear? Will you lend the money?"

To this question the Jew replied: "Signior[1] Antonio, on the Rialto many a time and often[2] you have railed at me about my monies[3] and my usuries, and I have borne it with a patient shrug, for sufferance[4] is the badge[5] of all our tribe; and then you have called me unbeliever, cut-throat[6] dog, and spit upon my Jewish garments, and spurned[7] at me with your foot, as if I was a cur[8]. Well then, it now appears you need my help; and you come to me, and say, *Shylock, lend me monies*. * Has a dog money? Is it possible a cur should lend three thousand ducats? Shall I bend low and say, Fair sir, you spit upon me on Wednesday last, another time you called me dog, and for these courtesies I am to lend you monies.[vi]"

Antonio replied: "I am as like to call you so again, to spit on you again, and spurn you too. * If you will lend me this money, lend it not to me as to a friend, but rather lend it to me as to an enemy, that, if I break, you may with better face exact the penalty.[vii]" "Why, look you," said Shylock, "how you storm[9]! I would be friends with you, and have your love. I will forget the shames you have put upon me. I will supply your wants, and take no interest for my money." This seemingly kind offer greatly surprised Antonio; and then Shylock, still pretending kindness, and that all he did was to gain Antonio's love, again said he would lend him the three thousand ducats, and take no interest for his money; only Antonio should go with him to a lawyer, and there sign in merry sport[10] a bond[11], that if he did not repay the money by a certain day, he would forfeit[12] a pound of flesh, to be cut off from any part of his body that Shylock pleased.

"Content," said Antonio. "I will sign to this bond, and say there is much kindness in the Jew."

Bassanio said Antonio should not sign to such a bond for him; but still Antonio insisted that he would sign it, for that before the day of payment came, his ships would return laden with many times the value of the money.

Shylock, hearing this debate, exclaimed: "* O, father Abraham[13], what suspicious[14] people these Christians are! Their own hard dealings teach them to suspect the thoughts of others.[viii] I pray you tell me this, Bassanio: if he should break this day[15], what should I gain by the exaction[16]

---

① Signior ['siːnjɔː] *n*. 先生(意大利语对男子的尊称);绅士
② many a time and often 很多次,频繁
③ monies ['mʌnɪz] *n*.〈古〉(money 的复数形式)货币;钱币
④ sufferance ['sʌfrəns] *n*. 忍耐 patience, endurance, tolerance
⑤ badge [bædʒ] *n*. 标识 mark, sign, token, brand, indicator
⑥ cut-throat ['kʌt θrəʊt] *adj*. 残忍的 cruel, bloody, murderous
⑦ spurn [spɜːn] *v*. 一脚踢开;冷落 reject, rebuff, repulse, despise
⑧ cur [kɜː(r)] *n*. 野狗
⑨ storm [stɔːm] *v*. 大发雷霆 rage, thunder, fly off the handle
⑩ in merry sport 开玩笑地,闹着玩儿地 in a jesting manner
⑪ bond [bɒnd] *n*. 协定 agreement, promise, contract
⑫ forfeit ['fɔːfɪt] *v*. 丧失 lose, relinquish, surrender, give up
⑬ father Abraham 我祖亚伯拉罕(据《旧约·创世纪》,亚伯拉罕是犹太人的祖先)
⑭ suspicious [sə'spɪʃəs] *adj*. 怀疑的,可疑的 distrustful, skeptical, doubtful
⑮ break this day 违约,到期还不了债
⑯ exaction [ɪg'zækʃn] *n*. 勒索,强求 demand, imposition, extortion

of the forfeiture①? A pound of man's flesh, taken from a man, is not so estimable②, nor profitable neither, as the flesh of mutton or beef. I say, to buy his favour I offer this friendship: if he will take it, so; if not, adieu③."

At last, against the advice of Bassanio, who, notwithstanding④ all the Jew had said of his kind intentions, did not like his friend should run the hazard⑤ of this shocking penalty⑥ for his sake, Antonio signed the bond, thinking it really was (as the Jew said) merely in sport⑦.

The rich heiress that Bassanio wished to marry lived near Venice, at a place called Belmont: * her name was Portia, and in the graces of her person and her mind she was nothing inferior⑧ to that Portia, of whom we read, who was Cato's daughter, and the wife of Brutus.[ix]

Bassanio being so kindly supplied with money by his friend Antonio, at the hazard of his life, set out for Belmont with a splendid train⑨, and attended by a gentleman of the name of Gratiano.

* Bassanio proving successful in his suit⑩, Portia in a short time consented⑪ to accept of him for a husband.[x]

Bassanio confessed⑫ to Portia that he had no fortune, and that his high birth and noble ancestry⑬ was all that he could boast⑭ of; * she, who loved him for his worthy qualities, and had riches enough not to regard⑮ wealth in a husband, answered with a graceful modesty, that she would wish herself a thousand times more fair, and ten thousand times more rich, to be more worthy of him;[xi] and then the accomplished⑯ Portia prettily dispraised⑰ herself, and said * she was an unlessoned⑱ girl, unschooled, unpractised⑲, yet not so old but that she could learn, and that she would commit her gentle spirit to be directed and governed by him in all things;[xii] and she said: "* Myself and what is mine, to you and yours is now converted⑳.[xiii] But yesterday, Bassanio, I was the lady of this fair mansion㉑, queen of myself, and mistress over these servants; and now this house, these servants, and myself, are yours, my lord; I give them with this ring," presenting a ring to Bassanio.

---

① forfeiture [ˈfɔːfɪtʃə(r)] *n*. 丧失,没收 loss, giving up, surrender
② estimable [ˈestɪməbl] *adj*. 有价值的 valuable, worthy, precious
③ adieu [əˈdjuː] *int*. 再见,告别 farewell, goodbye, so long, au revoir
④ notwithstanding [ˌnɒtwɪθˈstændɪŋ] *prep*. 尽管 despite, in spite of
⑤ hazard [ˈhæzəd] *n*. 危险 danger, risk, threat, menace, peril
⑥ penalty [ˈpenəlti] *n*. 惩罚 punishment, fine
⑦ in sport 开玩笑地 jokingly, sportively
⑧ inferior [ɪnˈfɪəriə(r)] *adj*. 较差的 lower, junior, minor, secondary
⑨ train [treɪn] *n*. 队伍 queue, procession
⑩ suit [suːt] *n*. 追求 courtship, wooing, pursuit, solicitation
⑪ consent [kənˈsent] *v*. 同意 agree, approve, permit, assent
⑫ confess [kənˈfes] *v*. 坦白 admit, acknowledge, disclose
⑬ ancestry [ˈænsestri] *n*. 祖先 origin, family, blood, parentage
⑭ boast [bəʊst] *v*. 自夸 brag, vaunt, flaunt, talk big, show off
⑮ regard [rɪˈgɑːd] *v*. 考虑 consider, value, account, esteem
⑯ accomplished [əˈkʌmplɪʃt] *adj*. 有才华的 able, talented, gifted
⑰ dispraise [dɪsˈpreɪz] *v*. 贬损 defame, devalue, speak ill of
⑱ unlessoned [ʌnˈlesənd] *adj*. 未受教育的 unschooled, uneducated
⑲ unpractised [ʌnˈpræktɪst] *adj*. 无经验的 untrained, inexperienced
⑳ convert [kənˈvɜːt] *v*. 改变 change, turn, transform, alter, adapt
㉑ mansion [ˈmænʃn] *n*. 宅邸 residence, manor, hall, villa, abode

Bassanio was so overpowered[1] with gratitude[2] and wonder at the gracious[3] manner in which the rich and noble Portia accepted of a man of his humble[4] fortunes, that he could not express his joy and reverence[5] to the dear lady who so honoured him, by anything but broken words of love and thankfulness; and taking the ring, he vowed[6] never to part with it.

Gratiano and Nerissa, Portia's waiting-maid, were in attendance upon their lord and lady, when Portia so gracefully promised to become the obedient[7] wife of Bassanio; and Gratiano, wishing Bassanio and the generous lady joy, desired permission to be married at the same time.

"With all my heart, Gratiano," said Bassanio, "if you can get a wife."

Gratiano then said that he loved the lady Portia's fair waiting gentlewoman Nerissa, and that she had promised to be his wife, if her lady married Bassanio. Portia asked Nerissa if this was true. Nerissa replied: "Madam, it is so, if you approve of it." Portia willingly consenting, Bassanio pleasantly said: "Then our wedding-feast shall be much honoured by your marriage, Gratiano."

The happiness of these lovers was sadly crossed[8] at this moment by the entrance of a messenger, who brought a letter from Antonio containing fearful tidings[9]. When Bassanio read Antonio's letter, Portia feared it was to tell him of the death of some dear friend, he looked so pale; and inquiring[10] what was the news which had so distressed[11] him, he said: "O sweet Portia, here are a few of the unpleasantest words that ever blotted[12] paper; gentle lady, when I first imparted[13] my love to you, * I freely told you all the wealth I had ran in my veins[14]; but I should have told you that I had less than nothing, being in debt.[xiv]" Bassanio then told Portia what has been here related, of his borrowing the money of Antonio, and of Antonio's procuring[15] it of Shylock the Jew, and of the bond by which Antonio had engaged[16] to forfeit a pound of flesh, if it was not repaid by a certain day—and then Bassanio read Antonio's letter—the words of which were: "*Sweet Bassanio, my ships are all lost, my bond to the Jew is forfeited, and since in paying*

---

① overpower [ˌəʊvəˈpaʊə(r)] *v*. 征服,克服 overcome, overwhelm, overthrow
② gratitude [ˈɡrætɪtjuːd] *n*. 感激 gratefulness, appreciation
③ gracious [ˈɡreɪʃəs] *adj*. 优雅的 courteous, elegant, graceful
④ humble [ˈhʌmbl] *adj*. 卑微的 mean, commonplace, insignificant
⑤ reverence [ˈrevərəns] *n*. 尊敬 respect, honour, admiration
⑥ vow [vaʊ] *v*. 发誓 promise, pledge, swear, avow
⑦ obedient [əˈbiːdiənt] *adj*. 顺从的 submissive, compliant, dutiful
⑧ cross [krɒs] *v*. 打断 interrupt, disturb, break in, cut off
⑨ tidings [ˈtaɪdɪŋz] *n*. 消息 news, report, message, intelligence
⑩ inquire [ɪnˈkwaɪə(r)] *v*. 询问 ask, question, query, interrogate
⑪ distress [dɪˈstres] *v*. 使苦恼 upset, worry, trouble, bother
⑫ blot [blɒt] *v*. 弄脏,涂污 stain, spot
⑬ impart [ɪmˈpɑːt] *v*. 透露 communicate, convey, reveal, relate
⑭ vein [veɪn] *n*. 静脉;血管 blood vessel
⑮ procure [prəˈkjʊə(r)] *v*.获得 get, obtain, gain, acquire, come by
⑯ engage [ɪnˈɡeɪdʒ] *v*. 承诺 promise, vow, guarantee, pledge

it is impossible I should live, I could wish to see you at my death; * *notwithstanding use your pleasure; if your love for me do not persuade you to come, let not my letter.*[xv]" "O, my dear love," said Portia, "despatch① all business, and begone②; you shall have gold to pay the money twenty times over, before this kind friend shall lose a hair by my Bassanio's fault; and * as you are so dearly③ bought, I will dearly love you.[xvi]" Portia then said she would be married to Bassanio before he set out, to give him a legal right to her money; and that same day they were married, and Gratiano was also married to Nerissa; and Bassanio and Gratiano, the instant they were married, set out in great haste④ for Venice, where Bassanio found Antonio in prison.

The day of payment being past, the cruel Jew would not accept of the money which Bassanio offered him, but insisted upon having a pound of Antonio's flesh. * A day was appointed to try this shocking cause⑤ before the duke of Venice, and Bassanio awaited in dreadful⑥ suspense⑦ the event of the trial⑧.[xvii]

When Portia parted with her husband, she spoke cheeringly to him, and bade⑨ him bring his dear friend along with him when he returned; yet she feared it would go hard with⑩ Antonio, and when she was left alone, she began to think and consider within herself, if she could by any means be instrumental⑪ in saving the life of her dear Bassanio's friend; and * notwithstanding when she wished to honour her Bassanio, she had said to him with such a meek⑫ and wifelike grace, that she would submit⑬ in all things to be governed by his superior wisdom, yet being now called forth⑭ into action by the peril⑮ of her honoured husband's friend, she did nothing doubt her own powers, and by the sole guidance of her own true and perfect judgement, at once resolved⑯ to go herself to Venice, and speak in Antonio's defence.[xviii]

Portia had a relation who was a counsellor⑰ in the law; to this gentleman, whose name was Bellario, she wrote, and stating the case to him, desired his opinion, and that with his advice he would also send her the dress worn by a counsellor. When the messenger returned, he brought

---

① despatch [dɪ'spætʃ] (=dispatch) *v*. 迅速处理 perform, dispose of
② begone [bɪ'gɒn] *v*. 走开 go away, leave, depart
③ dearly ['dɪəli] *adv*. 非常,深深地 very much, greatly
④ haste [heɪst] *n*. 匆忙 speed, rapidity, urgency, quickness
⑤ cause [kɔːz] *n*. 诉讼案 case, lawsuit, litigation, prosecution
⑥ dreadful ['dredfl] *adj*. 可怕的 terrible, horrible, fearful, frightful
⑦ suspense [sə'spens] *n*. 焦虑,担心 anxiety, tension, apprehension
⑧ trial ['traɪəl] *n*. 审理,审判 hearing, inquiry, lawsuit, court case
⑨ bid [bɪd] *v*. (bade, bidden) 吩咐 ask, charge, require, instruct
⑩ go hard with 对……不利,使痛苦
⑪ instrumental [ˌɪnstrə'mentl] *adj*. 有帮助的 helpful, serviceable
⑫ meek [miːk] *adj*. 温顺的 submissive, yielding, docile
⑬ submit [səb'mɪt] *v*. 顺从 give in, surrender, yield, comply
⑭ call forth 唤起 evoke, arouse, provoke, stimulate, inspire
⑮ peril ['perəl] *n*. 危险 danger, risk, threat, hazard, jeopardy
⑯ resolve [rɪ'zɒlv] *v*. 决定 decide, determine, intend
⑰ counsellor ['kaʊnsələ(r)] *n*. 律师 lawyer, solicitor

letters from Bellario of advice how to proceed①, and also everything necessary for her equipment.

Portia dressed herself and her maid Nerissa in men's apparel②, and putting on the robes of a counsellor, she took Nerissa along with her as her clerk; and setting out immediately, they arrived at Venice on the very day of the trial. The cause was just going to be heard③ before the duke and senators④ of Venice in the senate-house, when Portia entered this high court of justice, and presented a letter from Bellario, in which that learned counsellor wrote to the duke, saying, he would have come himself to plead⑤ for Antonio, but that he was prevented by sickness, and he requested that the learned young doctor Balthasar (so he called Portia) might be permitted to plead in his stead⑥. This the duke granted⑦, much wondering at the youthful appearance of the stranger, who was prettily disguised⑧ by her counsellor's robes and her large wig⑨.

And now began this important trial. Portia looked around her, and she knew the merciless⑩ Jew; and she saw Bassanio, but he knew her not in her disguise⑪. He was standing beside Antonio, in an agony⑫ of distress⑬ and fear for his friend.

The importance of the arduous⑭ task Portia had engaged⑮ in gave this tender lady courage, and she boldly proceeded in the duty she had undertaken⑯ to perform—and first of all she addressed herself to Shylock; and allowing⑰ that he had a right by the Venetian law to have the forfeit⑱ expressed in the bond, she spoke so sweetly of the noble quality of *mercy*, as would have softened any heart but the unfeeling⑲ Shylock's; saying, that * it dropped as the gentle rain from heaven upon the place beneath; and how mercy was a double blessing, it blessed him that gave, and him that received it; and how it became⑳ monarchs㉑ better than their crowns㉒, being an attribute㉓ of God Himself; and that earthly㉔ power came nearest to God's, in proportion㉕ as

---

① proceed [prəˈsiːd] *v*. 着手 advance, go ahead, carry on/out
② apparel [əˈpærəl] *n*. 衣服 garment, clothes, dress, costume
③ hear [hɪə(r)] *v*. (heard) 听审 judge, examine
④ senator [ˈsenətə(r)] *n*. 参议员 congressman, lawmaker
⑤ plead [pliːd] *v*. 辩护 argue, defend
⑥ stead [sted] *n*. 代替 position, place, lieu
⑦ grant [grɑːnt] *v*. 同意 accept, allow, permit, authorize
⑧ disguise [dɪsˈgaɪz] *v*. 掩饰 hide, cover, conceal, camouflage
⑨ wig [wɪg] *n*. 假发 false hair, hairpiece, periwig, peruke, toupee
⑩ merciless [ˈmɜːsɪləs] *adj*. 无情的 cruel, heartless, pitiless, inhumane
⑪ disguise [dɪsˈgaɪz] *n*. 假扮 mask, costume, false appearance
⑫ agony [ˈægəni] *n*. 痛苦,悲伤 suffering, pain, distress, misery, woe
⑬ distress [dɪˈstres] *n*. 忧虑
⑭ arduous [ˈɑːdjuəs] *adj*. 艰难的 difficult, hard, tough, exhausting
⑮ engage [ɪnˈgeɪdʒ] *v*. 参与 join/participate in, enter into
⑯ undertake [ˌʌndəˈteɪk] *v*. (undertook, undertaken) 承担 take on
⑰ allow [əˈlaʊ] *v*. 承认 accept, admit, acknowledge, recognize
⑱ forfeit [ˈfɔːfɪt] *n*. 罚金;没收物 fine, loss, penalty, forfeiture
⑲ unfeeling [ʌnˈfiːlɪŋ] *adj*. 无情的 pitiless, heartless, cruel, hardhearted
⑳ become [bɪˈkʌm] *v*. (became, become) 适合 suit, match, agree/harmonize with
㉑ monarch [ˈmɒnək] *n*. 君主 ruler, sovereign, emperor
㉒ crown [kraʊn] *n*. 王冠 coronet, tiara, diadem, coronal
㉓ attribute [ˈætrɪbjuːt] *n*. 属性 quality, feature, property
㉔ earthly [ˈɜːθli] *adj*. 尘世的 worldly, secular, mortal, temporal
㉕ proportion [prəˈpɔːʃn] *n*. 比例 ratio

mercy tempered① justice;[xix] and she bid Shylock remember that as we all pray for mercy, that same prayer should teach us to show mercy. Shylock only answered her by desiring to have the penalty forfeited in the bond.

"Is he not able to pay the money?" asked Portia. Bassanio then offered the Jew the payment of the three thousand ducats as many times over as he should desire; which Shylock refusing, and still insisting upon having a pound of Antonio's flesh, Bassanio begged the learned young counsellor would endeavour② to wrest③ the law a little, to save Antonio's life. But Portia gravely④ answered, that laws once established must never be altered. Shylock hearing Portia say that the law might not be altered, it seemed to him that she was pleading in his favour, and he said: "* A Daniel is come to judgement! O wise young judge, how I do honour you! How much elder are you than your looks![xx]"

Portia now desired Shylock to let her look at the bond; and when she had read it, she said: "This bond is forfeited, and by this the Jew may lawfully claim a pound of flesh, to be by him cut off nearest Antonio's heart." Then she said to Shylock: "Be merciful: take the money, and bid me tear the bond." But no mercy would the cruel Shylock show; and he said: "By my soul I swear, there is no power in the tongue of men to alter me." "Why then, Antonio," said Portia, "you must prepare your bosom⑤ for the knife"—and while Shylock was sharpening a long knife with great eagerness to cut off the pound of flesh, Portia said to Antonio: "Have you anything to say?" Antonio with a calm resignation⑥ replied, that he had but little to say, for that he had prepared his mind for death. Then he said to Bassanio: "Give me your hand, Bassanio! Fare you well⑦! Grieve⑧ not that I am fallen into this misfortune for you. Commend⑨ me to your honourable wife, and tell her how I have loved you!" Bassanio in the deepest affliction⑩ replied: "Antonio, I am married to a wife, who is as dear to me as life itself; but life itself, my wife, and all the world, are not esteemed⑪ with me above your life; I would lose all, I would sacrifice⑫ all to this devil here, to deliver you."

Portia hearing this, though the kind-hearted lady was not at all offended⑬ with her husband

---

① temper [ˈtempə(r)] *v*. 使缓和 moderate, soften, allay
② endeavour [ɪnˈdevə(r)] *v*. 尽力,努力 try, attempt, strive
③ wrest [rest] *v*. 歪曲 twist, wind, bend, wrench, wring, distort
④ gravely [ˈgreɪvli] *adv*. 严肃地 seriously, severely, solemnly
⑤ bosom [ˈbʊzəm] *n*. 胸部 breast, chest, front, bust, thorax
⑥ resignation [ˌrezɪgˈneɪʃn] *n*. 屈从 acceptance, submission
⑦ fare you well 祝你平安;再见,永别了
⑧ grieve [griːv] *v*. 悲伤 mourn, lament, bemoan, take it hard
⑨ commend [kəˈmend] *v*. 代问好 remember, say hello to
⑩ affliction [əˈflɪkʃn] *n*. 痛苦 suffering, distress, misery, torment
⑪ esteem [ɪˈstiːm] *v*. 尊重 respect, admire, honor, think highly of
⑫ sacrifice [ˈsækrɪfaɪs] *v*. 献出 offer, present, give, hold out to
⑬ offend [əˈfend] *v*. 冒犯 upset, slight, provoke, insult, displease

for expressing the love he owed to so true a friend as Antonio in these strong terms①, yet could not help answering: "Your wife would give you little thanks, if she were present, to hear you make this offer." And then Gratiano, who loved to copy what his lord did, thought he must make a speech like Bassanio's, and he said, in Nerissa's hearing, who was writing in her clerk's dress by the side of Portia: "I have a wife, whom I protest② I love; * I wish she were in heaven, if she could but entreat③ some power there to change the cruel temper of this currish④ Jew.[xxi]" "It is well you wish this behind her back, else you would have but an unquiet house," said Nerissa.

Shylock now cried out impatiently: "We trifle⑤ time; I pray pronounce⑥ the sentence." And now all was awful⑦ expectation in the court, and every heart was full of grief for Antonio.

Portia asked if the scales⑧ were ready to weigh the flesh; and she said to the Jew: "Shylock, you must have some surgeon by, lest⑨ he bleed to death." Shylock, whose whole intent⑩ was that Antonio should bleed to death, said: "It is not so named in the bond." Portia replied: "* It is not so named in the bond, but what of that? It were good you did so much for charity⑪.[xxii]" To this all the answer Shylock would make was: "I cannot find it; it is not in the bond." "Then," said Portia, "a pound of Antonio's flesh is thine⑫. The law allows it, and the court awards⑬ it. And you may cut this flesh from off his breast. The law allows it and the court awards it." Again Shylock exclaimed⑭: "O wise and upright⑮ judge! A Daniel is come to judgement!" And then he sharpened his long knife again, and looking eagerly on Antonio, he said: "Come, prepare!"

"Tarry⑯ a little, Jew," said Portia, "there is something else. This bond here gives you no drop of blood; the words expressly⑰ are 'a pound of flesh'. If in the cutting off the pound of flesh you shed⑱ one drop of Christian blood, your lands and goods are by the law to be confiscated⑲ to the state of Venice." Now as it was utterly⑳ impossible for Shylock to cut off the pound of flesh without shedding some of Antonio's blood, this wise discovery of Portia's, that it was flesh and not blood that was named in the bond, saved the life of Antonio; and all admiring the wonderful

---

① term [tɜːm] *n*. 措辞 language, terminology, phraseology
② protest [prəˈtest] *v*. 声明 assert, insist, declare, vow, profess
③ entreat [ɪnˈtriːt] *v*. 恳求 beg, petition, implore, beseech
④ currish [ˈkɜːrɪʃ] *adj*. 下贱的 low-down
⑤ trifle [ˈtraɪfl] *v*. 虚度,浪费 dally, waste, idle, fritter, dawdle
⑥ pronounce [prəˈnaʊns] *v*. 宣布 declare, announce, proclaim
⑦ awful [ˈɔːfl] *adj*. 可怕的 terrible, horrible, dreadful
⑧ scale [skeɪl] *n*. 天平 balance, weigh beam, weighing machine
⑨ lest [lest] *conj*. 以防万一 in case, for fear that, in order to avoid
⑩ intent [ɪnˈtent] *n*. 意图 intention, aim, purpose, goal, target
⑪ charity [ˈtʃærəti] *n*. 仁爱 kindness, humanity, compassion
⑫ thine [ðaɪn] *pron*. 〈古〉(第二人称单数的物主代词)你的
⑬ award [əˈwɔːd] *v*. 判给,裁定 grant, render, assign, confer
⑭ exclaim [ɪkˈskleɪm] *v*. 呼喊 cry, call, shout
⑮ upright [ˈʌpraɪt] *adj*. 正直的 honest, principled, just, high-minded
⑯ tarry [ˈtæri] *v*. 等待 wait, linger, loiter
⑰ expressly [ɪkˈspresli] *adv*. 清楚地 clearly, plainly, explicitly, distinctly
⑱ shed [ʃed] *v*. 使流(血) let drop, let flow
⑲ confiscate [ˈkɒnfɪskeɪt] *v*. 没收 seize, expropriate
⑳ utterly [ˈʌtəli] *adv*. 完全地 fully, totally, entirely, completely, absolutely

sagacity[1] of the young counsellor, who had so happily[2] thought of this expedient[3], plaudits[4] resounded[5] from every part of the senate-house; and Gratiano exclaimed, in the words which Shylock had used: "O wise and upright judge! Mark[6], Jew, a Daniel is come to judgement!"

Shylock, finding himself defeated in his cruel intent, said with a disappointed look, that he would take the money; and Bassanio, rejoiced[7] beyond measure at Antonio's unexpected deliverance, cried out: "Here is the money!" But Portia stopped him, saying: "Softly; there is no haste[8]; the Jew shall have nothing but the penalty—*therefore prepare, Shylock, to cut off the flesh; but mind you shed no blood—nor do not cut off more nor less than just a pound; be it more or less by one poor scruple[9], nay if the scale turn but by the weight of a single hair, you are condemned[10] by the laws of Venice to die, and all your wealth is forfeited to the senate.[xxiii]" "Give me my money, and let me go," said Shylock. "I have it ready," said Bassanio, "here it is."

Shylock was going to take the money, when Portia again stopped him, saying: "*Tarry, Jew; I have yet another hold[11] upon you.[xxiv] By the laws of Venice, your wealth is forfeited to the state, for having conspired[12] against the life of one of its citizens, and your life lies at the mercy of[13] the duke; therefore, down on your knees, and ask him to pardon you."

The duke then said to Shylock: "*That you may see the difference of our Christian spirit, I pardon you your life before you ask it;[xxv] half your wealth belongs to Antonio, the other half comes to the state."

The generous Antonio then said that he would give up his share of Shylock's wealth, if Shylock would sign a deed[14] to make it over[15] at his death to his daughter and her husband; for Antonio knew that the Jew had an only daughter who had lately married against his consent[16] to a young Christian, named Lorenzo, a friend of Antonio's, which had so offended[17] Shylock, that he had disinherited[18] her.

The Jew agreed to this—and being thus disappointed in his revenge[19], and despoiled[20] of his riches, he said: "I am ill. Let me go home; send the deed after me, and I will sign over[21] half my

---

① sagacity [sə'gæsəti] *n*. 智慧 wisdom, shrewdness
② happily ['hæpɪli] (=aptly) *adv*. 巧妙地 cleverly, expertly, skilfully
③ expedient [ɪk'spiːdiənt] *n*. 权宜之计 means, measure, method
④ plaudit ['plɔːdɪt] *n*. 喝彩 clapping, applause
⑤ resound [rɪ'zaʊnd] *v*. 回响 echo, resonate
⑥ mark [mɑːk] *v*. 注意 mind, observe, attend, pay attention
⑦ rejoiced [rɪ'dʒɔɪst] *adj*. 高兴的 glad, happy, overjoyed, delighted
⑧ haste [heɪst] *n*. 匆忙 speed, rapidity, urgency, expedition
⑨ scruple ['skruːpl] *n*. 微量
⑩ condemn [kən'dem] *v*. 判处,判决 sentence, judge
⑪ hold [həʊld] *n*. 控制 control
⑫ conspire [kən'spaɪə(r)] *v*. 图谋 plot, scheme, intrigue, contrive
⑬ at the mercy of 由……支配 in the power of, under the control of
⑭ deed [diːd] *n*. 契约 document, contract, certificate, papers
⑮ make sth. over 移交 transfer, turn/hand sth. over, pass sth. on
⑯ consent [kən'sent] *n*. 同意 agreement, approval, permission
⑰ offend [ə'fend] *v*. 冒犯 upset, slight, displease
⑱ disinherit [ˌdɪsɪn'herɪt] *v*. 剥夺继承权 dispossess
⑲ revenge [rɪ'vendʒ] *n*. 报复 retaliation, vengeance, reprisal
⑳ despoil [dɪ'spɔɪl] *v*. 掠夺 rob, plunder, destroy, deprive
㉑ sign over 签字转让

riches to my daughter." "Get thee gone, then," said the duke, "and sign it; and if you repent① your cruelty and turn Christian, the state will forgive you the fine of the other half of your riches."

The duke now released② Antonio, and dismissed the court. He then highly praised the wisdom and ingenuity③ of the young counsellor, and invited him home to dinner. Portia, who meant to return to Belmont before her husband, replied: "I humbly④ thank your grace⑤, but I must away directly." The duke said he was sorry he had not leisure⑥ to stay and dine with him; and turning to Antonio, he added: "Reward this gentleman; for in my mind you are much indebted⑦ to him."

The duke and his senators left the court; and then Bassanio said to Portia: "Most worthy gentleman, I and my friend Antonio have by your wisdom been this day acquitted of⑧ grievous⑨ penalties, and I beg you will accept of the three thousand ducats due unto the Jew." "And * we shall stand indebted to you over and above," said Antonio, "in love and service evermore⑩.[xxvi]"

Portia could not be prevailed⑪ upon to accept the money; but upon Bassanio still pressing her to accept of some reward, she said: "Give me your gloves; I will wear them for your sake"; and then Bassanio taking off his gloves, she espied⑫ the ring which she had given him upon his finger: * now it was the ring the wily⑬ lady wanted to get from him to make a merry jest when she saw her Bassanio again, that made her ask him for his gloves;[xxvii] and she said, when she saw the ring, "and for your love I will take this ring from you." Bassanio was sadly distressed⑭ that the counsellor should ask him for the only thing he could not part with, and he replied in great confusion, that he could not give him that ring, because it was his wife's gift, and he had vowed⑮ never to part with it; but that he would give him the most valuable ring in Venice, and find it out by proclamation⑯. On this Portia affected⑰ to be affronted⑱, and left the court, saying: "* You teach me, sir, how a beggar should be answered.[xxviii]"

"Dear Bassanio," said Antonio, "let him have the ring, * let my love and the great service he has done for me be valued against your wife's displeasure.[xxix]" Bassanio, ashamed to appear so ungrateful⑲, yielded⑳, and sent Gratiano after Portia with the ring; and then the clerk Nerissa,

---

① repent [rɪ'pent] *v*. 忏悔 regret, rue
② release [rɪ'liːs] *v*. 释放 free, discharge, deliver, set free, let out
③ ingenuity [ˌɪndʒə'njuːəti] *n*. 聪明才智 genius, inventiveness
④ humbly ['hʌmbli] *adv*. 恭顺地 meekly, modestly, respectfully
⑤ your grace 阁下;大人 your excellence/lordship
⑥ leisure ['leʒə(r)] *n*. 闲暇 spare/free time, ease
⑦ indebted [ɪn'detɪd] *adj*. 蒙恩的,感激的 grateful, obliged
⑧ acquit of 使免受 protect/save from
⑨ grievous ['griːvəs] *adj*. 使人痛苦的 painful, distressing
⑩ evermore [ˌevə'mɔː(r)] *adv*. 始终,永远 always, eternally, forever
⑪ prevail [prɪ'veɪl] *v*. 说服 persuade, convince, talk into
⑫ espy [ɪ'spaɪ] *v*. 看见 catch sight of, discover, spot, notice
⑬ wily ['waɪli] *adj*. 诡计多端的 sly, crafty, tricky, cunning, foxy, artful
⑭ distressed [dɪ'strest] *adj*. 苦恼的 upset, worried, troubled, afflicted
⑮ vow [vaʊ] *v*. 发誓 promise, pledge, swear
⑯ by proclamation 公开征求
⑰ affect [ə'fekt] *v*. 假装 put on, assume, pretend, imitate, feign
⑱ affront [ə'frʌnt] *v*. 冒犯 offend, anger, irritate, provoke, insult
⑲ ungrateful [ʌn'greɪtfl] *adj*. 忘恩负义的 unappreciative, thankless
⑳ yield [jiːld] *v*. 让步 give in, surrender, concede

who had also given Gratiano a ring, she begged his ring, and Gratiano (not choosing to be outdone[1] in generosity by his lord) gave it to her. And there was laughing among these ladies to think, when they got home, how they would tax[2] their husbands with giving away their rings, and swear that they had given them as a present to some woman.

* Portia, when she returned, was in that happy temper of mind which never fails to attend the consciousness[3] of having performed a good action;[xxx] her cheerful spirits enjoyed everything she saw: the moon never seemed to shine so bright before; and when that pleasant moon was hid behind a cloud, then a light which she saw from her house at Belmont as well pleased her charmed[4] fancy, and she said to Nerissa: "* That light we see is burning in my hall; how far that little candle throws its beams, so shines a good deed in a naughty world[xxxi]"; and hearing the sound of music from her house, she said: "Methinks[5] that music sounds much sweeter than by day."

And now Portia and Nerissa entered the house, and dressing themselves in their own apparel[6], they awaited[7] the arrival of their husbands, who soon followed them with Antonio; and Bassanio presenting his dear friend to the lady Portia, the congratulations and welcomings of that lady were hardly over, when they perceived Nerissa and her husband quarrelling in a corner of the room. "A quarrel already?" said Portia. "What is the matter?" Gratiano replied: "* Lady, it is about a paltry[8] gilt[9] ring that Nerissa gave me, with words upon it like the poetry on a cutler's[10] knife: *Love me, and leave me not*.[xxxii]"

"What does the poetry or the value of the ring signify[11]?" said Nerissa. "You swore[12] to me when I gave it to you, that you would keep it till the hour of death; and now you say you gave it to the lawyer's clerk. I know you gave it to a woman." "By this hand," replied Gratiano, "I gave it to a youth, a kind of boy, a little scrubbed[13] boy, no higher than yourself; he was clerk to the young counsellor that by his wise pleading saved Antonio's life: this prating[14] boy begged it for a fee, and I could not for my life deny him." Portia said: "You were to blame, Gratiano, to part with your wife's first gift. I gave my lord Bassanio a ring, and I am sure he would not part with it for all the world." Gratiano, in excuse for his fault, now said: "My lord Bassanio gave his ring away to the counsellor, and then the boy, his clerk, that took some pains in writing, he begged my ring."

Portia, hearing this, seemed very angry, and reproached[15] Bassanio for giving away her ring;

---

① outdo [ˌaʊt'duː] *v*. (outdid, outdone) 胜过 beat, defeat, surpass, top, overcome
② tax [tæks] *v*. 指责 accuse, charge, blame, confront, impeach
③ consciousness ['kɒnʃəsnəs] *n*. 意识 awareness
④ charmed [tʃɑːmd] *adj*. 喜悦的 delighted, gladdened, overjoyed
⑤ methinks [mɪ'θɪŋks] *v*. 我想 meseems, I think, to my mind
⑥ apparel [ə'pærəl] *n*. 衣服 garment, clothes, dress, costume
⑦ await [ə'weɪt] *v*. 等待,期待 expect, wait for, look forward to
⑧ paltry ['pɔːltri] *adj*. 微不足道的 petty, slight, worthless
⑨ gilt [gɪlt] *adj*. 镀金的 gilded, golden
⑩ cutler ['kʌtlə(r)] *n*. 刀匠
⑪ signify ['sɪgnɪfaɪ] *v*. 意味着 indicate, mean, suggest, imply
⑫ swear [sweə(r)] *v*. (swore, sworn) 发誓 vow, avow, promise
⑬ scrubbed ['skrʌbɪd] *adj*. 矮小的 short, dwarf, stunted
⑭ prate [preɪt] *v*. 唠叨 chatter, babble, blather
⑮ reproach[rɪ'prəʊtʃ] *v*. 责备 blame, criticize, condemn, scold

and she said, Nerissa had taught her what to believe, and that she knew some woman had the ring. Bassanio was very unhappy to have so offended his dear lady, and he said with great earnestness: "No, by my honour, no woman had it, but a civil doctor①, who refused three thousand ducats of me, and begged the ring, which when I denied him, he went displeased away. What could I do, sweet Portia? I was so beset② with shame for my seeming ingratitude③, that I was forced to send the ring after him. * Pardon me, good lady; had you been there, I think you would have begged the ring of me to give the worthy doctor.[xxxiii]"

"Ah!" said Antonio. "I am the unhappy cause of these quarrels."

Portia bid Antonio not to grieve at that, for that he was welcome notwithstanding; and then Antonio said: "I once did lend my body for Bassanio's sake; and but for him to whom your husband gave the ring, I should have now been dead. * I dare be bound④ again, my soul upon the forfeit, your lord will never more break his faith with you.[xxxiv]"

"* Then you shall be his surety⑤," said Portia, "give him this ring, and bid him keep it better than the other.[xxxv]"

When Bassanio looked at this ring, he was strangely surprised to find it was the same he gave away; and then Portia told him how she was the young counsellor, and Nerissa was her clerk; and Bassanio found, to his unspeakable wonder and delight, that it was by the noble courage and wisdom of his wife that Antonio's life was saved.

And Portia again welcomed Antonio, and gave him letters which by some chance had fallen into her hands, which contained an account⑥ of Antonio's ships, that were supposed lost, being safely arrived in the harbour. So these tragical⑦ beginnings of this rich merchant's story were all forgotten in the unexpected good fortune which ensued⑧; and there was leisure⑨ to laugh at the comical⑩ adventure of the rings, and the husbands that did not know their own wives: Gratiano merrily swearing, in a sort of rhyming⑪ speech, that

—* While he lived, he'd fear no other thing
So sore, as keeping safe Nerissa's ring.[xxxvi]

---

① civil doctor 法学博士 doctor of law
② beset [bɪˈset] v. 困扰 trouble, plague, harass
③ ingratitude [ɪnˈɡrætɪtjuːd] n. 忘恩负义 ungratefulness
④ bound [baʊnd] adj. 受约束的 compelled, obliged
⑤ surety [ˈʃʊərəti] n. 担保 guarantee, guarantor
⑥ account [əˈkaʊnt] n. 描述 description, depiction, relation
⑦ tragical [ˈtrædʒɪkəl] adj. 悲惨的 sad, pitiable, tragic, miserable
⑧ ensue [ɪnˈsjuː] v. 接着发生 follow, proceed, come after
⑨ leisure [ˈleʒə(r)] n. 闲暇 free/spare time, ease, relaxation
⑩ comical [ˈkɒmɪkl] adj. 可笑的 funny, amusing, laughable
⑪ rhyme [raɪm] v. 押韵 match, accord, harmonize

i He was one in whom the ancient Roman honour more appeared than in any that drew breath in Italy. 所有生活在意大利的人当中，没有哪个比他更能发扬古罗马的光荣品质。(...whom... that...：定语从句中嵌套定语从句；ancient Roman honour：指古罗马人拥有的正直、诚实等可贵品质)

ii In her father's lifetime he used to visit at her house, when he thought he had observed this lady had sometimes from her eyes sent speechless messages, that seemed to say he would be no unwelcome suitor. 她(鲍西娅)父亲在世的时候，他(巴萨尼奥)经常到她家拜访。当时他觉得他曾注意到这位小姐有时会含情脉脉地看着他，好像在说，如果他向她求婚，是会受到欢迎的。(when...observed (that)...messages, that...say (that)...：状语从句中嵌套宾语从句，宾语从句中嵌套同位语从句，同位语从句中嵌套宾语从句；he thought：插入语)

iii Not having money to furnish himself with an appearance befitting the lover of so rich an heiress, he besought Antonio to add to the many favours he had shown him, by lending him three thousand ducats. 因为没有钱来摆出相称的排场去和继承了这么多财产的小姐谈恋爱，他就恳求安东尼奥在过去帮过他的许多忙之外再帮他一把：借他三千块金币。(not having...：现在分词否定形式作原因状语；befitting...＝that befitted：现在分词作后置定语)

iv If I can once catch him on the hip, I will feed fat the ancient grudge I bear him. 要是让我抓住一回他的把柄，我一定要狠狠报一报往日的仇怨。(catch him on the hip：抓住他的把柄)

v Cursed be my tribe if I forgive him! 要是我饶恕了他，我的民族不得好死！(犹太人有很深的民族意识，并且非常团结)

vi Has a dog money? Is it possible a cur should lend three thousand ducats? Shall I bend low and say, Fair sir, you spit upon me on Wednesday last, another time you called me dog, and for these courtesies I am to lend you monies. 一条狗能有钱借吗？一条野狗能借得出三千块金币吗？我应不应该哈着腰说："好先生，您上星期三啐过我，又有一回您管我叫狗。为了报答您的这些好意，我得借钱给您。"

vii If you will lend me this money, lend it not to me as to a friend, but rather lend it to me as to an enemy, that, if I break, you may with better face exact the penalty. 你要是借钱给我，不要当作借给一个朋友，宁可当作借给一个仇人。这样，如果我违约了，你就可以拉下脸来按照约定惩罚我。

viii O, father Abraham, what suspicious people these Christians are! Their own hard dealings teach them to suspect the thoughts of others. 老祖宗啊！这些基督教徒疑心病有多重呀！他们自己待人刻薄，所以会怀疑别人有这种想法。

ix Her name was Portia, and in the graces of her person and her mind she was nothing inferior to that Portia, of whom we read, who was Cato's daughter, and the wife of Brutus. 她的名字叫鲍

西娅，在品貌和才智上她都比得上我们在书上读过的那个鲍西娅——凯图的女儿，勃鲁托斯的妻子。（“那个鲍西娅”指的是莎士比亚悲剧《裘力斯·凯撒》中的同名人物，她非常机智和贤惠）

x Bassanio proving successful in his suit, Portia in a short time consented to accept of him for a husband. 巴萨尼奥求婚很顺利，没多久，鲍西娅就答应嫁给他了。（Bassanio proving…：独立主格结构作状语）

xi She, who loved him for his worthy qualities, and had riches enough not to regard wealth in a husband, answered with a graceful modesty, that she would wish herself a thousand times more fair, and ten thousand times more rich, to be more worthy of him. 她（鲍西娅）本来就是为了他那可贵的品德而爱他（巴萨尼奥），她自己很有钱，因而不在乎丈夫有没有钱。于是她很谦逊大方地说，她但愿自己有一千倍的美丽、一万倍的富有，这样才配得上他。

xii She was an unlessoned girl, unschooled, unpractised, yet not so old but that she could learn, and that she would commit her gentle spirit to be directed and governed by him in all things. 她是个没受过多少教育、没念过多少书、没有什么经验的女孩子，幸而她还年轻，还能学习。她要把自己柔顺的心灵委托给他，事事都受他的指导、管教。（not so old but that she could learn：岁数还没大到不能学习）

xiii Myself and what is mine, to you and yours is now converted. 我自己和我所有的一切，现在都成为你的了。

xiv I freely told you all the wealth I had ran in my veins; but I should have told you that I had less than nothing, being in debt. 我坦诚地告诉过你我的贵族血统是我仅有的财产；可是我本应该说，我不但什么都没有，而且还负着债呢。（freely＝frankly；should have done：本应该做，但当时并没有做）

xv Notwithstanding use your pleasure; if your love for me do not persuade you to come, let not my letter. 然而事情也要看你的兴致，要是咱们的友谊不足以让你来，那么你也不要因为这封信而来。（use your pleasure：看你的兴致；let not my letter：后面省略了 persuade you to come）

xvi As you are so dearly bought, I will dearly love you. 你既然是用这么大的代价赎来的，我一定要格外珍爱你。（dearly：一语双关）

xvii A day was appointed to try this shocking cause before the duke of Venice, and Bassanio awaited in dreadful suspense the event of the trial. 由威尼斯公爵审判这件骇人案子的日子已经确定下来了，巴萨尼奥怀着极度的不安等候着这场审判。（in dreadful suspense：忐忑不安，提心吊胆；event＝result）

xviii Notwithstanding when she wished to honour her Bassanio, she had said to him with such a meek and wifelike grace, that she would submit in all things to be governed by his superior wisdom, yet being now called forth into action by the peril of her honoured husband's friend, she did nothing doubt her own powers, and by the sole guidance of her own true and perfect judgement, at once resolved to go herself to Venice, and speak in Antonio's defence. 尽管鲍西娅为了尊重她的巴萨尼奥，曾经用一个贤惠妻子的那种温顺对他说，她会在所有事情上服从他那卓越智慧的指引；可是眼看她所敬重的丈夫的朋友就要送命，她非得去挽救一下不可。她一点儿也不怀疑自己的本领，而且单凭她自己那真实完美的判断力的指点，她立刻就决定亲自到威尼斯去替安东尼奥辩护。（notwithstanding＝although：和 yet 搭配；did nothing doubt：毫不怀疑；nothing＝not…in the least）

xix It dropped as the gentle rain from heaven upon the place beneath; and how mercy was a double blessing, it blessed him that gave, and him that received it; and how it became monarchs better than their crowns, being an attribute of God Himself; and that earthly power came nearest to God's, in proportion as mercy tempered justice. 它(仁慈)就像从天空降到地上的甘霖;仁慈是双重的赐福,它赐福于给予仁慈的人和接受仁慈的人;仁慈是上帝的一大特征,它比皇冠更与君王相称;公正越是受到仁慈的调和,世俗权威就越是接近上帝的权威。

xx A Daniel is come to judgement! O wise young judge, how I do honour you! How much elder are you than your looks! 真是一个如但以理一般的裁判啊! 啊,聪明的年轻律师,我是多么敬重你呀! 你的学问比你的年纪要高多啦!(is come=has come;Daniel:但以理,古代以色列的先知。在《旧约·次经》中,年轻的但以理担任法官,他靠自己的才干从两个坏长老的手中挽救了名为苏撒拿的女子,成为人们推崇的法官)

xxi I wish she were in heaven, if she could but entreat some power there to change the cruel temper of this currish Jew. 假如她能去求求上帝改一改这个铁石心肠的犹太人的脾气,我宁愿她已经上了天堂。(wish...were...:虚拟语气表示希望或愿望)

xxii It is not so named in the bond, but what of that? It were good you did so much for charity. 契约上没有这一条又有什么关系呢? 行点儿善总是好的。

xxiii Therefore prepare, Shylock, to cut off the flesh; but mind you shed no blood—nor do not cut off more nor less than just a pound; be it more or less by one poor scruple, nay if the scale turn but by the weight of a single hair, you are condemned by the laws of Venice to die, and all your wealth is forfeited to the senate. 因此,夏洛克,准备好割那块肉吧。可是你当心别让他流出血来。你割的肉不能比一磅多,也不能比一磅少。要是比一磅多一点点或者少一点点,分量上哪怕只差一丝一毫,就要按照威尼斯的法律判你死罪,你的全部财产就都要充公归给元老院。(nor...nor...:强调否定;be it...:即使……)

xxiv Tarry, Jew; I have yet another hold upon you. 等一等,犹太人。我手中还有你一个把柄。

xxv That you may see the difference of our Christian spirit, I pardon you your life before you ask it. 为了让你看看我们基督教徒在精神上跟你的不同,我不等你开口请求就饶你的命。(that=in order that)

xxvi We shall stand indebted to you over and above, in love and service evermore. 除此之外,我们对您还是感恩不尽的,您的恩德,您替我们出的力,我们是永远也忘不了的。

xxvii Now it was the ring the wily lady wanted to get from him to make a merry jest when she saw her Bassanio again, that made her ask him for his gloves. 原来这位睿智的夫人是想把那枚戒指弄到手,好在再见到巴萨尼奥的时候跟他开开玩笑,因此她才向他要手套。(it was the ring (that)...when..., that...:强调句中嵌套定语从句和状语从句)

xxviii You teach me, sir, how a beggar should be answered. 先生,你教会我如何去对付一个乞丐了。(鲍西娅把巴萨尼奥拒绝自己的要求比喻成打发一个乞丐)

xxix Let my love and the great service he has done for me be valued against your wife's displeasure. 看在我的友情和他帮了我大忙的分上,就开罪一次你的夫人吧。

xxx Portia, when she returned, was in that happy temper of mind which never fails to attend the consciousness of having performed a good action. 鲍西娅回到家之后心情非常愉快,一个人做了一件好事之后总会这样。

xxxi That light we see is burning in my hall; how far that little candle throws its beams, so shines a good deed in a naughty world. 我们看见的这道灯光是从我家门厅里射出来的；小小一只蜡烛的光辉照得多么远啊！同样，一件好事在这个罪恶的世界上也能发出很大的光辉。（比喻修辞；典故出自《圣经·新约·马太福音》：You are the light of the world. A town built on a hill cannot be hidden. Neither do people light a lamp and put it under a bowl. Instead they put it on its stand, and it gives light to everyone in the house. In the same way, let your light shine before others, that they may see your good deeds and glorify your Father in heaven. 你们是世上的光。城造在山上，是不能隐藏的。人点灯，不放在斗底下，是放在灯台上，就照亮一家的人。你们的光也当这样照在人前，叫他们看见你们的好行为，便将荣耀归给你们在天上的父。）

xxxii Lady, it is about a paltry gilt ring that Nerissa gave me, with words upon it like the poetry on a cutler's knife: *Love me, and leave me not*. 夫人，都是为了尼莉莎给我的一枚不值几个大钱的镀金戒指。上面刻着诗句，就跟刀匠刻在刀子上的一样：爱我，不要离开我。（刻在刀身上的诗句是没有多大价值的）

xxxiii Pardon me, good lady; had you been there, I think you would have begged the ring of me to give the worthy doctor. 饶恕我吧，好夫人。要是你在场的话，我想你一定也会央求我把戒指送给那位可敬的律师的。（had you been...= if you had been...：与过去事实相反的虚拟语气，省略 if 的倒装结构）

xxxiv I dare be bound again, my soul upon the forfeit, your lord will never more break his faith with you. 现在我敢再立一张字据，用我的灵魂担保，您的丈夫再也不会失信于您了。

xxxv Then you shall be his surety, give him this ring, and bid him keep it better than the other. 那么您就是他的担保人了，请您把这枚戒指给他，叫他保存得比那一枚更当心些。

xxxvi While he lived, he'd fear no other thing /So sore, as keeping safe Nerissa's ring. 他活着的每一天，不怕别的事，就怕丢了尼莉莎的戒指。（押尾韵）

第十二夜
Twelfth Night

Act III. Sc. 4.

O spirit of love, how quick and fresh art thou,
That, notwithstanding thy capacity
Receiveth as the sea, nought enters there,
Of what validity and pitch soe'er,
But falls into abatement and low price
Even in a minute. So full of shapes is fancy
That it alone is high fantastical.

爱情的精灵呀！你是多么敏感而活泼；
虽然你有海一样的容量，
可是无论怎样高贵超越的事物，
一进了你的范围，
便会在顷刻间失去了它的价值。
爱情是这样充满了意象，
在一切事物中是最富于幻想的。

莎士比亚了解人的思想，知道它最细微的内部变化，他没有一个词或一个思想用得不恰当：如果我们不理解他，那就是我们的过错……他头脑中最零星的想法也常常与最完美、最规范和最一致的整体有关。

——柯勒律治

《第十二夜》被公正地认为是莎士比亚所有喜剧中最令人快乐的一部，全剧充满了甜美可爱……莎士比亚的喜剧天才和蜜蜂一样，在于它从杂草恶花中收集蜜糖的能力，而不在于留下一根蜇人的刺。

——威廉·黑兹利特

这部喜剧通过巨大的设计和创造，将错综复杂的剧情和形色各异的人物融为一体……该剧特别提醒我们，莎士比亚使用的“虚幻”这个词具有双重意义，即虚幻和爱情……这些喜剧场景十分可笑，但其构思同样美妙，且意味深长。

——奥古斯特·施莱格尔

迷人、可爱的薇奥拉！率真、洒脱的奥利维亚！

——傅光明

主要人物

Orsino　奥西诺　伊利里亚公爵
Sebastian　西巴斯辛　薇奥拉之兄
Antonio　安东尼奥　船长，西巴斯辛之友
Valentine　凡伦丁　公爵侍臣
Curio　丘里奥　公爵侍臣
Malvolio　马伏里奥　奥丽维娅的管家
Olivia　奥丽维娅　富有的伯爵小姐
Viola　薇奥拉　热恋公爵者
Maria　玛利娅　奥丽维娅的侍女

地点　伊利里亚某城及其附近海滨

Twelfth Night

Sebastian and his sister Viola, a young gentleman and lady of Messaline, were twins, and (which was accounted① a great wonder) from their birth they so much resembled② each other, that, but for the difference in their dress, they could not be known apart. * They were both born in one hour, and in one hour they were both in danger of perishing③, for they were shipwrecked④ on the coast of Illyria, as they were making a sea-voyage together.[i] The ship, on board of which they were, split on a rock in a violent storm, and a very small number of the ship's company escaped with their lives. The captain of the vessel⑤, with a few of the sailors that were saved, got to land in a small boat, and with them they brought Viola safe on shore, where she, poor lady, instead of rejoicing⑥ at her own deliverance⑦, began to lament her brother's loss; but * the captain comforted her with the assurance that he had seen her brother, when the ship split, fasten⑧ himself to a strong mast⑨, on which, as long as he could see anything of him for the distance, he perceived him borne up above the waves.[ii] Viola was much consoled⑩ by the hope this account gave her, and now considered how she was to dispose of⑪ herself in a strange country, so far from home; and she asked the captain if he knew anything of Illyria. "Ay, very well, madam," replied the captain, "for I was born not three hours' travel from this place." "Who governs here?" said Viola. The captain told her, Illyria was governed by Orsino, a duke noble in nature as well as dignity⑫. Viola said, she had heard her father speak of Orsino, and that he was unmarried then. "And he is so now," said the captain, "or was so very lately, for, but a month

① account [ə'kaʊnt] *v*. 视为 consider, think, deem, regard as
② resemble [rɪ'zembl] *v*. 相像 mirror, look like, take after
③ perish ['perɪʃ] *v*. 死亡 die, be killed, decease, lose one's life
④ shipwrecked ['ʃɪprekt] *adj*. 遭遭海难的
⑤ vessel ['vesl] *n*. 船,舰 ship, boat, craft, barque
⑥ rejoice [rɪ'dʒɔɪs] *v*. 非常高兴 delight, be happy, jump for joy
⑦ deliverance [dɪ'lɪvərəns] *n*. 释放,解救 release, rescue, liberation
⑧ fasten ['fɑːsn] *v*. 系牢 tie, bind, lace, secure
⑨ mast [mɑːst] *n*. 桅杆
⑩ console [kən'səʊl] *v*. 安慰 comfort, relieve, soothe
⑪ dispose of 应付 deal/cope with, handle
⑫ dignity ['dɪgnəti] *n*. 高贵 honour, station, rank, status

ago, I went from here, and then it was the general talk (as you know what great ones do, the people will prattle① of) that Orsino sought the love of fair Olivia, a virtuous maid, the daughter of a count② who died twelve months ago, leaving Olivia to the protection of her brother, who shortly after died also; and for the love of this dear brother, they say, she has abjured③ the sight and company④ of men." Viola, who was herself in such a sad affliction⑤ for her brother's loss, wished she could live with this lady, who so tenderly⑥ mourned⑦ a brother's death. She asked the captain if he could introduce her to Olivia, saying she would willingly serve this lady. But he replied, this would be a hard thing to accomplish, because the lady Olivia would admit no person into her house since her brother's death, not even the duke himself. Then Viola formed another project in her mind, which was, in a man's habit⑧, to serve the duke Orsino as a page⑨. * It was a strange fancy in a young lady to put on male attire⑩, and pass for⑪ a boy; but the forlorn⑫ and unprotected state of Viola, who was young and of uncommon beauty, alone, and in a foreign land, must plead⑬ her excuse. [iii]

She having observed a fair behaviour in the captain, and that he showed a friendly concern⑭ for her welfare⑮, entrusted⑯ him with her design, and he readily engaged⑰ to assist her. Viola gave him money, and directed him to furnish⑱ her with suitable apparel⑲, ordering her clothes to be made of the same colour and in the same fashion her brother Sebastian used to wear, and * when she was dressed in her manly garb⑳, she looked so exactly like her brother that some strange errors happened by means of their being mistaken for each other; for, as will afterwards appear, Sebastian was also saved. [iv]

Viola's good friend, the captain, when he had transformed this pretty lady into a gentleman, having some interest at court, got her presented to Orsino under the feigned㉑ name of Cesario. * The duke was wonderfully pleased with the address㉒ and graceful deportment㉓ of this handsome

---

① prattle [ˈprætl] *v*. 喋喋不休 chatter, babble, rattle on
② count [kaʊnt] *n*. 伯爵
③ abjure [əbˈdʒʊə(r)] *v*. 发誓放弃 abandon, forswear, give up
④ company [ˈkʌmpəni] *n*. 陪伴
⑤ affliction [əˈflɪkʃn] *n*. 痛苦 suffering, distress, misery
⑥ tenderly [ˈtendəli] *adv*. 温柔地 gently, mildly, affectionately
⑦ mourn [mɔːn] *v*. 哀悼 miss, lament, weep/wail/grieve for
⑧ habit [ˈhæbɪt] *n*. 衣服 clothes, attire, garment, apparel, garb
⑨ page [peɪdʒ] *n*. 男侍 attendant, pageboy, footboy, servant
⑩ attire [əˈtaɪə(r)] *n*. 服装 clothes, wear, dress, habit, raiment
⑪ pass for 扮作 impersonate, disguise as, dress up as
⑫ forlorn [fəˈlɔːn] *adj*. 被遗弃的，孤独的 pitiful, helpless, miserable
⑬ plead [pliːd] *v*. 恳求 beg, appeal, petition, solicit, beseech
⑭ concern [kənˈsɜːn] *n*. 关心 care, consideration
⑮ welfare [ˈwelfeə(r)] *n*. 幸福 wellbeing, happiness
⑯ entrust [ɪnˈtrʌst] *v*. 委托 confide, commit, turn over
⑰ engage [ɪnˈgeɪdʒ] *v*. 承诺 promise, undertake, go in for
⑱ furnish [ˈfɜːnɪʃ] *v*. 提供 supply, offer, provide, present
⑲ apparel [əˈpærəl] *n*. 衣服 garment, clothes, dress, costume
⑳ garb [gɑːb] *n*. 衣服 clothes, attire, habit, habiliment, uniform
㉑ feigned [feɪnd] *adj*. 假装的 false, fake, pretended
㉒ address [əˈdres] *n*. 谈吐
㉓ deportment [dɪˈpɔːtmənt] *n*. 风度，举止 air, bearing, conduct

youth, and made Cesario one of his pages that being the office Viola wished to obtain①[v] —and she so well fulfilled② the duties of her new station③, and showed such a ready observance④ and faithful attachment to her lord, that she soon became his most favoured attendant⑤. To Cesario Orsino confided⑥ the whole history of his love for the lady Olivia. * To Cesario he told the long and unsuccessful suit⑦ he had made to one who, rejecting⑧ his long services, and despising his person, refused to admit him to her presence; and for the love of this lady who had so unkindly treated him, the noble Orsino, forsaking⑨ the sports of the field and all manly exercises in which he used to delight, passed his hours in ignoble⑩ sloth⑪, listening to the effeminate⑫ sounds of soft music, gentle airs⑬, and passionate⑭ love-songs;[vi] and neglecting⑮ the company of the wise and learned lords with whom he used to associate⑯, he was now all day long conversing⑰ with young Cesario. * Unmeet⑱ companion no doubt his grave⑲ courtiers thought Cesario was for their once noble master, the great duke Orsino.[vii]

* It is a dangerous matter for young maidens to be the confidantes⑳ of handsome young dukes, which Viola too soon found to her sorrow, for all that Orsino told her he endured㉑ for Olivia, she presently perceived she suffered for the love of him; and much it moved her wonder, that Olivia could be so regardless of this her peerless㉒ lord and master, whom she thought no one could behold㉓ without the deepest admiration, and she ventured㉔ gently to hint㉕ to Orsino, that it was a pity he should affect㉖ a lady who was so blind to his worthy㉗ qualities;[viii] and she said: " * If a lady were to love you, my lord, as you love Olivia (and perhaps there may be one who does), if you could not love her in return, would you not tell her that you could not love, and must she not

---

① obtain [əb'teɪn] *v*. 获得 get, gain, acquire, attain, procure
② fulfill [fʊl'fɪl] *v*. 履行 perform, execute, carry out
③ station ['steɪʃn] *n*. 身份 position, rank, status
④ observance [əb'zɜːvəns] *n*. 专注 attentiveness
⑤ attendant [ə'tendənt] *n*. 侍者 assistant, servant
⑥ confide[kən'faɪd] *v*. 吐露 reveal, confess, disclose
⑦ suit [suːt] *n*. 追求 courtship, wooing, pursuit
⑧ reject [rɪ'dʒekt] *v*. 拒绝 refuse, decline, repulse, turn down
⑨ forsake [fə'seɪk] *v*. 抛弃 desert, abandon, quit, cast off
⑩ ignoble [ɪg'nəʊbl] *adj*. 不光彩的 infamous, disgraceful
⑪ sloth [sləʊθ] *n*. 懒散 laziness, idleness, indolence
⑫ effeminate [ɪ'femɪnət] *adj*. 女人气的 womanly, feminine
⑬ air [eə(r)] *n*. 曲调 tune, theme, melody, strain
⑭ passionate ['pæʃənət] *adj*. 热情的 ardent, excited, enthusiastic
⑮ neglect [nɪ'glekt] *v*. 忽视 ignore, overlook, pass over
⑯ associate [ə'səʊsieɪt] *v*. 交往 mix, befriend, socialize
⑰ converse [kən'vɜːs] *v*. 交谈 talk, speak, chat, communicate
⑱ unmeet [ˌʌn'miːt] *adj*. 不合适的 unfit, improper, inappropriate
⑲ grave [greɪv] *adj*.严肃的,庄重的 serious, solemn
⑳ confidante ['kɒnfɪdænt] *n*. 知己,密友 close/bosom friend
㉑ endure [ɪn'djʊə(r)] *v*. 忍受 stand, tolerate, bear, put up with
㉒ peerless ['pɪələs] *adj*. 无与伦比的 matchless, incomparable
㉓ behold [bɪ'həʊld] *v*. 看,注视 see, look/gaze at, watch, observe
㉔ venture ['ventʃə(r)] *v*. 冒险,敢于去 dare, risk, chance, stake, hazard
㉕ hint [hɪnt] *v*. 暗示 suggest, indicate, imply, intimate, insinuate
㉖ affect [ə'fekt] *v*. 喜欢 like, love, adore, go for, be fond of
㉗ worthy ['wɜːði] *adj*. 有价值的 deserving

be content with this answer? [ix]"

But Orsino would not admit of this reasoning①, for he denied that it was possible for any woman to love as he did. He said, * no woman's heart was big enough to hold so much love, and therefore② it was unfair to compare the love of any lady for him, to his love for Olivia.[x] Now, though Viola had the utmost③ deference④ for the duke's opinions, she could not help thinking this was not quite true, for she thought her heart had full as much love in it as Orsino's had; and she said: "Ah, but I know, my lord."

"What do you know, Cesario?" said Orsino. "Too well I know," replied Viola, "what love women may owe⑤ to men. They are as true of heart as we are. * My father had a daughter loved a man, as I perhaps, were I a woman, should love your lordship.[xi]" "And what is her history?" said Orsino. "A blank, my lord," replied Viola, "* she never told her love, but let concealment⑥, like a worm in the bud, feed on her damask⑦ cheek. She pined⑧ in thought, and with a green and yellow melancholy, she sat like Patience on a monument, smiling at Grief.[xii]" * The duke inquired⑨ if this lady died of her love, but to this question Viola returned an evasive⑩ answer; as probably she had feigned⑪ the story, to speak words expressive⑫ of the secret love and silent grief she suffered for Orsino.[xiii]

While they were talking, a gentleman entered whom the duke had sent to Olivia, and he said: "* So please you, my lord, I might not be admitted to the lady, but by her handmaid⑬ she returned you this answer: Until seven years hence⑭, the element itself shall not behold⑮ her face; but like a cloistress⑯ she will walk veiled⑰, watering her chamber with her tears for the sad remembrance⑱ of her dead brother.[xiv]" On hearing this, the duke exclaimed⑲: "* O she that has a

---

① reasoning ['riːzənɪŋ] *n*. 推理
② therefore ['ðeəfɔː(r)] *adv*. 因此 so, thus, consequently, as a result
③ utmost ['ʌtməʊst] *adj*. 最大的,极度的 greatest, highest, maximum
④ deference ['defərəns] *n*. 敬重 respect, esteem, reverence
⑤ owe [əʊ] (=own) *v*. 拥有 possess, have, keep, hold
⑥ concealment [kən'siːlmənt] *n*. 隐藏 cover, hiding
⑦ damask ['dæməsk] *adj*. 粉红色的 pink
⑧ pine [paɪn] *v*. 悲哀,难过
⑨ inquire [ɪn'kwaɪə(r)] *v*. 询问 ask, question, query, interrogate
⑩ evasive[ɪ'veɪsɪv] *adj*. 逃避的
⑪ feign [feɪn] *v*. 编造 invent, fabricate, devise, forge, make up
⑫ expressive [ɪk'spresɪv] *adj*. 意味深长的,有表现力的 indicative, suggestive
⑬ handmaid ['hændmeɪd] *n*. 侍女 housemaid, chambermaid
⑭ hence [hens] *adv*. 从此以后 hereafter, from now on, in the future
⑮ behold [bɪ'həʊld] *v*. 看到 see, watch, observe
⑯ cloistress ['klɔɪstrɪs] *n*. 修女 nun, abbess, religious woman
⑰ veil [veɪl] *v*. 使戴面纱 cover, screen, mask
⑱ remembrance [rɪ'membrəns] *n*. 回想,记忆 memory, recollection
⑲ exclaim [ɪk'skleɪm] *v*. 惊叫 cry out, call, shout, yell

heart of this fine frame①, to pay this debt of love to a dead brother, how will she love, when the rich golden shaft② has touched her heart![xv]" And then he said to Viola: "You know, Cesario, I have told you all the secrets of my heart; therefore, good youth, go to Olivia's house. * Be not denied③ access④; stand at her doors, and tell her, there your fixed foot shall grow till you have audience⑤.[xvi]" "And if I do speak to her, my lord, what then?" said Viola. "* O then," replied Orsino, "unfold⑥ to her the passion⑦ of my love. Make a long discourse⑧ to her of my dear faith. It will well become you to act my woes⑨, for she will attend⑩ more to you than to one of graver⑪ aspect⑫.[xvii]"

Away then went Viola; * but not willingly did she undertake this courtship⑬, for she was to woo⑭ a lady to become a wife to him she wished to marry[xviii] —but having undertaken the affair,

she performed it with fidelity⑮; and Olivia soon heard that a youth was at her door who insisted upon being admitted to her presence. "I told him," said the servant, "that you were sick—he said he knew you were, and therefore he came to speak with you. I told him that you were asleep—he seemed to have a foreknowledge⑯ of that too, and said, that therefore he must speak with you. What is to be said to him, lady? for he seems fortified⑰ against all denial⑱, and will speak with you, whether you will or no."

Olivia, curious to see who this peremptory⑲ messenger might be, desired he might be admitted; and throwing her veil over her face, she said she would once more hear Orsino's embassy⑳, not doubting but that he came from the duke, by his importunity㉑. Viola, entering, put on the most manly air

① frame [freɪm] n. 框架，结构 form, structure, construction
② the golden shaft（爱神丘比特的）金箭
③ deny [dɪˈnaɪ] v. 拒绝给予 refuse, decline, disallow, reject
④ access [ˈækses] n. 进入 entry, admission, passage, admittance
⑤ audience [ˈɔːdiəns] n. 正式会见 interview, meeting, reception
⑥ unfold [ʌnˈfəʊld] v. 展示 show, reveal, present, make known
⑦ passion [ˈpæʃn] n. 强烈情感 emotion, zest, ardour, fervour
⑧ discourse [ˈdɪskɔːs] n. 交谈 chat, conversation, communication
⑨ woe [wəʊ] n. 痛苦 misery, suffering, grief, sadness, sorrow
⑩ attend [əˈtend] v. 注意 mind, pay attention, take to heart
⑪ grave [greɪv] adj. 严肃的 serious, severe, grim-faced, unsmiling
⑫ aspect [ˈæspekt] n. 外表 appearance, countenance, feature
⑬ courtship [ˈkɔːtʃɪp] n. 追求，求爱 wooing, courting, dating, (pur)suit
⑭ woo [wuː] v. 追求 court, date, chase, pursue, seek the hand of
⑮ fidelity [fɪˈdeləti] n. 忠诚 loyalty, faith
⑯ foreknowledge [fɔːˈnɒlɪdʒ] n. 预知 foresight, prevision
⑰ fortify [ˈfɔːtɪfaɪ] v. 防御 protect, defend, secure
⑱ denial [dɪˈnaɪəl] n. 拒绝 refusal, rejection, rebuff, repulse
⑲ peremptory [pəˈremptəri] adj. 专横的 bossy, imperious, arbitrary
⑳ embassy [ˈembəsi] n. 信使；消息 messenger, message
㉑ importunity [ˌɪmpɔːˈtjuːnətɪ] n. 强求

she could assume, and affecting[1] the fine courtier[2] language of great men's pages, she said to the veiled lady: "* Most radiant[3], exquisite[4], and matchless beauty, I pray you tell me if you are the lady of the house; for I should be sorry to cast away[5] my speech upon another; for besides that it is excellently well penned, I have taken great pains to learn[6] it.[xix]" "Whence[7] come you, sir?" said Olivia. "I can say little more than I have studied," replied Viola, "and that question is out of my part." "Are you a comedian[8]?" said Olivia. "No," replied Viola, "and yet I am not that which I play"; meaning that she, being a woman, feigned herself to be a man. And again she asked Olivia if she were the lady of the house.

Olivia said she was; and then Viola, having more curiosity to see her rival's features, than haste[9] to deliver her master's message, said: "Good madam, let me see your face." With this bold[10] request Olivia was not averse[11] to comply[12]; for this haughty[13] beauty, whom the duke Orsino had loved so long in vain[14], at first sight conceived[15] a passion[16] for the supposed page, the humble[17] Cesario.

When Viola asked to see her face, Olivia said: "Have you any commission[18] from your lord and master to negotiate[19] with my face?" And then, forgetting her determination[20] to go veiled for seven long years, she drew aside her veil, saying: "* But I will draw the curtain and show the picture. Is it not well done?[xx]" Viola replied: "* It is beauty truly mixed; the red and white upon your cheeks is by Nature's own cunning[21] hand laid on.[xxi] * You are the most cruel[22] lady living, if you will lead these graces[23] to the grave, and leave the world no copy.[xxii]" "O, sir," replied Olivia, "I will not be so cruel. * The world may have an inventory[24] of my beauty. As, *item*, two lips, indifferent red; *item*, two grey eyes, with lids to them; one neck; one chin; and so forth.[xxiii] Were you sent here to praise me?"

Viola replied: "I see what you are: you are too proud, but you are fair. My lord and master

---

① affect [ə'fekt] *v*. 假装 assume, feign, pretend, imitate, put on
② courtier ['kɔːtiə(r)] *n*. 奉承者 flatterer, fawner, bootlicker
③ radiant ['reɪdiənt] *adj*. 容光焕发的 bright, brilliant, glorious
④ exquisite [ɪk'skwɪzɪt] *adj*. 优雅的，精致的 graceful, elegant
⑤ cast away 扔掉，抛弃
⑥ learn [lɜːn] *v*. 记住 remember, memorize, learn by heart
⑦ whence [wens] *adv*. 〈古〉从何处，从哪里 from where
⑧ comedian [kə'miːdiən] *n*. 喜剧演员 joker, jester, clown
⑨ haste [heɪst] *n*. 匆忙 speed, rapidity, urgency, swiftness
⑩ bold [bəʊld] *adj*. 大胆的 brave, courageous, daring, fearless
⑪ averse [ə'vɜːs] *adj*. 厌恶的，反对的 opposed, hostile
⑫ comply [kəm'plaɪ] *v*. (～ with) 顺从 obey, follow, abide by
⑬ haughty ['hɔːti] *adj*. 傲慢的 proud, arrogant, lofty, contemptuous
⑭ in vain 徒劳 to no avail
⑮ conceive [kən'siːv] *v*. 构想 imagine, envisage, fancy, think up
⑯ passion ['pæʃn] *n*. 爱情 love, fondness, affection
⑰ humble ['hʌmbl] *adj*. 卑微的 mean, low-born
⑱ commission [kə'mɪʃn] *n*. 委托，命令 duty, task, mission
⑲ negotiate [nɪ'gəʊʃieɪt] *v*. 谈判 discuss, debate, hold talks
⑳ determination [dɪˌtɜːmɪ'neɪʃn] *n*. 决定 decision, resolution
㉑ cunning ['kʌnɪŋ] *adj*. 巧妙的 skilled, skilful, masterly, expert
㉒ cruel ['kruːəl] *adj*. 残忍的 merciless, inhuman, cold-blooded
㉓ grace [greɪs] *n*. 优雅 elegance, refinement, gracefulness
㉔ inventory ['ɪnvəntri] *n*. 清单 list, catalogue, directory

loves you. * O such a love could but be recompensed①, though you were crowned② the queen of beauty—for Orsino loves you with adoration③ and with tears, with groans④ that thunder⑤ love, and sighs⑥ of fire.[xxiv]" "Your lord," said Olivia, "knows well my mind. I cannot love him; yet I doubt not he is virtuous; I know him to be noble and of high estate⑦, of fresh and spotless⑧ youth. * All voices proclaim⑨ him learned, courteous⑩, and valiant⑪; yet I cannot love him, he might have taken his answer long ago.[xxv]"

"* If I did love you as my master does," said Viola, "I would make me a willow⑫ cabin at your gates, and call upon your name, I would write complaining sonnets⑬ on Olivia, and sing them in the dead of the night; your name should sound among the hills, and I would make Echo, the babbling⑭ gossip⑮ of the air, cry out *Olivia*.[xxvi] * O you should not rest between the elements of earth and air, but you should pity me.[xxvii]" "You might do much," said Olivia, "what is your parentage⑯?" Viola replied: "* Above my fortunes, yet my state is well.[xxviii] I am a gentleman."

Olivia now reluctantly⑰ dismissed Viola, saying: "Go to your master, and tell him, I cannot love him. Let him send no more, unless perchance⑱ you come again to tell me how he takes it." And Viola departed⑲, bidding the lady farewell⑳ by the name of Fair Cruelty㉑.

When she was gone, Olivia repeated the words, *Above my fortunes, yet my state is well. I am a gentleman*. And she said aloud: "I will be sworn㉒ he is; his tongue, his face, his limbs, action, and spirit, plainly show he is a gentleman." And then she wished Cesario was the duke; and * perceiving the fast㉓ hold he had taken on her affections, she blamed herself for her sudden love: but the gentle blame which people lay upon their own faults has no deep root;[xxix] and presently * the noble lady Olivia so far forgot the inequality between her fortunes and those of this seeming㉔

---

① recompense [ˈrekəmpens] *v*. 酬谢，回报
② crown [kraʊn] *v*. 加冕
③ adoration [ˌædəˈreɪʃn] *n*. 崇拜 worship, admiration, idolization
④ groan [grəʊn] *n*. 呻吟 cry, sigh, moan, grumble
⑤ thunder [ˈθʌndə(r)] *v*. 打雷，发出雷鸣般的响声 rumble, crack, blast, explode, roar
⑥ sigh [saɪ] *n*. 叹息 moan, groan, grumble, whine, exhalation
⑦ estate [ɪˈsteɪt] *n*. 身份 class, rank, caste, status, position
⑧ spotless [ˈspɒtləs] *adj*. 纯洁的 clean, pure, faultless, unstained
⑨ proclaim [prəˈkleɪm] *v*. 宣布 announce, declare, profess
⑩ courteous [ˈkɜːtiəs] *adj*. 有礼貌的 polite, civil, well-mannered
⑪ valiant [ˈvæliənt] *adj*. 英勇的 brave, heroic, courageous, fearless
⑫ willow [ˈwɪləʊ] *n*. 柳树(象征单相思)
⑬ sonnet [ˈsɒnɪt] *n*. 十四行诗
⑭ babble [ˈbæbl] *v*. 喋喋不休 chatter, prattle
⑮ gossip [ˈgɒsɪp] *n*. 多嘴的人 babbler, prattler, chatterbox
⑯ parentage [ˈpeərəntɪdʒ] *n*. 出身 family, birth, origin, descent
⑰ reluctantly [rɪˈlʌktəntli] *adv*. 不情愿地 unwillingly, hesitantly
⑱ perchance [pəˈtʃɑːns] *adv*. 或许 perhaps, maybe, by chance
⑲ depart [dɪˈpɑːt] *v*. 离去 leave, withdraw, retire, quit, go away
⑳ bid sb. farewell 向某人告别 bid farewell to sb., say goodbye to sb.
㉑ Fair Cruelty 狠心的美人
㉒ swear [sweə(r)] *v*. (swore, sworn) 发誓 vow, promise, warrant
㉓ fast [fɑːst] *adj*. 紧紧的，稳固的 firm, tight, fixed, secure, sound
㉔ seeming [ˈsiːmɪŋ] *adj*. 表面上的 apparent, outward

page, as well as the maidenly① reserve② which is the chief ornament③ of a lady's character, that she resolved to court the love of young Cesario, and sent a servant after him with a diamond ring, under the pretence④ that he had left it with her as a present from Orsino.[xxx] She hoped by thus artfully⑤ making Cesario a present of the ring, she should give him some intimation⑥ of her design; and truly it did make Viola suspect⑦; for knowing that Orsino had sent no ring by her, she began to recollect⑧ that Olivia's looks and manner were expressive of admiration, and she presently guessed her master's mistress had fallen in love with her.

"*Alas," said she, "the poor lady might as well love a dream.[xxxi] *Disguise⑨ I see is wicked⑩, for it has caused Olivia to breathe as fruitless sighs for me as I do for Orsino.[xxxii]"

Viola returned to Orsino's palace, and related⑪ to her lord the ill success of the negotiation⑫, repeating the command of Olivia, that the duke should trouble her no more. Yet still the duke persisted⑬ in hoping that the gentle Cesario would in time⑭ be able to persuade⑮ her to show some pity, and therefore he bade⑯ him he should go to her again the next day. In the meantime⑰, to pass away⑱ the tedious⑲ interval⑳, he commanded a song which he loved to be sung; and he said: "My good Cesario, when I heard that song last night, methought it did relieve㉑ my passion much. Mark it, Cesario, it is old and plain㉒. *The spinsters㉓ and the knitters when they sit in the sun, and the young maids that weave㉔ their thread with bone, chant㉕ this song.[xxxiii] It is

---

① maidenly [ˈmeɪdnli] *adj*. 少女的 girlish
② reserve [rɪˈzɜːv] *n*. 矜持 shyness, modesty
③ ornament [ˈɔːnəmənt] *n*. 装饰 decoration, adornment
④ pretence [prɪˈtens] *n*. 托词,借口 excuse, pretext
⑤ artfully [ˈɑːtfəli] *adv*. 巧妙地 skillfully, cleverly, smartly, ingeniously
⑥ intimation [ˌɪntɪˈmeɪʃn] *n*. 暗示 hint, suggestion, indication
⑦ suspect [səˈspekt] *v*. 怀疑 distrust, doubt, mistrust
⑧ recollect [ˌrekəˈlekt] *v*. 回忆 remember, recall, look back on
⑨ disguise [dɪsˈgaɪz] *n*. 伪装 mask, deception, concealment
⑩ wicked [ˈwɪkɪd] *adj*. 邪恶的 evil, vile, vicious, immoral, devilish
⑪ relate [rɪˈleɪt] *v*. 讲述 tell, recount, describe, report, narrate
⑫ negotiation [nɪˌgəʊʃiˈeɪʃn] *n*. 谈判 bargaining, debate
⑬ persist [pəˈsɪst] *v*. 坚持 persevere, press on, stand firm
⑭ in time 最终,终究 eventually, sooner or later
⑮ persuade [pəˈsweɪd] *v*. 说服 talk/argue into, prevail upon
⑯ bid [bɪd] *v*. (bade, bidden) 吩咐 ask, order, charge, command
⑰ in the meantime 与此同时 at the same time
⑱ pass away 消磨(时间) kill, pass, spend, while away
⑲ tedious [ˈtiːdiəs] *adj*. 枯燥乏味的 boring, dull, dreary, tiresome
⑳ interval [ˈɪntəvl] *n*. 间歇 break, interlude, intermission, pause
㉑ relieve [rɪˈliːv] *v*. 缓解 ease, soothe, alleviate, relax, soften
㉒ plain [pleɪn] *adj*. 简单的,朴素的 clear, simple, unadorned
㉓ spinster [ˈspɪnstə(r)] (=spinner) *n*. 纺线者
㉔ weave [wiːv] *v*. 编织
㉕ chant [tʃɑːnt] *v*. 吟唱 sing, chorus, recite, intone

silly, yet I love it, for it tells of the innocence① of love in the old times."

SONG

* Come away, come away, Death,
And in sad cypress② let me be laid;
Fly away, fly away, breath,
I am slain③ by a fair cruel maid.
My shroud④ of white stuck all with yew⑤, O prepare it!
My part of death no one so true did share it.
Not a flower, not a flower sweet,
On my black coffin let there be strewn⑥—
Not a friend, not a friend greet
My poor corpse⑦, where my bones shall be thrown.
A thousand thousand sighs to save, lay me O where
Sad true lover never find my grave, to weep⑧ there! [xxxiv]

* Viola did not fail to mark the words of the old song, which in such true simplicity⑨ described⑩ the pangs⑪ of unrequited⑫ love, and she bore testimony⑬ in her countenance⑭ of feeling what the song expressed.[xxxv] Her sad looks were observed by Orsino, who said to her: "* My life upon it, Cesario, though you are so young, your eye has looked upon some face that it loves: has it not, boy?[xxxvi]" "A little, with your leave⑮," replied Viola. "And what kind of woman, and of what age is she?" said Orsino. "Of your age and of your complexion⑯, my lord," said Viola, which made the duke smile to hear this fair young boy loved a woman so much older than himself, and of a man's dark complexion; but Viola secretly meant Orsino, and not a woman like him.

When Viola made her second visit to Olivia, she found no difficulty in gaining access to her. Servants soon discover when their ladies delight⑰ to converse⑱ with handsome young messengers; and the instant Viola arrived, the gates were thrown wide open, and the duke's page was shown into Olivia's apartment with great respect; and when Viola told Olivia that she was come once

---

① innocence [ˈɪnəsns] *n*. 天真 naiveté, simplicity, inexperience
② cypress [ˈsaɪprəs] *n*. 柏树（象征悲哀）
③ slay [sleɪ] *v*.（slew, slain）杀死 kill, slaughter, massacre
④ shroud [ʃraʊd] *n*. 裹尸布 winding sheet, grave clothes
⑤ yew [juː] *n*. 紫杉(象征不朽)
⑥ strew [struː] *v*.（strewed, strewn）散播，撒满 scatter, spread, litter
⑦ corpse [kɔːps] *n*. 尸体 body, remains, cadaver, dead body
⑧ weep [wiːp] *v*. 哭泣 cry, sob, shed tears
⑨ simplicity [sɪmˈplɪsəti] *n*. 简单 plainness, naturalness, purity
⑩ describe [dɪˈskraɪb] *v*. 描述 relate, express, illustrate, depict
⑪ pang [pæŋ] *n*. 剧痛，痛苦 pain, stab, sting, ache, throe
⑫ unrequited [ˌʌnrɪˈkwaɪtɪd] *adj*. 得不到回应的 unanswered
⑬ bear testimony 证明
⑭ countenance [ˈkaʊntənəns] *n*. 面容 face, feature, expression
⑮ with your leave 对不起，请您原谅
⑯ complexion [kəmˈplekʃn] *n*. 肤色 skin, color, hue, skin tone
⑰ delight [dɪˈlaɪt] *v*. 非常高兴 joy, rejoice, exult
⑱ converse [kənˈvɜːs] *v*. 交谈 talk, speak, chat, communicate

more to plead① in her lord's behalf, this lady said: "*I desired you never to speak of him again; but if you would undertake another suit②, I had rather hear you solicit③, than music from the spheres④.[xxxvii]"

This was pretty plain⑤ speaking, but Olivia soon explained herself still more plainly, and openly confessed⑥ her love; and when she saw displeasure with perplexity⑦ expressed⑧ in Viola's face, she said: "*O what a deal of scorn⑨ looks beautiful in the contempt⑩ and anger of his lip![xxxviii] Cesario, by the roses of the spring, by maidhood⑪, honour, and by truth, I love you so, that, in spite of your pride, I have neither wit nor reason to conceal⑫ my passion."

But in vain the lady wooed⑬; Viola hastened⑭ from her presence, threatening never more to come to plead Orsino's love; and all the reply she made to Olivia's fond solicitation⑮ was, a declaration⑯ of a resolution⑰ *Never to love any woman.*

*No sooner had Viola left the lady than a claim⑱ was made upon her valour⑲.[xxxix] A gentleman, a rejected⑳ suitor of Olivia, who had learned how that lady had favoured㉑ the duke's messenger, challenged㉒ him to fight a duel㉓. *What should poor Viola do, who, though she carried a manlike outside, had a true woman's heart, and feared to look on her own sword?[xl]

When she saw her formidable㉔ rival advancing㉕ towards her with his sword drawn, she began

---

① plead [pliːd] *v*. 恳求 beg, appeal, petition, solicit, beseech
② suit [suːt] *n*. 追求 courtship, courting, wooing, pursuit
③ solicit [səˈlɪsɪt] *v*. 请求 petition, beseech, entreat, implore
④ sphere [sfɪə(r)] *n*. 天体 globe, orb, planet
⑤ plain [pleɪn] *adj*. 清楚的,显而易见的 clear, obvious, evident, manifest
⑥ confess [kənˈfes] *v*. 坦白 admit, acknowledge, disclose
⑦ perplexity [pəˈpleksəti] *n*. 困惑 confusion, puzzlement
⑧ express [ɪkˈspres] *v*. 表现 show, exhibit, depict, demonstrate
⑨ scorn [skɔːn] *n*. 轻蔑,蔑视 disdain, contempt
⑩ contempt [kənˈtempt] *n*. 鄙视 disdain, scorn, mockery
⑪ maidhood [ˈmeɪdhʊd] *n*. 贞洁 purity, chasteness, virginity
⑫ conceal [kənˈsiːl] *v*. 隐藏 hide, bury, cover
⑬ woo [wuː] *v*. 追求 court, date, chase, pursue, make love to
⑭ hasten [ˈheɪsn] *v*. 赶往 rush, run, race, hurry
⑮ solicitation [səˌlɪsɪˈteɪʃn] *n*. 恳求 plea, appeal, suit
⑯ declaration [ˌdekləˈreɪʃn] *n*. 宣布 announcement
⑰ resolution [ˌrezəˈluːʃn] *n*. 决心 resolve, determination
⑱ claim [kleɪm] *n*. 要求 demand, application, request
⑲ valour [ˈvælə(r)] *n*. 英勇 bravery, courage, heroism, boldness
⑳ reject [rɪˈdʒekt] *v*. 拒绝 refuse, repulse, decline, turn down
㉑ favour [ˈfeɪvə(r)] *v*. 偏爱 prefer, like better, incline towards
㉒ challenge [ˈtʃælɪndʒ] *v*. 挑战 provoke, defy
㉓ duel [ˈdjuːəl] *n*. 决斗 fight, battle, single combat
㉔ formidable [ˈfɔːmɪdəbl] *adj*. 可怕的 horrible, terrifying, fearful
㉕ advance [ədˈvɑːns] *v*. 行进 progress, go forward, press on

to think of confessing that she was a woman; but * she was relieved① at once from her terror②, and the shame of such a discovery, by a stranger that was passing by, who made up to them, and as if he had been long known to her, and were her dearest friend, [xli] said to her opponent③: "* If this young gentleman has done offence④, I will take the fault on me; and if you offend him, I will for his sake defy⑤ you.[xlii]"

Before Viola had time to thank him for his protection, or to inquire⑥ the reason of his kind interference⑦, her new friend met with an enemy where his bravery was of no use to him; for the officers of justice⑧ coming up in that instant, apprehended⑨ the stranger in the duke's name⑩, to answer for⑪ an offence he had committed⑫ some years before—and he said to Viola: "This comes with seeking you"—and then he asked her for a purse, saying: "* Now my necessity⑬ makes me ask for my purse, and it grieves⑭ me much more for what I cannot do for you, than for what befalls⑮ myself. You stand amazed⑯, but be of comfort.[xliii]"

His words did indeed amaze Viola, and she protested⑰ she knew him not, nor had ever received a purse from him; but for the kindness he had just shown her, she offered him a small sum of money, being nearly the whole she possessed⑱. And now the stranger spoke severe⑲ things, charging⑳ her with ingratitude㉑ and unkindness. He said: "* This youth, whom you see here, I snatched㉒ from the jaws of death and for his sake alone I came to Illyria, and have fallen into this danger.[xliv]"

But the officers cared little for hearkening㉓ to the complaints㉔ of their prisoner, and they hurried him off, saying: "What is that to us?" And as he was carried away, he called Viola by the name of Sebastian, reproaching the supposed㉕ Sebastian for disowning㉖ his friend, as long as he

---

① relieved [rɪ'liːvd] *adj*. 感到宽慰的 happy, pleased, comforted
② terror ['terə(r)] *n*. 恐惧 fear, alarm, dread, fright, panic
③ opponent [ə'pəʊnənt] *n*. 对手 rival, adversary, foe
④ offence [ə'fens] *n*. 冒犯 insult, rudeness
⑤ defy [dɪ'faɪ] *v*. 反抗 resist, oppose, confront, stand up to
⑥ inquire [ɪn'kwaɪə(r)] *v*. 询问 ask, question, query, interrogate
⑦ interference [ˌɪntə'fɪərəns] *n*. 干涉 intrusion, intervention
⑧ officer of justice 司法官员
⑨ apprehend [ˌæprɪ'hend] *v*. 逮捕 arrest, catch, capture, seize
⑩ in sb.'s name 以某人的名义 on behalf of sb.
⑪ answer for 对……负责 be responsible for, take the blame for
⑫ commit [kə'mɪt] *v*. 犯(罪或错等) do, perform, execute
⑬ necessity [nə'sesəti] *n*. 必须,必要 need
⑭ grieve [griːv] *v*. 使悲伤 sadden, distress, break the heart of
⑮ befall [bɪ'fɔːl] *v*. 降临到……头上 happen to, fall upon, occur in
⑯ amazed [ə'meɪzd] *adj*. 吃惊的 astonished, astounded
⑰ protest [prə'test] *v*. 坚决表示,申明 argue, insist, assert, maintain
⑱ possess [pə'zes] *v*. 拥有 own, have, hold, be in possession of
⑲ severe [sɪ'vɪə(r)] *adj*. 严重的 serious, critical, terrible
⑳ charge [tʃɑːdʒ] *v*. 指责 blame, accuse, reproach
㉑ ingratitude [ɪn'grætɪtjuːd] *n*. 忘恩负义 ungratefulness
㉒ snatch [snætʃ] *v*. 拯救 save, free, rescue, salvage
㉓ hearken ['hɑːkən] *v*. 倾听 listen, hear, give ears
㉔ complaint [kəm'pleɪnt] *n*. 抱怨 accusation
㉕ supposed [sə'pəʊzd] *adj*. 所谓的 so-called, assumed, claimed
㉖ disown [dɪs'əʊn] *v*. 否认 deny, reject, disclaim

was within hearing. * When Viola heard herself called Sebastian, though the stranger was taken away too hastily[1] for her to ask an explanation[2], she conjectured[3] that this seeming mystery[4] might arise[5] from her being mistaken for[6] her brother; and she began to cherish[7] hopes that it was her brother whose life this man said he had preserved[8].[xiv] And so indeed it was. The stranger, whose name was Antonio, was a sea-captain. He had taken Sebastian up into his ship, when, almost exhausted[9] with fatigue[10], he was floating[11] on the mast to which he had fastened himself in the storm. * Antonio conceived[12] such a friendship for Sebastian, that he resolved[13] to accompany[14] him whithersoever[15] he went; and when the youth expressed a curiosity to visit Orsino's court, Antonio, rather than part from him, came to Illyria, though he knew, if his person should be known there, his life would be in danger, because in a sea-fight he had once dangerously wounded the duke Orsino's nephew.[xlvi] This was the offence for which he was now made a prisoner.

Antonio and Sebastian had landed together but a few hours before Antonio met Viola. He had given his purse to Sebastian, desiring him to use it freely if he saw anything he wished to purchase[16], telling him he would wait at the inn, while Sebastian went to view the town; but Sebastian not returning at the time appointed[17], Antonio had ventured[18] out to look for him, and Viola being dressed the same, and in face so exactly resembling[19] her brother, Antonio drew his sword (as he thought) in defence of[20] the youth he had saved, and when Sebastian (as he supposed) disowned him, and denied him his own purse, no wonder[21] he accused[22] him of ingratitude[23].

---

① hastily ['heɪstɪli] *adv*. 匆忙地 quickly, rapidly, speedily, hurriedly
② explanation [ˌekspləˈneɪʃn] *n*. 解释 account
③ conjecture [kənˈdʒektʃə(r)] *v*. 猜测 guess, suppose
④ mystery ['mɪstri] *n*. 谜 puzzle, riddle, enigma
⑤ arise [əˈraɪz] *v*. 发生 happen, occur, come about
⑥ mistake...for... 把……错认为…… confuse...with...
⑦ cherish ['tʃerɪʃ] *v*. 抱有 hold, harbour, keep in mind
⑧ preserve [prɪˈzɜːv] *v*. 保护 protect, defend, safeguard
⑨ exhausted [ɪgˈzɔːstɪd] *adj*. 筋疲力尽的 tired, worn out, fatigued
⑩ fatigue [fəˈtiːg] *n*. 疲劳 tiredness, weariness, lethargy
⑪ float [fləʊt] *v*. 漂浮 hang, hover, stay afloat
⑫ conceive [kənˈsiːv] *v*. 构想 imagine, suppose, fancy, think up
⑬ resolve [rɪˈzɒlv] *v*. 决定 decide, determine, make up sb's mind
⑭ accompany [əˈkʌmpəni] *v*. 陪同
⑮ whithersoever [ˌwɪðəsəʊˈevə(r)] *adv*.〈古〉无论到何方 wherever
⑯ purchase ['pɜːtʃəs] 购买 buy, gain, obtain, acquire, pay for
⑰ appoint [əˈpɔɪnt] *v*. 约定 decide, set, determine, settle, fix
⑱ venture ['ventʃə] *v*. 敢于去 go, travel, wander, stray, set out
⑲ resemble [rɪˈzembl] *v*. 相像 mirror, look like, take after
⑳ in defence of 保卫 protection, safeguard, security
㉑ no wonder 难怪,怪不得,不足为怪 it is no wonder that
㉒ accuse [əˈkjuːz] *v*. (~ sb. of sth.) 控诉 charge with, indict for
㉓ ingratitude [ɪnˈgrætɪtjuːd] *n*. 忘恩负义 ungratefulness

Viola, when Antonio was gone, fearing a second invitation to fight, slunk① home as fast as she could. She had not been long gone, when her adversary② thought he saw her return; but it was her brother Sebastian, who happened to arrive at this place, and he said: "Now, sir, have I met with you again? There's for you"; and struck him a blow. * Sebastian was no coward③; he returned the blow with interest④, and drew his sword.[xlvii]

A lady now put a stop to this duel, for Olivia came out of the house, and she too mistaking Sebastian for Cesario, invited him to come into her house, expressing much sorrow at the rude attack he had met with. * Though Sebastian was as much surprised at the courtesy⑤ of this lady as at the rudeness of his unknown foe⑥, yet he went very willingly⑦ into the house, and Olivia was delighted⑧ to find Cesario (as she thought him) become more sensible⑨ of her attentions; for though their features⑩ were exactly the same, there was none of the contempt⑪ and anger to be seen in his face, which she had complained of when she told her love to Cesario.[xlviii]

Sebastian did not at all object⑫ to the fondness⑬ the lady lavished⑭ on him. * He seemed to take it in very good part, yet he wondered how it had come to pass, and he was rather inclined⑮ to think Olivia was not in her right senses⑯; but perceiving that she was mistress of a fine house, and that she ordered her affairs and seemed to govern her family discreetly⑰, and that in all but her sudden love for him she appeared in the full possession of her reason, he well approved of the courtship; and Olivia finding Cesario in this good humour⑱, and fearing he might change his mind, proposed⑲ that, as she had a priest⑳ in the house, they should be instantly married.[xlix] Sebastian assented㉑ to this proposal; and when the marriage ceremony was over, he left his lady for a short time, intending

---

① slink [slɪŋk] *v*. (slunk) 偷偷溜走 creep, steal, sneak, slip
② adversary ['ædvəsəri] *n*. 对手 opponent, rival, opposer
③ coward ['kaʊəd] *n*. 胆小鬼 weakling, craven, faint heart
④ interest ['ɪntrəst] *n*. 利息 returns, profits, gain, earnings
⑤ courtesy ['kɜːtəsi] *n*. 礼貌 politess, civility, good manners
⑥ foe [fəʊ] *n*. 仇敌 enemy, opponent, adversary, antagonist
⑦ willingly ['wɪlɪŋli] *adv*. 乐意地 readily, voluntarily, with pleasure
⑧ delighted [dɪ'laɪtɪd] *adj*. 高兴的 pleased, overjoyed, over the moon
⑨ sensible ['sensəbl] *adj*. 能感觉到的 aware, conscious, sensitive
⑩ features ['fiːtʃəz] *n*. 容貌 look, appearance, countenance
⑪ contempt [kən'tempt] *n*. 鄙视 disdain, scorn, disrespect
⑫ object [əb'dʒekt] *v*. (~ to) 反对 oppose, disagree, protest
⑬ fondness ['fɒndnəs] *n*. 喜爱 liking, affection, preference
⑭ lavish ['lævɪʃ] *v*. 慷慨(或过度)给予
⑮ inclined [ɪn'klaɪnd] *adj*. 有……意向,倾向于…… ready, prone, likely, liable
⑯ sense [sens] *n*. 意识 understanding, awareness
⑰ discreetly [dɪ'skriːtli] *adv*. 谨慎地 carefully, cautiously, warily, prudently
⑱ in a good humour 心情好
⑲ propose [prə'pəʊz] *v*. 提议 advise, suggest, recommend
⑳ priest [priːst] *n*. 牧师 father, pastor, churchman, clergyman
㉑ assent [ə'sent] *v*. 同意 approve, agree/consent to

to go and tell his friend Antonio the good fortune that he had met with. In the meantime Orsino came to visit Olivia: and at the moment he arrived before Olivia's house, the officers of justice brought their prisoner, Antonio, before the duke. * Viola was with Orsino, her master; and when Antonio saw Viola, whom he still imagined to be Sebastian, he told the duke in what manner he had rescued this youth from the perils of the sea; and after fully relating all the kindness he had really shown to Sebastian, he ended his complaint with saying, that for three months, both day and night, this ungrateful① youth had been with him.[l] But now the lady Olivia coming forth from her house, the duke could no longer attend to② Antonio's story; and he said: "* Here comes the countess③: now Heaven walks on earth![li] but for thee, fellow, thy words are madness. Three months has this youth attended on④ me"—and then he ordered Antonio to be taken aside.

* But Orsino's heavenly⑤ countess soon gave the duke cause to accuse Cesario as much of ingratitude as Antonio had done, for all the words he could hear Olivia speak were words of kindness to Cesario—and when he found his page⑥ had obtained⑦ this high place in Olivia's favour⑧, he threatened⑨ him with all the terrors⑩ of his just⑪ revenge⑫;[lii] and as he was going to depart⑬, he called Viola to follow him, saying: "Come, boy, with me. * My thoughts are ripe for mischief⑭.[liii]" * Though it seemed in his jealous⑮ rage⑯ he was going to doom⑰ Viola to instant death, yet her love made her no longer a coward, and she said she would most joyfully suffer death to give her master ease.[liv]

But Olivia would not so lose her husband, and she cried: "Where goes my Cesario?" Viola replied: "* After him I love more than my life.[lv]" Olivia, however, prevented⑱ their departure⑲ by loudly proclaiming⑳ that Cesario was her husband, and sent for the priest, who declared that

---

① ungrateful [ʌnˈgreɪtfl] *adj*. 忘恩负义的 thankless, unthankful
② attend to 专注,关注 pay attention to
③ countess [ˈkaʊntəs] *n*. 伯爵夫人
④ attend on 照料 look after, care for, take care of
⑤ heavenly [ˈhevnli] *adj*. 神圣的 holy
⑥ page [peɪdʒ] *n*. 男侍 attendant, footboy, servant
⑦ obtain [əbˈteɪn] *v*. 获得 get, gain, acquire, attain, get hold of
⑧ favour [ˈfeɪvə(r)] *n*. 偏爱 liking, preference
⑨ threaten [ˈθretn] *v*. 威胁 warn, intimidate, bully, menace
⑩ terror [ˈterə(r)] *n*. 恐怖 fear, alarm, dread, fright, panic, anxiety
⑪ just [dʒʌst] *adj*. 正义的 fair, right, righteous, impartial
⑫ revenge [rɪˈvendʒ] *n*. 报复 retaliation, vengeance, reprisal
⑬ depart [dɪˈpɑːt] *v*. 离去 leave, withdraw, retire, quit, go away
⑭ mischief [ˈmɪstʃɪf] *n*. 恶作剧 prank
⑮ jealous [ˈdʒeləs] *adj*. 妒忌的 envious, green-eyed
⑯ rage [reɪdʒ] *n*. 狂怒 anger, fury, passion, wrath
⑰ doom [duːm] *v*. 判决 condemn, sentence
⑱ prevent [prɪˈvent] *v*. 阻止 stop, obstruct, hinder, restrain
⑲ departure [dɪˈpɑːtʃə(r)] *n*. 离开 retreat
⑳ proclaim [prəˈkleɪm] *v*. 宣布 announce, declare

not two hours had passed since he had married the lady Olivia to this young man. * In vain Viola protested she was not married to Olivia; the evidence① of that lady and the priest made Orsino believe that his page had robbed him of the treasure he prized above his life.[lvi] * But thinking that it was past recall②, he was bidding farewell to his faithless③ mistress, and the young dissembler④, her husband, as he called Viola, warning her never to come in his sight again, when (as it seemed to them) a miracle⑤ appeared! [lvii] For another Cesario entered, and addressed⑥ Olivia as his wife. This new Cesario was Sebastian, the real husband of Olivia; and * when their wonder had a little ceased⑦ at seeing two persons with the same face, the same voice, and the same habit, the brother and sister began to question each other; for Viola could scarce⑧ be persuaded that her brother was living, and Sebastian knew not how to account for⑨ the sister he supposed drowned⑩ being found in the habit of a young man.[lviii] But Viola presently acknowledged⑪ that she was indeed Viola, and his sister, under that disguise.

When all the errors were cleared up which the extreme⑫ likeness between this twin brother and sister had occasioned⑬, they laughed at the lady Olivia for the pleasant mistake she had made in falling in love with a woman; and Olivia showed no dislike to her exchange, when she found she had wedded⑭ the brother instead of the sister.

* The hopes of Orsino were for ever at an end by this marriage of Olivia, and with his hopes, all his fruitless love seemed to vanish⑮ away, and all his thoughts were fixed on the event of his favourite, young Cesario, being changed into a fair lady.[lix] He viewed Viola with great attention, and he remembered how very handsome he had always thought Cesario was, and he concluded⑯ she would look very beautiful in a woman's attire; and * then he remembered how often she had said she loved him, which at the time seemed only the dutiful⑰ expressions⑱ of a faithful page; but now he guessed that something more was meant, for many of her pretty sayings, which were like riddles⑲ to him, came now into his mind, and he no sooner remembered all these things than he resolved to make Viola his wife;[lx] and he said to her (he still could not help calling her Cesario and boy): "* Boy, you have said to me a thousand times that you should never love a woman like

---

① evidence ['evɪdəns] n. 证词,证据 testimony
② past recall 不能挽回的
③ faithless ['feɪθləs] adj. 不忠诚的 disloyal, unreliable, false-hearted
④ dissembler [dɪ'semblə(r)] n. 伪善者 fraud, deceiver, pretender
⑤ miracle ['mɪrəkl] n. 奇迹 wonder
⑥ address [ə'dres] v. 称呼
⑦ cease [siːs] v. 停止 stop, end, finish, come to an end
⑧ scarce [skeəs] adv. 几乎不 scarcely, hardly, barely, almost not
⑨ account for 解释 explain, justify, clarify, clear up
⑩ drown [draʊn] v. 淹死
⑪ acknowledge [ək'nɒlɪdʒ] v. 承认 admit, concede, confess
⑫ extreme [ɪk'striːm] adj. 极度的 greatest, supreme, maximum
⑬ occasion [ə'keɪʒn] v. 引起 cause, bring about, give rise to
⑭ wed [wed] v. 结婚 marry, get married, tie the knot
⑮ vanish ['vænɪʃ] v. 突然消失 disappear, fade away, die out
⑯ conclude [kən'kluːd] v. 断定 reason out
⑰ dutiful ['djuːtɪfl] adj. 忠实的;顺从的 devoted, obedient, compliant
⑱ expression [ɪk'spreʃn] n. 表达 statement, declaration, utterance
⑲ riddle ['rɪdl] n. 谜 puzzle, problem, enigma, question, mystery

to me, and for the faithful service you have done for me so much beneath① your soft and tender② breeding③, and since you have called me master so long, you shall now be your master's mistress④, and Orsino's true duchess⑤.[lxi]"

Olivia, perceiving Orsino was making over that heart, which she had so ungraciously⑥ rejected, to Viola, invited them to enter her house, and offered the assistance of the good priest, who had married her to Sebastian in the morning, to perform the same ceremony in the remaining part of the day for Orsino and Viola. * Thus⑦ the twin brother and sister were both wedded on the same day: the storm and shipwreck⑧, which had separated⑨ them, being the means of bringing to pass⑩ their high and mighty⑪ fortunes.[lxii] Viola was the wife of Orsino, the duke of Illyria, and Sebastian the husband of the rich and noble countess, the lady Olivia.

Malvolio. Sweet lady, ho, ho.
Olivia. Smil'st thou?
I sent for thee upon a sad occasion.
Act III. Scene IV.

① beneath [bɪ'ni:θ] *prep*. 在……下面 under, below, underneath
② tender ['tendə(r)] *adj*. 温柔的 gentle, considerate, soft-hearted
③ breeding ['bri:dɪŋ] *n*. 教养 refinement, manner, elegance
④ mistress ['mɪstrəs] *n*. 女主人
⑤ duchess ['dʌtʃəs] *n*. 公爵夫人
⑥ ungraciously [ʌn'greɪʃəsli] *adv*. 不礼貌地 rudely, impolitely, discourteously
⑦ thus [ðʌs] *adv*.这样 so, in this way/manner/fashion
⑧ shipwreck ['ʃɪprek] *n*. 海难
⑨ separate ['sepəreɪt] *v*. 分开 divide, disconnect, keep apart
⑩ bring to pass 引起 lead to, result in, bring about, give rise to
⑪ mighty ['maɪti] *adj*. 巨大的,非凡的 huge, massive, extraordinary

i They were both born in one hour, and in one hour they were both in danger of perishing, for they were shipwrecked on the coast of Illyria, as they were making a sea-voyage together. 他们是在同一个时辰生下来的,又在同一个时辰遇到性命危险。因为当他们一起在海上航行的时候,他们的船在伊利里亚海岸失事了。

ii The captain comforted her with the assurance that he had seen her brother, when the ship split, fasten himself to a strong mast, on which, as long as he could see anything of him for the distance, he perceived him borne up above the waves. 船长安慰她说,船身破裂的时候他看见她哥哥把自己绑在一根结实的桅杆上,漂浮在波浪上面,直到远得看不见了。(...assurance that...:同位语从句;...mast, on which...:定语从句)

iii It was a strange fancy in a young lady to put on male attire, and pass for a boy; but the forlorn and unprotected state of Viola, who was young and of uncommon beauty, alone, and in a foreign land, must plead her excuse. 一位年轻的姑娘竟要穿上男装,假扮成男孩子,这是一个奇怪的想法;然而这位年轻而且异常美丽的薇奥拉是处在一种孤苦伶仃、无依无靠的情况下,又是一个人在外乡漂泊,这么做也算是情有可原吧。(must plead her excuse:也算是情有可原吧)

iv When she was dressed in her manly garb, she looked so exactly like her brother that some strange errors happened by means of their being mistaken for each other; for, as will afterwards appear, Sebastian was also saved. 她穿起男装来就跟她哥哥一模一样。后来由于他们被人认错,产生了一些离奇的误会。因为,后面我们会知道,西巴斯辛也被救了。(so...that...:如此……以至于……;as...:定语从句)

v The duke was wonderfully pleased with the address and graceful deportment of this handsome youth, and made Cesario one of his pages that being the office Viola wished to obtain. 公爵对这个俊秀少年的谈吐和文雅的举止十分满意,就叫西萨里奥当他的侍从,那正是薇奥拉想得到的差使。

vi To Cesario he told the long and unsuccessful suit he had made to one who, rejecting his long services, and despising his person, refused to admit him to her presence; and for the love of this lady who had so unkindly treated him, the noble Orsino, forsaking the sports of the field and all manly exercises in which he used to delight, passed his hours in ignoble sloth, listening to the effeminate sounds of soft music, gentle airs, and passionate love-songs. 他告诉西萨里奥,他向奥丽维娅求爱已经求了好多日子,一直也没有成功。他向她献了许久的殷勤,她都拒绝了,她看不起他这个人,不准他去见她。高贵的奥西诺为了向这位对他这么冷淡的姑娘求爱,连他一向所喜欢的野外游戏和一切男人的运动都放弃了,整天没精打采地消磨时光,听着靡靡之音,比如轻柔的音乐、哀伤的曲调和热烈的情歌。(suit (that)...one who...:定语从句中嵌套定语从句)

vii Unmeet companion no doubt his grave courtiers thought Cesario was for their once noble master, the great duke Orsino. 那些严肃的朝臣无疑都认为对于他们这位曾经非常高贵的主人——大公爵奥西诺来说,西萨里奥不是一个好伴侣。(unmeet...:表语提前的倒装结构)

viii It is a dangerous matter for young maidens to be the confidantes of handsome young dukes, which Viola too soon found to her sorrow, for all that Orsino told her he endured for Olivia, she presently perceived she suffered for the love of him; and much it moved her wonder, that Olivia could be so regardless of this her peerless lord and master, whom she thought no one could behold without the deepest admiration, and she ventured gently to hint to Orsino, that it was a pity he should affect a lady who was so blind to his worthy qualities. 年轻的姑娘给年轻漂亮的公爵当知音是件危险的事情，薇奥拉很快就发现了这一点，她十分难过。奥西诺把奥丽维娅加给他的折磨都告诉了她，而她因为爱上了公爵，这一切折磨她也都尝到了。她觉得像她的主人这样没人能比的贵族，谁见了都要深深爱慕，而奥丽维娅居然对他这样毫不理睬，真是莫名其妙。她温和地对奥西诺暗示说，可惜他偏偏爱上了一位丝毫不能赏识到他可贵品德的姑娘。(it…, that…, whom…：主语从句中嵌套定语从句)

ix If a lady were to love you, my lord, as you love Olivia (and perhaps there may be one who does), if you could not love her in return, would you not tell her that you could not love, and must she not be content with this answer? 大人，要是有一位姑娘爱上了您，正像您爱上了奥丽维娅(也许真的有这么个人)，要是您不能转过来去爱她，您不也就干脆告诉她，您不能爱她；她得到这个答复，不也得认为满足了吗？(if…were to/could…, would…：与将来相反的虚拟语气)

x No woman's heart was big enough to hold so much love, and therefore it was unfair to compare the love of any lady for him, to his love for Olivia. 没有一个女人的心里装得下那么多的爱，因此，用别的女人对他的爱跟他对奥丽维娅的爱来比较是不公平的。

xi My father had a daughter loved a man, as I perhaps, were I a woman, should love your lordship. 我父亲有个女儿，她爱上了一个男人，正像假如我是女的，也许会爱上您一样。(…daughter (who/that)…：定语从句中省略了作主语的关系代词，在现代英语中一般不可省略；were I…, should…＝if I were…, I should…：与现在事实相反的虚拟语气，倒装结构)

xii She never told her love, but let concealment, like a worm in the bud, feed on her damask cheek. She pined in thought, and with a green and yellow melancholy, she sat like Patience on a monument, smiling at Grief. 她从来没有表白过她的爱，只让这个秘密像花蕾里的虫子一样，侵蚀着她绯红的面颊。她因相思而憔悴，疾病和忧愁折磨着她，她像纪念碑上刻着的"忍耐"的化身那样坐着，向着"悲哀"微笑。(比喻和拟人修辞)

xiii The duke inquired if this lady died of her love, but to this question Viola returned an evasive answer; as probably she had feigned the story, to speak words expressive of the secret love and silent grief she suffered for Orsino. 公爵问起这位姑娘是不是害相思病死掉了，薇奥拉对这个问题回答得很含糊，因为这故事多半是她编的，为了表示她对奥西诺的隐秘爱情和她默默忍受的痛苦。(在莎士比亚的原剧中，薇奥拉是这样回答的：I am all the daughters of my father's house,/And all the brothers too—and yet I know not.)

xiv So please you, my lord, I might not be admitted to the lady, but by her handmaid she returned you this answer: Until seven years hence, the element itself shall not behold her face; but like a cloistress she will walk veiled, watering her chamber with her tears for the sad remembrance of her dead brother. 禀告大人，那位小姐不许我进去见她，只叫侍女传出这样一个答复给您：七年以内，就是大自然也见不到她的脸。她要像一个修女那样蒙着面纱走路，以此哀悼她死去的哥哥，她要把她的绣房洒满泪水。(the element：指空气)

xv O she that has a heart of this fine frame, to pay this debt of love to a dead brother, how will she love, when the rich golden shaft has touched her heart! 啊，她有这么好的一颗心，对她死去的哥哥这样念念不忘，要是有一天她的心被爱情这支富丽的金箭射中，她会爱得多么炽热啊！

xvi Be not denied access; stand at her doors, and tell her, there your fixed foot shall grow till you have audience. 不要被挡回来；站在她的门口，告诉她，你将一直站在那儿，直到脚下生根，直到她接见你。

xvii O then, unfold to her the passion of my love. Make a long discourse to her of my dear faith. It will well become you to act my woes, for she will attend more to you than to one of graver aspect. 那么，让她知道我多么爱她。把我的一片真心实意详详细细地告诉她。你替我去诉说我的相思苦恼，真是再合适不过了，因为比起那些板着面孔的人，她对你会更欢迎些。

xviii But not willingly did she undertake this courtship, for she was to woo a lady to become a wife to him she wished to marry. 但是她心里并不情愿替公爵去求爱，因为她是替一个她想嫁的男人去向另外一个女人求婚。（...not...did she...：否定词开头的部分倒装结构；...him (who/that)...：定语从句中省略了作宾语的关系代词）

xix Most radiant, exquisite, and matchless beauty, I pray you tell me if you are the lady of the house; for I should be sorry to cast away my speech upon another; for besides that it is excellently well penned, I have taken great pains to learn it. 最灿烂、卓绝、无与伦比的美人，请问您就是这府上的小姐吗？我不情愿把话白白说给别人听，因为我要说的话，不但写得很漂亮，而且是我费了好大的劲儿才背下来的。

xx But I will draw the curtain and show the picture. Is it not well done? 好吧，我把帷幕拉开，让你看看这幅画吧，画得好吗？

xxi It is beauty truly mixed; the red and white upon your cheeks is by Nature's own cunning hand laid on. 这幅画太美了。您脸颊上的红与白都刚好合适，只有大自然的巧手才能涂抹出这样的色彩。

xxii You are the most cruel lady living, if you will lead these graces to the grave, and leave the world no copy. 要是您甘心让这样的美埋没到坟墓里，不给世间留个副本，那么您就是世界上心肠最狠的人了。（copy：一语双关，既可以指美丽的画像，又可以指孩子）

xxiii The world may have an inventory of my beauty. As, *item*, two lips, indifferent red; *item*, two grey eyes, with lids to them; one neck; one chin; and so forth. 我可以给世界开一张我的美丽的清单，例如：红得恰到好处的嘴唇两片，附带眼睑的灰色眼睛一双，脖子一个，下巴一个，等等。（indifferent＝somewhat：有点，稍微，有几分）

xxiv O such a love could but be recompensed, though you were crowned the queen of beauty—for Orsino loves you with adoration and with tears, with groans that thunder love, and sighs of fire. 啊，尽管您是位绝色美人，但是这样的爱只能被酬谢，因为奥西诺是用崇敬的心和眼泪爱着您，他用雷鸣般的呻吟和烈火一样的叹息诉说着他的爱。（could but＝could not but：只有，只能）

xxv All voices proclaim him learned, courteous, and valiant; yet I cannot love him, he might have taken his answer long ago. 大家都说他学问好、懂礼貌而且勇敢，可是我不能爱他。这一点他早就该知道了。（might have done：本可能）

xxvi If I did love you as my master does, I would make me a willow cabin at your gates, and call upon your name, I would write complaining sonnets on Olivia, and sing them in the dead of the night; your name should sound among the hills, and I would make Echo, the babbling gossip of the air, cry out *Olivia*. 我要是像我主人那样爱您，我就用柳木在您家大门前头搭一间小屋，大声喊着您的名字；我要写一些拿奥丽维娅作主题的十四行诗，在深夜里歌唱；您的名字将响彻群山，我要让空中那个多嘴的厄科叫喊着"奥丽维娅"。

(willow:杨柳,象征单相思,此处薇奥拉既是在替公爵求婚,也是在倾吐自己单相思的酸涩苦楚;Echo:厄科,希腊神话中的山林女神,因受到天后赫拉的惩罚而不能正常说话,只能重复别人说的最后几个字)

xxvii O you should not rest between the elements of earth and air, but you should pity me. 你在天地间将得不到安宁,除非你怜悯我。(but=unless)

xxviii Above my fortunes, yet my state is well. 比我眼下的身份要高(超过我目前的境遇),不过我眼下的地位也不算低了。(state:社会地位)

xxix Perceiving the fast hold he had taken on her affections, she blamed herself for her sudden love: but the gentle blame which people lay upon their own faults has no deep root. 奥丽维娅意识到那个侍从牢牢地抓住了她的心,她责备自己不该这么突然地爱上了他,可是人们对自身过失的这种轻微责备没有很深的根基。

xxx The noble lady Olivia so far forgot the inequality between her fortunes and those of this seeming page, as well as the maidenly reserve which is the chief ornament of a lady's character, that she resolved to court the love of young Cesario, and sent a servant after him with a diamond ring, under the pretence that he had left it with her as a present from Orsino. 这位高贵的奥丽维娅小姐很快就把她跟这个乔装的侍从在地位上的差距,以及一个少女的腼腆(这是一个淑女品德的主要装饰)忘得干干净净,她竟决心去向年轻的西萨里奥求爱了。她派仆人拿着一枚钻石戒指追上西萨里奥,假装说那是西萨里奥留在她那儿的奥西诺的礼物。(...so far..., ...which..., that...: 结果状语从句中嵌套定语从句;...pretence that...: 同位语从句)

xxxi Alas, the poor lady might as well love a dream. 唉,这位可怜的姑娘还不如爱上一场梦。(may/might as well: 不妨,何妨;倒不如)

xxxii Disguise I see is wicked, for it has caused Olivia to breathe as fruitless sighs for me as I do for Orsino. 如今我明白了,女扮男装并不是什么好事情,因为这样做白白地叫奥利维娅为我害单相思,正像我白白地为奥西诺害单相思一样。

xxxiii The spinsters and the knitters when they sit in the sun, and the young maids that weave their thread with bone, chant this song. 纺线和编织的姑娘坐着晒太阳的时候唱它,年轻的姑娘用骨头针织东西的时候也唱它。

xxxiv

Come away, come away, Death,	过来吧,过来吧,死神!
And in sad cypress let me be laid;	让我横陈在凄凉的柏棺的中央;
Fly away, fly away, breath,	飞去吧,飞去吧,浮生!
I am slain by a fair cruel maid.	我被害于一个狠心的美貌姑娘。
My shroud of white stuck all with yew,	为我罩上白色的殓衾铺满紫杉;
O prepare it!	
My part of death no one so true did share it.	没有一个真心的人为我而悲哀。
Not a flower, not a flower sweet,	莫让一朵花儿甜柔,
On my black coffin let there be strewn—	撒上了我那黑色的、黑色的棺材;
Not a friend, not a friend greet	没有一个朋友迓候
My poor corpse, where my bones shall be thrown.	我尸身,不久我的骨骼将会散开。
A thousand thousand sighs to save, lay me O where	免得多情的人们千万次的感伤,
Sad true lover never find my grave, to weep there!	请把我埋葬在无从凭吊的荒场。

xxxv Viola did not fail to mark the words of the old song, which in such true simplicity described the pangs of unrequited love, and she bore testimony in her countenance of feeling what the song expressed. 薇奥拉果然留意了这支古老歌曲的歌词，它用真实、朴素的语言写出了单恋的痛苦，她的脸上流露出了这首歌所表现的感情。（which...：非限制性定语从句；what...：宾语从句）

xxxvi My life upon it, Cesario, though you are so young, your eye has looked upon some face that it loves: has it not, boy? 我用生命来起誓，西萨里奥，你虽然年纪很轻，但你的眼睛已经见到了你所爱之人。对不对，孩子？

xxxvii I desired you never to speak of him again; but if you would undertake another suit, I had rather hear you solicit, than music from the spheres. 我求你永远不要再提他了；但如果你要替另一个人求婚，我倒愿意听听你的请求，比听天上的音乐还要高兴。（had rather＝would rather；music from the spheres：天体的音乐，古希腊哲学家毕达哥拉斯认为各天体在按一定轨道围绕地球运行时必会产生一种和谐的音乐）

xxxviii O what a deal of scorn looks beautiful in the contempt and anger of his lip! 啊，他嘴角流露的轻蔑和怒气看起来是多么美丽！

xxxix No sooner had Viola left the lady than a claim was made upon her valour. 薇奥拉刚辞别奥丽维娅，就有人来试探她的胆量。（No sooner...than...＝Hardly/Scarcely...when...：倒装结构，刚……就……）

xl What should poor Viola do, who, though she carried a manlike outside, had a true woman's heart, and feared to look on her own sword? 可怜的薇奥拉怎么办好呢？她外表虽然是个男子，内心却完全是个女人，她都不敢去看自己身上佩的剑。

xli She was relieved at once from her terror, and the shame of such a discovery, by a stranger that was passing by, who made up to them, and as if he had been long known to her, and were her dearest friend. 这时候一个过路的陌生人立刻消除了她这种恐惧，也使她避免了暴露女人身份的耻辱。这个人走过来，就像是跟她认识多年的最亲密的朋友似的。（...that..., who...：双重定语从句；as if...：非真实方式状语从句）

xlii If this young gentleman has done offence, I will take the fault on me; and if you offend him, I will for his sake defy you. 要是这位年轻的先生冒犯了你，我替他担个不是；要是你冒犯了他，那么我就替他来跟你拼一下。

xliii Now my necessity makes me ask for my purse, and it grieves me much more for what I cannot do for you, than for what befalls myself. You stand amazed, but be of comfort. 我现在有了需要，不得不向你讨回我那只钱袋了。比起自己的遭遇，无法为你尽力更让我难过。你站在那里像是很吃惊，可是你尽管放心吧。

xliv This youth, whom you see here, I snatched from the jaws of death and for his sake alone I came to Illyria, and have fallen into this danger. 你们眼前的这个小伙子是我从死神的手中救出来的。全都是为了他，我才到伊利里亚来的，如今却落到这样危险的地步。

xlv When Viola heard herself called Sebastian, though the stranger was taken away too hastily for her to ask an explanation, she conjectured that this seeming mystery might arise from her being mistaken for her brother; and she began to cherish hopes that it was her brother whose life this man said he had preserved. 薇奥拉听到这个人叫她“西巴斯辛”，虽然衙吏匆忙地把那个陌生人带走了，使她来不及问个究竟，可是她猜想这件看似奇怪的事情可能是因

为那人错把她当成她哥哥了。她希望那个人所说的他搭救过的人就是她哥哥。(when..., though...:时间状语从句中嵌套让步状语从句;hopes that...whose...:同位语从句中嵌套定语从句)

xlvi Antonio conceived such a friendship for Sebastian, that he resolved to accompany him whithersoever he went; and when the youth expressed a curiosity to visit Orsino's court, Antonio, rather than part from him, came to Illyria, though he knew, if his person should be known there, his life would be in danger, because in a sea-fight he had once dangerously wounded the duke Orsino's nephew. 安东尼奥和西巴斯辛产生了深刻的友谊,他决定不论西巴斯辛去哪儿,他都要陪伴在侧。安东尼奥曾经在一场海战中让奥西诺公爵的侄子受过重伤。当西巴斯辛表示好奇,想看看奥西诺的宫廷的时候,安东尼奥明明知道如果他被发现在这里,一定性命难保,然而他宁可陪西巴斯辛到伊利里亚来,也不肯跟他分开。(such... that...结构;if...should..., ...would...:与将来相反的虚拟语气)

xlvii Sebastian was no coward; he returned the blow with interest, and drew his sword. 西巴斯辛并不是个懦夫,他用加倍的力气还了那个人一拳,然后拔出剑来。(returned the blow with interest:加倍回击)

xlviii Though Sebastian was as much surprised at the courtesy of this lady as at the rudeness of his unknown foe, yet he went very willingly into the house, and Olivia was delighted to find Cesario (as she thought him) become more sensible of her attentions; for though their features were exactly the same, there was none of the contempt and anger to be seen in his face, which she had complained of when she told her love to Cesario. 虽然西巴斯辛对这位姑娘的款待正像对他那个素不相识的仇敌的无礼一样摸不着头脑,可是他欢欢喜喜地进了奥丽维娅的家。奥丽维娅很高兴"西萨里奥"(她以为是西萨里奥)肯接受她的殷勤了。尽管两个人长得一模一样,她在西巴斯辛的脸上却看不到一点儿当初她向西萨里奥示爱时所看到的轻蔑和愤怒(那曾使她感到很委屈)。

xlix He seemed to take it in very good part, yet he wondered how it had come to pass, and he was rather inclined to think Olivia was not in her right senses; but perceiving that she was mistress of a fine house, and that she ordered her affairs and seemed to govern her family discreetly, and that in all but her sudden love for him she appeared in the full possession of her reason, he well approved of the courtship; and Olivia finding Cesario in this good humour, and fearing he might change his mind, proposed that, as she had a priest in the house, they should be instantly married. 他看起来乐意接受这一切,尽管他疑惑为什么会这样。他心想奥丽维娅也许是神经错乱了,然而看到她有那么华丽的住宅,家里的事情都归她调动,而且家务也打理得井井有条——除了她忽然爱上他这一点以外,她的精神看起来是十分正常的,所以他就高兴地同意了这个婚姻。奥丽维娅看见"西萨里奥"正在兴头上,怕他待会儿又变卦,就说她家里有一位神父,她提议两人马上结婚。(in very good part:很乐意;...perceiving that..., and that..., and that...:现在分词作状语,包含三个并列的宾语从句;...proposed that, as...:宾语从句中嵌套状语从句)

l Viola was with Orsino, her master; and when Antonio saw Viola, whom he still imagined to be Sebastian, he told the duke in what manner he had rescued this youth from the perils of the sea; and after fully relating all the kindness he had really shown to Sebastian, he ended his complaint with saying, that for three months, both day and night, this ungrateful youth had been with him. 薇奥拉和她的主人奥西诺一道来了。安东尼奥仍然认为薇奥拉就是西巴斯辛,他一看到薇奥拉,就告诉公爵他是怎样把这个少年从海上的险境里救出来的。他把他确实给过西巴斯辛的种种好处说完之后,埋怨说三个月来,这个忘恩负义的小伙子日日夜夜一直跟他在一起。(...when..., whom...:状语从句中嵌套定语从句)

li Here comes the countess: now Heaven walks on earth! 伯爵小姐出来了,简直是天仙下凡。(比喻、夸张修辞)

lii But Orsino's heavenly countess soon gave the duke cause to accuse Cesario as much of ingratitude as Antonio had done, for all the words he could hear Olivia speak were words of kindness to Cesario; and when he found his page had obtained this high place in Olivia's favour, he threatened him with all the terrors of his just revenge. 可是奥西诺奉为天仙的伯爵小姐很快就使公爵像安东尼奥一样责怪起西萨里奥的忘恩负义了,因为他听到奥丽维娅对西萨里奥说的都是温柔的话。当他发现他的侍从在奥丽维娅心里取得了这样高的地位,就恫吓要照他罪有应得的狠狠报复他。

liii My thoughts are ripe for mischief. 我要痛痛快快地收拾你一顿。

liv Though it seemed in his jealous rage he was going to doom Viola to instant death, yet her love made her no longer a coward, and she said she would most joyfully suffer death to give her master ease. 看来公爵对薇奥拉又妒又恨,要马上把她处死,可是爱情的力量叫薇奥拉也不再胆小了。她说为了叫她的主人消气,她甘愿赴死。

lv After him I love more than my life. 我要跟着那个比我自己的生命还重要的人走。(him (who/that)...:定语从句中省略了作宾语的关系代词)

lvi In vain Viola protested she was not married to Olivia; the evidence of that lady and the priest made Orsino believe that his page had robbed him of the treasure he prized above his life. 薇奥拉怎样否认她没跟奥丽维娅结婚也不成。奥丽维娅和神父的见证使奥西诺相信他的侍从已经把他看得比自己的生命还宝贵的情人夺去了。

lvii But thinking that it was past recall, he was bidding farewell to his faithless mistress, and the young dissembler, her husband, as he called Viola, warning her never to come in his sight again, when (as it seemed to them) a miracle appeared! 可是想到事情已经无可挽回了,公爵就和他那不讲信义的情人及她的丈夫——那个年轻的伪君子(他这样叫薇奥拉)分了手,警告薇奥拉永远不要出现在他面前。就在这时,一个奇迹(在他们看来是奇迹)出现了。

lviii When their wonder had a little ceased at seeing two persons with the same face, the same voice, and the same habit, the brother and sister began to question each other; for Viola could scarce be persuaded that her brother was living, and Sebastian knew not how to account for the sister he supposed drowned being found in the habit of a young man. 大家对这两个相貌、声音和服装都一模一样的人感到一阵惊讶之后,兄妹俩也彼此盘问起来了。薇奥拉几乎不敢相信她的哥哥还活在人间,西巴斯辛也不明白他认为已经淹死了的妹妹怎么会穿着年轻男子的服装出现。

lix The hopes of Orsino were for ever at an end by this marriage of Olivia, and with his hopes, all his fruitless love seemed to vanish away, and all his thoughts were fixed on the event of his favourite, young Cesario, being changed into a fair lady. 奥丽维娅结婚以后,奥西诺的希望也就永远落空了;他的希望一落空,他那徒然的爱情好像也消逝了。这时候,他的一切念头就放在他所宠爱的年轻的西萨里奥变成了一位美丽的姑娘这件事情上。

lx Then he remembered how often she had said she loved him, which at the time seemed only the dutiful expressions of a faithful page; but now he guessed that something more was meant, for many of her pretty sayings, which were like riddles to him, came now into his mind, and he no sooner remembered all these things than he resolved to make Viola his wife. 然后他又记起薇奥拉时常说她爱他，那时候他认为这不过是一个忠实的侍从理所应当的表示，可是现在他猜出了深意。她那许多甜蜜的话当时听来都像谜语似的，现在他恍然大悟了。他一想起这一切，就决定娶薇奥拉做他的妻子。(...remembered (that)..., which...：宾语从句中嵌套定语从句；for..., which...：原因状语从句中嵌套定语从句；no sooner... than...：刚一……就……)

lxi Boy, you have said to me a thousand times that you should never love a woman like to me, and for the faithful service you have done for me so much beneath your soft and tender breeding, and since you have called me master so long, you shall now be your master's mistress, and Orsino's true duchess. 孩子，你对我说过千百回你永远不会像爱我这样来爱一个女人。你既然不顾自己娇弱的身子和娴雅的教养，忠心地服侍了我，你既然管我叫了这么些日子的"主人"，现在你就成为你主人的主妇——奥西诺真正的公爵夫人吧。

lxii Thus the twin brother and sister were both wedded on the same day: the storm and shipwreck, which had separated them, being the means of bringing to pass their high and mighty fortunes. 就这样，这一对孪生兄妹在同一天结了婚。一度把他们拆散的风暴和沉船，如今却促成了他们的好运道。(the storm and shipwreck, which..., being...：独立主格结构中嵌套定语从句)

Sir Andrew Aguecheek. For the love of Heaven, a surgeon! send one presently to Sir Toby.
Olivia. What's the matter?
Act V. Scene I.

仲夏夜之梦
A Midsummer Night's Dream

The lunatic, the lover, and the poet	疯子、情人和诗人,
Are of imagination all compact.	都是空想的产儿:
One sees more devils than vast hell can hold—That is the madman.	疯子眼中所见的鬼,多过于广大的地狱所能容纳;
The lover, all as frantic,	情人,同样是那么疯狂,
Sees Helen's beauty in a brow of Egypt.	能从埃及人的黑脸上看见海伦的美貌
The poet's eye, in fine frenzy rolling,	诗人的眼睛在神奇的狂放的一转中,
Doth glance from heaven to Earth, from Earth to heaven.	便能从天上看到地下,从地下看到天上。

上帝梦见了世界,就像莎士比亚梦见了他的戏剧。

——博尔赫斯

《仲夏夜之梦》是莎士比亚涉足神仙世界的一出最有特色的作品。他在其中找到了一种声音和形式,用以表达人的幻想中那最闲适和最难确定的运动。

——托马斯·肯尼

《仲夏夜之梦》作为一部整体的诗,是莎士比亚所创作的最温柔、最富独创性和最完美的作品之一。

——勃兰兑斯

在所有莎剧中,《仲夏夜之梦》给我留下的印象最深,它至少有一次使我感到,在这悲苦的尘世曾有过一个快乐的人。

——莉莉·贝丝·坎贝尔

主要人物

Egeus　伊吉斯　赫米娅的父亲
Theseus　忒修斯　雅典公爵
Hermia　赫米娅　伊吉斯的女儿,恋爱着拉山德
Demetrius　狄米特律斯　恋爱着赫米娅
Lysander　拉山德　恋爱着赫米娅
Helena　海丽娜　恋爱着狄米特律斯
Bottom　波顿　织工
Oberon　奥布朗　仙王
Titania　提泰妮娅　仙后
Puck　迫克　又名好人罗宾(Robin Goodfellow)

地点　雅典及附近的森林

A Midsummer Night's Dream

There was a law in the city of Athens which gave to its citizens the power of compelling① their daughters to marry whomsoever they pleased; for upon a daughter's refusing to marry the man her father had chosen to be her husband, the father was empowered② by this law to cause her to be put to death; but as fathers do not often desire the death of their own daughters, even though they do happen to prove a little refractory③, this law was seldom or never put in execution④, though perhaps the young ladies of that city were not unfrequently threatened by their parents with the terrors⑤ of it.

There was one instance, however, of an old man, whose name was Egeus, who actually did come before Theseus (at that time the reigning duke of Athens), to complain that his daughter Hermia, whom he had commanded to marry Demetrius, a young man of a noble Athenian family, refused to obey him, because she loved another young Athenian, named Lysander. Egeus demanded justice of Theseus, and desired that this cruel law might be put in force against his daughter.

Hermia pleaded⑥ in excuse for her disobedience⑦, that Demetrius had formerly professed⑧ love for her dear friend Helena, and that Helena loved Demetrius to distraction⑨; but this honourable reason, which Hermia gave for not obeying her father's command, moved not the stern⑩ Egeus.

---

① compel [kəmˈpel] v. 强迫 force, pressure, drive, impel
② empower [ɪmˈpaʊə(r)] v. 授权 authorize, permit, sanction
③ refractory [rɪˈfræktəri] adj. 不听话的 unruly, stubborn, disobedient
④ execution [ˌeksɪˈkjuːʃn] n. 实施 realization, carrying out
⑤ terror [ˈterə(r)] n. 恐怖 fear, dread, fright, panic, intimidation
⑥ plead [pliːd] v. 辩护 defend, argue
⑦ disobedience [ˌdɪsəˈbiːdiəns] n. 不服从 revolt
⑧ profess [prəˈfes] v. 声称 claim, state, declare, announce
⑨ distraction [dɪˈstrækʃn] n. 心烦意乱 disturbance, confusion
⑩ stern [stɜːn] adj. 严厉的 strict, hard, harsh

Theseus, though a great and merciful[1] prince, had no power to alter the laws of his country; therefore he could only give Hermia four days to consider of it: and at the end of that time, if she still refused to marry Demetrius, she was to be put to death.

When Hermia was dismissed[2] from the presence of the duke, she went to her lover Lysander, and told him the peril she was in, and that she must either give him up and marry Demetrius, or lose her life in four days.

Lysander was in great affliction[3] at hearing these evil tidings[4]; but recollecting[5] that he had an aunt who lived at some distance from Athens, and that at the place where she lived the cruel law could not be put in force against Hermia (this law not extending[6] beyond the boundaries[7] of the city), he proposed to Hermia that she should steal out of her father's house that night, and go with him to his aunt's house, where he would marry her. "I will meet you," said Lysander, "in the wood a few miles without[8] the city; in that delightful wood where we have so often walked with Helena in the pleasant month of May."

To this proposal Hermia joyfully agreed; and she told no one of her intended flight but her friend Helena. * Helena (as maidens will do foolish things for love) very ungenerously resolved[9] to go and tell this to Demetrius, though she could hope no benefit from betraying her friend's secret, but the poor pleasure of following her faithless lover to the wood;[ii] for she well knew that Demetrius would go thither[10] in pursuit of Hermia.

The wood in which Lysander and Hermia proposed to meet was the favourite haunt[11] of those little beings known by the name of Fairies.

Oberon the king, and Titania the queen of the fairies, with all their tiny train[12] of followers, in this wood held their midnight revels[13].

Between this little king and queen of sprites[14] there happened, at this time, a sad disagreement; * they never met by moonlight in the shady walks of this pleasant wood, but they were quarrelling, till all their fairy elves[15] would creep[16] into acorn-cups and hide themselves for fear.[iii]

* The cause of this unhappy disagreement was Titania's refusing to give Oberon a little

---

① merciful [ˈmɜːsɪfl] *adj*. 仁慈的 sympathetic, compassionate
② dismiss [dɪsˈmɪs] *v*. 使离开 free, release, discharge, let go
③ affliction [əˈflɪkʃn] *n*. 痛苦 suffering, distress, misery
④ tidings [ˈtaɪdɪŋz] *n*. 消息 news, message, information
⑤ recollect [ˌrekəˈlekt] *v*. 想起 remember, recall, call to mind
⑥ extend [ɪkˈstend] *v*. 延伸 stretch, spread
⑦ boundary [ˈbaʊndri] *n*. 边界 limit, bound, confine, border
⑧ without [wɪˈðaʊt] *prep*. 在……外面 outside of
⑨ resolve[rɪˈzɒlv] *v*. 决定 decide, make up one's mind
⑩ thither [ˈðɪðə(r)] *adv*. 〈古〉向那边 there
⑪ haunt [hɔːnt] *n*. 常去的地方 meeting place, rendezvous
⑫ train [treɪn] *n*. 队伍 queue, procession
⑬ revel [ˈrevl] *n*. 狂欢 merrymaking, celebration, festivity
⑭ sprite [spraɪt] *n*. 精灵 spirit, fairy, elf, goblin
⑮ elf [elf] *n*.(双耳尖尖的)小精灵 fairy, sprite, puck, goblin
⑯ creep [kriːp] *v*. 爬行,蹑手蹑脚地移动 crawl, inch, sneak, steal

changeling[1] boy, whose mother had been Titania's friend; and upon her death the fairy queen stole the child from its nurse, and brought him up[2] in the woods.[iv]

The night on which the lovers were to meet in this wood, as Titania was walking with some of her maids of honour[3], she met Oberon attended[4] by his train of fairy courtiers.

"Ill met by moonlight, proud Titania," said the fairy king. The queen replied: "What, jealous Oberon, is it you? Fairies, skip hence[5]; I have foresworn[6] his company." "Tarry, rash fairy," said Oberon, "am not I thy lord? Why does Titania cross[7] her Oberon? Give me your little changeling boy to be my page."

"* Set your heart at rest," answered the queen, "your whole fairy kingdom buys not the boy of me.[v]" She then left her lord in great anger. "* Well, go your way," said Oberon, "before the morning dawns I will torment[8] you for this injury.[vi]"

Oberon then sent for Puck, his chief favourite and privy counsellor[9].

Puck (or as he was sometimes called, Robin Goodfellow) was a shrewd[10] and knavish[11] sprite, that used to play comical pranks[12] in the neighbouring villages; sometimes getting into the dairies and skimming[13] the milk, sometimes plunging[14] his light and airy form into the butter-churn, and while he was dancing his fantastic shape in the churn, in vain the dairymaid would labour[15] to change her cream into butter—nor had the village swains[16] any better success; whenever Puck chose to play his freaks[17] in the brewing[18] copper, the ale was sure to be spoiled[19]. * When a few good neighbours were met to drink some comfortable ale together, Puck would jump into the bowl of ale in the likeness[20] of a roasted crab, and when some old goody was going to drink he would

---

① changeling [ˈtʃeɪndʒlɪŋ] *n*. 被(仙女)偷换后留下的孩童

② bring sb. up 抚养,养大 rear, raise

③ maids of honour 女王(或王后、公主)的未婚侍女

④ attend [əˈtend] *v*. 陪伴 escort, accompany

⑤ skip hence 快快离开这儿

⑥ forswear [fɔːˈsweə(r)] *v*. (forswore, forsworn) 发誓抛弃,坚决放弃 renounce, reject, deny, abandon

⑦ cross [krɒs] *v*. 反对

⑧ torment [tɔːˈmɛnt] *v*. 折磨 torture, afflict, agonize

⑨ privy counselor 枢密院大臣或官员

⑩ shrewd [ʃruːd] *adj*. 精明的 astute, clever, sharp, smart

⑪ knavish [ˈneɪvɪʃ] *adj*. 狡诈的 tricky, deceitful

⑫ prank [præŋk] *n*. 恶作剧 trick

⑬ skim [skɪm] *v*. (从液体表面)撇去(浮物) remove

⑭ plunge [plʌndʒ] *v*. 跳入 fall, drop, sink, dive, go down

⑮ labour [ˈleɪbə(r)] *v*. 努力做 work hard, toil, strive, endeavor

⑯ swain [sweɪn] *n*. 情郎 admirer, suitor

⑰ freak [friːk] *n*. 怪异的事 whim, fancy

⑱ brew [bruː] *v*. 酿造

⑲ spoil [spɔɪl] *v*. 破坏 ruin, destroy, wreck, damage

⑳ likeness [ˈlaɪknəs] *n*. 相似 resemblance

bob[1] against her lips, and spill the ale over her withered[2] chin; [vii] and * presently after, when the same old dame was gravely seating herself to tell her neighbours a sad and melancholy[3] story, Puck would slip her three-legged stool from under her, and down toppled[4] the poor old woman, and then the old gossips[5] would hold their sides and laugh at her, and swear they never wasted a merrier hour.[viii]

"Come hither[6], Puck," said Oberon to this little merry wanderer of the night, "fetch me the flower which maids call *Love in Idleness*[7]; the juice of that little purple flower laid on the eyelids of those who sleep, will make them, when they awake, dote[8] on the first thing they see. Some of the juice of that flower I will drop on the eyelids of my Titania when she is asleep; and * the first thing she looks upon when she opens her eyes she will fall in love with, even though it be a lion or a bear, a meddling[9] monkey, or a busy ape; [ix] and before I will take this charm[10] from off her sight, which I can do with another charm I know of, I will make her give me that boy to be my page."

* Puck, who loved mischief[11] to his heart, was highly diverted[12] with this intended frolic[13] of his master, and ran to seek the flower; [x] and while Oberon was waiting the return of Puck, he observed Demetrius and Helena enter the wood: he overheard[14] Demetrius reproaching Helena for following him, and after many unkind words on his part, and gentle expostulations[15] from Helena, reminding him of his former love and professions of true faith to her, he left her (as he said) to the mercy of the wild beasts, and she ran after him as swiftly as she could.

[Love in Idleness.]

The fairy king, who was always friendly to true lovers, felt great compassion[16] for Helena; and perhaps, as Lysander said they used to walk by moonlight in this pleasant wood, Oberon might have seen Helena in those happy times when she was beloved by Demetrius. However, that might be, when Puck returned with the little purple flower, Oberon said to his favourite: "Take a part of this flower; there has been a sweet Athenian lady here, who

---

① bob [bɒb] *v*. 上下快速摆动 bounce, seesaw
② wither ['wɪðə(r)] *v*. 枯萎,干枯 wilt, decay, shrivel
③ melancholy ['melənkəli] *adj*. 悲伤的 sad, sorrowful, miserable
④ topple ['tɒpl] *v*. 倾倒 fall over, tip over, collapse, tumble
⑤ gossip ['gɒsɪp] *n*. 爱说长道短者 busybody, prattler
⑥ hither ['hɪðə(r)] *adv*. 〈古〉向此处,到此处 here
⑦ Love in Idleness 爱懒花
⑧ dote [dəʊt] *v*. 宠爱,溺爱 adore, admire, idolize, worship
⑨ meddle ['medl] *v*. 干涉,管闲事 interfere, intervene, intrude
⑩ charm [tʃɑːm] *n*. 魔法 spell, magic, sorcery, witchery
⑪ mischief ['mɪstʃɪf] *n*. 恶作剧 prank
⑫ divert [daɪ'vɜːt] *v*. 娱乐,供消遣 entertain, amuse, delight
⑬ frolic ['frɒlɪk] *n*. 嬉闹 merriment, amusement, fun
⑭ overhear [ˌəʊvə'hɪə(r)] *v*. (overheard) 偷听到 listen in, eavesdrop
⑮ expostulation [ɪkˌspɒstʃə'leɪʃn] *n*. 劝告
⑯ compassion [kəm'pæʃn] *n*. 同情 sympathy, pity, mercy

is in love with a disdainful[1] youth; if you find him sleeping, drop some of the love-juice in his eyes, but contrive[2] to do it when she is near him, that the first thing he sees when he awakes may be this despised[3] lady. You will know the man by the Athenian garments which he wears." Puck promised to manage this matter very dexterously[4]—and then Oberon went, unperceived[5] by Titania, to her bower[6], where she was preparing to go to rest. Her fairy bower was a bank, where grew wild thyme[7], cowslips[8], and sweet violets[9], under a canopy[10] of wood-bine[11], musk-roses[12], and eglantine[13]. There Titania always slept some part of the night; her coverlet[14] the enamelled[15] skin of a snake, which, though a small mantle[16], was wide enough to wrap a fairy in.

He found Titania giving orders to her fairies, how they were to employ themselves while she slept. "* Some of you," said her majesty, "must kill cankers[17] in the muskrose buds, and some wage[18] war with the bats for their leathern[19] wings, to make my small elves coats; and some of you keep watch that the clamorous[20] owl, that nightly hoots[21], come not near me: but first sing me to sleep.[xi]" Then they began to sing this song:

"* You spotted snakes with double tongue,
Thorny hedgehogs, be not seen;
Newts and blind-worms do no wrong,
Come not near our Fairy Queen.
Philomel, with melody,
Sing in our sweet lullaby,
Lulla, lulla, lullaby; lulla, lulla, lullaby;
Never harm, nor spell, nor charm,
Come our lovely lady nigh;
So good night with lullaby.[xii]"

When the fairies had sung their queen asleep with this pretty lullaby, they left her to perform

---

① disdainful [dɪs'deɪnfl] *adj*. 轻蔑的，倨傲的 arrogant, haughty
② contrive [kən'traɪv] *v*. 设法做到 manage, succeed
③ despise [dɪ'spaɪz] *v*. 鄙视 scorn, disdain, look down on
④ dexterously ['dekstrəsli] *adv*. 敏捷地 nimbly, adroitly
⑤ unperceived [ʌnpə'siːvd] *adj*. 未被察觉的 unnoticed, overlooked
⑥ bower ['baʊə(r)] *n*. 树荫；凉亭 arbour
⑦ thyme [taɪm] *n*. 百里香
⑧ cowslip ['kaʊslɪp] *n*. 樱草
⑨ violet ['vaɪələt] *n*. 紫罗兰
⑩ canopy ['kænəpi] *n*. 顶篷，华盖；（顶篷似的）树荫 awning, covering
⑪ wood-bine ['wuːd baɪn] *n*. 忍冬
⑫ musk-rose ['mʌsk rəʊz] *n*. 麝香蔷薇
⑬ eglantine ['egləntaɪn] *n*. 多花蔷薇
⑭ coverlet ['kʌvələt] *n*. 床罩 bedcover, bedspread
⑮ enamelled [ɪ'næmld] *adj*. 涂瓷釉的
⑯ mantle ['mæntl] *n*. 斗篷；覆盖物 veil, covering
⑰ canker ['kæŋkə(r)] *n*. （植物和树木的）溃疡病，枝枯病
⑱ wage [weɪdʒ] *v*. 发动
⑲ leathern ['leðən] *adj*. 皮革制的，似皮革的
⑳ clamorous ['klæmərəs] *adj*. 吵闹的 noisy, loud, deafening
㉑ hoot [huːt] *n*. 鸣叫

the important services she had enjoined① them. Oberon then softly drew near his Titania, and dropped some of the love-juice on her eyelids, saying:

"* What thou seest when thou dost wake,

Do it for thy true-love take.[xiii]"

But to return to Hermia, who made her escape out of her father's house that night, to avoid the death she was doomed② to for refusing to marry Demetrius. When she entered the wood, she found her dear Lysander waiting for her, to conduct her to his aunt's house; but * before they had passed half through the wood, Hermia was so much fatigued③, that Lysander, who was very careful of this dear lady, who had proved her affection for him even by hazarding④ her life for his sake, persuaded her to rest till morning on a bank of soft moss⑤, and lying down himself on the ground at some little distance, they soon fell fast asleep.[xiv] Here they were found by Puck, who, seeing a handsome young man asleep, and perceiving that his clothes were made in the Athenian fashion, and that a pretty lady was sleeping near him, concluded that this must be the Athenian maid and her disdainful lover whom Oberon had sent him to seek; and he naturally enough conjectured⑥ that, as they were alone together, she must be the first thing he would see when he awoke; so, without more ado⑦, he proceeded⑧ to pour some of the juice of the little purple flower into his eyes. But it so fell out⑨, that Helena came that way, and, instead of Hermia, was the first object Lysander beheld⑩ when he opened his eyes; and strange to relate, so powerful was the love-charm, all his love for Hermia vanished⑪ away, and Lysander fell in love with Helena.

* Had he first seen Hermia when he awoke, the blunder⑫ Puck committed would have been of no consequence, for he could not love that faithful lady too well;[xv] but for poor Lysander to be forced by a fairy love-charm to forget his own true Hermia, and to run after another lady, and leave Hermia asleep quite alone in a wood at midnight, was a sad chance indeed.

Thus this misfortune⑬ happened. Helena, as has been before related, endeavoured⑭ to keep pace with Demetrius when he ran away so rudely from her; but * she could not continue this unequal race long, men being always better runners in a long race than ladies.[xvi] Helena soon lost sight of Demetrius; and as she was wandering about, dejected⑮ and forlorn⑯, she arrived at the place where Lysander was sleeping. "Ah!" said she, "this is Lysander lying on the ground: is he

---

① enjoin [ɪn'dʒɔɪn] *v*. 吩咐,命令 order, command, instruct
② doom [duːm] *v*. 注定 predestine
③ fatigued [fə'tiːgd] *adj*. 精疲力竭的 tired, exhausted, worn out
④ hazard ['hæzəd] *v*. 使处于危险 endanger, risk, imperil
⑤ moss [mɒs] *n*. 苔藓,地衣 lichen
⑥ conjecture [kən'dʒektʃə(r)] *v*. 猜测 guess, speculate, assume
⑦ ado [ə'duː] *n*. 麻烦,困难;纷扰,忙乱 fuss, trouble, bother
⑧ proceed [prə'siːd] *v*. 继续做 continue, progress, go ahead
⑨ fall out 发生 happen, occur, take place, come to pass
⑩ behold [bɪ'həʊld] *v*. (beheld) 看见 see, observe, perceive
⑪ vanish ['vænɪʃ] *v*. 突然消失 disappear, fade away
⑫ blunder ['blʌndə(r)] *n*. 错误,疏忽 mistake, fault, error, slip
⑬ misfortune [ˌmɪs'fɔːtʃuːn] *n*. 不幸 adversity, mischance
⑭ endeavour [ɪn'devə(r)] *v*. 努力 try, attempt, take pains
⑮ dejected [dɪ'dʒektɪd] *adj*. 沮丧的 depressed, downhearted
⑯ forlorn [fə'lɔːn] *adj*. 被遗弃的;绝望的;孤独的 miserable, helpless

dead or asleep?" Then, gently touching him, she said: "Good sir, if you are alive, awake." Upon this Lysander opened his eyes, and (the love-charm beginning to work) immediately addressed her in terms of extravagant① love and admiration; * telling her she as much excelled② Hermia in beauty as a dove③ does a raven, and that he would run through fire for her sweet sake;[xvii] and many more such lover-like speeches. Helena, knowing Lysander was her friend Hermia's lover, and that he was solemnly④ engaged⑤ to marry her, was in the utmost rage⑥ when she heard herself addressed in this manner; for she thought (as well she might⑦) that Lysander was making a jest⑧ of her. "Oh!" said she, "why was I born to be mocked⑨ and scorned by every one? Is it not enough, is it not enough, young man, that I can never get a sweet look or a kind word from Demetrius; but you, sir, must pretend in this disdainful manner to court me? I thought, Lysander, you were a lord of more true gentleness." Saying these words in great anger, she ran away; and Lysander followed her, quite forgetful of his own Hermia, who was still asleep.

When Hermia awoke, she was in a sad fright⑩ at finding herself alone. She wandered about the wood, not knowing what was become of Lysander, or which way to go to seek for him. In the meantime Demetrius, not being able to find Hermia and his rival Lysander, and fatigued with his fruitless search, was observed by Oberon fast asleep. Oberon had learnt by some questions he had asked of Puck, that he had applied the love-charm to the wrong person's eyes; and now having found the person first intended, he touched the eyelids of the sleeping Demetrius with the love-juice, and he instantly awoke; and the first thing he saw being Helena, he, as Lysander had done before, began to address love-speeches to her; and just at that moment Lysander, followed by Hermia (for through Puck's unlucky mistake it was now become Hermia's turn to run after her lover) made his appearance; and then * Lysander and Demetrius, both speaking together, made love to Helena, they being each one under the influence of the same potent⑪ charm.[xviii]

The astonished⑫ Helena thought that Demetrius, Lysander, and her once dear friend Hermia, were all in a plot⑬ together to make a jest of her.

Hermia was as much surprised as Helena; she knew not why Lysander and Demetrius, who both before loved her, were now become the lovers of Helena; and to Hermia the matter seemed to be no jest.

The ladies, who before had always been the dearest of friends, now fell to high words⑭ together.

---

① extravagant [ɪk'strævəgənt] *adj.*过分的,不切实际的 excessive, exaggerated
② excel [ɪk'sel] *v.* 胜过 beat, outdo, surpass, be superior to
③ dove [dʌv] *n.* 鸽子 pigeon
④ solemnly ['sɒləmli] *adv.* 庄严地,郑重地 seriously, earnestly, gravely
⑤ engaged [ɪn'geɪdʒd] *adj.* 订婚的 betrothed
⑥ rage [reɪdʒ] *n.* 狂怒 anger, fury, madness, frenzy, temper
⑦ as well she might 她有理由那样想,这也怪不得她
⑧ jest [dʒest] *n.* 笑话,玩笑 joke, banter, prank, pleasantry
⑨ mock [mɒk] *v.* 嘲笑 tease, scorn, sneer, laugh at, make fun of
⑩ fright [fraɪt] *n.* 惊吓 fear, shock, alarm, horror, panic, terror
⑪ potent ['pəʊtnt] *adj.* 强大的,有力的;药效强的 strong, powerful, mighty, effective
⑫ astonished [ə'stɒnɪʃt] *adj.* 十分惊讶的 amazed, surprised, shocked
⑬ plot [plɒt] *n.* 密谋 plan, scheme, intrigue, conspiracy
⑭ fall to high words 怒言相向 exchanged hot/hard words

“Unkind Hermia,” said Helena, “* it is you have set Lysander on to vex① me with mock② praises; and your other lover Demetrius, who used almost to spurn③ me with his foot, have you not bid④ him call me Goddess, Nymph⑤, rare, precious, and celestial⑥?[xix] He would not speak thus to me, whom he hates, if you did not set him on⑦ to make a jest of me. Unkind Hermia, to join with men in scorning your poor friend. Have you forgot our school-day friendship? * How often, Hermia, have we two, sitting on one cushion, both singing one song, with our needles working the same flower, both on the same sampler⑧ wrought⑨; growing up together in fashion of a double cherry, scarcely seeming parted! [xx] Hermia, it is not friendly in you, it is not maidenly⑩ to join with men in scorning your poor friend.”

“I am amazed at your passionate words,” said Hermia. “I scorn you not; it seems you scorn me.” “* Ay, do,” returned Helena, “persevere⑪, counterfeit⑫ serious looks, and make mouths at me when I turn my back; then wink⑬ at each other, and hold the sweet jest up.[xxi] * If you had any pity, grace, or manners, you would not use me thus.[xxii]”

While Helena and Hermia were speaking these angry words to each other, Demetrius and Lysander left them, to fight together in the wood for the love of Helena.

When they found the gentlemen had left them, they departed, and once more wandered weary in the wood in search of their lovers.

As soon as they were gone, the fairy king, who with little Puck had been listening to their quarrels, said to him: “This is your negligence⑭, Puck; or did you do this willfully⑮?” “Believe me, king of shadows⑯,” answered Puck, “it was a mistake; did not you tell me I should know the man by his Athenian garments? However, I am not sorry this has happened, for I think their jangling⑰ makes excellent sport⑱.”

“You heard,” said Oberon, “that Demetrius and Lysander are gone to seek a convenient place to fight in. I command you to overhang⑲ the night with a thick fog, and lead these quarrelsome lovers so astray⑳ in the dark, that they shall not be able to find each other. Counterfeit each of

---

① vex [veks] *v*. 使恼火 annoy, bother, irritate, offend, displeasure
② mock [mɒk] *adj*. 虚假的,假装的 false, fake, pretended, feigned, artificial
③ spurn [spɜːn] *v*. 唾弃,冷落
④ bid [bɪd] *v*. 吩咐 order, charge, command, instruct
⑤ Nymph [nɪmf] *n*. 仙女,女神 fairy, goddess
⑥ celestial [sə'lestiəl] *adj*. 天上的;天国的 heavenly, angelic
⑦ set sb. on 唆使,煽动 urge, encourage, prompt
⑧ sampler ['sɑːmplə(r)] *n*. 刺绣样本 embroidery sample
⑨ wrought [rɔːt] *adj*. 做成的,加工的 made, created, constructed
⑩ maidenly ['meɪdnli] *adj*. 文雅的 modest, decent, decorous
⑪ persevere [ˌpɜːsə'vɪə(r)] *v*. 坚持 continue, persist, hold/hang on
⑫ counterfeit ['kaʊntəfɪt] *v*. 假装,伪造 pretend, fake, feign
⑬ wink [wɪŋk] *v*. 眨眼(示意) blink, twinkle
⑭ negligence['neglɪdʒəns] *n*. 疏忽 neglect, carelessness
⑮ willfully ['wɪlfəli] *adv*. 蓄意地,有意地 intentionally, purposefully, deliberately
⑯ king of shadows 精灵之王
⑰ jangle ['dʒæŋgl] *v*. 发出刺耳声 rattle, clatter, jingle
⑱ sport [spɔːt] *n*. 娱乐,乐趣 amusement, recreation, entertainment
⑲ overhang [ˌəʊvə'hæŋ] *v*. 悬于……之上 hang over, tower above
⑳ astray [ə'streɪ] *adv*. 迷途地,迷失地 off course, off the right track

their voices to the other, and with bitter taunts① provoke② them to follow you, while they think it is their rival's tongue they hear. * See you do this, till they are so weary they can go no farther; [xxiii] and when you find they are asleep, drop the juice of this other flower into Lysander's eyes, and when he awakes he will forget his new love for Helena, and return to his old passion for Hermia; and then the two fair ladies may each one be happy with the man she loves, and they will think all that has passed a vexatious③ dream. About this quickly④, Puck, and I will go and see what sweet love my Titania has found."

Titania was still sleeping, and Oberon seeing a clown⑤ near her, who had lost his way in the wood, and was likewise⑥ asleep—"This fellow," said he, "shall be my Titania's true love"; and * clapping⑦ an ass's head over the clown's, it seemed to fit him as well as if it had grown upon his own shoulders.[xxiv] Though Oberon fixed the ass's head on very gently, it awakened him, and rising up, unconscious⑧ of what Oberon had done to him, he went towards the bower where the fairy queen slept.

"Ah! What angel is that I see?" said Titania, opening her eyes, and the juice of the little purple flower beginning to take effect. "* Are you as wise as you are beautiful?[xxv]"

"* Why, mistress," said the foolish clown, "if I have wit enough to find the way out of this wood, I have enough to serve my turn.[xxvi]"

"Out of the wood do not desire to go," said the enamoured⑨ queen. "I am a spirit of no common rate⑩. I love you. Go with me, and I will give you fairies to attend upon⑪ you."

She then called four of her fairies: their names were Pease-blossom, Cobweb⑫, Moth⑬, and Mustard-seed⑭.

"Attend," said the queen, "upon this sweet gentleman; hop⑮ in his walks, and gambol⑯ in his sight; feed him with grapes and apricots⑰, and steal for him the honey-bags from the bees. Come, sit with me," said she to the clown, "and let me play with your amiable⑱ hairy cheeks, my beautiful ass! and kiss your fair large ears, my gentle joy!"

"Where is Pease-blossom?" said the ass-headed clown, not much regarding the fairy queen's courtship, but very proud of his new attendants.

---

① taunt [tɔːnt] *n*. 嘲笑 teasing, jeer, mockery, ridicule
② provoke [prəˈvəʊk] *v*. 激起 rouse, cause, incite, motivate
③ vexatious [vekˈseɪʃəs] *adj*. 烦人的 annoying, irritating
④ about this quickly 快点办去吧
⑤ clown [klaʊn] *n*. 粗鲁笨拙者；乡下人，乡巴佬；小丑
⑥ likewise [ˈlaɪkwaɪz] *adv*. 同样地 also, as well, in like manner
⑦ clap [klæp] *v*. 有力地放置，急速地放置
⑧ unconscious [ʌnˈkɒnʃəs] *adj*. 未意识到的 unaware, ignorant
⑨ enamoured [ɪˈnæməd] *adj*. 倾心的，迷恋的
⑩ rate [reɪt] *n*. 等级 grade, class, rank
⑪ attend upon 照料 look after, take care of
⑫ cobweb [ˈkɒbweb] *n*. 蜘蛛网
⑬ moth [mɒθ] *n*. 飞蛾
⑭ mustard-seed [ˈmʌstəd siːd] *n*. 芥菜籽
⑮ hop [hɒp] *v*. 跳跃 jump, spring, bound, leap, skip
⑯ gambol [ˈgæmbl] *v*. 嬉戏 frolic
⑰ apricot [ˈeɪprɪkɒt] *n*. 杏子
⑱ amiable [ˈeɪmiəbl] *adj*. 和蔼可亲的 pleasant, lovable

"Here, sir," said little Pease-blossom.

"Scratch① my head," said the clown. "Where is Cobweb?"

"Here, sir," said Cobweb.

"* Good Mr Cobweb," said the foolish clown, "kill me the red humble-bee② on the top of that thistle③ yonder④; and, good Mr Cobweb, bring me the honey-bag. Do not fret⑤ yourself too much in the action, Mr Cobweb, and take care the honey-bag break not; I should be sorry to have you over-flown with a honey-bag.[xxvii] Where is Mustard-seed?"

"Here, sir," said Mustard-seed, "what is your will?"

"Nothing," said the clown, "good Mr Mustard-seed, but to help Mr Pease-blossom to scratch; I must go to a barber's, Mr Mustard-seed, for methinks I am marvelous hairy about the face."

"* My sweet love," said the queen, "what will you have to eat? I have a venturous⑥ fairy shall seek the squirrel's hoard⑦, and fetch you some new nuts.[xxviii]"

"I had rather have a handful of dried pease," said the clown, who with his ass's head had got an ass's appetite⑧. "But, I pray, let none of your people disturb me, for I have a mind to sleep."

"Sleep, then," said the queen, "and I will wind⑨ you in my arms. O how I love you! how I dote⑩ upon you!"

When the fairy king saw the clown sleeping in the arms of his queen, he advanced within her sight, and reproached her with having lavished⑪ her favours upon an ass.

This she could not deny, as the clown was then sleeping within her arms, with his ass's head crowned⑫ by her with flowers.

When Oberon had teased⑬ her for some time, he again demanded the changeling boy; which she, ashamed of being discovered by her lord with her new favourite, did not dare to refuse him.

* Oberon, having thus obtained the little boy he had so long wished for to be his page, took

---

① scratch [skrætʃ] v. 挠，搔 rub, scrape
② humble-bee [ˈhʌmbl biː] n. 大黄蜂
③ thistle [ˈθɪsl] n. 蓟
④ yonder [ˈjɒndə(r)] adv.〈古〉在那边
⑤ fret [fret] v. 烦恼 worry
⑥ venturous [ˈventʃərəs] adj.大胆的 brave, bold, courageous
⑦ hoard [hɔːd] n. 贮藏物 store, stock, reserve, reservoir
⑧ appetite [ˈæpɪtaɪt] n. 食欲
⑨ wind [waɪnd] v. 缠绕；拥抱 coil, encircle; hug, embrace
⑩ dote [dəʊt] v. 宠爱 adore, admire
⑪ lavish [ˈlævɪʃ] v. 慷慨(或过度)给予
⑫ crown [kraʊn] v. 为……加冕
⑬ tease [tiːz] v. 揶揄 mock, ridicule, make fun of, pull one's leg

pity on[1] the disgraceful[2] situation into which, by his merry contrivance[3], he had brought his Titania and threw some of the juice of the other flower into her eyes; and the fairy queen immediately recovered her senses, and wondered at her late dotage[4], saying how she now loathed[5] the sight of the strange monster.[xxix]

* Oberon likewise took the ass's head from off the clown, and left him to finish his nap with his own fool's head upon his shoulders.[xxx]

Oberon and his Titania being now perfectly reconciled[6], he related to her the history of the lovers, and their midnight quarrels; and she agreed to go with him and see the end of their adventures.

The fairy king and queen found the lovers and their fair ladies, at no great distance from each other, sleeping on a grass-plot[7]; for Puck, to make amends[8] for his former mistake, had contrived[9] with the utmost diligence to bring them all to the same spot, unknown to each other—and he had carefully removed the charm from off the eyes of Lysander with the antidote[10] the fairy king gave to him.

Hermia first awoke, and finding her lost Lysander asleep so near her, was looking at him and wondering at his strange inconstancy[11]. * Lysander presently opening his eyes, and seeing his dear Hermia, recovered his reason which the fairy charm had before clouded, and with his reason, his love for Hermia; and they began to talk over the adventures of the night, doubting if these things had really happened, or if they had both been dreaming the same bewildering[12] dream.[xxxi]

Helena and Demetrius were by this time awake; and a sweet sleep having quieted Helena's disturbed and angry spirits, she listened with delight to the professions of love which Demetrius still made to her, and which, to her surprise as well as pleasure, she began to perceive were sincere.

These fair night-wandering ladies, now no longer rivals, became once more true friends; all the unkind words which had passed were forgiven, and they calmly consulted together what was best to be done in their present situation. It was soon agreed that, as Demetrius had given up his pretensions[13] to Hermia, he should endeavour to prevail[14] upon her father to revoke[15] the cruel sentence of death which had been passed against her. Demetrius was preparing to return to Athens for this friendly purpose, when they were surprised with the sight of Egeus, Hermia's father, who

---

① take pity on 同情 pity, have mercy on, show mercy to
② disgraceful [dɪs'greɪsfl] *adj*. 不光彩的,可耻的 shameful, dishonorable
③ contrivance [kən'traɪvəns] *n*. 计谋 plot, plan, trick, scheme
④ dotage ['dəʊtɪdʒ] *n*. 溺爱 fondness, affection, attachment
⑤ loathe [ləʊð] *v*. 厌恶 hate, dislike, detest, despise, abominate
⑥ reconcile ['rekənsaɪl] *v*. 使和解 reunite, make peace between
⑦ grass-plot [grɑːs plɒt] *n*. 草地 lawn, meadow, grassland
⑧ amends [ə'mendz] *n*. 赔偿 compensation
⑨ contrive [kən'traɪv] *v*. 设法做到 manage, succeed
⑩ antidote ['æntidəʊt] *n*. 解毒药 remedy, cure, antitoxin
⑪ inconstancy [ɪn'kɒnstənsi] *n*. 反复无常
⑫ bewildering [bɪ'wɪldərɪŋ] *adj*. 令人困惑的 confusing, puzzling
⑬ pretension [prɪ'tenʃn] *n*. 声称 statement, claim, declaration
⑭ prevail [prɪ'veɪl] *v*. 说服 persuade, convince, talk into
⑮ revoke [rɪ'vəʊk] *v*. 取消,撤销 cancel, recall, withdraw, take back

came to the wood in pursuit of① his runaway daughter.

When Egeus understood that Demetrius would not now marry his daughter, he no longer opposed her marriage with Lysander, but gave his consent that they should be wedded on the fourth day from that time, being the same day on which Hermia had been condemned② to lose her life; and on that same day Helena joyfully agreed to marry her beloved and now faithful Demetrius.

The fairy king and queen, who were invisible spectators③ of this reconciliation④, and now saw the happy ending of the lovers' history, brought about through the good offices⑤ of Oberon, received so much pleasure, that these kind spirits resolved⑥ to celebrate the approaching nuptials⑦ with sports and revels⑧ throughout their fairy kingdom.

And now, if any are offended⑨ with this story of fairies and their pranks, as judging it incredible⑩ and strange, they have only to think that they have been asleep and dreaming, and that all these adventures were visions⑪ which they saw in their sleep—and * I hope none of my readers will be so unreasonable as to be offended with a pretty harmless Midsummer Night's Dream.[xxxii]

① in pursuit of 追逐
② condemn [kən'dem] *v*. 判处 sentence
③ spectator [spek'teɪtə(r)] *n*. 旁观者 onlooker, observer, looker-on
④ reconciliation [ˌrekənsɪli'eɪʃn] *n*. 和解
⑤ good offices 调解 mediation, arbitration, intervention
⑥ resolve [rɪ'zɒlv] *v*. 决定 decide, determine, make up sb's mind
⑦ nuptial ['nʌpʃl] *n*. 婚礼 wedding, marriage ceremony
⑧ revel ['revl] *n*. 狂欢 merrymaking, celebration, festivity
⑨ offend [ə'fend] *v*. 得罪,冒犯 upset, insult, annoy, irritate, displease
⑩ incredible [ɪn'kredəbl] *adj*. 难以置信的 unbelievable
⑪ vision ['vɪʒn] *n*. 幻想,想象 dream, fancy, fantasy, delusion

Titania. Out of this wood do not desire to go:
Thou shalt remain here, whether thou wilt or no.
I am a spirit of no common rate.
Act III. Scene I.

i Hermia pleaded in excuse for her disobedience, that Demetrius had formerly professed love for her dear friend Helena, and that Helena loved Demetrius to distraction; but this honourable reason, which Hermia gave for not obeying her father's command, moved not the stern Egeus. 赫米娅替自己辩解说，她违背父亲的意思是因为狄米特律斯曾经向她的好朋友海丽娜示爱，并且海丽娜也疯狂地爱着狄米特律斯。可是尽管赫米娅提出这个正大光明的理由来说明她为什么违背父亲的命令，这并没能感动严苛的伊吉斯。（moved not＝did not move：中世纪英语的否定结构常把 not 直接置于动词之后）

ii Helena (as maidens will do foolish things for love) very ungenerously resolved to go and tell this to Demetrius, though she could hope no benefit from betraying her friend's secret, but the poor pleasure of following her faithless lover to the wood. 海丽娜（正如姑娘们会为了爱情做出傻事来）非常不厚道地决定跑去把这件事告诉狄米特律斯，尽管她并不能从泄露朋友的秘密当中得到什么好处，她只是希望能跟着她那不忠实的爱人到树林里去罢了。

iii They never met by moonlight in the shady walks of this pleasant wood, but they were quarrelling, till all their fairy elves would creep into acorn-cups and hide themselves for fear. 月光下，每当他们在这片宜人森林的树荫小径上相遇时，他们总是吵架，直吵到他们的

小仙子都害怕地爬到橡果壳里躲起来。(but:强调一贯事实)

ⅳ The cause of this unhappy disagreement was Titania's refusing to give Oberon a little changeling boy, whose mother had been Titania's friend; and upon her death the fairy queen stole the child from its nurse, and brought him up in the woods. 这次闹翻是由于提泰妮娅不肯把她偷偷换来的小男孩送给奥布朗——这个小男孩的母亲是提泰妮娅的朋友,她去世后,仙后就把孩子从保姆那儿偷走,带到了树林里。(在欧洲,传说仙人常常在半夜把人类家中的聪明美丽的孩子偷去,用愚蠢的妖童替换)

ⅴ Set your heart at rest, your whole fairy kingdom buys not the boy of me. 你就死了这条心吧,你的整个仙国也买不走我的这个孩子。"

ⅵ Well, go your way, before the morning dawns I will torment you for this injury. 好,去你的吧,为了报复这次的侮辱,我要在天亮以前给你苦头吃。

ⅶ When a few good neighbours were met to drink some comfortable ale together, Puck would jump into the bowl of ale in the likeness of a roasted crab, and when some old goody was going to drink he would bob against her lips, and spill the ale over her withered chin. 当几个要好的街坊聚在一起舒舒服服地喝几杯麦酒的时候,迫克就变成一个烤熟的野苹果,跳进酒杯里去。趁老太婆要喝的当儿,他就蹦到她的嘴唇上,把麦酒洒遍了她那干瘪的下巴。(crab =crab apple:野生苹果树上的果实;goody:goodwife 的缩写,这里指地位低下的老妇人)

ⅷ Presently after, when the same old dame was gravely seating herself to tell her neighbours a sad and melancholy story, Puck would slip her three-legged stool from under her, and down toppled the poor old woman, and then the old gossips would hold their sides and laugh at her, and swear they never wasted a merrier hour. 过了一会儿,老太婆正要庄重地坐下来,讲个悲惨的故事给街坊们听,迫克就会从她身底下抽出她的三脚凳,把可怜的老太婆重重地摔在地上。于是那些闲谈的人都对她捧腹大笑,并发誓说他们从来没有这么开心过。

ⅸ The first thing she looks upon when she opens her eyes she will fall in love with, even though it be a lion or a bear, a meddling monkey, or a busy ape. 不管她一睁开眼睛看见的是狮子、熊、好捣乱的猴子还是忙手忙脚的无尾猿,她都会爱上的。

ⅹ Puck, who loved mischief to his heart, was highly diverted with this intended frolic of his master, and ran to seek the flower. 迫克打心眼里喜欢恶作剧,他对主人要玩的这个鬼把戏感到非常开心,就赶忙跑去找花了。

ⅹⅰ Some of you, must kill cankers in the muskrose buds, and some wage war with the bats for their leathern wings, to make my small elves coats; and some of you keep watch that the clamorous owl, that nightly hoots, come not near me: but first sing me to sleep. 你们当中,有些去杀死麝香蔷薇花蕾中的害虫,有些去和蝙蝠打仗,用它们的皮翅膀来为我的小仙子们做外衣,还有些去监视那每天晚上都吵吵闹闹的猫头鹰,不要让它们靠近我。不过,现在,先唱歌把我哄睡着了吧。

ⅹⅱ
You spotted snakes with double tongue,	两舌的花蛇
Thorny hedgehogs, be not seen;	多刺的猬,不要打扰着她的安睡;
Newts and blind-worms do no wrong,	蝾螈和蜥蜴,不要行近,
Come not near our Fairy Queen.	仔细毒害了她的宁静。
Philomel, with melody,	夜莺,鼓起你的清弦,
Sing in our sweet lullaby,	为我们唱一曲催眠:

Lulla, lulla, lullaby; lulla, lulla, lullaby;
Never harm, nor spell, nor charm,
Come our lovely lady nigh;
So good night with lullaby.

睡啦,睡啦,睡睡吧! 睡啦,睡啦,睡睡吧!
一切害物远走高飏,
不会行近她的身旁;
晚安,睡睡吧!

xiii What thou seest when thou dost wake,/Do it for thy true-love take. 你醒来时看到什么,什么就是你的真爱。(thou=you;seest=see;dost=do;thy=your)

xiv Before they had passed half through the wood, Hermia was so much fatigued, that Lysander, who was very careful of this dear lady, who had proved her affection for him even by hazarding her life for his sake, persuaded her to rest till morning on a bank of soft moss, and lying down himself on the ground at some little distance, they soon fell fast asleep. 他们俩还没走完半个树林子,赫米娅就已经累坏了。拉山德对这位亲爱的姑娘照顾得十分周到。赫米娅为了他甚至不顾自己的性命,可见她对拉山德的爱有多么真挚。拉山德劝她在一片软草地上休息一下,等天亮再走,他自己也在离她不远的地上躺了下去,他俩很快就睡着了。(so...that...结构;...who..., who...:定语从句的嵌套)

xv Had he first seen Hermia when he awoke, the blunder Puck committed would have been of no consequence, for he could not love that faithful lady too well. 如果他(拉山德)醒来第一眼看到的是赫米娅,那么迫克犯的错误就没有什么关系了,因为拉山德已经对那位忠诚的姑娘十分痴情了。(Had he...=If he had seen..., ...would have been...:与过去事实相反的虚拟语气,省略 if 的倒装结构)

xvi She could not continue this unequal race long, men being always better runners in a long race than ladies. 在这场力量不均等的赛跑中,她(海丽娜)坚持不下去了,因为在长距离赛跑中男人总是比女人强。(being...:独立主格结构作原因状语)

xvii Telling her she as much excelled Hermia in beauty as a dove does a raven, and that he would run through fire for her sweet sake. 告诉她,她比赫米娅漂亮得多,就像鸽子比乌鸦漂亮一样,而且他会为了可爱的海丽娜赴汤蹈火。(telling her (that)..., and that...:并列的宾语从句,比喻和夸张修辞)

xviii Lysander and Demetrius, both speaking together, made love to Helena, they being each one under the influence of the same potent charm. 拉山德和狄米特律斯同时开口向海丽娜示爱,因为他们都受到同一种强大魔法的影响。(they being...:独立主格结构作原因状语)

xix It is you have set Lysander on to vex me with mock praises; and your other lover Demetrius, who used almost to spurn me with his foot, have you not bid him call me Goddess, Nymph, rare, precious, and celestial? 是你让拉山德用虚伪的赞美之辞来使我生气。而你的另一个情人狄米特律斯,过去恨不得把我踩在脚底下,难道你没有让他管我叫什么女神、仙女、绝世美人、宝贝和天人吗?(it is you (who/that) have...:强调句中省略了 who/that,属于 16 世纪英语文法,在现代英语中不能省略)

xx How often, Hermia, have we two, sitting on one cushion, both singing one song, with our needles working the same flower, both on the same sampler wrought; growing up together in fashion of a double cherry, scarcely seeming parted! 赫米娅,有多少次咱们俩坐在同一张椅垫上,唱着同一支歌,绣着从同一个花样上描下来的花,像并蒂的樱桃一样一块儿长大,看起来就像是一个人!

xxi Ay, do, persevere, counterfeit serious looks, and make mouths at me when I turn my back;

then wink at each other, and hold the sweet jest up. 唉,你们尽管装下去吧,装出一副正经样子,等我一转过身去就对我做鬼脸;然后你们又挤眉弄眼,继续把这个有趣的玩笑开下去。

xxii If you had any pity, grace, or manners, you would not use me thus. 只要你们稍微还有点怜悯之心,稍微懂得点风度或是礼数,你们就不会这样对待我。(If…had…, …would…:与现在事实相反的虚拟语气)

xxiii See you do this, till they are so weary they can go no farther. 你务必这么做,直到他们累得再也走不动了。(see=see that:务必,保证;so…that…结构中省略了 that)

xxiv Clapping an ass's head over the clown's, it seemed to fit him as well as if it had grown upon his own shoulders. 把驴头套在乡巴佬的头上,驴头大小正合适,仿佛原来就长在他的脖子上。(as if…had grown…:非真实虚拟语气)

xxv Are you as wise as you are beautiful? 你的聪明是跟你的美貌一样超凡吗?

xxvi Why, mistress, if I have wit enough to find the way out of this wood, I have enough to serve my turn. 啊,女士,要是俺有足够的智慧,能够走出这座树林子,那俺就已经很知足了。

xxvii Good Mr Cobweb, kill me the red humble-bee on the top of that thistle yonder; and, good Mr Cobweb, bring me the honey-bag. Do not fret yourself too much in the action, Mr Cobweb, and take care the honey-bag break not; I should be sorry to have you over-flown with a honey-bag. 好蛛网先生,把那荆树上红颜色的小蜜蜂给俺杀死;好蛛网先生,把蜜囊给俺拿来。蛛网先生,做事的时候不要太慌张,留心不要把蜜囊弄破了。你要是打翻了蜜囊,俺就难过啦。(kill me=kill for me)

xxviii My sweet love, what will you have to eat? I have a venturous fairy shall seek the squirrel's hoard, and fetch you some new nuts. 温柔的情人呀,你想吃点什么呢? 我有一个胆子大的仙子,他能找到松鼠的存粮,给你捡些新鲜的干果。(…fairy (who/that) shall…:定语从句中省略了作主语的关系代词,在现代英语中一般不可省略)

xxix Oberon, having thus obtained the little boy he had so long wished for to be his page, took pity on the disgraceful situation into which, by his merry contrivance, he had brought his Titania and threw some of the juice of the other flower into her eyes; and the fairy queen immediately recovered her senses, and wondered at her late dotage, saying how she now loathed the sight of the strange monster. 奥布朗就这样终于把要了那么久的小孩子弄到手,做他的侍从。于是他就可怜起提泰妮娅来,觉得都是他开的玩笑害得她落到这样见不得人的地步。奥布朗往她眼睛里滴了一些另外一种花的汁液。仙后马上神志清醒了,对自己刚才的钟情感到很惊奇,说她现在非常讨厌这个畸形的怪物。(having obtained…:现在分词完成式作时间状语;situation into which…:定语从句;saying…:现在分词作伴随状语)

xxx Oberon likewise took the ass's head from off the clown, and left him to finish his nap with his own fool's head upon his shoulders. 奥布朗也把驴头从乡巴佬脖子上取了下来,让他继续睡他的觉,他肩上仍旧顶着自己那个愚蠢的脑袋。

xxxi Lysander presently opening his eyes, and seeing his dear Hermia, recovered his reason which the fairy charm had before clouded, and with his reason, his love for Hermia; and they began to talk over the adventures of the night, doubting if these things had really happened, or if they had both been dreaming the same bewildering dream. 不久,拉山德睁开眼睛,一看到赫米娅,他那先前被仙人用魔法蒙蔽的神志又清醒过来了;神志一清醒,他

也恢复了对赫米娅的爱。他俩谈起夜里的奇遇，搞不清究竟这些事是真的发生过，还是他俩做了同样的莫名其妙的梦。（which…：定语从句；with his reason，his love for Hermia＝with his reason，he recovered his love for Hermia：此处为省略句）

xxxii I hope none of my readers will be so unreasonable as to be offended with a pretty harmless Midsummer Night's Dream. 我希望没有一个读者会这么不讲理，竟会为这场美妙的、无伤大雅的仲夏夜之梦而生起气来。（当时人们认为，在仲夏夜所做的梦往往是离奇古怪的）

Oberon. Welcome, good Robin. See'st thou this sweet sight?
Her dotage now I do begin to pity.
Act IV. Scene I.

TRAGEDY 悲剧

哈姆莱特
Hamlet

What a piece of work is a man!	人类是一件多么了不得的杰作!
How noble in reason, how infinite in faculty!	多么高贵的理性!多么伟大的力量!
In form and moving how express and admirable!	多么优美的仪表!多么文雅的举动!
In action how like an angel!	在行为上多么像一个天使!
In apprehension how like a god!	在智慧上多么像一个天神!
The beauty of the world, the paragon of animals.	宇宙的精华!万物的灵长!

莎士比亚具有敏锐的洞察力、超常的语言表现力和伟大的创造力。

——哈罗德·布鲁姆

倘若你没读《哈姆莱特》便终了此生，那么你等于在煤矿深处度过一生。

——贝多芬

《哈姆莱特》是那位前无古人后无来者、全人类所加冕的戏剧诗人之王的灿烂王冠上的一颗最辉煌的宝石。

——别林斯基

哈姆莱特像我们每一个人一样真实，但又要比我们伟大。他是一个巨人，却是一个真实的人。因为哈姆莱特不是你，也不是我，而是我们大家。哈姆莱特不是某一个人，而是人。

——雨果

《哈孟雷特》一剧尤沉痛悲怆为莎翁四大悲剧之冠。读 Hamlet 的独白，to be or not to be, that is a question，不啻读屈子离骚。

——田汉

莎士比亚旨在向我们阐释这样一个真理：行动是存在的主要目的。人的智力天才不管如何高明，与行动比起来都是无足轻重的；相反，如果思想使我们退缩或讨厌行动，那么思想无异于灾难。

——柯勒律治

主要人物

Hamlet　哈姆莱特　前王之子，今王之侄
Claudius　克劳狄斯　丹麦国王
Gertrude　乔特鲁德　丹麦王后，哈姆莱特之母
Polonius　波洛涅斯　御前大臣
Ophelia　奥菲利娅　波洛涅斯之女
Laertes　雷欧提斯　波洛涅斯之子
Horatio　霍拉旭　哈姆莱特之友
Marcellus　马西勒斯　军官
Ghost of the late king　前王之鬼魂

地点　艾尔西诺

Hamlet

Gertrude, queen of Denmark①, becoming a widow by the sudden death of King Hamlet, in less than two months after his death married his brother Claudius, which was noted by all people at the time for a strange act of indiscretion②, or unfeelingness, or worse: for * this Claudius did no ways resemble her late husband in the qualities of his person or his mind, but was as contemptible③ in outward④ appearance, as he was base⑤ and unworthy in disposition⑥;[i] and * suspicions did not fail to arise in the minds of some, that he had privately made away with⑦ his brother, the late king, with the view of marrying his widow, and ascending⑧ the throne⑨ of Denmark, to the exclusion of⑩ young Hamlet, the son of the buried king, and lawful successor⑪ to the throne.[ii]

* But upon no one did this unadvised⑫ action of the queen make such impression as upon this young prince, who loved and venerated⑬ the memory of his dead father almost to idolatry⑭, and

---

① Denmark [ˈdenmɑːk] *n*. 丹麦(北欧国家)
② indiscretion [ˌɪndɪˈskreʃn] *n*. 轻率 rashness, imprudence
③ contemptible [kənˈtemptəbl] *adj*. 可鄙的 base, mean, despicable
④ outward [ˈaʊtwəd] *adj*. 表面的 apparent, outside, external
⑤ base [beɪs] *adj*. 卑鄙的 mean, despicable
⑥ disposition [ˌdɪspəˈzɪʃn] *n*. 性情 character, nature, temper
⑦ make away with 杀死 kill, murder, destroy
⑧ ascend [əˈsend] *v*. 登上 climb, scale, mount, go/move up
⑨ throne [θrəʊn] *n*. 王位 crown, sovereignty
⑩ to the exclusion of 把……排除在外
⑪ successor [səkˈsesə(r)] *n*. 继任者 heir, inheritor
⑫ unadvised [ˌʌnədˈvaɪzd] *adj*. 轻率的 rash, careless, ill-advised
⑬ venerate [ˈvenəreɪt] *v*. 敬重 respect, esteem, look up to
⑭ idolatry [aɪˈdɒlətri] *n*. 崇拜 worship, adoration

being of a nice sense of honour, and a most exquisite① practiser of propriety② himself, did sorely take to heart③ this unworthy conduct of his mother Gertrude [iii] —insomuch④ that, between grief for his father's death and shame for his mother's marriage, this young prince was overclouded with a deep melancholy⑤, and lost all his mirth⑥ and all his good looks; all his customary pleasure in books forsook⑦ him, his princely exercises and sports, proper to his youth, were no longer acceptable; * he grew weary of the world, which seemed to him an unweeded⑧ garden, where all the wholesome⑨ flowers were choked up, and nothing but weeds could thrive⑩. [iv] * Not that the prospect⑪ of exclusion⑫ from the throne, his lawful inheritance⑬, weighed so much upon his spirits, though that to a young and high-minded prince was a bitter wound and a sore indignity⑭; but what so galled⑮ him, and took away all his cheerful spirits, was, that his mother had shown herself so forgetful to his father's memory; and such a father! who had been to her so loving and so gentle a husband! [v] and then she always appeared as loving and obedient⑯ a wife to him, and would hang upon him as if her affection grew to him—and now within two months, or as it seemed to young Hamlet, less than two months, she had married again, married his uncle, her dear husband's brother, in itself a highly improper and unlawful marriage, from the nearness of relationship, but made much more so by the indecent⑰ haste with which it was concluded, and the unkingly character of the man whom she had chosen to be the partner of her throne and bed. * This it was, which more than the loss of ten kingdoms, dashed⑱ the spirits and brought a cloud over the mind of this honourable young prince. [vi]

* In vain was all that his mother Gertrude or the king could do to contrive⑲ to divert⑳ him; he still appeared in court in a suit of deep black, as mourning for the king his father's death, which mode of dress he had never laid aside, not even in compliment to his mother upon the day she was married, nor could he be brought to join in any of the festivities㉑ or rejoicings of that (as appeared to him) disgraceful day. [vii]

What mostly troubled him was an uncertainty about the manner of his father's death. It was

---

① exquisite [ɪk'skwɪzɪt] *adj*. 精致的,精美的 elegant, graceful
② propriety [prə'praɪəti] *n*. 礼节 courtesy, decorum, decency
③ take to heart 对……耿耿于怀 take...seriously/personally
④ insomuch [ˌɪnsəʊ'mʌtʃ] *adv*. 至如此程度 to such an extent
⑤ melancholy ['melənkəli] *n*. 忧郁 depression, gloom
⑥ mirth [mɜːθ] *n*. 欢笑,欢乐 merriment, amusement, rejoicing, gaiety
⑦ forsake [fə'seɪk] *v*. (forsook, forsaken) 抛弃 desert, abandon
⑧ unweeded [ʌn'wiːdɪd] *adj*.未除杂草的
⑨ wholesome ['həʊlsəm] *adj*. 健全的,健康的 healthy, sanitary, salutary
⑩ thrive [θraɪv] *v*. 茁壮成长 prosper, boom, flourish
⑪ prospect ['prɒspekt] *n*. 前景 possibility, promise
⑫ exclusion [ɪk'skluːʒn] *n*. 排斥,排除在外 exception, removal
⑬ inheritance [ɪn'herɪtəns] *n*. 继承 heritage
⑭ indignity [ɪn'dɪgnəti] *n*. 侮辱 insult, humiliation, dishonor
⑮ gall [gɔːl] *v*. 使气恼 annoy, madden, make sb's blood boil
⑯ obedient [ə'biːdiənt] *adj*. 顺从的 submissive, compliant, docile
⑰ indecent [ɪn'diːsnt] *adj*. 不得体的 improper, indecorous
⑱ dash [dæʃ] *v*. 使破灭 smash, shatter
⑲ contrive [kən'traɪv] *v*. 策划 plan, plot, design, devise
⑳ divert [daɪ'vɜːt] *v*. 使娱乐 delight, amuse, entertain, recreate
㉑ festivity[fe'stɪvəti] *n*. 欢庆 celebration, amusement, entertainment

given out by Claudius that a serpent① had stung② him; but young Hamlet had shrewd suspicions that Claudius himself was the serpent; in plain English, that he had murdered him for his crown, and that the serpent who stung his father did now sit on the throne.

How far he was right in this conjecture③, and what he ought to think of his mother, how far she was privy④ to this murder, and whether by her consent or knowledge, or without, it came to pass, were the doubts which continually harassed⑤ and distracted⑥ him.

A rumour⑦ had reached the ear of young Hamlet, that an apparition⑧, exactly resembling the dead king his father, had been seen by the soldiers upon watch, on the platform before the palace at midnight, for two or three nights successively⑨. The figure came constantly clad⑩ in the same suit of armour⑪, from head to foot, which the dead king was known to have worn—and they who saw it (Hamlet's bosom friend⑫ Horatio was one) agreed in their testimony⑬ as to the time and manner of its appearance: that it came just as the clock struck twelve; that it looked pale, with a face more of sorrow than of anger; that its beard was grisly⑭, and the colour a *sable silvered*, as they had seen it in his lifetime: that it made no answer when they spoke to it; yet once they thought it lifted up its head, and addressed itself to motion, as if it were about to speak; but in that moment the morning cock crew⑮, and it shrunk⑯ in haste⑰ away, and vanished out of their sight.

The young prince, strangely amazed at their relation, which was too consistent⑱ and agreeing with itself to disbelieve, concluded that it was his father's ghost which they had seen, and determined to take his watch with the soldiers that night, that he might have a chance of seeing it; for he reasoned with himself, that such an appearance did not come for nothing, but that the

---

① serpent ['sɜːpənt] *n*. 蛇 snake
② sting [stɪŋ] *v*. (stung) 叮,刺,蜇 prick, bite
③ conjecture [kən'dʒektʃə(r)] *n*. 猜测 guess, speculation, supposition
④ privy ['prɪvi] *adj*. 私人的,不公开的
⑤ harass ['hærəs] *v*. 骚扰 annoy, trouble, bother, worry, disturb
⑥ distract [dɪ'strækt] *v*. 困扰 confuse, puzzle, agitate, confound
⑦ rumour ['ruːmə(r)] *n*. 传闻,谣言 gossip, hearsay
⑧ apparition [ˌæpə'rɪʃn] *n*. 幽灵,鬼魂 ghost, spirit, phantom, spectre
⑨ successively [sək'sesɪvli] *adv*. 相继地 continuously, in succession
⑩ clad [klæd] *adj*. 穿衣的;覆盖的 dressed, clothed, appareled
⑪ armour ['ɑːmə(r)] *n*. 甲胄,盔甲 shield, plate
⑫ bosom friend 密友 crony, confidant, close friend
⑬ testimony ['testɪməni] *n*. 证明 proof, evidence, witness
⑭ grisly ['grɪzli] *adj*. 可怕的
⑮ crow [krəʊ] *v*. (crowed/crew, crowed) 啼叫 cry, squawk
⑯ shrink [ʃrɪŋk] *v*. (shrank/shrunk, shrunk) 退缩 recoil
⑰ in haste 急速 hastily, hurriedly
⑱ consistent [kən'sɪstənt] *adj*. 一致的

ghost had something to impart[1], and though it had been silent hitherto[2], yet it would speak to him. And he waited with impatience for the coming of night.

When night came he took his stand with Horatio, and Marcellus, one of the guard, upon the platform, where this apparition was accustomed to walk—and it being a cold night, and the air unusually raw[3] and nipping[4], Hamlet and Horatio and their companion fell into some talk about the coldness of the night, which was suddenly broken off by Horatio announcing that the ghost was coming.

At the sight of his father's spirit, Hamlet was struck with a sudden surprise and fear. He at first called upon the angels and heavenly ministers[5] to defend them, for he knew not whether it were a good spirit or bad; whether it came for good or evil: but he gradually assumed more courage; and his father (as it seemed to him) looked upon him so piteously[6], and as it were desiring to have conversation with him, and did in all respects appear so like himself as he was when he lived, that * Hamlet could not help addressing him: he called him by his name, *Hamlet*, *King*, *Father*! and conjured[7] him that he would tell the reason why he had left his grave[8], where they had seen him quietly bestowed[9], to come again and visit the earth and the moonlight—and besought[10] him that he would let them know if there was anything which they could do to give peace to his spirit.[viii] And the ghost beckoned[11] to Hamlet, that he should go with him to some more removed[12] place, where they might be alone; and Horatio and Marcellus would have dissuaded[13] the young prince from following it, for they feared lest it should be some evil spirit, who would tempt[14] him to the neighbouring sea, or to the top of some dreadful cliff, and there put on some horrible shape which might deprive[15] the prince of his reason. * But their counsels[16] and entreaties[17] could not alter Hamlet's determination, who cared too little about life to fear the

---

① impart [ɪm'pɑːt] *v*. 透露，告知 tell, reveal, convey, disclose
② hitherto [ˌhɪðə'tuː] *adv*. 迄今 so far, up to now
③ raw [rɔː] *adj*. 阴冷的 chilly, cold, freezing, bleak
④ nipping ['nɪpɪŋ] *adj*. 刺骨的 cutting, biting, piercing, sharp, bitter
⑤ heavenly minister 天使 angel
⑥ piteously ['pɪtiəsli] *adv*. 可怜地 pitifully, pitiably, miserably
⑦ conjure ['kʌndʒə(r)] *v*. 恳求 beg, implore, beseech,
⑧ grave [ɡreɪv] *n*. 坟墓 tomb, sepulchre, burying place
⑨ bestow [bɪ'stəʊ] *v*. 存放，贮藏 place, put, set, settle, deposit
⑩ beseech [bɪ'siːtʃ] *v*. (besought) 恳求 beg, petition, plead
⑪ beckon ['bekən] *v*. 示意 sign, signal, motion, gesture, gesticulate
⑫ removed [rɪ'muːvd] *adj*. 偏僻的，遥远的 remote, distant, faraway, lonely
⑬ dissuade [dɪ'sweɪd] *v*. 劝阻 discourage, talk out of
⑭ tempt [tempt] *v*. 引诱 attract, invite, allure, entice, seduce
⑮ deprive [dɪ'praɪv] *v*. 剥夺 rob, strip, dispossess
⑯ counsel ['kaʊnsl] *n*. 劝告 advice, suggestion, warning
⑰ entreaty [ɪn'triːti] *n*. 恳求 plea, petition, appeal

losing of it; and as to his soul, he said, what could the spirit do to that, being a thing immortal① as itself? [ix] And he felt as hardy② as a lion, and bursting③ from them, who did all they could to hold him, he followed whithersoever④ the spirit led him.

And when they were alone together, the spirit broke silence, and told him that he was the ghost of Hamlet, his father, who had been cruelly murdered, and he told the manner of it; that it was done by his own brother Claudius, Hamlet's uncle, as Hamlet had already but too much suspected, for the hope of succeeding⑤ to his bed and crown. That as he was sleeping in his garden, his custom always in the afternoon, * his treasonous⑥ brother stole upon him in his sleep, and poured the juice of poisonous henbane⑦ into his ears, which has such an antipathy⑧ to the life of man, that swift as quicksilver⑨ it courses through all the veins⑩ of the body, baking up⑪ the blood, and spreading a crust-like leprosy⑫ all over the skin[x] —thus sleeping, by a brother's hand he was cut off at once from his crown, his queen, and his life—and he adjured⑬ Hamlet, if he did ever his dear father love, that he would revenge his foul⑭ murder. * And the ghost lamented to his son, that his mother should so fall off from virtue⑮, as to prove false to the wedded⑯ love of her first husband, and to marry his murderer; but he cautioned Hamlet, howsoever⑰ he proceeded⑱ in his revenge against his wicked uncle, by no means to act any violence against the person of his mother, but to leave her to heaven, and to the stings and thorns⑲ of conscience⑳.[xi] And Hamlet promised to observe the ghost's direction in all things, and the ghost vanished.

And when Hamlet was left alone, he took up a solemn㉑ resolution, that all he had in his memory, all that he had ever learned by books or observation, should be instantly forgotten by him, and nothing live in his brain but the memory of what the ghost had told him, and enjoined him to do. And Hamlet related the particulars of the conversation which had passed to none but his dear friend Horatio; and he enjoined both to him and Marcellus the strictest secrecy as to what they had seen that night.

* The terror which the sight of the ghost had left upon the senses of Hamlet, he being weak

---

① immortal [ɪ'mɔːtl] *adj*. 不朽的,不死的
② hardy ['hɑːdi] *adj*. 坚强的,吃苦耐劳的 strong, robust, brave, courageous
③ burst [bɜːst] *v*. 冲,闯 rush, run, dash
④ whithersoever [ˌwɪðəsəʊ'evə(r)] *adv*.〈古〉无论到何方 wherever
⑤ succeed [sək'siːd] *v*. 继承 inherit, take over
⑥ treasonous ['triːzənəs] *adj*. 谋反的 disloyal, treacherous
⑦ henbane ['henbeɪn] *n*. 天仙子(野生毒草)
⑧ antipathy [æn'tɪpəθi] *n*. 不相容
⑨ quicksilver ['kwɪksɪlvə(r)] *n*. 汞,水银 mercury, hydrargyrum
⑩ vein [veɪn] *n*. 静脉
⑪ bake up 烤干 warm up
⑫ leprosy ['leprəsi] *n*. 麻风,麻风病 Hansen's disease
⑬ adjure [ə'dʒʊə(r)] *v*. 恳请,恳求 beg, beseech
⑭ foul [faʊl] *adj*. 不正当的,不道德的
⑮ virtue ['vɜːtʃuː] *n*. 美德 goodness, morality
⑯ wedded ['wedɪd] *adj*. 婚姻的,结婚的 married, marital, nuptial, conjugal
⑰ howsoever [haʊsəʊ'evə] *adv*. 不管怎样 however, no matter how
⑱ proceed [prə'siːd] *v*. 着手,开始进行 begin, carry on, get under way
⑲ thorn [θɔːn] *n*. 刺,荆棘 prickle, spine, spur
⑳ conscience ['kɒnʃəns] *n*. 良心 moral sense
㉑ solemn ['sɒləm] *adj*. 郑重的,庄严的 serious, earnest, grave, sober

and dispirited① before, almost unhinged② his mind, and drove him beside his reason.[xii] * And he, fearing that it would continue to have this effect, which might subject③ him to observation, and set his uncle upon his guard, if he suspected that he was meditating anything against him, or that Hamlet really knew more of his father's death than he professed, took up a strange resolution, from that time to counterfeit as if he were really and truly mad; thinking that he would be less an object of suspicion④ when his uncle should believe him incapable of any serious project, and that this real perturbation⑤ of mind would be best covered and pass concealed under a disguise of pretended lunacy⑥.[xiii]

From this time Hamlet affected a certain wildness and strangeness in his apparel, his speech, and behaviour, and did so excellently counterfeit the madman, that the king and queen were both deceived⑦, and not thinking his grief for his father's death a sufficient cause to produce such a distemper⑧, for they knew not of the appearance of the ghost, they concluded that his malady⑨ was love, and they thought they had found out the object.

Before Hamlet fell into the melancholy way which has been related, he had dearly loved a fair maid called Ophelia, the daughter of Polonius, the king's chief counsellor⑩ in affairs of state. He had sent her letters and rings, and made many tenders⑪ of his affection to her, and importuned⑫ her with love in honourable fashion—and she had given belief to his vows and importunities⑬. * But the melancholy which he fell into latterly⑭ had made him neglect her, and from the time he conceived⑮ the project of counterfeiting madness, he affected to treat her with unkindness, and a sort of rudeness—but she good lady, rather than reproach him with being false to her, persuaded herself that it was nothing but the disease in his mind, and no settled unkindness, which had made him less observant⑯ of her than formerly;[xiv] and * she compared the faculties⑰ of his once noble mind and excellent understanding, impaired⑱ as

---

① dispirited [dɪ'spɪrɪtɪd] *adj*. 沮丧的 depressed, dejected, disheartened
② unhinge [ʌn'hɪndʒ] *v*. 使精神失常 unsettle, madden, derange
③ subject [səb'dʒekt] *v*. 使经受 expose, submit, put through
④ suspicion [sə'spɪʃn] *n*. 怀疑 doubt, distrust, mistrust, scepticism
⑤ perturbation [ˌpɜːtə'beɪʃn] *n*. 不安 worry, unease, anxiety
⑥ lunacy ['luːnəsi] *n*. 精神失常 madness, craziness
⑦ deceive [dɪ'siːv] *v*. 欺骗 trick, fool, cheat, entrap, take in
⑧ distemper [dɪ'stempə(r)] *n*. 坏脾气 touchiness
⑨ malady ['mælədi] *n*. 疾病 illness, disease, disorder
⑩ counsellor ['kaʊnsələ(r)] *n*. 顾问 adviser, consultant, solicitor
⑪ tender ['tendə(r)] *n*. 提出,提供 offer, proposal
⑫ importune [ˌɪmpɔː'tjuːn] *v*. 强求,纠缠 press, pester, plague, harass
⑬ importunity [ˌɪmpɔː'tjuːnəti] *n*. 强求
⑭ latterly ['lætəli] *adv*. 最近,近来 recently, lately
⑮ conceive [kən'siːv] *v*. 构想 design, contrive, think up
⑯ observant [əb'zɜːvənt] *adj*. 善于观察的,观察力敏锐的 watchful, mindful, attentive
⑰ faculty ['fækltі] *n*. 才能 ability, talent, capacity, capability
⑱ impaired [ɪm'peəd] *adj*. 受损的 damaged, imperfect, unsound

they were with the deep melancholy that oppressed him, to sweet bells which in themselves are capable of most exquisite music, but when jangled① out of tune, or rudely handled, produce only a harsh and unpleasing sound.[xv]

Though * the rough business which Hamlet had in hand, the revenging of his father's death upon his murderer, did not suit with the playful state of courtship, or admit of the society of so idle② a passion as love now seemed to him,[xvi] yet * it could not hinder③ but that soft thoughts of his Ophelia would come between, and in one of these moments, when he thought that his treatment of this gentle lady had been unreasonably harsh, he wrote her a letter full of wild starts of passion, and in extravagant terms, such as agreed with his supposed madness, but mixed with some gentle touches of affection, which could not but show to this honoured lady that a deep love for her yet lay at the bottom of his heart.[xvii] * He bade her to doubt the stars were fire, and to doubt that the sun did move, to doubt truth to be a liar, but never to doubt that he loved; with more of such extravagant phrases.[xviii] This letter Ophelia dutifully showed to her father, and the old man thought himself bound④ to communicate it to the king and queen, who from that time supposed that the true cause of Hamlet's madness was love. And * the queen wished that the good beauties of Ophelia might be the happy cause of his wildness, for so she hoped that her virtues might happily restore him to his accustomed way again, to both their honours.[xix]

But Hamlet's malady lay deeper than she supposed, or than could be so cured. His father's ghost, which he had seen, still haunted⑤ his imagination, and the sacred⑥ injunction⑦ to revenge his murder gave him no rest till it was accomplished. Every hour of delay seemed to him a sin, and a violation of his father's commands. * Yet how to compass⑧ the death of the king, surrounded as he constantly was with his guards, was no easy matter. Or if it had been, the presence of the queen, Hamlet's mother, who was generally with the king, was a restraint⑨ upon his purpose, which he could not break through.[xx] Besides, the very circumstance that the usurper was his mother's husband filled him with some remorse⑩, and still blunted⑪ the edge of his purpose. * The mere act of putting a fellow-creature to death was in itself odious⑫ and terrible to a disposition⑬ naturally so gentle as Hamlet's was.[xxi] * His very melancholy, and the dejection⑭ of spirits he had so long been in, produced an irresoluteness⑮ and wavering⑯ of purpose, which kept him from

---

① jangle [ˈdʒæŋgl] *v*. 使发出刺耳声
② idle [ˈaɪdl] *adj*. 无聊的 empty
③ hinder [ˈhɪndə(r)] *v*. 阻碍 stop, check, block, prevent, hold up
④ bound [baʊnd] *adj*. 有义务的 compelled, obliged, committed
⑤ haunt [hɔːnt] *v*. 萦绕 possess, plague, torment
⑥ sacred [ˈseɪkrɪd] *adj*. 神圣的 holy, divine, hallowed, consecrated
⑦ injunction [ɪnˈdʒʌŋkʃn] *n*. 命令 order, command, dictate
⑧ compass [ˈkʌmpəs] *v*. 图谋完成,达到 achieve, accomplish, attain, obtain
⑨ restraint [rɪˈstreɪnt] *n*. 束缚 limit, check, curb
⑩ remorse [rɪˈmɔːs] *n*. 自责,懊悔 regret, contrition, self-reproach
⑪ blunt [blʌnt] *v*. 使变钝 dull
⑫ odious [ˈəʊdiəs] *adj*. 可憎的 nasty, foul, offensive, disgusting
⑬ disposition [ˌdɪspəˈzɪʃn] *n*. 性格 character, nature, temper
⑭ dejection [dɪˈdʒekʃn] *n*. 沮丧 gloom, depression, despondency
⑮ irresoluteness [ɪrezəˈluːtnəs] *n*. 犹豫 hesitation, irresolution
⑯ wavering [ˈweɪvərɪŋ] *n*. 犹豫,摇摆不定 hesitation, indecisiveness

proceeding to extremities.[xxii] Moreover, he could not help having some scruples① upon his mind, whether the spirit which he had seen was indeed his father, or whether it might not be the devil, who he had heard has power to take any form he pleases, and who might have assumed his father's shape only to take advantage of② his weakness and his melancholy, to drive him to the doing of so desperate an act as murder. And he determined that he would have more certain grounds to go upon than a vision, or apparition③, which might be a delusion④.

While he was in this irresolute⑤ mind there came to the court certain players, in whom Hamlet formerly used to take delight, and particularly to hear one of them speak a tragical speech, describing the death of old Priam⑥, King of Troy⑦, with the grief of Hecuba⑧ his queen. Hamlet welcomed his old friends, the players, and remembering how that speech had formerly given him pleasure, requested the player to repeat it; * which he did in so lively a manner, setting forth⑨ the cruel murder of the feeble⑩ old king, with the destruction of his people and city by fire, and the mad grief of the old queen, running barefoot up and down the palace, with a poor clout⑪ upon that head where a crown had been, and with nothing but a blanket upon her loins⑫, snatched⑬ up in haste, where she had worn a royal robe; that not only it drew tears from all that stood by, who thought they saw the real scene, so lively was it represented, but even the player himself delivered it with a broken voice and real tears.[xxiii]

* This put Hamlet upon thinking, if that player could so work himself up to passion by a mere fictitious⑭ speech, to weep for one that he had never seen, for Hecuba, that had been dead so many hundred years, how dull was he, who having a real motive⑮ and cue⑯ for passion, a real king and a dear father murdered, was yet so little moved, that his revenge all this while had seemed to have slept in dull and muddy forgetfulness! [xxiv] and * while he meditated on actors and acting, and the powerful effects which a good play, represented to the life⑰, has upon the spectator, he remembered the instance of some murderer, who seeing a murder on the stage, was by the mere force of the scene and resemblance⑱ of circumstances so affected, that on the spot he confessed the crime which he had committed.[xxv] And he determined that these players should play something like the murder of his father before his uncle, and he would watch narrowly what effect

---

① scruple [ˈskruːpl] *n*. 顾忌 uneasiness, misgiving, hesitation
② take advantage of 利用 use, exploit
③ apparition [ˌæpəˈrɪʃn] *n*. 幽灵，鬼魂 ghost, spirit, phantom, spectre
④ delusion [dɪˈluːʒn] *n*. 错觉 fancy, illusion, hallucination
⑤ irresolute [ɪˈrezəluːt] *adj*. 踌躇不定的 indecisive, undetermined
⑥ Priam [ˈpraɪəm] *n*. 普里阿摩斯（希腊传说中的特洛伊国王）
⑦ Troy [trɔɪ] *n*. 特洛伊（小亚细亚西北部的古城）
⑧ Hecuba [ˈhekjʊbə] *n*. 赫卡柏（普里阿摩斯之妻）
⑨ set forth 阐述，提出 explain, describe, illustrate, spell out
⑩ feeble [ˈfiːbl] *adj*. 虚弱的 weak, delicate, powerless, frail, infirm
⑪ clout [klaʊt] *n*. 破布 rag, tatter, shred, wiper, dishrag
⑫ loin [lɔɪn] *n*. 腰部；臀部
⑬ snatch [snætʃ] *v*. 抓住 seize, grab, grip, grasp, take hold of
⑭ fictitious [fɪkˈtɪʃəs] *adj*. 虚构的 unreal, artificial, invented, made-up
⑮ motive [ˈməʊtɪv] *n*. 动机 cause, motivation
⑯ cue [kjuː] *n*. 暗示 signal, sign, hint, suggestion
⑰ to the life 逼真地 vividly
⑱ resemblance [rɪˈzembləns] *n*. 相似 similarity, alikeness

it might have upon him, and from his looks he would be able to gather with more certainty if he were the murderer or not. To this effect① he ordered a play to be prepared, to the representation of which he invited the king and queen.

The story of the play was of a murder done in Vienna② upon a duke. The duke's name was Gonzago, his wife Baptista. The play showed how one Lucianus, a near relation to the duke, poisoned him in his garden for his estate, and how the murderer in a short time after got the love of Gonzago's wife.

At the representation of this play, the king, who did not know the trap which was laid for him, was present, with his queen and the whole court: Hamlet sitting attentively near him to observe his looks. The play began with a conversation between Gonzago and his wife, in which the lady made many protestations③ of love, and of never marrying a second husband, if she should outlive Gonzago; wishing she might be accursed④ if she ever took a second husband, and adding that no woman did so, but those wicked women who kill their first husbands. Hamlet observed the king his uncle change colour at this expression, and that it was as bad as wormwood⑤ both to him and to the queen. * But when Lucianus, according to the story, came to poison Gonzago sleeping in the garden, the strong resemblance which it bore⑥ to his own wicked act upon the late king, his brother, whom he had poisoned in his garden, so struck upon the conscience of this usurper, that he was unable to sit out the rest of the play, but on a sudden calling for lights to his chamber, and affecting or partly feeling a sudden sickness, he abruptly⑦ left the theatre.[xxvi] The king being departed, the play was given over. Now Hamlet had seen enough to be satisfied⑧ that the words of the ghost were true, and no illusion⑨; and * in a fit⑩ of gaiety⑪, like that which comes over a man who suddenly has some great doubt or scruple resolved, he swore to Horatio, that he would take the ghost's word for a thousand pounds.[xxvii] But before he could make up his resolution as to what measures of revenge he should take, now he was certainly informed that his uncle was his father's murderer, he was sent for by the queen his mother, to a private conference in her closet.

* It was by desire of the king that the queen sent for Hamlet, that she might signify⑫ to her

① to this effect 为此目的
② Vienna [vɪ'enə] *n*. 维也纳(奥地利首都)
③ protestation [ˌprɒtə'steɪʃn] *n*. 誓言 vow, oath
④ accursed [ə'kɜːsɪd] *adj*. 被诅咒的 cursed
⑤ wormwood ['wɜːmwʊd] *n*. 苦艾草(此处指令人苦恼的事)
⑥ bear [beə(r)] *v*. (bore, borne) 具有 hold, exhibit, maintain
⑦ abruptly [ə'brʌptli] *adv*. 突然 suddenly, all of a sudden
⑧ satisfied ['sætɪsfaɪd] *adj*. 确信的 sure, certain, convinced
⑨ illusion [ɪ'luːʒn] *n*. 错觉 delusion, fancy, fantasy
⑩ fit [fɪt] *n*. 一阵
⑪ gaiety ['geɪəti] *n*. 高兴,快乐 glee, gladness, happiness, cheerfulness
⑫ signify ['sɪgnɪfaɪ] *v*. 表达,显示 express

son how much his late behaviour had displeased them both, and the king, wishing to know all that passed at that conference, and thinking that the too partial① report of a mother might let slip some part of Hamlet's words, which it might much import② the king to know, Polonius, the old counsellor of state, was ordered to plant himself behind the hangings in the queen's closet, where he might unseen hear all that passed.[xxviii] * This artifice③ was particularly adapted to the disposition of Polonius, who was a man grown old in crooked④ maxims⑤ and policies of state, and delighted to get at the knowledge of matters in an indirect and cunning way.[xxix]

* Hamlet being come to his mother, she began to tax⑥ him in the roundest⑦ way with his actions and behaviour, and she told him that he had given great offence to his father, meaning the king, his uncle, whom, because he had married her, she called Hamlet's father.[xxx] Hamlet, sorely⑧ indignant⑨ that she should give so dear and honoured a name as father seemed to him, to a wretch⑩ who was indeed no better than the murderer of his true father, with some sharpness replied: "Mother, you have much offended⑪ my father." The queen said that was but an idle answer. "* As good as the question deserved,[xxxi]" said Hamlet. The queen asked him if he had forgotten who it was he was speaking to? "Alas!" replied Hamlet, "I wish I could forget. You are the queen, your husband's brother's wife; and you are my mother: I wish you were not what you are." "Nay; then," said the queen, "if you show me so little respect, * I will set those to you that can speak,[xxxii]" and was going to send the king or Polonius to him. * But Hamlet would not let her go, now he had her alone, till he had tried if his words could not bring her to some sense of her wicked life; and, taking her by the wrist, he held her fast, and made her sit down.[xxxiii] She, affrighted at his earnest manner, and fearful lest in his lunacy he should do her a mischief⑫, cried out; and a voice was heard from behind the hangings: "Help, help, the queen!" * which Hamlet hearing, and verily thinking that it was the king himself there concealed, he drew his sword and stabbed⑬ at the place where the voice came from, as he would have stabbed a rat that ran there, till the voice ceasing⑭, he concluded the person to be dead.[xxxiv] But when he dragged for the body, it was not the king, but Polonius, the old officious⑮ counsellor, that had planted himself as a spy behind the hangings. "Oh me!" exclaimed the queen, "what a rash⑯ and bloody deed have you done!" "A bloody deed, mother," replied Hamlet, "but not so bad as yours, who killed a king,

① partial [ˈpɑːʃl] *adj*. 偏袒的 unfair, prejudiced, discriminatory
② import [ɪmˈpɔːt] *v*. 具有重要性
③ artifice [ˈɑːtɪfɪs] *n*. 诡计,欺骗 trick, craft, tactic, stratagem
④ crooked [ˈkrʊkɪd] *adj*. 不正直的 dishonest
⑤ maxim [ˈmæksɪm] *n*. 格言 saying, motto, proverb, axiom
⑥ tax [tæks] *v*. 指责 accuse, charge, blame
⑦ round [raʊnd] *adj*. 兜圈子的 roundabout, indirect, evasive
⑧ sorely [ˈsɔːli] *adv*. 非常 badly, extremely
⑨ indignant [ɪnˈdɪgnənt] *adj*. 愤怒的 angry
⑩ wretch [retʃ] *n*. 坏蛋,恶棍 villain, rogue, rascal, knave, bad egg
⑪ offend [əˈfend] *v*. 得罪 insult, upset, annoy, irritate, displease
⑫ mischief [ˈmɪstʃɪf] *n*. 伤害 harm, damage, injury, detriment
⑬ stab [stæb] *v*. 刺,戳 pierce, cut, jab, stick, thrust
⑭ cease [siːs] *v*. 停止 stop, finish, come to an end
⑮ officious [əˈfɪʃəs] *adj*. 多管闲事的 overbusy
⑯ rash [ræʃ] *adj*. 鲁莽的 hasty, reckless, ill-advised, hot-headed

and married his brother." * Hamlet had gone too far to leave off[①] here.[xxxv] He was now in the humour[②] to speak plainly to his mother, and he pursued[③] it. And * though the faults of parents are to be tenderly[④] treated by their children, yet in the case of great crimes the son may have leave to speak even to his own mother with some harshness, so as that harshness is meant for her good, and to turn her from her wicked ways, and not done for the purpose of upbraiding[⑤].[xxxvi] And now this virtuous prince did in moving terms represent to the queen the heinousness[⑥] of her offence, in being so forgetful of the dead king, his father, as in so short a space of time to marry with his brother and reputed[⑦] murderer—*such an act as, after the vows which she had sworn to her first husband, was enough to make all vows of women suspected, and all virtue to be accounted hypocrisy[⑧], wedding contracts to be less than gamesters'[⑨] oaths[⑩], and religion[⑪] to be a mockery[⑫] and a mere form of words.[xxxvii] He said she had done such a deed, that the heavens blushed at it, and the earth was sick of her because of it. * And he showed her two pictures, the one of the late king, her first husband, and the other of the present king, her second husband, and he bade her mark the difference; what a grace was on the brow of his father, how like a god he looked! the curls of Apollo, the forehead of Jupiter, the eye of Mars, and a posture[⑬] like to Mercury newly alighted[⑭] on some heaven-kissing hill! [xxxviii] this man, he said, *had been* her husband. And then he showed her whom she had got in his stead: how like a blight[⑮] or a mildew[⑯] he looked, for so he had blasted[⑰] his wholesome brother. And the queen was sore[⑱] ashamed that he should so turn her eyes inward upon her soul, which she now saw so black and deformed[⑲].

And he asked her how she could continue to live with this man, and be a wife to him, who had murdered her first husband, and got the crown by as false means as a thief—

① leave off 停止
② humour [ˈhjuːmə(r)] *n*. 心情,感觉 mood, temper
③ pursue [pəˈsjuː] *v*. 致力于,追求 work at, go in for
④ tenderly [ˈtendəli] *adv*. 温柔地 softly, mildly, gently
⑤ upbraid [ʌpˈbreɪd] *v*. 责骂,训斥 blame, scold, reproach, condemn
⑥ heinousness [ˈheɪnəsnəs] *n*. 十恶不赦 atrocity, enormity, hatefulness
⑦ reputed [rɪˈpjuːtɪd] *adj*. 号称的 supposed
⑧ hypocrisy [hɪˈpɒkrəsi] *n*. 伪善 falsity, insincerity
⑨ gamester [ˈgeɪmstə(r)] *n*. 赌徒 gambler, bettor
⑩ oath [əʊθ] *n*. 誓言 promise, pledge, vow
⑪ religion [rɪˈlɪdʒən] *n*. 宗教信仰 belief, faith, doctrine, creed
⑫ mockery [ˈmɒkəri] *n*. 嘲笑 contempt, scorn, disdain
⑬ posture [ˈpɒstʃə(r)] *n*. 姿势 pose, stance
⑭ alight [əˈlaɪt] *v*. 降落 land, descend, come down
⑮ blight [blaɪt] *n*. 枯萎病;荒芜
⑯ mildew [ˈmɪldjuː] *n*. 霉菌 mould, mold, mustiness
⑰ blast [blɑːst] *v*. 摧毁 destroy, ruin
⑱ sore [sɔː(r)] *adj*. 痛苦的 painful, burning
⑲ deformed [dɪˈfɔːmd] *adj*. 畸形的 distorted

and just as he spoke, the ghost of his father, such as he was in his lifetime, and such as he had lately seen it, entered the room, and Hamlet, in great terror, asked what it would have; and the ghost said that it came to remind him of the revenge he had promised, which Hamlet seemed to have forgot; and the ghost bade him speak to his mother, for the grief and terror she was in would else kill her. * It then vanished, and was seen by none but Hamlet, neither could he by pointing to where it stood, or by any description, make his mother perceive it, who was terribly frightened all this while to hear him conversing①, as it seemed to her, with nothing; and she imputed② it to the disorder of his mind.[xxxix] * But Hamlet begged her not to flatter③ her wicked soul in such a manner as to think that it was his madness, and not her own offences, which had brought his father's spirit again on the earth.[xl] And he bade her feel his pulse, how temperately④ it beat, not like a madman's. And he begged of her with tears, to confess herself to heaven for what was past, and for the future to avoid the company of the king, and be no more as a wife to him—and when she should show herself a mother to him, by respecting his father's memory, he would ask a blessing of her as a son. And she promising to observe his directions, the conference ended.

* And now Hamlet was at leisure⑤ to consider who it was that in his unfortunate rashness he had killed—and when he came to see that it was Polonius, the father of the lady Ophelia, whom he so dearly loved, he drew apart the dead body, and, his spirits being now a little quieter, he wept for what he had done.[xli]

The unfortunate death of Polonius gave the king a pretence⑥ for sending Hamlet out of the kingdom. He would willingly have put him to death, fearing him as dangerous; but he dreaded⑦ the people, who loved Hamlet, and the queen who, with all her faults, doted upon the prince, her son. * So this subtle⑧ king, under pretence of providing for Hamlet's safety, that he might not be called to account for Polonius' death, caused him to be conveyed on board a ship bound for⑨ England, under the care of two courtiers, by whom he despatched⑩ letters to the English court, which in that time was in subjection⑪ and paid tribute⑫ to Denmark, requiring for special reasons there pretended, that Hamlet should be put to death as soon as he landed on English ground.[xlii] Hamlet, suspecting some treachery⑬, in the nighttime secretly got at the letters, and skillfully erasing his own name, he in the stead of it put

① converse [kən'vɜːs] v. 交谈 talk, speak, chat, communicate
② impute [ɪm'pjuːt] v. 归咎于 attribute, ascribe, set down to
③ flatter ['flætə] v. 奉承，讨好 praise, compliment, butter up
④ temperately ['tempərətli] adv. 温和地，有节制地 moderately
⑤ at leisure 空闲的
⑥ pretence [prɪ'tens] n. 借口 excuse, pretext
⑦ dread [dred] v. 害怕 fear
⑧ subtle ['sʌtl] adj. 狡猾的 crafty, cunning, sly, wily, artful
⑨ bound for 去往…… headed for
⑩ despatch [dɪ'spætʃ] v. 发送，派遣 send
⑪ subjection [səb'dʒekʃn] n. 隶属
⑫ tribute ['trɪbjuːt] n. 贡品；敬意
⑬ treachery ['tretʃəri] n. 背叛，变节 betrayal

in the names of those two courtiers, who had the charge of him, to be put to death—then sealing① up the letters, he put them into their place again. * Soon after the ship was attacked by pirates, and a sea-fight commenced②; in the course of which Hamlet, desirous③ to show his valour④, with sword in hand singly boarded the enemy's vessel; while his own ship, in a cowardly manner, bore away⑤, and leaving him to his fate, the two courtiers made the best of their way to England, charged with those letters the sense of which Hamlet had altered to their own deserved destruction.[xliii]

* The pirates, who had the prince in their power, showed themselves gentle enemies; and knowing whom they had got prisoner, in the hope that the prince might do them a good turn at court in recompense⑥ for any favour they might show him, they set Hamlet on shore at the nearest port in Denmark.[xliv] From that place Hamlet wrote to the king, acquainting him with the strange chance which had brought him back to his own country, and saying that on the next day he should present himself before his majesty. When he got home, a sad spectacle⑦ offered itself the first thing to his eyes.

This was the funeral of the young and beautiful Ophelia, his once dear mistress. The wits⑧ of this young lady had begun to turn ever since her poor father's death. * That he should die a violent death, and by the hands of the prince whom she loved, so affected this tender young maid, that in a little time she grew perfectly distracted⑨, and would go about giving flowers away to the ladies of the court, and saying that they were for her father's burial, singing songs about love and about death, and sometimes such as had no meaning at all, as if she had no memory of what happened to her.[xlv] There was a willow which grew slanting⑩ over a brook⑪, and reflected its leaves on the stream. * To this brook she came one day when she was unwatched, with garlands⑫ she had been making, mixed up of daisies⑬ and nettles, flowers and weeds together, and clambering⑭ up to hang her garland upon the boughs⑮ of the willow, a bough broke, and precipitated⑯ this fair

---

① seal [siːl] *v*. 封上,密封
② commence [kəˈmens] *v*. 开始 start, proceed, kick off
③ desirous [dɪˈzaɪərəs] *adj*. 渴望的 eager
④ valour [ˈvælə(r)] *n*. 英勇 bravery, courage, gallantry
⑤ bear away 改变航向
⑥ recompense [ˈrekəmpens] *n*. 补偿 repayment, compensation
⑦ spectacle [ˈspektəkl] *n*. 景象 sight, scene
⑧ wit [wɪt] *n*. 头脑 mind, brain
⑨ distracted [dɪˈstræktɪd] *adj*. 心烦意乱的,注意力分散的
⑩ slanting [ˈslɑːntɪŋ] *adj*. 倾斜的 inclined, tilted
⑪ brook [brʊk] *n*. 小溪 stream, rivulet, rill, runnel, watercourse
⑫ garland [ˈɡɑːlənd] *n*. 花环,花冠 wreath
⑬ daisy [ˈdeɪzi] *n*. 雏菊
⑭ clamber [ˈklæmbə(r)] *v*. 攀爬 climb, scale, mount, scramble
⑮ bough [baʊ] *n*. 大树枝 branch, twig, sprig, limb
⑯ precipitate [prɪˈsɪpɪteɪt] *v*. 使陡然下落

young maid, garland, and all that she had gathered, into the water, where her clothes bore her up for a while, during which she chanted① scraps② of old tunes, like one insensible③ to her own distress, or as if she were a creature natural to that element④[xlvi]—but * long it was not before her garments, heavy with the wet, pulled her in from her melodious⑤ singing to a muddy and miserable death.[xlvii] It was the funeral of this fair maid which her brother Laertes was celebrating, the king and queen and whole court being present, when Hamlet arrived. He knew not what all this show imported⑥, but stood on one side, not inclining⑦ to interrupt the ceremony. He saw the flowers strewed⑧ upon her grave, as the custom was in maiden burials, which the queen herself threw in; and as she threw them she said: "* Sweets to the sweet! I thought to have decked⑨ thy bride-bed, sweet maid, not to have strewed thy grave.[xlviii] Thou shouldst have been my Hamlet's wife." And he heard her brother wish that violets might spring from her grave—and he saw him leap into the grave all frantic⑩ with grief⑪, and bid the attendants pile mountains of earth upon him, that he might be buried with her. And * Hamlet's love for this fair maid came back to him, and he could not bear that a brother should show so much transport⑫ of grief, for he thought that he loved Ophelia better than forty thousand brothers.[xlix] Then discovering himself⑬, he leaped into the grave where Laertes was, all as frantic or more frantic than he, and Laertes knowing him to be Hamlet, who had been the cause of his father's and his sister's death, grappled⑭ him by the throat as an enemy, till the attendants parted them—and * Hamlet, after the funeral, excused his hasty⑮ act in throwing himself into the grave as if to brave⑯ Laertes; but he said he could not bear that any one should seem to outgo⑰ him in grief for the death of the fair Ophelia.[l] And for the time these two noble youths seemed reconciled.

But out of the grief and anger of Laertes for the death of his father and Ophelia, the king, Hamlet's wicked uncle, contrived destruction for Hamlet. He set on Laertes, under cover of peace and reconciliation, to challenge Hamlet to a friendly trial of skill at fencing, which Hamlet accepting, a day was appointed to try the match. At this match all the court was present, and Laertes, by direction of the king, prepared a poisoned weapon. Upon this match great wagers⑱ were laid by the courtiers, as both Hamlet and Laertes were known to excel at this sword play;

---

① chant [tʃɑːnt] *v*. 吟唱 sing, chorus, intone, carol
② scrap [skræp] *n*. 片段 piece, part, fragment
③ insensible [ɪnˈsensəbl] *adj*. 无感觉的,麻木的 indifferent, unconscious
④ element [ˈelɪmənt] *n*. 元素,要素 part, component, constituent
⑤ melodious [məˈləʊdiəs] *adj*. 悦耳的 musical, sweet-sounding
⑥ import [ɪmˈpɔːt] *v*. 意指,表明 mean, indicate, signify, stand for
⑦ incline [ɪnˈklaɪn] *v*. 倾向于 tend, predispose, dispose
⑧ strew [struː] *v*. 散播 scatter, spread, sprinkle, disperse
⑨ deck [dek] *v*. 装饰 decorate, adorn, ornament
⑩ frantic [ˈfræntɪk] *adj*. 发狂的,紧张的 wild, mad, crazy
⑪ grief [griːf] *n*. 悲痛 sadness, sorrow, distress
⑫ transport [ˈtrænspɔːt] *n*. 强烈情感 passion, frenzy, fervour
⑬ discover oneself 某人显露真容
⑭ grapple [ˈgræpl] *v*. 扭打 fight, battle, combat, wrestle
⑮ hasty [ˈheɪsti] *adj*. 草率的 rash, reckless, imprudent, incautious
⑯ brave [breɪv] *v*. 挑战 challenge, stand up to
⑰ outgo [ˌaʊtˈgəʊ] *v*. 超过 outdo, exceed, surpass, be superior to
⑱ wager [ˈweɪdʒə(r)] *n*. 赌注 bet, stake, ante

and * Hamlet taking up the foils① chose one, not at all suspecting the treachery② of Laertes, or being careful to examine Laertes' weapon, who, instead of a foil or blunted③ sword, which the laws of fencing require, made use of one with a point, and poisoned.[li] * At first Laertes did but play with Hamlet, and suffered him to gain some advantages, which the dissembling④ king magnified⑤ and extolled⑥ beyond measure, drinking to Hamlet's success, and wagering rich bets upon the issue⑦[lii] —but after a few passes, Laertes growing warm made a deadly thrust at Hamlet with his poisoned weapon, and gave him a mortal⑧ blow. * Hamlet incensed⑨, but not knowing the whole of the treachery, in the scuffle⑩ exchanged his own innocent weapon for Laertes' deadly one, and with a thrust of Laertes' own sword repaid Laertes home, who was thus justly caught in his own treachery.[liii] In this instant the queen shrieked⑪ out that she was poisoned. She had inadvertently⑫ drunk out of a bowl which the king had prepared for Hamlet, in case, that being warm in fencing, he should call for drink—into this the treacherous king had infused⑬ a deadly poison, to make sure of Hamlet, if Laertes had failed. He had forgotten to warn the queen of the bowl, which she drank of, and immediately died, exclaiming with her last breath that she was poisoned. Hamlet, suspecting some treachery ordered the doors to be shut, while he sought it out. Laertes told him to seek no farther, for he was the traitor; and feeling his life go away with the wound which Hamlet had given him, he made confession of the treachery he had used, and now he had fallen a victim to it—and he told Hamlet of the envenomed⑭ point, and said that Hamlet had not half an hour to live, for no medicine could cure him; and begging forgiveness of Hamlet, he died, with his last words accusing the king of being the contriver⑮ of the mischief.

* When Hamlet saw his end draw near, there being yet some venom⑯ left upon the sword, he suddenly turned upon his false uncle, and thrust the point of it to his heart, fulfilling the promise which he had made to his father's spirit, whose injunction⑰ was now accomplished, and his foul murder revenged upon the murderer.[liv] Then Hamlet, feeling his breath fail and life departing, turned to his dear friend Horatio, who had been spectator of this fatal⑱ tragedy; and with his dying breath requested him that he would live to tell his story to the world (for Horatio had made

---

① foil [fɔɪl] *n*. 花剑
② treachery ['tretʃəri] *n*. 背叛 dishonesty, betrayal
③ blunted ['blʌntɪd] *adj*. 钝的,迟钝的 blunt, dull
④ dissemble [dɪ'sembl] *v*. 掩饰 hide, pretend, affect, falsify
⑤ magnify ['mægnɪfaɪ] *v*. 夸大 exaggerate, overstate, blow up
⑥ extol [ɪk'stəʊl] *v*. 赞扬,赞美 praise, acclaim, applaud
⑦ issue ['ɪʃuː] *n*. 结果,后果 result, outcome, conclusion
⑧ mortal ['mɔːtl] *adj*. 致命的 fatal, killing, terminal
⑨ incensed [ɪn'senst] *adj*. 激怒的 mad, furious, fuming, enraged
⑩ scuffle ['skʌfl] *n*. 混战,扭打 fight, fray, skirmish, commotion
⑪ shriek [ʃriːk] *v*. 尖叫 scream, cry, yell, howl, wail, squeal
⑫ inadvertently [ˌɪnəd'vɜːtntli] *adv*. 无意地,不经意地 accidentally, by accident
⑬ infuse [ɪn'fjuːz] *v*. 注入,使充满 add, fill, suffuse
⑭ envenomed [ɪn'venəmd] *adj*. 下毒的 poisoned, poisonous
⑮ contriver [kən'traɪvər] *n*. 策划人 planner, plotter, schemer
⑯ venom ['venəm] *n*. 毒液 poison, toxin, bane
⑰ injunction [ɪn'dʒʌŋkʃn] *n*. 命令 order, command, dictate
⑱ fatal ['feɪtl] *adj*. 毁灭性的,致命的 disastrous, devastating, catastrophic

a motion as if he would slay① himself to accompany the prince in death), and Horatio promised that he would make a true report, as one that was privy to all the circumstances. * And, thus satisfied, the noble heart of Hamlet cracked②; and Horatio and the bystanders with many tears commended the spirit of this sweet prince to the guardianship of angels.[lv] For * Hamlet was a loving and a gentle prince, and greatly beloved for his many noble and princelike qualities; and if he had lived, would no doubt have proved a most royal and complete king to Denmark.[lvi]

ⅰ This Claudius did no ways resemble her late husband in the qualities of his person or his mind, but was as contemptible in outward appearance, as he was base and unworthy in disposition. 不论从人品还是性情上看,这个克劳狄斯都跟她已故的丈夫没有一点点相同的地方:他的外貌是可憎的,正如他的性情是卑鄙下流的。(did:强调谓语动词)

ⅱ Suspicions did not fail to arise in the minds of some, that he had privately made away with his brother, the late king, with the view of marrying his widow, and ascending the throne of Denmark, to the exclusion of young Hamlet, the son of the buried king, and lawful successor to the throne. 有些人心里不免怀疑他是为了娶他的嫂子并且篡夺丹麦的王位,偷偷把他哥哥(已故的国王)害死的。这样一来,他就把先王的合法继承人——年轻的哈姆莱特撇到一边儿去了。(suspicions..., that...:同位语从句;with the view of:意欲)

---

① slay [sleɪ] v. 杀死 kill, murder, slaughter

② crack [kræk] v. 破裂 break, split, burst, go to pieces

iii But upon no one did this unadvised action of the queen make such impression as upon this young prince, who loved and venerated the memory of his dead father almost to idolatry, and being of a nice sense of honour, and a most exquisite practiser of propriety himself, did sorely take to heart this unworthy conduct of his mother Gertrude. 但是没有人比王子更受王后这个轻率举动的刺激。他爱他已故的父亲，差不多把他当作偶像来崇拜；哈姆莱特有很强的荣誉感，举止正派体面，他为母亲乔特鲁德的可耻行为感到非常难过。（did…make…：部分倒装结构；who…：非限制性定语从句；being…：分词作状语；did…：强调谓语动词）

iv He grew weary of the world, which seemed to him an unweeded garden, where all the wholesome flowers were choked up, and nothing but weeds could thrive. 他对这个世界感到厌倦，他把世界看作一个野草丛生的花园，一切新鲜的花草都枯死了，除了杂草，什么也长不出来。（which…, where…：定语从句的嵌套）

v Not that the prospect of exclusion from the throne, his lawful inheritance, weighed so much upon his spirits, though that to a young and high-minded prince was a bitter wound and a sore indignity; but what so galled him, and took away all his cheerful spirits, was, that his mother had shown herself so forgetful to his father's memory; and such a father! who had been to her so loving and so gentle a husband! 他觉得最沉重的还不是他不能按照法律继承本该由他来继承的王位——尽管这件事对于一个年轻高傲的王子来说是一个刺骨的创伤和一个惨痛的屈辱。让他气恼，让他再也打不起精神来的，是他母亲那么快就忘掉他的父亲——而且是多么好的一位父亲呀！他的父亲是多么温存体贴的一位丈夫呀！（not…, but…：不是……而是……；though…：让步状语从句；what…, was, that…who…：主语从句、表语从句和定语从句）

vi This it was, which more than the loss of ten kingdoms, dashed the spirits and brought a cloud over the mind of this honourable young prince. 正是这件事，比丢掉十个王国还要让这位可敬的年轻王子意气消沉，使他的心灵遮上了一层阴云。（This it was, which…＝It was this which…：强调句中表语提前，现代英语中不用 which 而用 that）

vii In vain was all that his mother Gertrude or the king could do to contrive to divert him; he still appeared in court in a suit of deep black, as mourning for the king his father's death, which mode of dress he had never laid aside, not even in compliment to his mother upon the day she was married, nor could he be brought to join in any of the festivities or rejoicings of that (as appeared to him) disgraceful day. 他母亲乔特鲁德和国王想尽了办法叫他快活起来，怎么也不成功。他在宫里仍然穿着深黑色的衣服来哀悼他父王的死。他从来也不肯脱去丧服，甚至在他母亲结婚的那天，他也不肯为了祝贺她而换一换衣裳。在那可耻的一天（在他看来是这样的），什么宴会、庆典他一概拒绝参加。（In vain was all that…：倒装结构、定语从句）

viii Hamlet could not help addressing him: he called him by his name, *Hamlet*, *King*, *Father*! and conjured him that he would tell the reason why he had left his grave, where they had seen him quietly bestowed, to come again and visit the earth and the moonlight—and besought him that he would let them know if there was anything which they could do to give peace to his spirit. 年轻的哈姆莱特禁不住叫出他的名字，对他说："哈姆莱特，国王，父亲！"恳求它告诉他，为什么要离开坟墓——他们曾看到它静静地躺在那里，回到人间来，在月光底下出现！他请鬼魂告诉他们怎样才可以替它安魂。（besought…that…if…which…：宾语从

句、宾语从句和定语从句的嵌套）

ⅸ But their counsels and entreaties could not alter Hamlet's determination, who cared too little about life to fear the losing of it; and as to his soul, he said, what could the spirit do to that, being a thing immortal as itself? 但是他们的劝告和恳求并不能改变哈姆莱特的决心，他早就把生命看得无所谓了，他并不怕死；至于他的灵魂，他说这个鬼魂怎么能够害它呢？因为灵魂和鬼魂同样都是永生不灭的。

ⅹ His treasonous brother stole upon him in his sleep, and poured the juice of poisonous henbane into his ears, which has such an antipathy to the life of man, that swift as quicksilver it courses through all the veins of the body, baking up the blood, and spreading a crust-like leprosy all over the skin. 他那起了歹心的弟弟就趁他睡着了，偷偷走到他身边，把毒草汁注入他的耳朵。那毒草汁是要人命的，它像水银一样迅速地流遍他全身的血管，把血烧干，使他的皮肤到处都长起一层硬壳似的癞。

ⅹⅰ And the ghost lamented to his son, that his mother should so fall off from virtue, as to prove false to the wedded love of her first husband, and to marry his murderer; but he cautioned Hamlet, howsoever he proceeded in his revenge against his wicked uncle, by no means to act any violence against the person of his mother, but to leave her to heaven, and to the stings and thorns of conscience. 鬼魂又对它的儿子哀叹说，他的母亲竟然堕落到这个地步，这样背弃同她恩爱一场的第一个丈夫，嫁了谋杀他的人。可是鬼魂嘱咐哈姆莱特在对他的坏叔叔进行报复的时候，千万不要伤害到他的母亲，只让上天去裁判她，让她自己的良心去刺痛她吧。（person＝body）

ⅹⅱ The terror which the sight of the ghost had left upon the senses of Hamlet, he being weak and dispirited before, almost unhinged his mind, and drove him beside his reason. 这之前哈姆莱特本来就身体虚弱而且情绪低落，鬼魂的出现在他心灵上留下的恐怖几乎使他神经错乱，失去了理智。（which..., he being...：定语从句中嵌套独立主格结构）

ⅹⅲ And he, fearing that it would continue to have this effect, which might subject him to observation, and set his uncle upon his guard, if he suspected that he was meditating anything against him, or that Hamlet really knew more of his father's death than he professed, took up a strange resolution, from that time to counterfeit as if he were really and truly mad; thinking that he would be less an object of suspicion when his uncle should believe him incapable of any serious project, and that this real perturbation of mind would be best covered and pass concealed under a disguise of pretended lunacy. 哈姆莱特担心这种情况会继续影响自己，从而引起他人的注意，并让他叔叔对他起戒心，如果他叔叔怀疑他在密谋对付自己，或者怀疑他比他声称的更了解他父亲之死。于是，哈姆莱特就做了一个奇怪的决定：从那时候起假装真的发了疯。他想，这样一来，他叔叔就会认为他无法有什么认真的图谋，就会更少怀疑他。而他心中真正的不安也可以在假装疯癫的掩饰下被更好地隐藏起来。（if...that..., or that...：条件状语从句中嵌套双重宾语从句；as if...：非真实状语从句）

ⅹⅳ But the melancholy which he fell into latterly had made him neglect her, and from the time he conceived the project of counterfeiting madness, he affected to treat her with unkindness, and a sort of rudeness—but she good lady, rather than reproach him with being false to her, persuaded herself that it was nothing but the disease in his mind, and no settled unkindness, which had made him less observant of her than formerly. 可是由于近来的苦闷，

他对她冷淡起来了。自从他定下装疯的计策,他就故意装得对她很无情,还有些粗鲁。可是这位好心的姑娘并没有责备他变了心,她竭力使自己相信,哈姆莱特之所以对她没有以前那样殷勤,并不是由于他本性冷酷无情,而完全是因为他的精神失常。(rather than:而不是;persuaded...that it was nothing but..., which...:宾语从句、强调句和定语从句的嵌套)

xv She compared the faculties of his once noble mind and excellent understanding, impaired as they were with the deep melancholy that oppressed him, to sweet bells which in themselves are capable of most exquisite music, but when jangled out of tune, or rudely handled, produce only a harsh and unpleasing sound. 她把他曾经高贵的心灵和卓越的理智比作美妙的铃铛,尽管被深切的忧郁压抑着,仍能够奏出非常动听的音乐,可是假如被摇得不成调子或是摇得很粗暴,就只能发出刺耳而令人不悦的声响。(compare...to...:把……比作……;...as...:让步状语从句的倒装结构)

xvi The rough business which Hamlet had in hand, the revenging of his father's death upon his murderer, did not suit with the playful state of courtship, or admit of the society of so idle a passion as love now seemed to him. 哈姆莱特手头要办的横暴之事,即向杀父仇人报仇,这件事和求爱的轻快心情很不相称,同时他也不能容许自己有像爱情这样对他来说过于悠闲的感情。

xvii It could not hinder but that soft thoughts of his Ophelia would come between, and in one of these moments, when he thought that his treatment of this gentle lady had been unreasonably harsh, he wrote her a letter full of wild starts of passion, and in extravagant terms, such as agreed with his supposed madness, but mixed with some gentle touches of affection, which could not but show to this honoured lady that a deep love for her yet lay at the bottom of his heart. 这并不能阻止他儿女情长,想到他的奥菲利娅。有一回,他觉得自己对这位温柔的姑娘残酷得毫无道理,便给她写了一封信,里面充满了狂热激动的话,而且措辞十分夸张,恰好符合他装疯的神态,但是字里行间也微微流露出一些柔情,使这位可敬的小姐无法不觉得哈姆莱特在内心深处仍然对她怀有深厚的爱。(but:强调一贯事实;wild starts of passion:狂热情感的迸发;extravagant=exaggerated)

xviii He bade her to doubt the stars were fire, and to doubt that the sun did move, to doubt truth to be a liar, but never to doubt that he loved; with more of such extravagant phrases. 他让她尽管怀疑星星是不是一团火,怀疑太阳会不会动,怀疑真理是不是谎言,但是永远不要怀疑他的爱,以及更多诸如此类的夸张措辞。(排比修辞)

xix The queen wished that the good beauties of Ophelia might be the happy cause of his wildness, for so she hoped that her virtues might happily restore him to his accustomed way again, to both their honours. 王后倒也很希望他是为了奥菲利娅的美貌才发起疯来的,那样,奥菲利娅的美德也可以幸运地叫哈姆莱特恢复到原来的样子,那对他们两个人都是有光彩的事。(happy=fortunate;happily=fortunately)

xx Yet how to compass the death of the king, surrounded as he constantly was with his guards, was no easy matter. Or if it had been, the presence of the queen, Hamlet's mother, who was generally with the king, was a restraint upon his purpose, which he could not break through. 可是国王身边成天都有卫兵保护着,杀死他真不是件容易的事。即使杀死国王好办,可是王后,哈姆莱特的母亲,总跟国王在一起,使他下不了手,这个障碍他没法冲破。

xxi The mere act of putting a fellow-creature to death was in itself odious and terrible to a disposition naturally so gentle as Hamlet's was. 对于哈姆莱特这样天生性格温厚的人来说，单是把一个同类活活害死这一举动本身就令人憎恶和恐惧。

xxii His very melancholy, and the dejection of spirits he had so long been in, produced an irresoluteness and wavering of purpose, which kept him from proceeding to extremities. 他自己长时间的忧郁和精神上的颓唐产生出了一种摇摆不定、踌躇不决的心态，使他一直没有能够采取最后的行动。

xxiii Which he did in so lively a manner, setting forth the cruel murder of the feeble old king, with the destruction of his people and city by fire, and the mad grief of the old queen, running barefoot up and down the palace, with a poor clout upon that head where a crown had been, and with nothing but a blanket upon her loins, snatched up in haste, where she had worn a royal robe; that not only it drew tears from all that stood by, who thought they saw the real scene, so lively was it represented, but even the player himself delivered it with a broken voice and real tears. 那个演员很生动地表演了一遍，演出了衰老的国王怎样被人残忍地谋害，城市和市民都被火烧毁，年老的王后难过得发了疯，光着脚在宫里跑来跑去，本来戴着王冠的头上只顶了一块破布，本来披着王袍的腰上只裹了一条慌忙中抓来的毯子。这一场戏表演得十分生动，不但使站在旁边的人都流下泪来，以为他们看的都是真实的情景，连演员说台词的时候嗓子也哑了，真的流出眼泪来。(so...was it..., but (that)...:部分倒装结构)

xxiv This put Hamlet upon thinking, if that player could so work himself up to passion by a mere fictitious speech, to weep for one that he had never seen, for Hecuba, that had been dead so many hundred years, how dull was he, who having a real motive and cue for passion, a real king and a dear father murdered, was yet so little moved, that his revenge all this while had seemed to have slept in dull and muddy forgetfulness! 这件事使哈姆莱特想到：要是那个演员仅通过念一段虚构的台词，就能动起感情来，替他从来没见过面的、千百年前的古人赫卡柏流下眼泪，那他自己是有多么迟钝，他有真正应该痛哭的理由和动机——一个真的国王，一个亲爱的父亲被谋杀了——然而他竟这么无动于衷，他的复仇心好像一直在醉生梦死。

xxv While he meditated on actors and acting, and the powerful effects which a good play, represented to the life, has upon the spectator, he remembered the instance of some murderer, who seeing a murder on the stage, was by the mere force of the scene and resemblance of circumstances so affected, that on the spot he confessed the crime which he had committed. 他想到演员和演技，想到演得维妙维肖的一出好戏给观众的影响有多大。这时候，他又记起有些凶手看到舞台上演的谋杀案后，会仅仅由于场面的感人和情节的相似而受到感动，当场把自己犯的罪招认出来。

xxvi But when Lucianus, according to the story, came to poison Gonzago sleeping in the garden, the strong resemblance which it bore to his own wicked act upon the late king, his brother, whom he had poisoned in his garden, so struck upon the conscience of this usurper, that he was unable to sit out the rest of the play, but on a sudden calling for lights to his chamber, and affecting or partly feeling a sudden sickness, he abruptly left the theatre. 可是当卢西亚努斯按照剧情来毒害睡在花园里的贡扎古的时候，这情景跟国王在花园里毒害他哥哥(已故的国王)的罪恶行为太相像了，这个篡位的人良心上受了强

烈的刺激，他无法坚持把戏看完。国王忽然喊人点上火把回宫，装作（也许一部分是真的）得了急病，匆忙离开了剧场。（...which...，whom...，so...，that...：双重定语从句和结果状语从句的嵌套）

xxvii In a fit of gaiety，like that which comes over a man who suddenly has some great doubt or scruple resolved，he swore to Horatio，that he would take the ghost's word for a thousand pounds. 像一个人心里怀着很大的疑问或顾虑而忽然得到了解决一样，哈姆莱特感到一阵高兴。他对霍拉旭说，鬼魂说的话一点儿也不假。

xxviii It was by desire of the king that the queen sent for Hamlet，that she might signify to her son how much his late behaviour had displeased them both，and the king，wishing to know all that passed at that conference，and thinking that the too partial report of a mother might let slip some part of Hamlet's words，which it might much import the king to know，Polonius，the old counsellor of state，was ordered to plant himself behind the hangings in the queen's closet，where he might unseen hear all that passed. 王后是奉国王的旨意叫哈姆莱特去的，他让王后向哈姆莱特表示，他刚才的举动让他们都很不高兴。国王想知道他们谈话的全部内容，同时又担心王后作为母亲的叙述会偏袒自己的儿子，会隐瞒一些可能对国王很重要的话，所以他又吩咐御前大臣老波洛涅斯躲在王后内宫的帏幕后面。这样，他可以偷听到全部对话，还不会被发现。（which it might much import the king to know：知道这些话可能对国王关系重大）

xxix This artifice was particularly adapted to the disposition of Polonius，who was a man grown old in crooked maxims and policies of state，and delighted to get at the knowledge of matters in an indirect and cunning way. 这个计策特别适合波洛涅斯的性格，他在朝廷勾心斗角的生活中混到晚年，喜欢用间接或是狡猾的手段来刺探内幕。（crooked maxims and policies of state：勾心斗角的政治活动）

xxx Hamlet being come to his mother，she began to tax him in the roundest way with his actions and behaviour，and she told him that he had given great offence to his father，meaning the king，his uncle，whom，because he had married her，she called Hamlet's father. 哈姆莱特来到他母亲面前。她先婉转地责备他的举动，说他已经深深得罪了他的父亲——她指的是国王，哈姆莱特的叔叔；因为他们结了婚，所以她把他叫作哈姆莱特的父亲。（being come＝having come）

xxxi As good as the question deserved. 你那样问，我就应该这样回答。

xxxii I will set those to you that can speak. 我会叫会说话的来跟你说话。

xxxiii But Hamlet would not let her go，now he had her alone，till he had tried if his words could not bring her to some sense of her wicked life；and，taking her by the wrist，he held her fast，and made her sit down. 可是哈姆莱特不让她走。现在，既然他单独跟她在一起了，他就想试着用言语叫她多少认识到自己过的堕落生活。他一把抓住他母亲的手腕，紧紧按着她，硬叫她坐下来。

xxxiv Which Hamlet hearing，and verily thinking that it was the king himself there concealed，he drew his sword and stabbed at the place where the voice came from，as he would have stabbed a rat that ran there，till the voice ceasing，he concluded the person to be dead. 哈姆莱特听到以后，认为一定是国王本人藏在那里，就拔出剑来，朝那个发出声音的地方扎去，假装是扎一只从那儿跑过的老鼠。后来没有了声音，他断定那个人已经死了。

(Hamlet hearing, ...thinking that it was...himself (who)...:独立主格结构中嵌套宾语从句、强调句、定语从句;as...that...:方式状语从句中嵌套定语从句)

xxxv Hamlet had gone too far to leave off here. 哈姆莱特一发难收了。

xxxvi Though the faults of parents are to be tenderly treated by their children, yet in the case of great crimes the son may have leave to speak even to his own mother with some harshness, so as that harshness is meant for her good, and to turn her from her wicked ways, and not done for the purpose of upbraiding. 尽管对于父母的错误,孩子应当尽量包涵,然而如果是严重的罪过,那么儿子也是可以相当严厉地斥责他的母亲的,只要这种严厉是为了她好,是为了让她改邪归正,而不是为了责备。(so as that=so long as)

xxxvii Such an act as, after the vows which she had sworn to her first husband, was enough to make all vows of women suspected, and all virtue to be accounted hypocrisy, wedding contracts to be less than gamesters' oaths, and religion to be a mockery and a mere form of words. 做出这样的事情,尤其是在她对她的第一个丈夫发过誓之后,足以使人怀疑一切女人的誓言。一切美德都将被算作伪善,结婚的誓约将比不上赌徒的诺言,宗教将不过是开玩笑的一片空话罢了。(...to be...:排比修辞)

xxxviii And he showed her two pictures, the one of the late king, her first husband, and the other of the present king, her second husband, and he bade her mark the difference; what a grace was on the brow of his father, how like a god he looked! the curls of Apollo, the forehead of Jupiter, the eye of Mars, and a posture like to Mercury newly alighted on some heaven-kissing hill! 哈姆莱特给她看两幅肖像,一幅是已故的国王,她的第一个丈夫,另外一幅是现在的国王,她的第二个丈夫。他要她注意他们之间的区别。他父亲的额头有多么慈祥,气概有多么非凡!他的卷发像阿波罗,前额像朱庇特,眼睛像玛尔斯,他的姿势像是刚落在吻着苍天的山峰上的墨丘利!(Apollo:希腊神话中的太阳神阿波罗;Jupiter:罗马神话中的主神朱庇特;Mars:罗马神话中的战神玛尔斯;Mercury:罗马神话中诸神的使者墨丘利)

xxxix It then vanished, and was seen by none but Hamlet, neither could he by pointing to where it stood, or by any description, make his mother perceive it, who was terribly frightened all this while to hear him conversing, as it seemed to her, with nothing; and she imputed it to the disorder of his mind. 然后,鬼魂就不见了。鬼魂只有哈姆莱特一个人看得见,不论是指出它站的地方,还是描述给她听,都不能使他母亲察觉到它的存在。她看到哈姆莱特对着空气说话(她以为是这样),感到非常害怕,认为这是因为他发了疯。(neither could he...:部分倒装结构;who..., as...:定语从句的嵌套)

xl But Hamlet begged her not to flatter her wicked soul in such a manner as to think that it was his madness, and not her own offences, which had brought his father's spirit again on the earth. 可是哈姆莱特要求她不要替自己那邪恶的灵魂找安慰,不要以为是由于他发疯才把他父亲的鬼魂引到人间,而不是由于王后自己的罪过。

xli And now Hamlet was at leisure to consider who it was that in his unfortunate rashness he had killed—and when he came to see that it was Polonius, the father of the lady Ophelia, whom he so dearly loved, he drew apart the dead body, and, his spirits being now a little quieter, he wept for what he had done. 现在哈姆莱特有闲情来看看是谁这么不幸,被他一时鲁莽杀死了。当他发现自己杀死的是他心爱的奥菲利娅的父亲波洛涅斯时,他把尸身拉开。这时

候，他的心神镇定了一些，他为他做的这件事哭了。

xlii So this subtle king, under pretence of providing for Hamlet's safety, that he might not be called to account for Polonius' death, caused him to be conveyed on board a ship bound for England, under the care of two courtiers, by whom he despatched letters to the English court, which in that time was in subjection and paid tribute to Denmark, requiring for special reasons there pretended, that Hamlet should be put to death as soon as he landed on English ground. 因此，这个诡计多端的国王假装是为了哈姆莱特的安全，让他避免为波洛涅斯的死受到处分，要哈姆莱特由两个朝臣陪着坐船到英国去。当时英国是向丹麦纳贡的属邦，国王给英国朝廷写了封信，交给这两个朝臣带去，信中编造了一些特殊理由，嘱咐他们等哈姆莱特在英国一上岸，就立刻把他处死。（pretence..., that...：同位语从句；by whom..., which...：非限制性定语从句的嵌套；requiring..., that...should...as soon as...：虚拟语气宾语从句中嵌套状语从句）

xliii Soon after the ship was attacked by pirates, and a sea-fight commenced; in the course of which Hamlet, desirous to show his valour, with sword in hand singly boarded the enemy's vessel; while his own ship, in a cowardly manner, bore away, and leaving him to his fate, the two courtiers made the best of their way to England, charged with those letters the sense of which Hamlet had altered to their own deserved destruction. 不久，船受到海盗的袭击，海战随即爆发。作战中，哈姆莱特为表现自己的勇敢，就独自持剑登上敌人的船，他自己坐的那艘船却怯懦地逃掉了。那两个朝臣把他丢下随他去，带着信急急忙忙赶到英国去了。信的内容已经被哈姆莱特改了，他们会得到应得的惩罚。（in the course of which...：定语从句；made the best of their way＝went as fast as they could；...the sense of which...：定语从句）

xliv The pirates, who had the prince in their power, showed themselves gentle enemies; and knowing whom they had got prisoner, in the hope that the prince might do them a good turn at court in recompense for any favour they might show him, they set Hamlet on shore at the nearest port in Denmark. 海盗俘获了王子以后，对这个高贵的敌人十分客气。既然晓得他们俘获的是什么人，他们就把哈姆莱特带到最近的一个丹麦港口，放他上了岸，希望王子在朝廷里可以帮他们些忙，来报答他们这番好意。

xlv That he should die a violent death, and by the hands of the prince whom she loved, so affected this tender young maid, that in a little time she grew perfectly distracted, and would go about giving flowers away to the ladies of the court, and saying that they were for her father's burial, singing songs about love and about death, and sometimes such as had no meaning at all, as if she had no memory of what happened to her. 波洛涅斯死得这样惨，而且竟然死在她所爱的王子手里，这件事伤透了这位温柔的年轻姑娘的心，她的精神很快就完全错乱了。她到处跑来跑去，把花撒给宫里的女人们，说是为了她父亲的葬礼撒的；又唱起关于爱情和死亡的歌，有时候唱一些毫无意义的歌，好像以前发生过什么事情她全记不得了。

xlvi To this brook she came one day when she was unwatched, with garlands she had been making, mixed up of daisies and nettles, flowers and weeds together, and clambering up to hang her garland upon the boughs of the willow, a bough broke, and precipitated this fair young maid, garland, and all that she had gathered, into the water, where her clothes bore her up for a while, during which she chanted scraps of old tunes, like one insensible to her own distress, or as if she were a creature natural to that element. 有一天，她趁没人看见的时候来到这条小河旁，用雏菊、荨麻、野花和杂草编成一个花环，然后爬到柳树上，想把这个花环挂到柳枝上。但是柳枝折断了，这个美丽、年轻的姑娘就跟她编的花环和她采的花草一起跌到河水里去了。她的衣服托着她在水上漂了一会儿，她还断断续续地唱了几句古老的曲调，好像一点儿也没有注意到自己所遇到的灾难，或者好像她本来就是生在水里的动物一样。(daisies：雏菊有“纯洁的童贞”或“生命之春”的含义；nettles：荨麻，喻指奥菲利娅的心被刺伤了；natural to that element：原本就生在水里的)

xlvii Long it was not before her garments, heavy with the wet, pulled her in from her melodious singing to a muddy and miserable death. 没过多久，她的衣服因被水浸泡而变得沉重，没等她唱完那支婉转的歌曲，她就被拖到污泥里悲惨地淹死了。(long it was not before...= it was not long before...：倒装结构)

xlviii Sweets to the sweet! I thought to have decked thy bride-bed, sweet maid, not to have strewed thy grave. 香花应当投给美人儿！我本来希望用鲜花来铺你的新婚之床的，可爱的姑娘，没想到却来撒在你的坟墓上了。

xlix Hamlet's love for this fair maid came back to him, and he could not bear that a brother should show so much transport of grief, for he thought that he loved Ophelia better than forty thousand brothers. 哈姆莱特对这位美丽姑娘的爱又恢复过来了，他不能容忍一个做哥哥的如此悲哀，因为他认为他对奥菲利娅的爱比四万个哥哥还要深。(夸张修辞)

l Hamlet, after the funeral, excused his hasty act in throwing himself into the grave as if to brave Laertes; but he said he could not bear that any one should seem to outgo him in grief for the death of the fair Ophelia. 葬礼结束以后，哈姆莱特道歉说，他刚才很鲁莽，叫人看了以为他是要跟雷欧提斯打架才跳进坟里去的，可是他说他不能容忍别人比他更为美丽的奥菲利娅之死而伤心。

li Hamlet taking up the foils chose one, not at all suspecting the treachery of Laertes, or being careful to examine Laertes' weapon, who, instead of a foil or blunted sword, which the laws of fencing require, made use of one with a point, and poisoned. 哈姆莱特挑了一把花剑，他一点儿没怀疑雷欧提斯有什么诡计，也没有留意去检查雷欧提斯的剑；可是雷欧提斯却没有使用击剑比赛所规定的花剑或钝剑，而是使用了一把尖头剑，上面还涂着毒药。

lii At first Laertes did but play with Hamlet, and suffered him to gain some advantages, which the dissembling king magnified and extolled beyond measure, drinking to Hamlet's success, and wagering rich bets upon the issue. 起初，雷欧提斯没有认真和哈姆莱特比剑，让他占了一些上风；国王就故意夸大哈姆莱特的胜利，满口喝着彩，为他的胜利干杯，并且下了很大的赌注，赌哈姆莱特一定会赢。

liii Hamlet incensed, but not knowing the whole of the treachery, in the scuffle exchanged his own innocent weapon for Laertes' deadly one, and with a thrust of Laertes' own sword repaid Laertes home, who was thus justly caught in his own treachery. 哈姆莱特被激怒了，但是还不知道全部的阴谋。在激战中他用自己那把没有毒的剑换过雷欧提斯的那把毒剑，然后用雷欧提斯的剑回刺了他一下，就这样，雷欧提斯罪有应得地中了他自己的阴谋奸计。(repaid Laertes home：回刺了雷欧提斯一下)

liv When Hamlet saw his end draw near, there being yet some venom left upon the sword, he suddenly turned upon his false uncle, and thrust the point of it to his heart, fulfilling the promise which he had made to his father's spirit, whose injunction was now accomplished, and his foul murder revenged upon the murderer. 哈姆莱特看到自己就要死了，而剑上还有些剩余的毒药，就猛地朝那个奸诈的叔叔扑去，把剑头刺进他的胸膛。这样，他就实践了对他父亲的鬼魂许下的诺言，完成了鬼魂吩咐他做的事，叫那个卑污地谋杀人的凶手遭到报应。

lv And, thus satisfied, the noble heart of Hamlet cracked; and Horatio and the bystanders with many tears commended the spirit of this sweet prince to the guardianship of angels. 这样，哈姆莱特满意了，他高贵的心碎裂了。霍拉旭和在场的人都流着泪把这个可爱的王子的灵魂委托给天使去保佑。

lvi Hamlet was a loving and a gentle prince, and greatly beloved for his many noble and princelike qualities; and if he had lived, would no doubt have proved a most royal and complete king to Denmark. 哈姆莱特是一位仁慈宽厚的王子。因为他那些高贵的美德，大家都十分喜爱他。要是没死的话，他一定会是一个最尊贵的、最完美的丹麦国王。

李尔王
King Lear

All blessed secrets,	一切神圣的秘密,
All you unpublished virtues of the earth,	一切地下潜伏的灵奇,
Spring with my tears	随着我的眼泪一起奔涌出来吧!
…	……
When we are born,	当我们生下地来的时候,
we cry that we are come to this great stage of fools.	我们因为来到了这个全是些傻瓜的广大的舞台之上,所以禁不住放声大哭。

莎士比亚是黑暗王国的一线光明，他指出了人类发展的几个新阶段，是人类认识的最高阶段的最充分的代表，他的作品表现出道德的最充分的理想。

——杜勃罗留波夫

《李尔王》是世界上最完美的戏剧诗的样本。

——雪莱

李尔之伟大不在他的巨大的身躯，而在他的思想伟大；他的激情爆发起来，像火山一样可怕；它像风暴一样搅起海浪，翻开海底——李尔的内心——展现出无穷无尽的宝藏。

——查尔斯·兰姆

《李尔王》经常被称为莎翁“最伟大的作品、他戏剧中最好的一部”，如果人们被迫不得不失去莎士比亚所有的作品，只保留一部，也许大部分最了解和欣赏莎士比亚的人会选择保留《李尔王》。

——布拉德雷

主要人物

Lear　李尔　不列颠国王
Goneril　高纳里尔　李尔的长女
Regan　里根　李尔的次女
Cordelia　考狄利娅　李尔的三女
Earl of Kent　肯特伯爵
Earl of Gloucester　葛罗斯特伯爵
Edgar　爱德伽　葛罗斯特伯爵的长子
Edmund　爱德蒙　葛罗斯特伯爵的私生子
Duke of Albany　奥本尼公爵　高纳里尔的丈夫
Duke of Cornwall　康华尔公爵　里根的丈夫
Duke of Burgundy　勃艮第公爵　考狄利娅的求婚者
King of France　法兰西国王　考狄利娅的求婚者
Fool　弄臣

地点　不列颠

King Lear

Lear, king of Britain, had three daughters; Goneril, wife to the duke of Albany; Regan, wife to the duke of Cornwall and Cordelia, a young maid, for whose love the king of France and duke of Burgundy were joint[1] suitors, and were at this time making stay for that purpose in the court of Lear.

* The old king, worn out with age and the fatigues of government, he being more than fourscore years old, determined to take no further part in state affairs, but to leave the management to younger strengths, that he might have time to prepare for death, which must at no long period ensue[2].[i] With this intent he called his three daughters to him, to know from their own lips which of them loved him best, that he might part[3] his kingdom among them in such proportions[4] as their affection for him should seem to deserve.

Goneril, the eldest, declared that she loved her father more than words could give out, that he was dearer to her than the light of her own eyes, dearer than life and liberty, * with a deal of such professing[5] stuff, which is easy to counterfeit where there is no real love, only a few fine words delivered with confidence being wanted in that case.[ii] The king, delighted to hear from her own mouth this assurance of her love, and thinking truly that her heart went with it, in a fit of fatherly fondness bestowed[6] upon her and her husband one-third of his ample[7] kingdom.

Then calling to him his second daughter, he demanded what she had to say. * Regan, who was made of the same hollow[8] metal as her sister, was not a whit[9] behind in her profession[10], but rather declared that what her sister had spoken came short of the love which she professed to bear

---

① joint [dʒɔɪnt] *adj*. 联合的 joined, shared, combined, united
② ensue [ɪn'sjuː] *v*. 接着发生 follow, succeed, come after
③ part [pɑːt] *v*. 分割 divide, separate, break, tear, split, rend
④ proportion [prə'pɔːʃn] *n*. 部分,比例 part, share
⑤ profess [prə'fes] *v*. 自称,声称 claim, allege, pretend, make out
⑥ bestow [bɪ'stəʊ] *v*. 给予 present, give, accord, award, grant
⑦ ample ['æmpl] *adj*. 硕大的 large, great, extensive, spacious
⑧ hollow ['hɒləʊ] *adj*. 中空的 empty, vacant, void, unfilled
⑨ not a whit 一点也不,完全不 not a bit, not at all
⑩ profession [prə'feʃn] *n*. 宣称 declaration, claim, statement

for his highness; insomuch that she found all other joys dead, in comparison with the pleasure which she took in the love of her dear king and father.[iii]

Lear blessed himself in having such loving children, as he thought; and could do no less, after the handsome assurances which Regan had made, than bestow a third of his kingdom upon her and her husband, equal in size to that which he had already given away to Goneril.

Then turning to his youngest daughter Cordelia, whom he called his joy, he asked what she had to say, thinking no doubt that she would glad his ears with the same loving speeches which her sisters had uttered①, or rather that her expressions would be so much stronger than theirs, as she had always been his darling, and favoured by him above either of them. * But Cordelia, disgusted with the flattery② of her sisters, whose hearts she knew were far from their lips, and seeing that all their coaxing③ speeches were only intended to wheedle④ the old king out of his dominions, that they and their husbands might reign in his lifetime, made no other reply but this—that she loved his majesty according to her duty, neither more nor less.[iv]

The king, shocked with this appearance of ingratitude in his favourite child, desired her to consider her words, and to mend⑤ her speech, lest⑥ it should mar⑦ her fortunes.

Cordelia then told her father, that he was her father, that he had given her breeding⑧, and loved her; that she returned those duties back as was most fit, and did obey him, love him, and most honour him. But that she could not frame her mouth to⑨ such large speeches as her sisters had done, or promise to love nothing else in the world. Why had her sisters husbands, if (as they said) they had no love for anything but their father? * If she should ever wed⑩, she was sure the lord to whom she gave her hand would want half her love, half of her care and duty; she should never marry like her sisters, to love her father all.[v]

* Cordelia, who in earnest loved her old father even almost as extravagantly as her sisters pretended to do, would have plainly told him so at any other time, in more daughter-like and loving terms, and without these qualifications, which did indeed sound a little ungracious⑪; but after the crafty flattering speeches of her sisters, which she had seen draw such extravagant

① utter [ˈʌtə(r)] *v*. 说 say, speak, state, articulate
② flattery [ˈflætəri] *n*. 奉承 fawning, sweet talk, false praise
③ coax [ˈkəʊks] *v*. 哄劝 persuade, beguile, prevail upon, wheedle
④ wheedle [ˈwiːdl] *v*. 哄骗,以甜言蜜语诱惑 coax, tempt, allure, seduce, entice
⑤ mend [mend] *v*. 改进 improve, better, reform, correct, revise
⑥ lest [lest] *conj*. 唯恐 in case, for fear that, in order to avoid
⑦ mar [mɑː] *v*. 损害 harm, damage, hurt, spoil, ruin, impair
⑧ breeding [ˈbriːdɪŋ] *n*. 抚养,教养 cultivation, rearing, raising, nurturing
⑨ frame mouth to 刻意地说
⑩ wed [wed] *v*. 结婚 marry, get married, be united, tie the knot
⑪ ungracious [ʌnˈɡreɪʃəs] *adj*. 失礼的,没礼貌的 rude, impolite, bad-mannered

rewards, she thought the handsomest thing she could do was to love and be silent.[vi] This put her affection out of suspicion of mercenary① ends, and showed that she loved, but not for gain; and that her professions, the less ostentatious② they were, had so much the more of truth and sincerity than her sisters'.

* This plainness of speech, which Lear called pride, so enraged the old monarch③—who in his best of times always showed much of spleen④ and rashness, and in whom the dotage⑤ incident⑥ to old age had so clouded over his reason, that he could not discern⑦ truth from flattery, nor a gay painted speech from words that came from the heart—that in a fury⑧ of resentment⑨ he retracted⑩ the third part of his kingdom, which yet remained, and which he had reserved for Cordelia, and gave it away from her, sharing it equally between her two sisters and their husbands, the dukes of Albany and Cornwall;[vii] whom he now called to him, and in presence of all his courtiers bestowing a coronet⑪ between them, invested⑫ them jointly with all the power, revenue, and execution of government, only retaining⑬ to himself the name of king; all the rest of royalty⑭ he resigned⑮; with this reservation, that himself, with a hundred knights for his attendants, was to be maintained⑯ by monthly course in each of his daughters' palaces in turn.

So preposterous⑰ a disposal⑱ of his kingdom, so little guided by reason, and so much by passion, filled all his courtiers with astonishment⑲ and sorrow; but * none of them had the courage to interpose⑳ between this incensed㉑ king and his wrath㉒, except the earl㉓ of Kent, who was beginning to speak a good word for Cordelia, when the passionate㉔ Lear on pain of㉕ death commanded him to desist㉖;[viii] but the good Kent was not so to be repelled㉗. * He had been ever loyal to Lear, whom he had honoured as a king, loved as a father, followed as a master; and he

---

① mercenary [ˈmɜːsənəri] *adj*. 唯利是图的 greedy
② ostentatious [ˌɒstenˈteɪʃəs] *adj*. 炫耀的,卖弄的 showy, pretentious
③ monarch [ˈmɒnək] *n*. 君主 ruler, king, sovereign, emperor
④ spleen [spliːn] *n*. 愤怒 anger, wrath
⑤ dotage [ˈdəʊtɪdʒ] *n*. 年老昏聩 senility
⑥ incident [ˈɪnsɪdənt] *adj*. 伴随的,由……产生的 incidental, accompanying
⑦ discern [dɪˈsɜːn] *v*. 识别,察觉 recognize, distinguish
⑧ fury [ˈfjʊəri] *n*. 盛怒 anger, wrath, rage, passion, irritation
⑨ resentment [rɪˈzentmənt] *n*. 怨恨 bitterness, ill will, bad blood
⑩ retract [rɪˈtrækt] *v*. 撤销,取消 unsay, recall, withdraw, take back
⑪ coronet [ˈkɒrənet] *n*. 王冠 crown, tiara, diadem
⑫ invest [ɪnˈvest] *v*. 授予 empower, authorize
⑬ retain [rɪˈteɪn] *v*. 保持 maintain, reserve, preserve, conserve
⑭ royalty [ˈrɔɪəlti] *n*. 王权,王位 kingship, supremacy
⑮ resign [rɪˈzaɪn] *v*. 放弃 give up, quit, abandon, relinquish
⑯ maintain [meɪnˈteɪn] *v*. 维持 continue, sustain, carry on
⑰ preposterous [prɪˈpɒstərəs] *adj*. 荒唐的,荒唐的 ridiculous, unreasonable
⑱ disposal [dɪˈspəʊzl] *n*. 分配,处理 distribution, allocation
⑲ astonishment [əˈstɒnɪʃmənt] *n*. 惊讶 surprise, amazement
⑳ interpose [ˌɪntəˈpəʊz] *v*. 介入,干预 intervene, step in
㉑ incensed [ɪnˈsenst] *adj*. 激怒的 enraged, infuriated
㉒ wrath [rɒθ] *n*. 盛怒 anger, fury, rage, irritation, indignation
㉓ earl [ɜːl] *n*. 伯爵
㉔ passionate [ˈpæʃənət] *adj*. 易怒的 fiery, irritable, hot-headed
㉕ on pain of (death) 如违反则处以(死刑)
㉖ desist [dɪˈzɪst] *v*. 停止 stop, cease, halt, terminate, break off
㉗ repel [rɪˈpel] *v*. 赶走 resist, repulse, drive off

had never esteemed① his life further than as a pawn② to wage against his royal master's enemies, nor feared to lose it when Lear's safety was the motive; nor now that Lear was most his own enemy, did this faithful servant of the king forget his old principles, but manfully opposed Lear, to do Lear good; and was unmannerly only because Lear was mad.[ix] *He had been a most faithful counsellor③ in times past to the king, and he besought him now, that he would see with his eyes (as he had done in many weighty matters), and go by his advice still; and in his best consideration recall this hideous④ rashness⑤[x]—for *he would answer with his life, his judgement that Lear's youngest daughter did not love him least, nor were those empty-hearted whose low sound gave no token⑥ of hollowness⑦.[xi] *When power bowed to flattery, honour was bound to plainness.[xii] For Lear's threats, what could he do to him, whose life was already at his service? That should not hinder duty from speaking.

The honest freedom of this good earl of Kent only stirred up the king's wrath the more, and like a frantic patient who kills his physician, and loves his mortal disease, he banished this true servant, and allotted⑧ him but five days to make his preparations for departure⑨; but if on the sixth his hated person was found within the realm⑩ of Britain, that moment was to be his death. And *Kent bade farewell to the king, and said, that since he chose to show himself in such fashion, it was but banishment to stay there; and before he went, he recommended Cordelia to the protection of the gods, the maid who had so rightly thought, and so discreetly⑪ spoken; and only wished that her sisters' large speeches might be answered with deeds of love; and then he went, as he said, to shape his old course to a new country.[xiii]

The king of France and duke of Burgundy were now called in to hear the determination of Lear about his youngest daughter, and to know whether they would persist⑫ in their courtship to Cordelia, now that she was under her father's displeasure, and had no fortune but her own person to recommend her—and the duke of Burgundy declined⑬ the match, and would not take her to wife upon such conditions; but *the king of

① esteem [ɪ'stiːm] *v.* 尊重 respect, cherish, think highly of
② pawn [pɔːn] *n.* 卒,兵
③ counsellor ['kaʊnsələ(r)] *n.* 顾问 adviser, consultant, counsel
④ hideous ['hɪdiəs] *adj.* 可怕的 terrible, horrible, dreadful
⑤ rashness['ræʃnəs] *n.* 鲁莽 hastiness, indiscretion
⑥ token ['təʊkən] *n.* 标志,象征 symbol, mark, sign, indication
⑦ hollowness ['hɒləʊnəs] *n.* 空洞,空虚 blankness, emptiness, vacancy
⑧ allot [ə'lɒt] *v.* 分配 assign, allocate, designate, distribute
⑨ departure [dɪ'pɑːtʃə(r)] *n.* 离开,起程 leaving, going away, setting out
⑩ realm [relm] *n.* 王国 kingdom, empire, state, nation
⑪ discreetly [dɪ'skriːtli] *adv.* 谨慎地,小心地 carefully, cautiously, guardedly, prudently
⑫ persist [pə'sɪst] *v.* 坚持 endure, persevere, hold on, keep up
⑬ decline [dɪ'klaɪn] *v.* 拒绝 refuse, reject, deny, turn down

France, understanding what the nature of the fault had been which had lost her the love of her father, that it was only a tardiness[1] of speech, and the not being able to frame her tongue to flattery like her sisters, took this young maid by the hand, and saying that her virtues were a dowry[2] above a kingdom, bade Cordelia to take farewell of her sisters and of her father, though he had been unkind, and she should go with him, and be queen of him and of fair France, and reign over fairer possessions than her sisters[xiv] —and * he called the duke of Burgundy in contempt a waterish duke, because his love for this young maid had in a moment run all away like water.[xv]

* Then Cordelia with weeping eyes took leave of her sisters, and besought them to love their father well, and make good their professions—and they sullenly[3] told her not to prescribe[4] to them, for they knew their duty; but to strive to content her husband, who had taken her (as they tauntingly expressed it) as Fortune's alms[5].[xvi] And Cordelia with a heavy heart departed, for she knew the cunning of her sisters, and she wished her father in better hands than she was about to leave him in.

* Cordelia was no sooner gone, than the devilish[6] dispositions of her sisters began to show themselves in their true colours.[xvii] Even before the expiration[7] of the first month, which Lear was to spend by agreement with his eldest daughter Goneril, the old king began to find out the difference between promises and performances. This wretch having got from her father all that he had to bestow, even to the giving away of the crown from off his head, began to grudge[8] even those small remnants[9] of royalty which the old man had reserved to himself, to please his fancy with the idea of being still a king. She could not bear to see him and his hundred knights. Every time she met her father, she put on a frowning countenance; and when the old man wanted to speak with her, she would feign sickness, or anything to get rid of the sight of him; for it was plain that she esteemed his old age a useless burden, and his attendants an unnecessary expense—* not only she herself slackened[10] in her expressions of duty to the king, but by her example, and (it is to be feared) not without her private instructions, her very servants affected to treat him with neglect,[xviii] and would either refuse to obey his orders, or still more contemptuously[11] pretend

---

① tardiness [ˈtɑːdinəs] *n*. 缓慢 delay, slowness, procrastination

② dowry [ˈdaʊri] *n*. 嫁妆 dower

③ sullenly [ˈsʌlənli] *adv*. 不高兴地 crossly, gloomily, sulkily

④ prescribe [prɪˈskraɪb] *v*. 指示，命令 specify, order, direct, command

⑤ alms [ɑːmz] *n*. 施舍(物)，救济(物) donation, relief, charity

⑥ devilish [ˈdevəlɪʃ] *adj*. 邪恶的，魔鬼似的 fiendish, diabolical, wicked, satanic

⑦ expiration [ˌekspəˈreɪʃn] *n*. 期满 expiry, end, finish, conclusion

⑧ grudge [grʌdʒ] *v*. 吝惜；妒忌

⑨ remnant [ˈremnənt] *n*. 剩余物 remainder, remains, leftover

⑩ slacken [ˈslækən] *v*. 松弛，松懈

⑪ contemptuously [kənˈtemptjuəsli] *adv*. 轻蔑地 scornfully, disdainfully not to hear them. * Lear could not but perceive this alteration[1] in the behaviour of his daughter, but he shut his eyes against it as long as he could, as people commonly are unwilling to believe the unpleasant consequences which their own mistakes and obstinacy[2] have brought upon them.[xix]

* True love and fidelity[3] are no more to be estranged[4] by ill, than falsehood and hollow-heartedness can be conciliated[5] by good usage.[xx] This eminently appears in the instance of the good earl of Kent, who, though banished by Lear, and his life made forfeit[6] if he were found in Britain, chose to stay and abide[7] all consequences, as long as there was a chance of his being useful to the king his master. * See to what mean[8] shifts[9] and disguises[10] poor loyalty[11] is forced to submit sometimes; yet it counts[12] nothing base or unworthy[13], so as it can but do service where it owes an obligation[14]![xxi] * In the disguise of a serving man, all his greatness and pomp laid aside[15], this good earl proffered[16] his services to the king, who, not knowing him to be Kent in that disguise, but pleased with a certain plainness[17], or rather bluntness[18] in his answers, which the earl put on (so different from that smooth oily flattery which he had so much reason to be sick of, having found the effects not answerable in his daughter), a bargain was quickly struck, and Lear took Kent into his service by the name of Caius, as he called himself, never suspecting him to be his once great favourite, the high and mighty[19] earl of Kent.[xxii]

This Caius quickly found means to show his fidelity and love to his royal master—for Goneril's steward[20] that same day behaving in a disrespectful[21] manner to Lear, and giving him saucy[22] looks and language, as no doubt he was secretly encouraged to do by his mistress, Caius, not enduring[23]

---

① alteration [ˌɔːltəˈreɪʃn] *n*. 改变 change, modification
② obstinacy [ˈɒbstɪnəsi] *n*. 固执 stubbornness, doggedness
③ fidelity [fɪˈdeləti] *n*. 忠诚 loyalty, faithfulness, trustworthiness
④ estrange [ɪsˈtreɪndʒ] *v*. 使疏远 alienate, separate
⑤ conciliate [kənˈsɪlieɪt] *v*. 安抚 pacify, calm, soothe, appease
⑥ forfeit [ˈfɔːfɪt] *adj*. 没收的,丧失的
⑦ abide [əˈbaɪd] *v*. 忍受 tolerate, stand, endure, put up with
⑧ mean [miːn] *adj*. 卑劣的 base, vile, despicable
⑨ shift [ʃɪft] *n*. 计谋 scheme, trick, craft
⑩ disguise [dɪsˈɡaɪz] *n*. 伪装 mask, cover, false appearance
⑪ loyalty [ˈlɔɪəlti] *n*. 忠诚 faithfulness, true-heartedness, fidelity
⑫ count [kaʊnt] *v*. 视为 consider, regard, think of, look upon
⑬ unworthy [ʌnˈwɜːði] *adj*. 不值得的,无价值的 degrading, disgraceful
⑭ obligation [ˌɒblɪˈɡeɪʃn] *n*. 责任 duty, mission, responsibility
⑮ lay aside 抛开,放置一边 ast aside
⑯ proffer [ˈprɒfə(r)] *v*. 提供 offer, give, present
⑰ plainness [ˈpleɪnnəs] *n*. 正直
⑱ bluntness [ˈblʌntnəs] *n*. 率直 frankness, outspokenness
⑲ mighty [ˈmaɪti] *adj*. 强大的 forceful, powerful
⑳ steward [ˈstjuːəd] *n*. 管家 keeper, caretaker
㉑ disrespectful [ˌdɪsrɪˈspektfl] *adj*. 无礼的 impolite, discourteous
㉒ saucy [ˈsɔːsi] *adj*. 粗鲁的 rude, impudent
㉓ endure [ɪnˈdjʊə(r)] *v*. 忍耐 stand, bear, tolerate, put up with

to hear so open an affront① put upon his majesty, made no more ado but presently tripped up his heels, and laid the unmannerly slave in the kennel②; for which friendly service Lear became more and more attached to him.

Nor was Kent the only friend Lear had. *In his degree, and as far as so insignificant a personage③ could show his love, the poor fool, or jester④, that had been of his palace while Lear had a palace, as it was the custom of kings and great personages at that time to keep a fool (as he was called) to make them sport after serious business: this poor fool clung to⑤ Lear after he had given away his crown, and by his witty⑥ sayings would keep up his good humour, though he could not refrain sometimes from jeering⑦ at his master for his imprudence⑧ in uncrowning⑨ himself, and giving all away to his daughters; [xxiii] at which time, as he rhymingly⑩ expressed it, these daughters

*For sudden joy did weep
And I for sorrow sung,
That such a king should play bo-peep⑪
And go the fools among.[xxiv]

And in such wild sayings, and scraps⑫ of songs, of which he had plenty, this pleasant honest fool poured out his heart even in the presence of Goneril herself, in many a bitter taunt and jest which cut to the quick⑬—such as *comparing the king to the hedge-sparrow, who feeds the young of the cuckoo⑭ till they grow old enough, and then has its head bit off for its pains;[xxv] and saying, that *an ass may know when the cart draws the horse (meaning that Lear's daughters, that ought to go behind, now ranked before their father);[xxvi] and that Lear was no longer Lear, but the shadow of Lear—for which free speeches he was once or twice threatened to be whipped⑮.

The coolness and falling off of respect which Lear had begun to perceive, were not all which this foolish fond father was to suffer from his unworthy daughter—she now plainly told him that his staying in her palace was inconvenient so long as he insisted upon keeping up an establishment of a hundred knights; that this establishment was useless and expensive, and only served to fill her court with riot⑯ and feasting⑰; and she prayed him that he would lessen their number, and keep

---

① affront [ə'frʌnt] *n*. 侮辱,冒犯 insult, abuse, offence
② kennel ['kenl] *n*. 狗窝 doghouse
③ personage ['pɜːsənɪdʒ] *n*. 人物,要人
④ jester ['dʒestə(r)] *n*. 小丑 joker, prankster
⑤ cling to 依附于 stick/attach to
⑥ witty ['wɪti] *adj*. 诙谐的 humorous, funny
⑦ jeer [dʒɪə(r)] *v*. 嘲弄 mock, ridicule, taunt, tease, sneer, scoff
⑧ imprudence [ɪm'pruːdns] *n*. 轻率 rashness, carelessness, incaution
⑨ uncrown [ʌn'kraʊn] *v*. 废黜 unseat, dethrone, depose
⑩ rhymingly ['raɪmɪŋli] *adv*. 押韵地
⑪ bo-peep [ˌbəu'piːp] *n*. 捉迷藏游戏
⑫ scrap [skræp] *n*. 碎片 piece, fragment, shred, bit
⑬ cut to the quick 触及痛处,深深伤害
⑭ cuckoo ['kʊkuː] *n*. 杜鹃
⑮ whip [wɪp] *v*. 鞭打 lash, cane, flog, beat, thrash
⑯ riot ['raɪət] *n*. 喧闹 row, disorder, confusion, turmoil, uproar
⑰ feasting ['fiːstɪŋ] *n*. 盛宴 banquet, repast, carousal

none but old men about him, such as himself, and fitting his age.

Lear at first could not believe his eyes or ears, nor that it was his daughter who spoke so unkindly. * He could not believe that she who had received a crown from him could seek to cut off his train, and grudge him the respect due to his old age.[xxvii] * But she persisting in her undutiful demand, the old man's rage was so excited, that he called her a detested① kite②, and said that she spoke an untruth; and so indeed she did, for the hundred knights were all men of choice③ behaviour and sobriety④ of manners, skilled in all particulars of duty, and not given to rioting or feasting, as she said.[xxviii] And he bid his horses to be prepared, for he would go to his other daughter, Regan, he and his hundred knights; and * he spoke of ingratitude, and said it was a marble-hearted⑤ devil, and showed more hideous in a child than the sea-monster.[xxix] And he cursed his eldest daughter Goneril so as was terrible to hear; praying that she might never have a child, or if she had, that it might live to return that scorn and contempt upon her which she had shown to him—that she might feel how sharper than a serpent's tooth it was to have a thankless child. And Goneril's husband, the duke of Albany, beginning to excuse himself for any share which Lear might suppose he had in the unkindness, Lear would not hear him out, but in a rage ordered his horses to be saddled⑥, and set out with his followers for the abode⑦ of Regan, his other daughter. And Lear thought to himself how small the fault of Cordelia (if it was a fault) now appeared, in comparison with⑧ her sister's, and he wept; and then he was ashamed that such a creature as Goneril should have so much power over his manhood as to make him weep.

Regan and her husband were keeping their court in great pomp and state at their palace; and Lear despatched his servant Caius with letters to his daughter, that she might be prepared for his reception⑨, while he and his train followed after. But it seems that Goneril had been beforehand with him, sending letters also to Regan, accusing her father of waywardness⑩ and ill humours, and advising her not to receive so great a train as he was bringing with him. This messenger arrived at the same time with Caius, and Caius and he met—and * who should it be but Caius's old enemy the steward, whom he had formerly tripped up by the heels for his saucy behaviour to Lear.[xxx] * Caius not liking the fellow's look, and suspecting what he came for, began to revile⑪ him, and challenged him to fight, which the fellow refusing, Caius, in a fit of honest passion, beat him soundly, as such a mischief-maker⑫ and carrier of wicked messages deserved; which coming to the ears of Regan and her husband, they ordered Caius to be put in the stocks⑬, though he was a

---

① detest [dɪ'test] *v*. 厌恶 hate, loathe, despise, abominate
② kite [kaɪt] *n*. 鸢(猛禽)
③ choice [tʃɔɪs] *adj*. 优质的 best, selected, excellent, superior
④ sobriety [sə'braɪəti] *n*. 节制 temperance, moderation
⑤ marble-hearted [mɑːbl'hɑːtɪd] *adj*. 铁石心肠的 iron-hearted, stone-hearted
⑥ saddle ['sædl] *v*. 装以马鞍
⑦ abode [ə'bəʊd] *n*. 住所 home, house, residence, domicile
⑧ in comparison with 与……相比 compared to/with
⑨ reception [rɪ'sepʃn] *n*. 接待
⑩ waywardness ['weɪwədnəs] *n*. 任性 willfulness
⑪ revile [rɪ'vaɪl] *v*. 辱骂 abuse, reproach, bad-mouth
⑫ mischief-maker ['mɪstʃɪf meɪkə(r)] *n*. 挑拨离间者,搬弄是非者
⑬ stocks [stɒks] *n*.(旧时惩罚犯人用的)枷锁

messenger from the king her father, and in that character demanded the highest respect[xxxi] —so that the first thing the king saw when he entered the castle, was his faithful servant Caius sitting in that disgraceful situation.

This was but a bad omen① of the reception which he was to expect; but a worse followed, when, upon inquiry for his daughter and her husband, he was told they were weary with travelling all night, and could not see him; and when lastly, * upon his insisting in a positive and angry manner to see them, they came to greet him, whom should he see in their company but the hated Goneril, who had come to tell her own story, and set her sister against the king her father![xxxii]

This sight much moved the old man, and still more to see Regan take her by the hand; and he asked Goneril if she was not ashamed to look upon his old white beard. And Regan advised him to go home again with Goneril, and live with her peaceably, dismissing half of his attendants, and to ask her forgiveness; for he was old and wanted discretion②, and must be ruled and led by persons that had more discretion than himself. And Lear showed how preposterous that would sound, if he were to go down on his knees, and beg of his own daughter for food and raiment③, and he argued against such an unnatural dependence, declaring his resolution never to return with her, but to stay where he was with Regan, he and his hundred knights; for he said that she had not forgot the half of the kingdom which he had endowed her with, and that her eyes were not fierce④ like Goneril's, but mild and kind. And he said that rather than return to Goneril, with half his train cut off, he would go over to France, and beg a wretched⑤ pension⑥ of the king there, who had married his youngest daughter without a portion⑦.

But he was mistaken in expecting kinder treatment of Regan than he had experienced from her sister Goneril. As if willing to outdo her sister in unfilial⑧ behaviour, she declared that she thought fifty knights too many to wait upon him—that five-and-twenty were enough. Then Lear, nigh⑨ heart-broken, turned to Goneril and said that he would go back with her, for her fifty doubled five-and-twenty, and so her love was twice as much as Regan's. But Goneril excused herself, and said, what need of so many as five-and-twenty? or even ten? or five? when he might be waited upon by her servants, or her sister's servants? * So these two wicked daughters, as if they strove to exceed each other in cruelty to their old father, who had been so

---

① omen [ˈəʊmən] *n*. 征兆 portent, warning, writing on the wall
② discretion [dɪˈskreʃn] *n*. 谨慎 caution, prudence
③ raiment [ˈreɪmənt] *n*. 衣服 clothes, apparel, garment, attire
④ fierce [fɪəs] *adj*. 凶狠的 cruel, brutal, savage, ferocious
⑤ wretched [ˈretʃɪd] *adj*. 可怜的 unfortunate, pitiful, luckless
⑥ pension [ˈpenʃn] *n*. 养老金 annuity
⑦ portion [ˈpɔːʃn] *n*. 嫁妆 marriage portion, dowry, trousseau
⑧ unfilial [ʌnˈfɪljəl] *adj*. 不孝的 undutiful, disobedient
⑨ nigh [naɪ] *adv*. 几乎,接近 almost, nearly, close to

good to them, by little and little would have abated① him of all his train, all respect (little enough for him that once commanded a kingdom), which was left him to show that he had once been a king! xxxiii Not that a splendid② train is essential to happiness, but from a king to a beggar is a hard change, from commanding millions to be without one attendant; and * it was the ingratitude in his daughters' denying it, more than what he would suffer by the want of it, which pierced③ this poor king to the heart; xxxiv insomuch, that with this double ill-usage④, a vexation⑤ for having so foolishly given away a kingdom, his wits began to be unsettled, and * while he said he knew not what, he vowed revenge against those unnatural hags, and to make examples of them that should be a terror to the earth! xxxv

While he was thus idly⑥ threatening what his weak arm could never execute⑦, night came on, and a loud storm of thunder and lightning with rain; and his daughters still persisting in their resolution not to admit his followers, he called for his horses, and chose rather to encounter⑧ the utmost fury⑨ of the storm abroad⑩, than stay under the same roof with these ungrateful⑪ daughters—and they, saying that * the injuries which wilful⑫ men procure to themselves are their just punishment, xxxvi suffered⑬ him to go in that condition and shut their doors upon him.

* The winds were high, and the rain and storm increased, when the old man sallied⑭ forth to combat⑮ with the elements⑯, less sharp than his daughters' unkindness. xxxvii For many miles about there was scarce a bush; and there upon a heath⑰, exposed to the fury of the storm in a dark night, did king Lear wander out, and defy⑱ the winds and the thunder; and he bid the winds to blow the earth into the sea, or swell the waves of the sea till they drowned the earth, that no token might remain of any such ungrateful animal as man. * The old king was now left with

---

① abate [ə'beɪt] *v*. 减少 decrease, reduce, diminish, dwindle
② splendid ['splendɪd] *adj*. 华丽的 grand, gorgeous, magnificent
③ pierce [pɪəs] *v*. 穿透 penetrate, stick into
④ ill-usage [ˌɪl'juːzɪdʒ] *n*. 虐待 abuse, ill-treatment
⑤ vexation [vek'seɪʃn] *n*. 苦恼 annoyance, irritation, displeasure
⑥ idly ['aɪdli] *adv*. 漫不经心地,懒散地 lazily, casually
⑦ execute ['eksɪkjuːt] *v*. 执行 fulfill, perform, carry out
⑧ encounter [ɪn'kaʊntə(r)] *v*. 遭遇 experience, undergo
⑨ fury ['fjʊəri] *n*. 盛怒 anger, wrath, rage, irritation
⑩ abroad [ə'brɔːd] *adv*. 〈古〉户外 outdoors, in the open air
⑪ ungrateful [ʌn'greɪtfl] *adj*. 忘恩负义的 unappreciative, thankless
⑫ wilful ['wɪlfl] *adj*. 任性的,故意的 stubborn, headstrong, self-willed
⑬ suffer ['sʌfə(r)] *v*. 容忍 bear, tolerate, put up with
⑭ sally ['sæli] *v*. 冲出,突围 go forth, set out, rush
⑮ combat ['kɒmbæt] *v*. 搏斗 fight, battle
⑯ elements ['elɪmənts] *n*. 恶劣天气
⑰ heath [hiːθ] *n*. 荒地
⑱ defy [dɪ'faɪ] *v*. 反抗 resist, oppose, challenge, stand up to

no other companion than the poor fool, who still abided with him, with his merry conceits① striving to outjest② misfortune, saying it was but a naughty night to swim in, and truly the king had better go in and ask his daughters' blessing:[xxxviii]

* But he that has a little tiny wit,
With heigh ho, the wind and the rain!
Must make content with his fortunes fit,
Though the rain it raineth every day[xxxix] —

and * swearing it was a brave night to cool a lady's pride.[xl]

Thus poorly accompanied, this once great monarch was found by his ever-faithful servant the good earl of Kent, now transformed to Caius, who ever followed close at his side, though the king did not know him to be the earl; and he said: "Alas! sir, are you here? Creatures that love night, love not such nights as these. This dreadful storm has driven the beasts to their hiding places. Man's nature cannot endure the affliction③ or the fear." And Lear rebuked④ him and said, * these lesser evils were not felt, where a greater malady was fixed.[xli] * When the mind is at ease, the body has leisure to be delicate⑤, but the tempest⑥ in his mind did take all feeling else from his senses, but of that which beat at his heart.[xlii] And * he spoke of filial ingratitude, and said it was all one as if the mouth should tear the hand for lifting food to it; for parents were hands and food and everything to children.[xliii]

But the good Caius still persisting in his entreaties that the king would not stay out in the open air, at last persuaded him to enter a little wretched hovel⑦ which stood upon the heath, where the fool first entering, suddenly ran back terrified, saying that he had seen a spirit. But * upon examination this spirit proved to be nothing more than a poor Bedlam⑧ beggar,[xliv] who had crept⑨ into this deserted⑩ hovel for shelter, and with his talk about devils frighted⑪ the fool, one of those poor lunatics⑫ who are either mad, or feign to be so, the better to extort⑬ charity⑭ from the compassionate⑮ country people, who go about the country, * calling themselves poor Tom and poor Turlygood,[xlv] saying: "Who gives anything to poor Tom?" sticking pins and nails and sprigs⑯ of rosemary⑰ into their arms to make them bleed; and with such horrible actions, partly by

---

① conceit [kən'siːt] *n*. 巧妙言辞
② outjest [ˌaʊt'dʒest] *v*. 戏弄,逗笑
③ affliction [ə'flɪkʃn] *n*. 痛苦 pain, suffering, distress, misery
④ rebuke [rɪ'bjuːk] *v*. 指责 scold, reproach, blame
⑤ delicate['delɪkət] *adj*. 敏感的 sensitive, responsive, impressionable
⑥ tempest ['tempɪst] *n*. 暴风雨 storm, gale
⑦ hovel ['hɒvl] *n*. 小屋 hut, shed, cabin, shack, shanty, cottage
⑧ Bedlam ['bedləm] *n*. 疯人院,精神病院
⑨ creep [kriːp] *v*. (crept) 爬行 crawl
⑩ deserted [dɪ'zɜːtɪd] *adj*. 遗弃的,废弃的 abandoned, forsaken, cast-off
⑪ fright [fraɪt] *v*. 惊吓 scare, terrify, startle, frighten
⑫ lunatic ['luːnətɪk] *n*. 疯子 maniac, nutcase, headcase
⑬ extort [ɪk'stɔːt] *v*. 强要,索取 exact, force, squeeze, wring
⑭ charity ['tʃærəti] *n*. 施舍 help, assistance
⑮ compassionate [kəm'pæʃənət] *adj*. 有同情心的 sympathetic
⑯ sprig [sprɪg] *n*. 小树枝 spray, twig, branch, stick
⑰ rosemary ['rəʊzməri] *n*. 迷迭香

prayers, and partly with lunatic curses, they move or terrify the ignorant countryfolks into giving them alms. * This poor fellow was such a one; and the king seeing him in so wretched a plight①, with nothing but a blanket about his loins to cover his nakedness②, could not be persuaded but that the fellow was some father who had given all away to his daughters, and brought himself to that pass③—for nothing he thought could bring a man to such wretchedness④ but the having unkind daughters.[xlvi]

And from this and many such wild speeches which he uttered, the good Caius plainly perceived that he was not in his perfect mind, but that his daughters' ill usage had really made him go mad. And now the loyalty of this worthy earl of Kent showed itself in more essential services than he had hitherto found opportunity to perform. For with the assistance of some of the king's attendants who remained loyal, he had the person of his royal master removed at daybreak to the castle of Dover⑤, where his own friends and influence, as earl of Kent, chiefly lay; and himself embarking⑥ for France, hastened to the court of Cordelia, and * did there in such moving terms represent the pitiful condition of her royal father, and set out in such lively colours the inhumanity⑦ of her sisters, that this good and loving child with many tears besought the king her husband that he would give her leave to embark for England, with a sufficient power to subdue⑧ these cruel daughters and their husbands, and restore⑨ the old king her father to his throne;[xlvii] which being granted, she set forth, and with a royal army landed at Dover.

* Lear having by some chance escaped from the guardians which the good earl of Kent had put over him to take care of him in his lunacy, was found by some of Cordelia's train, wandering about the fields near Dover, in a pitiable condition, stark⑩ mad, and singing aloud to himself with a crown upon his head which he had made of straw, and nettles⑪, and other wild weeds that he had picked up in the corn-fields.[xlviii] By the advice of the physicians, Cordelia, though earnestly⑫ desirous⑬ of seeing her father, was prevailed upon to put off⑭ the meeting, till by sleep and the

① plight [plaɪt] *n*. 困境 difficulty, dilemma, straits, extremity
② nakedness [ˈneɪkɪdnəs] *n*. 赤裸 nudity, undress, bareness
③ pass [pɑːs] *n*. 不好的境遇 predicament, plight, straits
④ wretchedness [ˈretʃɪdnəs] *n*. 悲惨,不幸 misery, distress, misfortune
⑤ Dover [ˈdəʊvə(r)] *n*. 多佛(英国东南部的港口)
⑥ embark [ɪmˈbɑːk] *v*. 登(船) go aboard, board, go on board
⑦ inhumanity [ˌɪnhjuːˈmænəti] *n*. 无人性,残暴 cruelty, brutality
⑧ subdue [səbˈdjuː] *v*. 征服,制服 defeat, conquer, vanquish
⑨ restore [rɪˈstɔː(r)] *v*. 恢复 recover, re-establish, bring back
⑩ stark [stɑːk] *adv*. 完全地,彻底地 fully, totally, entirely, thoroughly, completely
⑪ nettle [ˈnetl] *n*. 荨麻
⑫ earnestly [ˈɜːnɪstli] *adv*. 热切地,认真地 seriously, sincerely, in all sincerity
⑬ desirous [dɪˈzaɪərəs] *adj*. 渴望的,想要的 wanting, eager, longing for
⑭ put off 推迟 delay, postpone, defer, suspend, put on ice

operation of herbs which they gave him, he should be restored to greater composure[1]. By the aid of these skilful physicians, to whom Cordelia promised all her gold and jewels for the recovery of the old king, Lear was soon in a condition to see his daughter.

A tender sight it was to see the meeting between this father and daughter; to see the struggles between the joy of this poor old king at beholding again his once darling child, and the shame at receiving such filial kindness from her whom he had cast off for so small a fault in his displeasure; both these passions struggling with the remains of his malady, which in his half-crazed brain sometimes made him that he scarce remembered where he was, or who it was that so kindly kissed him and spoke to him; and then he would beg the standers-by not to laugh at him, if he were mistaken in thinking this lady to be his daughter Cordelia! And then to see him fall on his knees to beg pardon of his child; and she, good lady, kneeling[2] all the while to ask a blessing of him, and telling him that it did not become[3] him to kneel, but it was her duty, for she was his child, his true and very child Cordelia! And she kissed him (as she said) to kiss away all her sisters' unkindness, and said that they might be ashamed of themselves, to turn their old kind father with his white beard out into the cold air, when her enemy's dog, though it had bit her (as she prettily expressed it), should have stayed by her fire such a night as that, and warmed himself. And she told her father how she had come from France with purpose to bring him assistance; and he said that she must forget and forgive, for he was old and foolish, and did not know what he did; but that to be sure she had great cause not to love him, but her sisters had none. And Cordelia said that she had no cause, no more than they had.

So we will leave this old king in the protection of his dutiful and loving child, where, * by the help of sleep and medicine, she and her physicians at length[4] succeeded in winding up[5] the untuned[6] and jarring[7] senses which the cruelty of his other daughters had so violently[8] shaken.[xlix] Let us return to say a word or two about those cruel daughters.

These monsters of ingratitude, who had been so false to their old father, could not be expected to prove more faithful to their own husbands. They soon grew tired of paying even the appearance of duty and affection, and in an open way showed they had fixed their loves upon another. It happened that the object of their guilty loves was the same. It was Edmund, a natural son of the late earl of Gloucester, who by his treacheries had succeeded in disinheriting[9] his brother Edgar, the lawful heir[10], from his earldom[11], and by his wicked practices was now earl himself; a wicked man, and a fit object for the love of such wicked creatures as Goneril and

---

① composure [kəm'pəʊʒə(r)] *n*. 镇静 calmness, tranquillity
② kneel [niːl] *v*. 跪 bow, kowtow, get down on sb's knees
③ become [bɪ'kʌm] *v*. 适合 fit, suit, match, go with
④ at length 最终 at last, finally, eventually, in the end
⑤ wind up 上紧发条
⑥ untuned [ʌn'tjuːnd] *adj*. 跑调的，不协调的 discordant, inharmonious
⑦ jarring ['dʒɑːrɪŋ] *adj*. 刺耳的
⑧ violently ['vaɪələntli] *adv*. 猛烈地 fiercely, intensely, forcefully
⑨ disinherit [ˌdɪsɪn'herɪt] *v*. 剥夺继承权
⑩ heir [eə(r)] *n*. 继承人 successor, inheritor
⑪ earldom ['ɜːldəm] *n*. 伯爵爵位

Regan. * It falling out① about this time that the duke of Cornwall, Regan's husband, died, Regan immediately declared her intention of wedding this earl of Gloucester, which rousing② the jealousy of her sister, to whom as well as to Regan this wicked earl had at sundry③ times professed love, Goneril found means to make away with④ her sister by poison;[l] but * being detected in her practices, and imprisoned by her husband, the duke of Albany, for this deed, and for her guilty passion for the earl which had come to his ears, she, in a fit of disappointed love and rage, shortly put an end to⑤ her own life.[li] Thus the justice of Heaven at last overtook⑥ these wicked daughters.

* While the eyes of all men were upon this event, admiring the justice displayed in their deserved deaths, the same eyes were suddenly taken off from this sight to admire at the mysterious ways of the same power in the melancholy fate of the young and virtuous daughter, the lady Cordelia, whose good deeds did seem to deserve a more fortunate conclusion—but it is an awful truth, that innocence and piety⑦ are not always successful in this world.[lii] The forces which Goneril and Regan had sent out under the command of the bad earl of Gloucester were victorious, and Cordelia, by the practices of this wicked earl, who did not like that any should stand between him and the throne, ended her life in prison. * Thus, Heaven took this innocent lady to itself in her young years, after showing her to the world an illustrious⑧ example of filial duty. Lear did not long survive this kind child.[liii]

* Before he died, the good earl of Kent, who had still attended his old master's steps from the first of his daughters' ill usage to this sad period of his decay⑨, tried to make him understand that it was he who had followed him under the name of Caius; but Lear's care-crazed brain at that time could not comprehend⑩ how that could be, or how Kent and Caius could be the same person[liv] —so Kent thought it needless to trouble him with explanations at such a time; and * Lear soon after expiring⑪, this faithful servant to the king, between age and grief for his old master's vexations⑫, soon followed him to the grave.[lv]

---

① fall out 发生 happen, occur, take place, come to pass
② rouse [raʊz] *v*. 激起 excite, arouse, stir, provoke, incite
③ sundry ['sʌndri] *adj*. 各种各样的 various, varied, different, diverse
④ make away with 除掉 get rid of
⑤ put an end to 结束 end, finish, cease, terminate, wind up
⑥ overtake [ˌəʊvə'teɪk] *v*. (overtook, overtaken)突然降临
⑦ piety ['paɪəti] *n*. 虔诚 faith, devotion, devoutness, piousness
⑧ illustrious [ɪ'lʌstriəs] *adj*. 杰出的,著名的 famous, remarkable, distinguished
⑨ decay [dɪ'keɪ] *n*. 衰落 decline, failing, collapse
⑩ comprehend [ˌkɒmprɪ'hend] *v*. 理解 understand, take in
⑪ expire [ɪk'spaɪə(r)] *v*. 断气 die, decease, perish, pass away
⑫ vexation [vek'seɪʃn] *n*. 烦恼 annoyance, frustration, displeasure

How the judgement of Heaven overtook the bad earl of Gloucester, whose treasons[1] were discovered, and himself slain in single combat with his brother, the lawful earl; and how Goneril's husband, the duke of Albany, who was innocent of the death of Cordelia, and had never encouraged his lady in her wicked proceedings[2] against her father, ascended the throne of Britain after the death of Lear, is needless here to narrate[3]; Lear and his three daughters being dead, whose adventures alone concern our story.

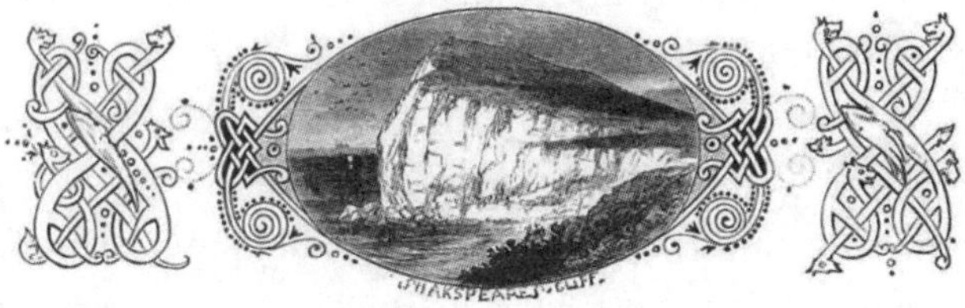

Cordelia. Who cover faults, at last shame them derides.
Well may you prosper!
France. Come, my fair Cordelia.
Act I. Scene I.

① treason [ˈtriːzn] *n*. 背叛 disloyalty, mutiny, treachery, betrayal

② proceeding [prəˈsiːdɪŋ] *n*. 行动 action

③ narrate [nəˈreɪt] *v*. 叙述 tell, relate, recount, describe, report

ⅰ The old king, worn out with age and the fatigues of government, he being more than fourscore years old, determined to take no further part in state affairs, but to leave the management to younger strengths, that he might have time to prepare for death, which must at no long period ensue. 老国王八十多岁了,由于上了年纪并且为国事操劳过度,身体衰弱下来。他决定把国事交给年轻有为的人去治理,自己就不再过问了,好让他有时间准备后事,因为死亡离他不远了。(he being...:独立主格结构;that=so that:引导目的状语从句)

ⅱ With a deal of such professing stuff, which is easy to counterfeit where there is no real love, only a few fine words delivered with confidence being wanted in that case. (她)用一堆花言巧语来表白。在没有真心的爱的时候,这种话很容易编造。其实这种场合只要老老实实说几句真心话就够了。(professing stuff:口不应心的花言巧语;which...where...:定语从句中嵌套地点状语从句)

ⅲ Regan, who was made of the same hollow metal as her sister, was not a whit behind in her profession, but rather declared that what her sister had spoken came short of the love which she professed to bear for his highness; insomuch that she found all other joys dead, in comparison with the pleasure which she took in the love of her dear king and father. 里根和她姐姐一样虚伪,表白得一点儿也不比她姐姐差。她说她姐姐的话还不足以表达她对父王的爱,世界上一切欢乐都提不起她的兴趣,只有在孝顺她亲爱的父王的时候,她才能感到无比的幸福。(who...:非限制性定语从句;hollow metal:中空的材料,喻指虚伪的本质;declared that what...which...:宾语从句中嵌套主语从句和定语从句)

ⅳ But Cordelia, disgusted with the flattery of her sisters, whose hearts she knew were far from their lips, and seeing that all their coaxing speeches were only intended to wheedle the old king out of his dominions, that they and their husbands might reign in his lifetime, made no other reply but this—that she loved his majesty according to her duty, neither more nor less. 可是考狄利娅十分讨厌她姐姐们的奉承,她知道她们嘴上说的跟心里想的完全不是一回事,她也看出她们的谄媚只是为了从年老的国王手里骗取国土,这样,她们和她们的丈夫就能在老国王还在世的时候掌握大权。因此,考狄利娅只这样回答:她的爱不多也不少,她就照着做女儿的本分去爱国王。

ⅴ If she should ever wed, she was sure the lord to whom she gave her hand would want half her love, half of her care and duty; she should never marry like her sisters, to love her father all. 她要是结婚的话,她确信她的丈夫会想要她一半的爱,以及一半的关心和责任。假使她光爱她父亲一个人的话,她就永远也不会像她姐姐们那样结婚了。(if she should..., ...would...:与将来相反的虚拟语气;all=exclusively:完全地)

ⅵ Cordelia, who in earnest loved her old father even almost as extravagantly as her sisters pretended to do, would have plainly told him so at any other time, in more daughter-like and loving terms, and without these qualifications, which did indeed sound a little ungracious; but after the crafty flattering speeches of her sisters, which she had seen draw such extravagant rewards, she thought the handsomest thing she could do was to love and be silent. 考狄利娅是真心诚意地爱她的老父亲,几乎像她姐姐们假装的那样真挚。换其他任何时候,她都会用更像女儿所说的、充满爱意的话语直接告诉他她的感情,而不会加上那些保留的话,那些话确实不大中听。可是听了她姐姐们那些虚伪的奉承,又看到她们从而得到的丰厚赏赐,她心里想,最好不声不响地爱她的父亲。(...who..., which...:双重定语从句;

would have...told...：与过去事实相反的虚拟语气 which..., thought (that)...thing (that)...：定语从句，宾语从句中嵌套定语从句）

vii This plainness of speech, which Lear called pride, so enraged the old monarch—who in his best of times always showed much of spleen and rashness, and in whom the dotage incident to old age had so clouded over his reason, that he could not discern truth from flattery, nor a gay painted speech from words that came from the heart—that in a fury of resentment he retracted the third part of his kingdom, which yet remained, and which he had reserved for Cordelia, and gave it away from her, sharing it equally between her two sisters and their husbands, the dukes of Albany and Cornwall. 老国王李尔把考狄利娅这番朴实的话语称作傲慢，他十分生气。国王年轻力壮的时候性情向来很急躁，动不动就发脾气；如今上了年纪，人更糊涂了，他不能分辨真话和奉承，也分不清花言巧语和心窝里的话。于是，一阵暴怒过后，他就把原来留给考狄利娅的那三分之一的国土收回来，不再给她，而是平分给她两个姐姐和她们的丈夫奥本尼公爵和康华尔公爵。（...speech..., which..., so enraded...that in...：so...that...结构中嵌套定语从句；monarch—who..., ...in whom...so clouded..., that he could not...：双重定语从句中嵌套 so...that...结构；dotage incident to old age：上了年纪，难免昏聩）

viii None of them had the courage to interpose between this incensed king and his wrath, except the earl of Kent, who was beginning to speak a good word for Cordelia, when the passionate Lear on pain of death commanded him to desist. 除了肯特伯爵，谁也不敢去冒犯这位正发着脾气的国王。肯特伯爵刚开始替考狄利娅说几句好话，暴跳如雷的李尔就叫他住嘴，不然就要他的命。

ix He had been ever loyal to Lear, whom he had honoured as a king, loved as a father, followed as a master; and he had never esteemed his life further than as a pawn to wage against his royal master's enemies, nor feared to lose it when Lear's safety was the motive, nor now that Lear was most his own enemy, did this faithful servant of the king forget his old principles, but manfully opposed Lear, to do Lear good; and was unmannerly only because Lear was mad. 他一向对李尔忠心耿耿，把他当国王来尊敬，当父亲来爱戴，当主人来追随。他从来不看重自己的生命，认为自己活着不过是为了当个小卒，好跟国王的敌人打仗；他也不怕舍弃生命，只要是为了保卫李尔的安全。如今，李尔就是自己最大的敌人，这个忠实的臣仆不曾忘记他一贯维护国王的精神，为了李尔的利益毅然起来反对李尔。只因为李尔发了疯，肯特才对他失礼。（...as..., ...as..., ...as...；and...never..., nor..., nor...：排比修辞）

x He had been a most faithful counsellor in times past to the king, and he besought him now, that he would see with his eyes (as he had done in many weighty matters), and go by his advice still; and in his best consideration recall this hideous rashness. 过去，他一向是国王最忠实的谏臣，所以他请求国王仍然接受他的意见（就像过去在许多重大的事情上那样），照他的劝告去做。他劝国王好好考虑一下，收回他那草率的成命。

xi He would answer with his life, his judgement that Lear's youngest daughter did not love him least, nor were those empty-hearted whose low sound gave no token of hollowness. 他敢用性命担保，李尔的小女儿对李尔的孝心绝不比姐姐们差。有些人不会说得天花乱坠，可他们并不是无情无义。（answer with his life：以他的性命担保；judgement that...：同位语从句；nor...：否定倒装结构；those...whose...：定语从句）

xii When power bowed to flattery, honour was bound to plainness. 当权力向谄媚低头的时候，

忠诚便不能不直言不讳。(借代修辞:当掌握大权的人向谄媚者低了头,正直的朝臣就只好把坦率的话说出来)

xiii Kent bade farewell to the king, and said, that since he chose to show himself in such fashion, it was but banishment to stay there; and before he went, he recommended Cordelia to the protection of the gods, the maid who had so rightly thought, and so discreetly spoken; and only wished that her sisters' large speeches might be answered with deeds of love; and then he went, as he said, to shape his old course to a new country. 肯特向国王告辞,说自己既然已经采取了那种态度,再留在那里也就跟流放在外头一个样子了。他走之前,又祈祷上天保佑考狄利娅这个思想正确、说话谨慎的姑娘;然后又说,但愿她的两个姐姐能用孝顺的行为来证实她们说过的大话。接着,肯特就走了,他说他要到一个新的国家去走他旧日走过的路。

xiv The king of France, understanding what the nature of the fault had been which had lost her the love of her father, that it was only a tardiness of speech, and the not being able to frame her tongue to flattery like her sisters, took this young maid by the hand, and saying that her virtues were a dowry above a kingdom, bade Cordelia to take farewell of her sisters and of her father, though he had been unkind, and she should go with him, and be queen of him and of fair France, and reign over fairer possessions than her sisters. 法兰西国王了解考狄利娅是由于什么样的过错失掉她父亲的宠爱的,他了解那只是因为她说话迟钝,不像她姐姐们那样巧舌如簧、善于谄媚。他拉住这位年轻姑娘的手说,她的品德是比一个王国还要贵重的一份嫁妆。他叫考狄利娅跟两个姐姐告别,也向她父亲告别——尽管她父亲待她那样坏;然后跟他走,做他的王后,也做锦绣的法兰西的王后,她统治的王国将要比她姐姐们的更灿烂。(understanding what...which..., that...:现在分词后的并列宾语从句中嵌套定语从句)

xv He called the duke of Burgundy in contempt a waterish duke, because his love for this young maid had in a moment run all away like water. 他又用轻蔑的口气把勃艮第公爵叫作"如水的公爵",因为他对这位年轻姑娘的爱一眨眼就像流水一般不见了。(waterish:语义双关,多水的,淡薄无味的)

xvi Then Cordelia with weeping eyes took leave of her sisters, and besought them to love their father well, and make good their professions—and they sullenly told her not to prescribe to them, for they knew their duty; but to strive to content her husband, who had taken her (as they tauntingly expressed it) as Fortune's alms. 于是,考狄利娅流着泪跟她的姐姐们告别,同时还嘱咐她们要好好爱护父亲,要照她们所表白的那样做。她的姐姐们绷着脸说,她们会尽自己的本分,用不着她指点,让她努力取悦自己的丈夫,既然他把她当作(她们用嘲笑的语气说)命运施舍给他的东西。(Fortune's alms:命运之神施舍的东西)

xvii Cordelia was no sooner gone, than the devilish dispositions of her sisters began to show themselves in their true colours. 考狄利娅刚走,她的姐姐们恶魔般的性情就露出真面目来。(no sooner...than...:刚一……就……)

xviii Not only she herself slackened in her expressions of duty to the king, but by her example, and (it is to be feared) not without her private instructions, her very servants affected to treat him with neglect. 不但她自己对国王越来越怠慢,而且由于她的榜样,(恐怕)还由于她暗地里的唆使,连她的仆人也对他冷淡起来了。(affected to treat him with neglect:公然对他不闻不问)

xix Lear could not but perceive this alteration in the behaviour of his daughter, but he shut his eyes against it as long as he could, as people commonly are unwilling to believe the unpleasant consequences which their own mistakes and obstinacy have brought upon them. 李尔也不会看不出他女儿一举一动的改变,可他还是尽量装作看不见。因为人们一般不肯相信他们自己的错误和固执所造成的不愉快的结果。(could not but...:不得不……,只能……)

xx True love and fidelity are no more to be estranged by ill, than falsehood and hollow-heartedness can be conciliated by good usage. 真实的爱与忠诚并不会被恶意所离间,正如虚假与空洞不能被善行所感化。(借代修辞:如果一个人的爱和忠诚是真实的,你待他坏也不能使他疏远;正如一个心地虚伪的人,你待他再好也不能将他感化)

xxi See to what mean shifts and disguises poor loyalty is forced to submit sometimes; yet it counts nothing base or unworthy, so as it can but do service where it owes an obligation! 看一看吧,可怜的忠诚有时被迫屈从于卑贱的计谋与伪装;然而这并不算是下贱或者卑微,只要是为了去服务它应尽的责任!(so as=so/as long as:只要……;...where...:地点状语从句)

xxii In the disguise of a serving man, all his greatness and pomp laid aside, this good earl proffered his services to the king, who, not knowing him to be Kent in that disguise, but pleased with a certain plainness, or rather bluntness in his answers, which the earl put on (so different from that smooth oily flattery which he had so much reason to be sick of, having found the effects not answerable in his daughter), a bargain was quickly struck, and Lear took Kent into his service by the name of Caius, as he called himself, never suspecting him to be his once great favourite, the high and mighty earl of Kent. 这个好心的伯爵就放弃了他的尊严和排场,乔装成一个仆人,请求国王雇用他。国王不知道他是肯特扮的,问话的时候肯特故意答得很直爽,甚至可以说有些粗鲁(与那种油腔滑调的谄媚大大不同,李尔因为看到自己的女儿说话不算数,已经对那种奉承感到厌恶了),可是这却让国王很高兴。于是,他们很快就谈妥了,李尔收下肯特做他的仆人,肯特说自己名叫卡厄斯。国王绝对没法料到,这就是当年他十分得意的宠臣,位高权重的肯特伯爵。(not knowing...; never suspecting...:现在分词否定形式作状语)

xxiii In his degree, and as far as so insignificant a personage could show his love, the poor fool, or jester, that had been of his palace while Lear had a palace, as it was the custom of kings and great personages at that time to keep a fool (as he was called) to make them sport after serious business—this poor fool clung to Lear after he had given away his crown, and by his witty sayings would keep up his good humour, though he could not refrain sometimes from jeering at his master for his imprudence in uncrowning himself, and giving all away to his daughters. 照当时的习俗,国王或是大人物身边都养着个"弄臣"(他们是这样叫的)。弄臣可以在他们忙完繁重公事以后,替他们解闷散心。李尔还拥有自己的王宫的时候,宫里也有这么个可怜的弄臣,一个逗乐的人。这样一个地位低微的人尽他所能地对李尔表示敬爱。在李尔放弃了他的王位之后,这个可怜的弄臣仍然跟着他,用他那机智的口才来叫国王开心,尽管有时候他不免也会讥笑国王放弃王位,把一切都给了女儿的这种轻率举动。

xxiv For sudden joy did weep
And I for sorrow sung,
That such a king should play bo-peep
And go the fools among.

(她们)高兴得眼泪盈眶,
我只好唱歌自遣哀愁,
可怜你堂堂一国之王,
却跟傻瓜们作伴嬉游。

xxv Comparing the king to the hedge-sparrow, who feeds the young of the cuckoo till they grow old enough, and then has its head bit off for its pains.(弄臣)把国王比作一只篱雀,它把幼小的杜鹃鸟养大,杜鹃鸟为了报答它的养育之恩,却一口把它的脑袋咬掉了。

xxvi An ass may know when the cart draws the horse (meaning that Lear's daughters, that ought to go behind, now ranked before their father). 一头驴也许知道什么时候车会拉着马走(意思是李尔的女儿本应该在后边的,如今却站到她们父亲前面去了)。

xxvii He could not believe that she who had received a crown from him could seek to cut off his train, and grudge him the respect due to his old age. 他不能相信她从他手里得到了王冠,却想裁掉他的侍从,并如此吝惜给予他一个老人家应得的尊重。

xxviii But she persisting in her undutiful demand, the old man's rage was so excited, that he called her a detested kite, and said that she spoke an untruth; and so indeed she did, for the hundred knights were all men of choice behaviour and sobriety of manners, skilled in all particulars of duty, and not given to rioting or feasting, as she said. 可是高纳里尔坚持她那不孝顺的要求,老人家就大发脾气,骂她是只"可恶的鸢",并且说她扯谎。这的确是事实,因为那一百名骑士都是品行端正、绝不胡作非为的人,他们在所有小事情上都训练有素,从来也不像她说的那样吵吵嚷嚷、大吃大喝。(she persisting...:独立主格结构)

xxix He spoke of ingratitude, and said it was a marble-hearted devil, and showed more hideous in a child than the sea-monster. 他谈到忘恩负义,说那是铁石心肠的魔鬼。一个孩子要是忘恩负义,那就比海里的妖怪还要可怕。

xxx Who should it be but Caius's old enemy the steward, whom he had formerly tripped up by the heels for his saucy behaviour to Lear. 他刚好就是卡厄斯的旧日对头,高纳里尔的那个管家,卡厄斯曾因为他对李尔态度蛮横而绊了他一跤。

xxxi Caius not liking the fellow's look, and suspecting what he came for, began to revile him, and challenged him to fight, which the fellow refusing, Caius, in a fit of honest passion, beat him soundly, as such a mischief-maker and carrier of wicked messages deserved; which coming to the ears of Regan and her husband, they ordered Caius to be put in the stocks, though he was a messenger from the king her father, and in that character demanded the highest respect. 卡厄斯很不喜欢这家伙的神气,也猜出了他的来意,于是就破口大骂,要跟他决斗。这家伙不肯决斗,卡厄斯一阵气愤,就把这个制造祸端、捎恶毒信件的家伙,照他罪有应得的狠狠揍了一顿。里根和她的丈夫听到这件事,就吩咐人给卡厄斯戴上镣铐,尽管他是父王派来的,本应受到最高礼遇。(in a fit of honest passion:出于一阵义愤)

xxxii Upon his insisting in a positive and angry manner to see them, they came to greet him, whom should he see in their company but the hated Goneril, who had come to tell her own story, and set her sister against the king her father! 由于他十分坚决,气冲冲地表示非见到他们不可,他们才出来接见他。可是陪他们一道接见他的不是别人,偏偏就是那个可恨的高纳里尔,她跑来向妹妹讲了一通自己的道理,并且挑拨她妹妹也反对自己的父王!

xxxiii So these two wicked daughters, as if they strove to exceed each other in cruelty to their old father, who had been so good to them, by little and little would have abated him of all his train, all respect (little enough for him that once commanded a kingdom), which was left him to show that he had once been a king! 这两个坏心肠的姐妹像是有意在虐待她们的老父亲这方面比赛似的,竟想一步步把表示他曾经是个国王的那些侍从和那点尊严(作

为曾经统治过一个王国的人来说，已所剩甚少）削弱，而他曾经对他们那么好。

xxxiv It was the ingratitude in his daughters' denying it, more than what he would suffer by the want of it, which pierced this poor king to the heart. 使这个可怜的国王伤透了心的，还不是他没有了侍从，而是他的女儿忘恩负义，拒绝了他的要求。

xxxv While he said he knew not what, he vowed revenge against those unnatural hags, and to make examples of them that should be a terror to the earth! 他一面说着连自己都不明白的话，一面发誓要向不孝的妖妇报仇，使她们成为警示，令全世界为之悚然！

xxxvi The injuries which wilful men procure to themselves are their just punishment. 固执的人给自己造成的伤害是他们应得的惩罚。

xxxvii The winds were high, and the rain and storm increased, when the old man sallied forth to combat with the elements, less sharp than his daughters' unkindness. 风刮得很猛，雷雨也更大了。风雨的袭击毕竟没有女儿们的狠毒那样叫人扎心，老人家冲出去，跟大自然搏斗了。（elements：古代炼金术士认为一切物质由土、风、水、火四大元素构成，此处用来指雷电和风雨）

xxxviii The old king was now left with no other companion than the poor fool, who still abided with him, with his merry conceits striving to outjest misfortune, saying it was but a naughty night to swim in, and truly the king had better go in and ask his daughters' blessing. 现在老国王身边只剩下那个可怜的弄臣了，他依然跟着国王，竭力想拿诙谐、怪诞的话来排遣这种不幸的遭遇。他说，在这样糟糕的夜晚来游泳真没意思，老实说，国王还不如进屋去向女儿们乞求庇护呢。（still＝always, ever；naughty＝bad）

xxxix

But he that has a little tiny wit,	只怪自己糊涂自己蠢，
With heigh ho, the wind and the rain!	嗨呵，一阵风来一阵雨，
Must make content with his fortunes fit,	背时倒运莫把天公恨，
Though the rain it raineth every day.	管它朝朝雨雨又风风。

xl Swearing it was a brave night to cool a lady's pride. （弄臣）发誓说，这是一个适合叫一个傲慢的女人懂得谦虚的晚上。（brave＝fine, glorious）

xli These lesser evils were not felt, where a greater malady was fixed. 一个人得了重病，就感觉不到小的痛苦。（where…：地点状语从句）

xlii When the mind is at ease, the body has leisure to be delicate, but the tempest in his mind did take all feeling else from his senses, but of that which beat at his heart. 只有心情安宁的时候，肉体才有闲暇变得敏感；可是他心里的暴风雨已经夺去了他的一切感觉，只剩下心脏跳动的感觉。

xliii He spoke of filial ingratitude, and said it was all one as if the mouth should tear the hand for lifting food to it; for parents were hands and food and everything to children. 他谈到儿女的忘恩，说那就像嘴把喂它的手咬了下来，因为对儿女来说，父母就是手、食物和一切。（比喻修辞；it was all one as if：正好像）

xliv Upon examination this spirit proved to be nothing more than a poor Bedlam beggar. 仔细一看，这个“鬼”原来只是一个可怜的疯乞丐。

xlv Calling themselves poor Tom and poor Turlygood. 他们给自己起名叫“可怜的汤姆”和“可怜的屠列古德”。（poor Tom：“可怜的汤姆”，疯乞丐乞讨时的用语，相当于“可怜的张三”“可怜的李四”；Turlygood：疯子，旧时意大利语中称疯子为 turlupin，英语中念成 turlygood）

xlvi This poor fellow was such a one; and the king seeing him in so wretched a plight, with nothing but a blanket about his loins to cover his nakedness, could not be persuaded but that the fellow was some father who had given all away to his daughters, and brought himself to that pass—for nothing he thought could bring a man to such wretchedness but the having unkind daughters. 这个可怜的家伙就是这种人。国王见他这样穷苦，浑身一丝不挂，只在腰间围着一条毯子，就断定这个人一定也是把自己所有的财产都分给女儿了，才落到这般田地。因为他认为除了养了狠毒的女儿，再没有别的事情可以把一个人弄得这样悲惨的了。

xlvii Did there in such moving terms represent the pitiful condition of her royal father, and set out in such lively colours the inhumanity of her sisters, that this good and loving child with many tears besought the king her husband that he would give her leave to embark for England, with a sufficient power to subdue these cruel daughters and their husbands, and restore the old king her father to his throne.（肯特伯爵）用感人的话叙述了她父王的悲惨情况，绘声绘色地讲出她两个姐姐的惨无人道的行为，以至于这个善良孝顺的孩子听了流下泪来。她要求国王（她的丈夫）准许她坐船回英国去，带上足够的人马去讨伐这两个残忍的姐姐和她们的丈夫，把父王重新扶上王位。（set out in such lively colours：生动逼真地叙述；power：指军事力量）

xlviii Lear having by some chance escaped from the guardians which the good earl of Kent had put over him to take care of him in his lunacy, was found by some of Cordelia's train, wandering about the fields near Dover, in a pitiable condition, stark mad, and singing aloud to himself with a crown upon his head which he had made of straw, and nettles, and other wild weeds that he had picked up in the corn-fields. 李尔钻了个空子，从好心的肯特伯爵派来照顾他的那些人手里逃了出来。当他正在多佛附近的田野里徘徊的时候，被考狄利娅的侍从发现了。当时他的情况真是凄惨，已经完全疯了，一个人大声唱着歌，头上戴着用稻草、荨麻和从麦地里捡来的其他野草编成的王冠。（having...escaped...guardians which...：现在分词完成式中嵌套定语从句；a crown...which..., ...weeds that...：定语从句的嵌套）

xlix By the help of sleep and medicine, she and her physicians at length succeeded in winding up the untuned and jarring senses which the cruelty of his other daughters had so violently shaken. 国王被他那两个狠毒的女儿折磨得精神完全错乱。在睡眠和药草的帮助下，考狄利娅和大夫们终于把他治好了。

l It falling out about this time that the duke of Cornwall, Regan's husband, died, Regan immediately declared her intention of wedding this earl of Gloucester, which rousing the jealousy of her sister, to whom as well as to Regan this wicked earl had at sundry times professed love, Goneril found means to make away with her sister by poison. 恰好这个时候里根的丈夫康华尔公爵死了，里根立刻宣布要和葛罗斯特伯爵结婚。这件事引起了她姐姐的嫉妒。因为这个卑鄙的伯爵不仅向里根示爱，还同时屡次向高纳里尔表示过爱意。于是高纳里尔想办法把自己的妹妹毒死了。（It falling..., which rousing...：独立主格结构的嵌套；to whom...：非限制性定语从句）

li Being detected in her practices, and imprisoned by her husband, the duke of Albany, for this deed, and for her guilty passion for the earl which had come to his ears, she, in a fit of disappointed love and rage, shortly put an end to her own life. 这件事被她的丈夫奥本尼公爵发现了。公爵因为知道了这件事，也因为知道了她和伯爵的暧昧关系，便把她关进监牢

里。她因为爱情遭受挫折，又气又恼，不久便自行了断了。（this deed：指代前面的动名词被动式短语 being detected...和 imprisoned...）

lii While the eyes of all men were upon this event, admiring the justice displayed in their deserved deaths, the same eyes were suddenly taken off from this sight to admire at the mysterious ways of the same power in the melancholy fate of the young and virtuous daughter, the lady Cordelia, whose good deeds did seem to deserve a more fortunate conclusion—but it is an awful truth, that innocence and piety are not always successful in this world. 大家都注意到这件事，说这两个人死得公道。忽然间，他们又移开视线，惊愕地看到同一股力量是怎样神秘地施展在年轻、品德高尚的女儿考狄利娅的悲惨命运上的。她的善行似乎应该得到更幸运的结局，然而这是个可怕的真理：世界上纯洁和孝顺的人并不一定总得好报。（admire at＝be astonished at：对……感到吃惊）

liii Thus, Heaven took this innocent lady to itself in her young years, after showing her to the world an illustrious example of filial duty. Lear did not long survive this kind child. 这样，上天叫这个纯洁无辜的女人给世界展示了尽孝的杰出榜样，然后在她年纪轻轻的时候就把她接回去了。这个善良的孩子走了没多久，李尔也去世了。

liv Before he died, the good earl of Kent, who had still attended his old master's steps from the first of his daughters' ill usage to this sad period of his decay, tried to make him understand that it was he who had followed him under the name of Caius; but Lear's care-crazed brain at that time could not comprehend how that could be, or how Kent and Caius could be the same person. 从李尔最初受到女儿虐待，到他最后令人难过地衰弱下去，好心的肯特伯爵一直陪伴着老主人。李尔去世前，肯特试图让国王知道，就是他一直用卡厄斯这个名字跟随着他，可是那时李尔已经气得发了疯，无法理解那样的事怎么可能发生，肯特和卡厄斯怎么会是一个人。（still＝always, ever；care-crazed：因忧虑而发疯的）

lv Lear soon after expiring, this faithful servant to the king, between age and grief for his old master's vexations, soon followed him to the grave. 过了不久，李尔死了。这位国王的忠仆，一方面因为自己上了年纪，一方面又因为老主人的痛苦而悲伤，很快也跟着进了坟墓。

麦克白
Macbeth

Act IV. Sc. 1.

Life's but a walking shadow; a poor player,
人生不过是一个行走的影子，

That struts and frets his hour upon the stage,
一个在舞台上指手画脚的拙劣的伶人，登场片刻，

And then is heard no more. It is a tale
就在无声无息中悄然退下；

Told by an idiot, full of sound and fury,
它是一个愚人所讲的故事，充满着喧哗和骚动，

Signifying nothing.
却找不到一点儿意义。

麦克白的灵魂从未消失在黑暗的阴影里。他是不会下雨的云，被风吹来吹去；他是一棵会枯萎的果子树，但甚至到了最后，却还没有被连根拔起。麦克白那阴暗的暴行是没有快乐可言的。

——爱德华·道登

莎士比亚把怜悯描写得多么出色，而他所写的恐怖又是多么有力啊！他使恐怖从罪恶之中浮现出来。我们也许可以像《圣经》谈到死亡那样，在谈莎士比亚所描写的罪恶时这样说，他是"恐怖之王"。在《麦克白》一剧中，人物的悔恨与随着悔恨而逐渐强烈起来的疑神疑鬼的心理，是结合得多么好啊！

——斯塔尔夫人

莎士比亚有一颗通天之心，能够了解一切人物和激情。

——约翰·德莱顿

莎士比亚笔下的麦克白是一个坏蛋，但却是一个具有深刻而强大的灵魂的坏蛋。因此，他唤起的不是反感，而是同情。你会看出他是这样一个人，他包含着胜利与失败两者的可能性，如果走向另外一个方面，他就可能变成另一个人。

——别林斯基

主要人物

Duncan　邓肯　苏格兰国王
Macbeth　麦克白　苏格兰军中大将
Banquo　班柯　苏格兰军中大将
Malcolm　马尔康　邓肯之子
Donalbain　道纳本　邓肯之子
Fleance　弗里恩斯　班柯之子
Macduff　麦克德夫　苏格兰贵族
Lady Macbeth　麦克白夫人
Ross　洛斯　苏格兰贵族
Angus　安格斯　苏格兰贵族
First/Second/Third Witch　三女巫

地点　苏格兰；英格兰

Macbeth

When Duncan the Meek[1] reigned king of Scotland, there lived a great thane[2] or lord, called Macbeth. This Macbeth was a near kinsman to the king, and in great esteem at court for his valour and conduct in the wars; an example of which he had lately given, in defeating a rebel[3] army assisted by the troops of Norway in terrible numbers.

The two Scottish generals, Macbeth and Banquo, returning victorious[4] from this great battle, their way lay over a blasted[5] heath, where they were stopped by the strange appearance of three figures like women, except that they had beards, and their withered[6] skins and wild attire made them look not like any earthly creatures. Macbeth first addressed them, when they, seemingly offended, laid each one her choppy[7] finger upon her skinny lips, in token of[8] silence; and the first of them saluted[9] Macbeth with the title of thane of Glamis. The general was not a little startled[10] to find himself known by such creatures; but how much more, when the second of them followed up that salute by giving him the title of thane of Cawdor, to which honour he had no pretensions[11];

---

① Duncan the Meek 温厚的邓肯(苏格兰国王)
② thane [θeɪn] *n*. 苏格兰的一种爵位
③ rebel [ˈrebl] *n*. 反叛者 revolutionary, insurgent
④ victorious [vɪkˈtɔːriəs] *adj*. 胜利的 winning, successful, triumphant
⑤ blasted [ˈblɑːstɪd] *adj*. 荒凉的 ruined, wasted, desolated
⑥ wither [ˈwɪðə(r)] *v*. 萎缩 wilt, shrink, decay, shrivel
⑦ choppy [ˈtʃɒpi] *adj*. 有裂痕的,支离破碎的 broken
⑧ in token of 作为……的标志
⑨ salute [səˈluːt] *v*. 致敬 greet
⑩ startled [ˈstɑːtld] *adj*. 震惊的 surprised, shocked
⑪ pretension [prɪˈtenʃn] *n*. 自负

and again the third bid him "* All hail①! King that shalt be hereafter②![i]" Such a prophetic③ greeting might well amaze him, who knew that while the king's sons lived he could not hope to succeed to the throne④. Then turning to Banquo, they pronounced⑤ him, in a sort of riddling⑥ terms, to be * lesser than Macbeth and greater! not so happy, but much happier![ii] And prophesied⑦ that though he should never reign, yet his sons after him should be kings in Scotland. They then turned into air, and vanished—by which the generals knew them to be the weird sisters⑧, or witches⑨.

While they stood pondering⑩ on the strangeness of this adventure, there arrived certain messengers from the king, who were empowered⑪ by him to confer⑫ upon Macbeth the dignity⑬ of thane of Cawdor—an event so miraculously⑭ corresponding with the prediction of the witches astonished Macbeth, and he stood wrapped in amazement, unable to make reply to the messengers; and in that point of time swelling⑮ hopes arose in his mind that the prediction of the third witch might in like manner have its accomplishment⑯, and that he should one day reign king in Scotland.

Turning to Banquo, he said: "Do you not hope that your children shall be kings, when what the witches promised to me has so wonderfully come to pass?" "* That hope," answered the general, "might enkindle⑰ you to aim at the throne; but oftentimes these ministers⑱ of darkness tell us truths in little things, to betray us into deeds of greatest consequence.[iii]"

But the wicked suggestions of the witches had sunk too deep into the mind of Macbeth to allow him to attend to the warnings of the good Banquo. From that time he bent all his thoughts on⑲ how to compass⑳ the throne of Scotland.

Macbeth had a wife, to whom he communicated the strange prediction of the weird sisters, and its partial㉑ accomplishment. * She was a bad, ambitious woman, and so as her husband and herself could arrive at greatness, she cared not much by what means.[iv] * She spurred㉒ on the

---

① hail [heɪl] *v*. 欢呼 applaud, clap, cheer
② hereafter [ˌhɪər'ɑːftə(r)] *adv*. 将来,以后 hence, in future, from now on
③ prophetic[prə'fetɪk] *adj*. 预言的 predictive, presaging, prescient
④ throne [θrəʊn] *n*. 王位 royalty, sovereignty
⑤ pronounce [prə'naʊns] *v*. 宣布 declare, announce, proclaim
⑥ riddling ['rɪdlɪŋ] *adj*. 谜一样的 enigmatic, mysterious, puzzling
⑦ prophesy ['prɒfəsaɪ] *v*. 预言 predict, forecast, foresee, foretell
⑧ weird sisters 神话中的命运三女神,此处指三女巫
⑨ witch [wɪtʃ] *n*. 女巫 enchantress, sorceress, necromancer
⑩ ponder['pɒndə(r)] *v*. 沉思 consider, muse, think about, reflect on
⑪ empower [ɪm'paʊə(r)] *v*. 授权 authorize, commission, qualify
⑫ confer [kən'fɜː(r)] *v*. 授予 grant, present, award, bestow
⑬ dignity ['dɪgnəti] *n*. 高贵 standing, station, rank, status
⑭ miraculously [mɪ'rækjələsli] *adv*. 奇迹般地 wonderfully, marvelously
⑮ swell [swel] *v*. 膨胀 increase, grow, expand, surge, well up
⑯ accomplishment [ə'kʌmplɪʃmənt] *n*. 实现 realization, fulfilment
⑰ enkindle [ɪn'kɪndl] *v*. 煽动 arouse, incite, inspire, stir
⑱ minister ['mɪnɪstə(r)] *n*. 公使;牧师;大臣
⑲ bend sth. on 倾注某物于,集中某物于 fix sth. on
⑳ compass ['kʌmpəs] *v*. 得到,图谋完成 get, gain, obtain, attain, secure
㉑ partial ['pɑːʃl] *adj*. 部分的 incomplete, limited, unfinished
㉒ spur [spɜː(r)] *v*. 激励 incite, drive, prompt, urge, stimulate

reluctant purpose of Macbeth, who felt compunction① at the thoughts of blood, and did not cease to represent the murder of the king as a step absolutely necessary to the fulfilment② of the flattering prophecy③.[v]

* It happened at this time that the king, who out of his royal condescension④ would oftentimes visit his principal⑤ nobility upon gracious terms, came to Macbeth's house, attended by his two sons, Malcolm and Donalbain, and a numerous⑥ train of thanes and attendants, the more to honour Macbeth for the triumphal⑦ success of his wars.[vi]

* The castle of Macbeth was pleasantly situated, and the air about it was sweet and wholesome, which appeared by the nests which the martlet⑧, or swallow, had built under all the jutting⑨ friezes⑩ and buttresses⑪ of the building, wherever it found a place of advantage; for where those birds most breed and haunt, the air is observed to be delicate.[vii] The king entered well-pleased with the place, and not less so with the attentions and respect of his honoured hostess, lady Macbeth, who had the art⑫ of covering treacherous purposes with smiles; and could look like the innocent⑬ flower, while she was indeed the serpent under it.

The king being tired with his journey, went early to bed, and in his state-room two grooms⑭ of his chamber (as was the custom) slept beside him. He had been unusually pleased with his reception⑮, and had made presents before he retired⑯ to his principal officers; and among the rest, had sent a rich diamond to lady Macbeth, greeting her by the name of his most kind hostess.

* Now was the middle of night, when over half the world nature seems dead, and wicked dreams abuse⑰ men's minds asleep, and none but the wolf and the murderer is abroad.[viii] This was the time when lady Macbeth waked to plot the murder of the king. * She would not have undertaken a deed so abhorrent⑱ to her sex, but that she feared her husband's nature, that it was too full of the milk of human kindness, to do a contrived⑲ murder.[ix] * She knew him to be ambitious, but withal⑳ to be scrupulous㉑, and not yet prepared for that height of crime which

---

① compunction [kəm'pʌŋkʃn] *n*. 内疚 guilt, remorse
② fulfilment [fʊl'fɪlmənt] *n*. 完成 accomplishment
③ prophecy ['prɒfəsi] *n*. 预言 prediction, forecast
④ condescension [ˌkɒndɪ'senʃn] *n*. 屈尊 patronage
⑤ principal ['prɪnsəpl] *adj*. 主要的 main, chief, prime, primary
⑥ numerous ['njuːmərəs] *adj*. 众多的 many, countless, innumerable
⑦ triumphal [traɪ'ʌmfl] *adj*. 凯旋的 victorious, triumphant
⑧ martlet ['mɑːtlɪt] *n*. 圣马丁鸟,无足鸟
⑨ jut [dʒʌt] *v*. 凸出 stick/stand/swell out, protrude, bulge
⑩ frieze [friːz] *n*. 檐壁饰带
⑪ buttress ['bʌtrəs] *n*. 扶壁
⑫ art [ɑːt] *n*. 诡计 trickery, deceit, cunning, guile, artifice
⑬ innocent ['ɪnəsnt] *adj*. 清白的 sinless, guiltless, blameless, naive
⑭ groom [gruːm] *n*. 马夫;王室侍从官 servant, stableman
⑮ reception [rɪ'sepʃn] *n*. 接待
⑯ retire [rɪ'taɪə(r)] *v*. 离去 withdraw, leave, depart
⑰ abuse [ə'bjuːz] *v*. 蒙骗 deceive, fool, trick, cheat, take in
⑱ abhorrent [əb'hɒrənt] *adj*. 可憎的;相抵触的
⑲ contrived [kən'traɪvd] *adj*. 预谋的 planned, intentional
⑳ withal [wɪ'ðɔːl] *adv*. 此外 besides, moreover, in addition
㉑ scrupulous ['skruːpjələs] *adj*. 正直的 moral, upright, high-minded

commonly in the end accompanies inordinate① ambition.[x] She had won him to consent to the murder, but she doubted his resolution; and she feared that the natural tenderness② of his disposition (more humane③ than her own) would come between④, and defeat the purpose. So with her own hands armed with a dagger, she approached the king's bed; having taken care to ply⑤ the grooms of his chamber so with wine, that they slept intoxicated⑥, and careless of their charge. There lay Duncan in a sound sleep after the fatigues of his journey, and as she viewed him earnestly, there was something in his face, as he slept, which resembled her own father; and she had not the courage to proceed.

She returned to confer with her husband. His resolution had begun to stagger⑦. He considered that there were strong reasons against the deed. In the first place, he was not only a subject, but a near kinsman to the king; and he had been his host and entertainer⑧ that day, whose duty, by the laws of hospitality⑨, it was to shut the door against his murderers, not bear the knife himself. * Then he considered how just and merciful a king this Duncan had been, how clear of offence to his subjects, how loving to his nobility, and in particular to him; that such kings are the peculiar⑩ care of Heaven, and their subjects doubly bound to revenge their deaths.[xi] Besides, by the favours of the king, Macbeth stood high in the opinion of all sorts of men, and how would those honours be stained⑪ by the reputation⑫ of so foul a murder!

In these conflicts of the mind lady Macbeth found her husband inclining⑬ to the better part, and resolving to proceed no further. * But she being a woman not easily shaken from her evil purpose, began to pour in at his ears words which infused⑭ a portion of her own spirit into his mind, assigning⑮ reason upon reason why he should not shrink⑯ from what he had undertaken; how easy the deed was; how soon it would be over; and how the action of one short night would give to all their nights and days to come sovereign⑰ sway⑱ and royalty![xii] Then she threw contempt on his change of purpose, and accused him of fickleness⑲ and cowardice⑳; and declared that * she had given suck㉑, and knew how tender it was to love the babe that milked her; but she

---

① inordinate [ɪn'ɔːdɪnət] *adj*. 过度的 excessive, intemperate
② tenderness ['tendənəs] *n*. 温柔 kindness, gentleness
③ humane [hjuː'meɪn] *adj*. 人道的,仁慈的 kind, merciful, sympathetic
④ come between 妨碍 hinder, hamper, impede, obstruct
⑤ ply [plaɪ] *v*. 不断供应 provide, supply
⑥ intoxicated [ɪn'tɒksɪkeɪtɪd] *adj*. 喝醉的 drunk, tipsy, unsober
⑦ stagger ['stæɡə(r)] *v*. 动摇;踉跄 totter, reel, sway, falter, waver, teeter
⑧ entertainer [ˌentə'teɪnə(r)] *n*. 款待者
⑨ hospitality [ˌhɒspɪ'tæləti] *n*. 好客 sociability, heartiness
⑩ peculiar [pɪ'kjuːliə(r)] *adj*. 特殊的 special, particular, unique, distinct
⑪ stain [steɪn] *v*. 玷污 mark, soil, tarnish, blemish, spot
⑫ reputation [ˌrepju'teɪʃn] *n*. 名声 name, fame, credit, renown
⑬ incline [ɪn'klaɪn] *v*. 倾向于 tend, predispose
⑭ infuse [ɪn'fjuːz] *v*. 注入 fill, charge, instil, add, inject, implant
⑮ assign [ə'saɪn] *v*. 分配 distribute, allocate, apportion, give out
⑯ shrink [ʃrɪŋk] *v*. 退缩 recoil, flinch, shy away, fight shy of
⑰ sovereign ['sɒvrɪn] *n*. 君主,元首 royal
⑱ sway [sweɪ] *n*. 影响,统治,势力 power, control, rule, influence, authority
⑲ fickleness ['fɪklnəs] *n*. 变化无常 inconstancy, changefulness
⑳ cowardice ['kaʊədɪs] *n*. 懦弱 cowardliness, faint-heartedness
㉑ give suck 喂奶,哺乳

would, while it was smiling in her face, have plucked① it from her breast, and dashed② its brains out, if she had so sworn to do it, as he had sworn to perform that murder.[xiii] Then she added, how practicable③ it was to lay the guilt of the deed upon the drunken sleepy grooms. And with the valour of her tongue she so chastised④ his sluggish⑤ resolutions, that he once more summoned⑥ up courage to the bloody business.

So, taking the dagger in his hand, he softly stole in the dark to the room where Duncan lay; and as he went, he thought he saw another dagger in the air, with the handle towards him, and on the blade⑦ and at the point of it drops of blood; but * when he tried to grasp at it, it was nothing but air, a mere phantasm⑧ proceeding⑨ from his own hot and oppressed⑩ brain and the business he had in hand.[xiv]

Getting rid of this fear, he entered the king's room, whom he despatched with one stroke⑪ of his dagger. Just as he had done the murder, one of the grooms, who slept in the chamber, laughed in his sleep, and the other cried "Murder", which woke them both; but they said a short prayer; one of them said: "God bless us!" and the other answered "Amen"; and addressed themselves⑫ to sleep again. * Macbeth, who stood listening to them, tried to say "Amen" when the fellow said "God bless us!" but, though he had most need of a blessing, the word stuck in his throat, and he could not pronounce it.[xv]

Again he thought he heard a voice which cried: "Sleep no more—Macbeth doth murder sleep, the innocent sleep, that nourishes⑬ life." Still it cried: "Sleep no more," to all the house. "Glamis hath murdered sleep, and therefore Cawdor shall sleep no more. Macbeth shall sleep no more."

With such horrible imaginations Macbeth returned to his listening wife, who began to think he had failed of his purpose, and that the deed was somehow frustrated⑭. * He came in so distracted⑮ a state, that she reproached him with his want⑯ of firmness, and sent him to wash his hands of the blood which stained⑰ them, while she took his dagger,

---

① pluck [plʌk] *v*. 猛拉 draw, catch, snatch, yank, pull out/off
② dash [dæʃ] *v*. 猛掷 throw, cast, pitch, toss, hurl, fling, sling
③ practicable ['præktɪkəbl] *adj*. 可行的 workable, doable, feasible
④ chastise [tʃæ'staɪz] *v*. 指责 scold, blame, chide, find fault with
⑤ sluggish ['slʌgɪʃ] *adj*. 迟缓的,迟钝的 inactive, slow, lethargic, unresponsive
⑥ summon ['sʌmən] *v*. 召唤,召集 call, gather, call together
⑦ blade [bleɪd] *n*. 刀刃
⑧ phantasm ['fæntæzəm] *n*. 幻觉 illusion, vision, hallucination
⑨ proceed [prə'siːd] *v*. 产生
⑩ oppressed [ə'prest] *adj*. 被压迫的 burdened
⑪ stroke [strəʊk] *n*. 一击 blow, hit, knock, rap, thump
⑫ address oneself 使自己镇静 settle/compose oneself
⑬ nourish ['nʌrɪʃ] *v*. 滋养 feed, supply, sustain, nurture
⑭ frustrate [frʌ'streɪt] *v*. 挫败,使懊恼 thwart, defeat
⑮ distracted [dɪ'stræktɪd] *adj*. 心烦意乱的 agitated, troubled
⑯ want [wɒnt] *n*. 缺乏 lack, shortage, absence, deficiency
⑰ stain [steɪn] *v*. 玷污 mark, soil, blemish, smirch, spot

with purpose to stain the cheeks of the grooms with blood, to make it seem their guilt.[xvi]

Morning came, and with it the discovery of the murder, which could not be concealed①; and * though Macbeth and his lady made great show of grief, and the proofs② against the grooms (the dagger being produced against them and their faces smeared③ with blood) were sufficiently④ strong, yet the entire suspicion⑤ fell upon Macbeth, whose inducements⑥ to such a deed were so much more forcible⑦ than such poor silly grooms could be supposed to have;[xvii] and Duncan's two sons fled. Malcolm, the eldest, sought for refuge in the English court; and the youngest, Donalbain, made his escape to Ireland.

The king's sons, who should have succeeded him, having thus vacated⑧ the throne, Macbeth as next heir was crowned⑨ king, and thus the prediction of the weird sisters was literally⑩ accomplished.

Though placed so high, Macbeth and his queen could not forget the prophecy of the weird sisters, that, though Macbeth should be king, yet not his children, but the children of Banquo, should be kings after him. * The thought of this, and that they had defiled⑪ their hands with blood, and done so great crimes, only to place the posterity⑫ of Banquo upon the throne, so rankled⑬ within them, that they determined to put to death both Banquo and his son, to make void⑭ the predictions of the weird sisters, which in their own case had been so remarkably brought to pass.[xviii]

For this purpose they made a great supper, to which they invited all the chief thanes; and, among the rest, with marks of particular respect, Banquo and his son Fleance were invited. The way by which Banquo was to pass to the palace at night was beset⑮ by murderers appointed by Macbeth, who stabbed Banquo; but in the scuffle⑯ Fleance escaped. * From that Fleance descended a race of monarchs⑰ who afterwards filled the Scottish throne, ending with James the Sixth of Scotland and the First of England, under whom the two crowns of England and Scotland were united.[xix]

At supper, the queen, whose manners were in the highest degree affable⑱ and royal, played

---

① conceal [kən'siːl] *v.* 隐瞒 hide, bury, cover, keep secret
② proof [pruːf] *n.* 证据 evidence, testimony, confirmation
③ smear [smɪə(r)] *v.* 涂抹,弄脏 smudge, soil, dirty, stain, sully, smirch
④ sufficiently [sə'fɪʃntli] *adv.* 足够地,充足地 adequately
⑤ suspicion [sə'spɪʃn] *n.* 嫌疑 doubt, distrust, scepticism
⑥ inducement [ɪn'djuːsmənt] *n.* 诱因 incentive, motive
⑦ forcible ['fɔːsəbl] *adj.* 有说服力的 convincing
⑧ vacate [və'keɪt] *v.* 空出 abandon, desert, quit, yield, relinquish
⑨ crown [kraʊn] *v.* 加冕
⑩ literally ['lɪtərəli] *adv.* 确实 exactly, precisely, to the letter
⑪ defile [dɪ'faɪl] *v.* 弄脏 dirty, soil, smear, taint, smirch
⑫ posterity [pɒ'sterəti] *n.* 后代 descendant, children, offspring
⑬ rankle ['ræŋkl] *v.* 使痛苦 annoy, embitter
⑭ make void 使无效
⑮ beset [bɪ'set] *adj.* 充满……的
⑯ scuffle ['skʌfl] *n.* 混战,扭打 fight, disturbance, fray, brawl, skirmish
⑰ monarch ['mɒnək] *n.* 帝王,君主 ruler, king, sovereign, emperor
⑱ affable ['æfəbl] *adj.* 和蔼可亲的 friendly, amiable, approachable

the hostess with a gracefulness① and attention which conciliated② every one present, and Macbeth discoursed③ freely with his thanes and nobles, saying, that * all that was honourable in the country was under his roof, if he had but his good friend Banquo present, whom yet he hoped he should rather have to chide④ for neglect, than to lament for any mischance⑤.[xx] Just at these words the ghost of Banquo, whom he had caused to be murdered, entered the room and placed himself on the chair which Macbeth was about to occupy. Though Macbeth was a bold man, and one that could have faced the devil without trembling, at this horrible sight his cheeks turned white with fear, and he stood quite unmanned⑥ with his eyes fixed upon the ghost. His queen and all the nobles, who saw nothing but perceived him gazing (as they thought) upon an empty chair, took it for a fit of distraction⑦; and she reproached him, whispering that it was but the same fancy which made him see the dagger in the air, when he was about to kill Duncan. * But Macbeth continued to see the ghost, and gave no heed⑧ to all they could say, while he addressed it with distracted⑨ words, yet so significant, that his queen, fearing the dreadful secret would be disclosed, in great haste dismissed the guests, excusing the infirmity⑩ of Macbeth as a disorder⑪ he was often troubled with.[xxi]

To such dreadful fancies Macbeth was subject⑫. His queen and he had their sleeps afflicted⑬ with terrible dreams, and * the blood of Banquo troubled them not more than the escape of Fleance, whom now they looked upon as father to a line of kings who should keep their posterity out of the throne.[xxii] With these miserable thoughts they found no peace, and Macbeth determined once more to seek out the weird sisters, and know from them the worst.

He sought them in a cave upon the heath, where they, who knew by foresight⑭ of his

① gracefulness [ˈgreɪsflnəs] n. 优雅 grace, elegance, refinement
② conciliate [kənˈsɪlieɪt] v. 安抚 pacify, soothe, calm
③ discourse [ˈdɪskɔːs] v. 交谈 confer, converse, communicate
④ chide [tʃaɪd] v. 斥责 scold, criticize, reproach
⑤ mischance [ˌmɪsˈtʃɑːns] n. 不幸 misfortune, ill luck
⑥ unmanned [ˌʌnˈmænd] adj. 失去男子气概的
⑦ distraction [dɪˈstrækʃn] n. 分心
⑧ heed [hiːd] n. 注意 attention, notice, observation
⑨ distracted [dɪˈstræktɪd] adj. 注意力分散的
⑩ infirmity [ɪnˈfɜːməti] n. 体弱,病弱 ailment, malady, ill health
⑪ disorder [dɪsˈɔːdə(r)] n. 疾病,紊乱 illness, sickness, disease, ailment, malady
⑫ subject [ˈsʌbdʒɪkt] adj. 受支配的 subordinate, submissive
⑬ afflict [əˈflɪkt] v. 折磨 torment, distress, oppress
⑭ foresight [ˈfɔːsaɪt] n. 预见,先见之明 forethought, far-sightedness

coming, were engaged in preparing their dreadful charms①, by which they conjured② up infernal③ spirits to reveal to them futurity④. * Their horrid⑤ ingredients⑥ were toads⑦, bats, and serpents, the eye of a newt⑧, and the tongue of a dog, the leg of a lizard⑨, and the wing of the night-owl, the scale⑩ of a dragon, the tooth of a wolf, the maw⑪ of the ravenous⑫ salt-sea shark, the mummy of a witch, the root of the poisonous hemlock⑬(this to have effect must be digged in the dark), the gall⑭ of a goat, and the liver of a Jew, with slips⑮ of the yew⑯ tree that roots itself in graves, and the finger of a dead child—all these were set on to boil in a great kettle, or cauldron⑰, which, as fast as it grew too hot, was cooled with a baboon's⑱ blood—to these they poured in the blood of a sow⑲ that had eaten her young, and they threw into the flame the grease⑳ that had sweaten from a murderer's gibbet㉑.[xxiii] By these charms they bound㉒ the infernal spirits to answer their questions.

It was demanded of Macbeth, whether he would have his doubts resolved by them, or by their masters, the spirits. He, nothing㉓ daunted㉔ by the dreadful ceremonies which he saw, boldly answered: "Where are they? Let me see them." And they called the spirits, which were three. * And the first arose in the likeness of an armed head, and he called Macbeth by name, and bid him beware of the thane of Fife; for which caution Macbeth thanked him; for Macbeth had

---

① charm [tʃɑːm] n. 魔法 spell, magic, sorcery, witchery
② conjure [ˈkʌndʒə(r)] v. 变魔术
③ infernal [ɪnˈfɜːnl] adj. 地狱的 hellish
④ futurity [fjuˈtjʊərəti] n. 将来 future, prospect
⑤ horrid [ˈhɒrɪd] adj. 可怕的 horrible, terrible, awful, dreadful
⑥ ingredient [ɪnˈgriːdiənt] n. 成分 component, constituent
⑦ toad [təʊd] n. 蟾蜍
⑧ newt [njuːt] n. 蝾螈
⑨ lizard [ˈlɪzəd] n. 蜥蜴
⑩ scale [skeɪl] n. 鳞片
⑪ maw [mɔː] n. 动物的胃
⑫ ravenous [ˈrævənəs] adj. 贪婪的 greedy, insatiable, avaricious
⑬ hemlock [ˈhemlɒk] n. 铁杉
⑭ gall [gɔːl] n. 胆汁
⑮ slip [slɪp] n. 嫩枝,小枝
⑯ yew [juː] n. 紫杉
⑰ cauldron [ˈkɔːldrən] n. 大锅
⑱ baboon [bəˈbuːn] n. 狒狒
⑲ sow [saʊ] n. 母猪
⑳ grease [griːs] n. 油脂 fat, lard, lubricant, oil, dripping, tallow
㉑ gibbet [ˈdʒɪbɪt] n. 绞刑架 gallows, scaffold
㉒ bind [baɪnd] v. (bound) 强迫 oblige, force, compel
㉓ nothing [ˈnʌθɪŋ] adv. 丝毫不,一点也不 not at all, by no means
㉔ daunt [dɔːnt] v. 使胆怯 alarm, frighten, scare, terrify

entertained① a jealousy of Macduff, the thane of Fife.[xxiv]

And the second spirit arose in the likeness of a bloody child, and * he called Macbeth by name, and bid him have no fear, but laugh to scorn the power of man, for none of woman born should have power to hurt him;[xxv] and he advised him to be bloody, bold, and resolute②. "* Then live, Macduff!" cried the king. "What need I fear of thee? But yet I will make assurance doubly sure. Thou shalt not live; that I may tell pale-hearted fear it lies, and sleep in spite of thunder.[xxvi]"

* That spirit being dismissed, a third arose in the form of a child crowned, with a tree in his hand.[xxvii] He called Macbeth by name, and comforted him against conspiracies③, saying, that * he should never be vanquished④, until the wood of Birnam to Dunsinane Hill should come against him.[xxviii] "Sweet bodements⑤! good!" cried Macbeth, "who can unfix⑥ the forest, and move it from its earth-bound roots? I see I shall live the usual period of man's life, and not be cut off by a violent death. But my heart throbs⑦ to know one thing. Tell me, if your art can tell so much, if Banquo's issue⑧ shall ever reign in this kingdom?" Here the cauldron sank into the ground, and a noise of music was heard, and eight shadows, like kings, passed by Macbeth, and Banquo last, who bore a glass which showed the figures of many more, and Banquo all bloody smiled upon Macbeth, and pointed to them; by which Macbeth knew that these were the posterity of Banquo, who should reign after him in Scotland; and the witches, with a sound of soft music, and with dancing, making a show of duty⑨ and welcome to Macbeth, vanished. And from this time the thoughts of Macbeth were all bloody and dreadful.

The first thing he heard when he got out of the witches' cave, was that Macduff, thane of Fife, had fled to England, to join the army which was forming against him under Malcolm, the eldest son of the late king, with intent to displace⑩ Macbeth, and set Malcolm, the rightful heir, upon the throne. Macbeth, stung⑪ with rage, set upon⑫ the castle of Macduff, and put his wife and children, whom the thane had left behind, to the sword, and extended the slaughter⑬ to all who claimed the least relationship to Macduff.

These and suchlike deeds alienated⑭ the minds of all his chief nobility from him. * Such as could, fled to join with Malcolm and Macduff, who were now approaching with a powerful army, which they had raised in England; and the rest secretly wished success to their arms, though for

---

① entertain [ˌentəˈteɪn] *v.* 心存,怀有 harbor, conceive of
② resolute [ˈrezəluːt] *adj.* 坚决的 determined, firm, persevering
③ conspiracy [kənˈspɪrəsi] *n.* 阴谋 plot, scheme, intrigue
④ vanquish [ˈvæŋkwɪʃ] *v.* 征服,击败 defeat, conquer, triumph over
⑤ bodement [ˈbəʊdmənt] *n.* 预兆 omen, presage, foretoken
⑥ unfix [ʌnˈfɪks] *v.* 解开 untie, unloose, release
⑦ throb [θrɒb] *v.* 搏动 pulsate, pound, beat, thump
⑧ issue [ˈɪʃuː] *n.* 后嗣,子女 children, offspring, descendant
⑨ duty [ˈdjuːti] *n.* 敬意 respect, honour, esteem, recognition
⑩ displace [dɪsˈpleɪs] *v.* 驱逐 expel, unsettle, force out
⑪ sting [stɪŋ] *v.* (stung) 激怒 anger, provoke, incense, inflame
⑫ set upon 袭击 attack, assail, assault, beat up, lay into
⑬ slaughter [ˈslɔːtə(r)] *n.* 杀戮 killing, murder, massacre, bloodshed
⑭ alienate [ˈeɪliəneɪt] *v.* 使疏远 estrange, disaffect

fear of Macbeth they could take no active part.[xxix] His recruits① went on slowly. Everybody hated the tyrant②; nobody loved or honoured him; but all suspected him, and * he began to envy the condition of Duncan, whom he had murdered, who slept soundly in his grave, against whom treason had done its worst—steel nor poison, domestic malice③ nor foreign levies④, could hurt him any longer.[xxx]

* While these things were acting, the queen, who had been the sole partner in his wickedness, in whose bosom⑤ he could sometimes seek a momentary⑥ repose⑦ from those terrible dreams which afflicted them both nightly, died, it is supposed, by her own hands, unable to bear the remorse of guilt, and public hate; by which event he was left alone, without a soul to love or care for him, or a friend to whom he could confide his wicked purposes.[xxxi]

He grew careless of life, and wished for death; but the near approach of Malcolm's army roused⑧ in him what remained of his ancient courage, and he determined to die (as he expressed it) "with armour⑨ on his back". Besides this, the hollow⑩ promises of the witches had filled him with a false confidence, and he remembered the sayings of the spirits, that none of woman born was to hurt him, and that he was never to be vanquished till Birnam wood should come to Dunsinane, which he thought could never be. * So he shut himself up in his castle, whose impregnable⑪ strength was such as defied a siege⑫[xxxii]—here he sullenly waited the approach of Malcolm. When, upon a day, there came a messenger to him, pale and shaking with fear, almost unable to report that which he had seen; for he averred⑬, that as he stood upon his watch on the hill, he looked towards Birnam, and to his thinking the wood began to move! "Liar and slave!" cried Macbeth, "* if thou speakest false, thou shalt hang alive upon the next tree, till famine⑭ end thee. If thy tale be true, I care not if thou dost as much by me[xxxiii]"—for Macbeth now began to faint in resolution, and to doubt the equivocal⑮ speeches of the spirits. He was not to fear till Birnam wood should come to Dunsinane; and now a wood did move! "However," said he, "if this

---

① recruit [rɪ'kruːt] *n*. 新兵
② tyrant ['taɪrənt] *n*. 暴君 dictator, oppressor, despot, autocrat
③ malice ['mælɪs] *n*. 恶意 spite, animosity, enmity, hate, ill will
④ levy ['levi] *n*. 征兵
⑤ bosom ['bʊzəm] *n*. 怀抱 breast, chest
⑥ momentary ['məʊməntri] *adj*. 短暂的 brief, temporary, transitory
⑦ repose [rɪ'pəʊz] *n*. 安宁 peace, quiet, ease, tranquility
⑧ rouse [raʊz] *v*. 唤醒 wake up, awaken, arouse
⑨ armour ['ɑːmə(r)] *n*. 甲胄 shield
⑩ hollow ['hɒləʊ] *adj*. 虚伪的 false, insincere, hollow-hearted
⑪ impregnable [ɪm'pregnəbl] *adj*. 坚不可摧的 indestructible
⑫ siege [siːdʒ] *n*. 围攻 blockade, closure, besiegement
⑬ aver [ə'vɜː(r)] *v*. 断言 state, maintain, declare, affirm, assert
⑭ famine ['fæmɪn] *n*. 饥饿 hunger, starvation
⑮ equivocal [ɪ'kwɪvəkl] *adj*. 模棱两可的 ambiguous, uncertain

which he avouches① be true, let us arm② and out. *There is no flying hence③, nor staying here.[xxxiv] I begin to be weary of the sun, and wish my life at an end." With these desperate speeches he sallied forth upon the besiegers④, who had now come up to the castle.

The strange appearance which had given the messenger an idea of a wood moving is easily solved. *When the besieging army marched through the wood of Birnam, Malcolm, like a skilful general, instructed⑤ his soldiers to hew⑥ down every one a bough and bear it before him, by way of concealing the true numbers of his host.[xxxv] This marching of the soldiers with boughs had at a distance the appearance which had frightened the messenger. Thus were the words of the spirit brought to pass, in a sense different from that in which Macbeth had understood them, and one great hold⑦ of his confidence was gone.

And now a severe skirmishing⑧ took place, in which Macbeth, though feebly⑨ supported by those who called themselves his friends, but in reality hated the tyrant and inclined to the party of Malcolm and Macduff, yet fought with the extreme of rage and valour, cutting to pieces all who were opposed to him, till he came to where Macduff was fighting. *Seeing Macduff, and remembering the caution of the spirit who had counselled him to avoid Macduff, above all men, he would have turned, but Macduff, who had been seeking him through the whole fight, opposed his turning, and a fierce contest ensued;[xxxvi] Macduff giving him many foul reproaches for the murder of his wife and children. *Macbeth, whose soul was charged⑩ enough with blood of that family already, would still have declined the combat⑪; but Macduff still urged him to it, calling him tyrant, murderer, hell-hound⑫, and villain⑬.[xxxvii]

Then Macbeth remembered the words of the spirit, how none of woman born should hurt him; and smiling confidently he said to Macduff: "*Thou losest thy labour, Macduff. As easily thou mayest impress⑭ the air with thy sword, as make me vulnerable⑮. I bear a charmed⑯ life, which must not yield to one of woman born.[xxxviii]"

"Despair⑰ thy charm," said Macduff, "and let that lying spirit whom thou hast served, tell thee, that *Macduff was never born of woman, never as the ordinary manner of men is to be born, but was untimely⑱ taken from his mother.[xxxix]"

---

① avouch [ə'vaʊtʃ] *v*. 断言 state, claim, maintain, declare, assert
② arm [ɑːm] *v*. 武装 equip, take up arms, prepare for war
③ hence [hens] *adv*. 〈古〉从这儿 from here, from this place
④ besieger [bɪ'siːdʒə(r)] *n*. 围攻者
⑤ instruct [ɪn'strʌkt] *v*. 命令 order, direct, command, bid, enjoin
⑥ hew [hjuː] *v*. 砍 cut, chop, hack, lop, cleave, fell
⑦ hold [həʊld] *n*. 支撑 foothold, footing, anchorage
⑧ skirmish ['skɜːmɪʃ] *v*. 冲突 fight, clash, collide
⑨ feebly ['fiːbli] *adv*. 无力地 weakly
⑩ charge [tʃɑːdʒ] *v*. 装载 fill, load, suffuse, stuff, make full
⑪ combat ['kɒmbæt] *n*. 战斗 fight, battle, conflict, warfare
⑫ hell-hound ['helhaʊnd] *n*. 地狱之犬;恶鬼
⑬ villain ['vɪlən] *n*. 恶棍,反派 evildoer, criminal, rogue, bad egg
⑭ impress [ɪm'pres] *v*. 压,压印
⑮ vulnerable ['vʌlnərəbl] *adj*. 易受伤害的 defenceless, open to attack
⑯ charmed [tʃɑːmd] *adj*. 被施魔法的 spellbound, enchanted
⑰ despair [dɪ'speə(r)] *v*. 绝望,丧失信心 lose hope/heart
⑱ untimely [ʌn'taɪmli] *adv*. 过早地,不合时宜地 prematurely, before time

"Accursed① be the tongue which tells me so," said the trembling Macbeth, who felt his last hold of confidence give way—"and * let never man in future believe the lying equivocations② of witches and juggling③ spirits, who deceive us in words which have double senses, and while they keep their promise literally, disappoint our hopes with a different meaning.[xl] I will not fight with thee."

"Then live!" said the scornful Macduff. "We will have a show of thee, as men show monsters, and a painted board, on which shall be written: 'Here men may see the tyrant!'"

"Never," said Macbeth, whose courage returned with despair; "* I will not live to kiss the ground before young Malcolm's feet, and to be baited④ with the curses of the rabble⑤.[xlii] * Though Birnam wood be come to Dunsinane, and thou opposed to me, who wast never born of woman, yet will I try the last.[xliii]" With these frantic words he threw himself upon Macduff, who, after a severe struggle, in the end overcame him, and cutting off his head, made a present of it to the young and lawful king, Malcolm; who took upon him the government which, by the machinations⑥ of the usurper, he had so long been deprived⑦ of, and ascended the throne of Duncan the Meek, amid⑧ the acclamations⑨ of the nobles and the people.

---

① accursed [ə'kɜːsɪd] *adj*. 被诅咒的 cursed, damned, ill-fated

② equivocation [ɪˌkwɪvə'keɪʃn] *n*. 含糊其辞 ambiguity

③ juggle ['dʒʌgl] *v*. 欺骗,歪曲 fool, trick, cheat, deceive, mislead

④ bait [beɪt] *v*. 逗弄 tease, provoke, annoy, irritate, mock, taunt

⑤ rabble ['ræbl] *n*. 乌合之众 mob

⑥ machination [ˌmæʃɪ'neɪʃn] *n*. 阴谋 plot, trick, scheme

⑦ deprive [dɪ'praɪv] *v*. 剥夺 rob, strip, divest, dispossess

⑧ amid [ə'mɪd] *prep*. 在……当中 among, in the middle/midst of

⑨ acclamation [ˌæklə'meɪʃn] *n*. 欢呼 applause, cheering

i All hail! King that shalt be hereafter! 万岁，未来的国王！（shalt：shall 的旧式用法，用于第二人称单数）

ii Lesser than Macbeth and greater! not so happy, but much happier!（班柯）将比麦克白低微，可是又比麦克白伟大！没有麦克白那样幸运，可是又比麦克白有福气得多！（happy＝fortunate）

iii That hope, might enkindle you to aim at the throne; but oftentimes these ministers of darkness tell us truths in little things, to betray us into deeds of greatest consequence. 那样的希望，可能会使你贪图王位；但这些幽冥的使者时常在小事上给我们透露一点点实情，结果却害得我们去做有严重后果的事情。（darkness：喻指地狱）

iv She was a bad, ambitious woman, and so as her husband and herself could arrive at greatness, she cared not much by what means. 她是个野心勃勃的坏女人，只要能使她的丈夫和她自己成为大人物，她可以不择手段。（so as＝so/as long as：只要）

v She spurred on the reluctant purpose of Macbeth, who felt compunction at the thoughts of blood, and did not cease to represent the murder of the king as a step absolutely necessary to the fulfilment of the flattering prophecy. 麦克白的意志还有些动摇，想到流血，他总感到良心不安；然而他的妻子竭力怂恿他，不断地告诉他要想实现那个恭维他的预言，就必须把国王杀死。

vi It happened at this time that the king, who out of his royal condescension would oftentimes visit his principal nobility upon gracious terms, came to Macbeth's house, attended by his two sons, Malcolm and Donalbain, and a numerous train of thanes and attendants, the more to honour Macbeth for the triumphal success of his wars. 国王时常屈尊到显要的贵族家中拜访，亲切地问候他们。刚好这时候，他在他两个儿子马尔康和道纳本的陪伴下，来到了麦克白家里。为表彰麦克白在战场上立下的赫赫战功，国王还带上了许多爵士和随从。

vii The castle of Macbeth was pleasantly situated, and the air about it was sweet and wholesome, which appeared by the nests which the martlet, or swallow, had built under all the jutting friezes and buttresses of the building, wherever it found a place of advantage; for where those birds most breed and haunt, the air is observed to be delicate. 麦克白住的城堡位置很好，周围的空气十分清新。因此在城堡的飞檐和扶壁上，只要是可以搭窝的地方，燕子都搭起窝来了。只要是燕子喜欢繁殖和常来常往的地方，那里的空气总是好的。（appeared＝was made clear；wherever...：让步状语从句；advantage＝convenience；where...：地点状语从句）

viii Now was the middle of night, when over half the world nature seems dead, and wicked dreams abuse men's minds asleep, and none but the wolf and the murderer is abroad. 这时候已经是半夜，大半个世界似乎都了无生气，噩梦趁着人们入睡扰乱着人们的心灵，只有狼和凶手还待在外面。

ix She would not have undertaken a deed so abhorrent to her sex, but that she feared her husband's nature, that it was too full of the milk of human kindness, to do a contrived murder. 她本不愿意去做这样一件对女人来说很可怕的行凶之事，但是她又怕她丈夫的心肠太软了，担心他不肯按照预先计划好的下手。（would not have undertaken...：与过去事实相反的虚拟语气；but that...：要不是……）

x She knew him to be ambitious, but withal to be scrupulous, and not yet prepared for that height of crime which commonly in the end accompanies inordinate ambition. 她知道他有野心，可是也知道他为人正直，杀人那样的恶事是要野心发展到了极点的时候才干得出的，麦克白还没有做好准备。（withal＝as well；inordinate＝unregulated，unbounded）

xi Then he considered how just and merciful a king this Duncan had been，how clear of offence to his subjects，how loving to his nobility，and in particular to him；that such kings are the peculiar care of Heaven，and their subjects doubly bound to revenge their deaths. 然后他又想到邓肯是个多么公正、慈祥的国王，从来没有欺负过老百姓，对贵族，尤其是对他自己，又是那么爱惜。上天对这样的国王一定会加以特别的保护，如果这样的国王被害死了，老百姓也要加倍替他报仇的。

xii But she being a woman not easily shaken from her evil purpose，began to pour in at his ears words which infused a portion of her own spirit into his mind，assigning reason upon reason why he should not shrink from what he had undertaken；how easy the deed was；how soon it would be over；and how the action of one short night would give to all their nights and days to come sovereign sway and royalty！可是她是一个定下奸计就不肯轻易罢手的女人，她开始在他耳边絮絮叨叨地讲着，把她自己的一部分精神灌注到他的心灵里，举出一条条的理由来说服他：既然答应去行凶，就不应该半路又退缩下来；这件事办起来很方便，很快就可以干完；短短一个晚上的行动就可以让他们在今后的日子里稳坐王位、掌握大权！

xiii She had given suck，and knew how tender it was to love the babe that milked her；but she would，while it was smiling in her face，have plucked it from her breast，and dashed its brains out，if she had so sworn to do it，as he had sworn to perform that murder. 她曾经给娃娃喂过奶，她懂得怎样温柔地去爱吃奶的娃娃。然而，她可以在娃娃正对着她微笑的时候把他从怀里揪开，摔出他的脑浆来，只要她曾经起过誓要那样做，正像麦克白已经起誓去行凶一样。（...would，...have plucked...，if...had...sworn...：与过去事实相反的虚拟语气）

xiv When he tried to grasp at it，it was nothing but air，a mere phantasm proceeding from his own hot and oppressed brain and the business he had in hand. 可是他伸手一抓，却什么也没有抓到，那只不过是他狂热、紧绷的大脑和当前他正要干的勾当使他产生的幻觉。（hot and oppressed brain：在莎士比亚《麦克白》原剧中为 heat-oppressed brain，意即"狂热的头脑"）

xv Macbeth，who stood listening to them，tried to say "Amen" when the fellow said "God bless us！" but，though he had most need of a blessing，the word stuck in his throat，and he could not pronounce it. 麦克白站在那里听着他们说话，当侍从说"上帝祝福我们！"的时候，他很想说"阿门"。虽然他非常需要祝福，但是这两个字却堵在了他的嗓子眼儿里，就是说不出来。

xvi He came in so distracted a state，that she reproached him with his want of firmness，and sent him to wash his hands of the blood which stained them，while she took his dagger，with purpose to stain the cheeks of the grooms with blood，to make it seem their guilt. 麦克白走进来时心神不宁，他的妻子责备他不够坚决，叫他去洗洗那染了血迹的手，然后她拿起他的匕首，去把血涂在侍从的脸上，好让人看起来觉得是他们行的凶。

xvii Though Macbeth and his lady made great show of grief，and the proofs against the grooms（the dagger being produced against them and their faces smeared with blood）were sufficiently strong，yet the entire suspicion fell upon Macbeth，whose inducements to such a deed were so much more forcible than such poor silly grooms could be supposed to have. 尽管麦克白和他的妻子装出十分悲恸的样子，并且两个侍从行凶的证据也很充分（匕首是从他们

身上搜出来的，他们脸上又涂满了血），然而大家的怀疑却集中在麦克白身上。因为比起这两个可怜而且愚蠢的侍从，麦克白干这件事会更加有利可图。（silly = simple-minded, innocent）

xviii The thought of this, and that they had defiled their hands with blood, and done so great crimes, only to place the posterity of Banquo upon the throne, so rankled within them, that they determined to put to death both Banquo and his son, to make void the predictions of the weird sisters, which in their own case had been so remarkably brought to pass. 想到这一点，又想到他们双手沾满血迹，犯下滔天大罪，却只不过是把班柯的子孙捧上王位，他们觉得十分不甘心。于是他们下定决心要把班柯和他的儿子一起杀死，好让女巫的预言无法完全实现，尽管关于麦克白自己那部分的预言已精神奇地应验了。（only to...：表示意料之外的结果）

xix From that Fleance descended a race of monarchs who afterwards filled the Scottish throne, ending with James the Sixth of Scotland and the First of England, under whom the two crowns of England and Scotland were united. 这个弗里恩斯的后代接连做了苏格兰的国王，一直延续到苏格兰的詹姆斯六世兼英国的詹姆斯一世。在詹姆斯的统治下，英国和苏格兰才合并起来。（詹姆斯六世为苏格兰国王，1567 年起统治苏格兰，1603 年又成为英国斯图亚特王朝第一代国王，加冕为英国的詹姆斯一世；其为班柯的后代是莎士比亚杜撰的）

xx All that was honourable in the country was under his roof, if he had but his good friend Banquo present, whom yet he hoped he should rather have to chide for neglect, than to lament for any mischance. 假如他的好朋友班柯在座，那么本国所有的贤士都聚在一堂了；他宁愿班柯是因为疏忽才没来，那只管责备他一顿就好，也不愿意班柯是遭到不幸而去哀悼他。（all that...：定语从句，相当于 what 引导的名词性从句；rather...than...：宁可……也不愿意……）

xxi But Macbeth continued to see the ghost, and gave no heed to all they could say, while he addressed it with distracted words, yet so significant, that his queen, fearing the dreadful secret would be disclosed, in great haste dismissed the guests, excusing the infirmity of Macbeth as a disorder he was often troubled with. 但是麦克白仍然能看到鬼魂，对于旁人说的话完全不理会，只跟鬼魂说着胡话。他虽然语无伦次，说的话却是意味深长，王后担心他这么一来会把那可怕的秘密泄露出来，就托词说麦克白犯了老毛病，赶紧把客人们打发走了。

xxii The blood of Banquo troubled them not more than the escape of Fleance, whom now they looked upon as father to a line of kings who should keep their posterity out of the throne. 弗里恩斯的逃跑给他们造成的威胁跟班柯的死一样严重，麦克白认为将来一定是这个弗里恩斯的子子孙孙做国王，他会让麦克白的子子孙孙永远做不了国王。

xxiii Their horrid ingredients were toads, bats, and serpents, the eye of a newt, and the tongue of a dog, the leg of a lizard, and the wing of the night-owl, the scale of a dragon, the tooth of a wolf, the maw of the ravenous salt-sea shark, the mummy of a witch, the root of the poisonous hemlock (this to have effect must be digged in the dark), the gall of a goat, and the liver of a Jew, with slips of the yew tree that roots itself in graves, and the finger of a dead child—all these were set on to boil in a great kettle, or cauldron, which, as fast as it grew too hot, was cooled with a baboon's blood—to these they poured in the blood of a sow that had eaten her young, and they threw into the flame the grease that had sweaten from a murderer's gibbet. 那符咒是由骇人的材料做成的，有癞蛤蟆、蝙蝠和蛇，有蝾螈的眼睛、狗的舌头、蜥蜴的腿、猫头鹰的翅膀、龙鳞、狼牙、盐海里贪婪的鲨鱼的胃、女巫的木乃伊、毒草根（必须在黑夜挖出来才有效）、山羊胆、犹太人的肝、长在坟墓上的紫杉枝和死孩子的手指头。她们把这些东西通通放到一口大锅里去熬，等到要开锅的时候就立刻浇上狒狒的血，叫它凉下去。然后再浇上吃过自己猪崽子的母猪的血，并且把杀人犯在绞刑架上流的油脂投到火里去。

xxiv And the first arose in the likeness of an armed head, and he called Macbeth by name, and bid him beware of the thane of Fife; for which caution Macbeth thanked him; for Macbeth had entertained a jealousy of Macduff, the thane of Fife. 第一个鬼魂看上去像是一个戴着头盔的脑袋。它叫着麦克白的名字，吩咐他要当心费辅爵士。麦克白听到这个忠告后就向它道了谢，因为麦克白一直嫉妒着费辅爵士麦克德夫。（“戴着头盔的脑袋”象征麦克白，他的头后来被麦克德夫砍下）

xxv He called Macbeth by name, and bid him have no fear, but laugh to scorn the power of man, for none of woman born should have power to hurt him. 它叫着麦克白的名字，吩咐他不必害怕，他大可不必把凡人的力量放在眼里，因为凡是女人生出来的都不能伤害他。

xxvi Then live, Macduff! What need I fear of thee? But yet I will make assurance doubly sure. Thou shalt not live; that I may tell pale-hearted fear it lies, and sleep in spite of thunder. 那么你就活着吧，麦克德夫！我何必怕你呢？然而我要做到万无一失，我还是要你死，那样我就可以不再提心吊胆了，就是打雷我也能安心睡觉。（make assurance doubly sure：确保万无一失；thou shalt＝you shall；that I may tell pale-hearted fear it lies：这样我可以说那胆怯的恐惧是谎言）

xxvii That spirit being dismissed, a third arose in the form of a child crowned, with a tree in his hand. 把这个鬼魂打发走以后，第三个又出现了。这个鬼魂是个戴了王冠的孩子，手里拿着树枝。（“戴王冠的孩子”象征马尔康；“手里拿着树枝”预示下文勃南的树林中的情节）

xxviii He should never be vanquished, until the wood of Birnam to Dunsinane Hill should come against him. 他永远不会被人打败，除非勃南的树林会冲着他向邓西嫩山移动。

xxix Such as could, fled to join with Malcolm and Macduff, who were now approaching with a powerful army, which they had raised in England; and the rest secretly wished success to their arms, though for fear of Macbeth they could take no active part. 马尔康和麦克德夫已经在英格兰组成一支强大的军队，现在正向这边逼来。凡是能逃到他们那里的人都逃去了，留下的人怕麦克白，不敢积极去参加，但也都在暗地里希望他们打胜仗。

xxx He began to envy the condition of Duncan, whom he had murdered, who slept soundly in his grave, against whom treason had done its worst—steel nor poison, domestic malice nor foreign levies, could hurt him any longer. 他开始羡慕起被他害死的邓肯：邓肯虽然遭到了叛逆者最毒辣的暗算，可是他现在却好好地睡在坟墓里；武器和毒药，国内的阴谋和国外的征兵都再也不能伤害到他了。（...nor...＝neither...nor...）

xxxi While these things were acting, the queen, who had been the sole partner in his wickedness, in whose bosom he could sometimes seek a momentary repose from those terrible dreams which afflicted them both nightly, died, it is supposed, by her own hands, unable to bear the remorse of guilt, and public hate; by which event he was left alone, without a soul to love or care for him, or a friend to whom he could confide his wicked purposes. 麦克白干这些坏事的时候，他唯一的同谋是王后。有时，在她的怀里，他可以从那些每晚折磨他们的噩梦中得到片刻的安宁。正当前边讲的那些事情发生的时候，王后死了。她大概是因为受不了良心的责备和民众的仇恨，自己寻死的。这样一来，麦克白就剩下孤身一人了，没有一个爱他、关怀他的人，也没有一个可以跟他谈谈他那些坏主意的知心朋友。（who...in whose...which...：多重定语从句的嵌套）

xxxii So he shut himself up in his castle, whose impregnable strength was such as defied a siege. 因此他把自己关在他的城堡里，那城堡牢不可破，经得起围攻。

xxxiii If thou speakest false, thou shalt hang alive upon the next tree, till famine end thee. If thy tale be true, I care not if thou dost as much by me. 如果你说的是假的，我要把你吊在旁边的那棵树上，叫你活活饿死；假如你说的是真的，你大可以也这样对我（把我吊死）。（thou speakest＝you speak；thou shalt＝you shall；next＝nearest；thee＝you；thy＝your；thou dost＝you do）

xxxiv There is no flying hence, nor staying here. 从这里逃不出去，待在这里等死也不是办法。（there is no doing...：无法……，不可能……）

xxxv When the besieging army marched through the wood of Birnam, Malcolm, like a skilful general, instructed his soldiers to hew down every one a bough and bear it before him, by way of concealing the true numbers of his host. 当包围军经过勃南的树林时，马尔康作为一个精于战术的将军，命令他的士兵每人砍一根树枝捧在面前，这样可以掩盖军队的实际人数。（by way of＝thereby, by that：由此，从而；host＝army）

xxxvi Seeing Macduff, and remembering the caution of the spirit who had counselled him to avoid Macduff, above all men, he would have turned, but Macduff, who had been seeking him through the whole fight, opposed his turning, and a fierce contest ensued. 望到麦克德夫，他记起鬼魂警告过他，在所有人当中，头一个要躲避的就是麦克德夫。麦克白很想掉头离开，可是麦克德夫在整场战斗中一直在找他，拦住了他的去路。于是，一场激烈的战斗就开始了。

xxxvii Macbeth, whose soul was charged enough with blood of that family already, would still have declined the combat; but Macduff still urged him to it, calling him tyrant, murderer, hell-hound, and villain. 麦克白的灵魂已经欠了那家人太多的血债，他本不想应战；可是麦克德夫骂他是暴君、凶手、恶魔和坏蛋，仍逼着他来交手。

xxxviii Thou losest thy labour, Macduff. As easily thou mayest impress the air with thy sword, as make me vulnerable. I bear a charmed life, which must not yield to one of woman born. 你白费力气，麦克德夫。你要是能够伤害我，你大概也能用宝剑在空中划出痕迹了。我有魔法护身，凡是女人生出来的，都伤不了我。（thou losest＝you lose；thou mayest＝you may；thy＝your）

xxxix Macduff was never born of woman, never as the ordinary manner of men is to be born, but was untimely taken from his mother. 麦克德夫不是女人生出来的，他不是跟平常人一样生出来的，他是不够月份就从他母亲肚子里取出来的。

xl Let never man in future believe the lying equivocations of witches and juggling spirits, who deceive us in words which have double senses, and while they keep their promise literally, disappoint our hopes with a different meaning. 愿人们以后再也不要相信那些巫婆和骗人的鬼魂所说的模棱两可的谎话，它们用双关的话来欺骗我们，尽管照字面上看句句都应验了，

然而跟我们所希望的却恰恰相反。

xli I will not live to kiss the ground before young Malcolm's feet, and to be baited with the curses of the rabble. 我不愿意为了苟活而低头去吻马尔康那小子脚下的泥土，挨贱民的咒骂。

xlii Though Birnam wood be come to Dunsinane, and thou opposed to me, who wast never born of woman, yet will I try the last. 尽管勃南的树林已经来到邓西嫩山上了，尽管不是女人生出来的你反抗我，我也还是要干到底。

奥瑟罗
Othello

'Tis yet to know—	世人还没有知道——
Which, when I know that boasting is an honor,	要是夸口是一件荣耀的事，
I shall promulgate. I fetch my life and being	我就要到处宣布——
From men of royal siege, and my demerits	我是高贵的祖先的后裔，
May speak unbonneted to as proud a fortune	我有充分的资格，
As this that I have reached.	享受我目前所得到的值得骄傲的幸运。

正是这个诗人，他无可比拟地把人的心底隐事和盘托出，震动了我们的心灵，他清楚的理智又掌握了全部奇异复杂的人生。

——弗里德里希·施莱格尔

我总有这样的感觉：我从来不曾读到过有哪一段文字，能像《奥瑟罗》最后一段伟大的说白那样，可怕地暴露了人类的弱点——人类的普遍的弱点。

——T. S. 艾略特

奥瑟罗有着敏捷而有力的想象力。这种天赋对于一个富于行动的人来说，要么成就其伟大，要么便造成灾难。

——哈利·格兰维尔-巴克

奥瑟罗从威尼斯转到塞浦路斯，从对苔丝狄蒙娜绝对的爱转到熄灭她生命的灯，再到杀死他自己，这便是莎士比亚为悲剧的人所写的话。

——阿尔文·克南

圈套给盲目出主意，热衷黑暗者给那黑人引路，欺骗负责给黑暗提供光明，虚情假意为猜忌当上了导盲犬……黑人奥瑟罗与叛徒伊阿古……互相对立。还有什么能比这更有力的呢？黑暗的暴行一致行动起来。这两个人是散布黑暗的化身，一个咆哮如雷，一个冷言冷语，合谋让光明悲惨地窒息而死。

——维克多·雨果

主要人物

Othello　奥瑟罗　摩尔族贵裔，供职威尼斯政府
Brabantio　勃拉班修　元老
Desdemona　苔丝狄蒙娜　勃拉班修之女
Cassio　凯西奥　奥瑟罗的副将
Iago　伊阿古　奥瑟罗的旗官
Emilia　爱米利娅　伊阿古之妻
Roderigo　罗德利哥　威尼斯绅士

地点　威尼斯；塞浦路斯岛

Othello

Brabantio, the rich senator① of Venice, had a fair daughter, the gentle Desdemona. She was sought to by divers② suitors, both on account of her many virtuous qualities, and for her rich expectations. But among the suitors of her own clime③ and complexion④, she saw none whom she could affect⑤: for * this noble lady, who regarded⑥ the mind more than the features of men, with a singularity⑦ rather to be admired than imitated⑧, had chosen for the object of her affections, a Moor⑨, a black, whom her father loved, and often invited to his house.[i]

Neither is Desdemona to be altogether condemned for the unsuitableness of the person whom she selected for her lover. Bating⑩ that Othello was black, the noble Moor wanted nothing which might recommend him to the affections of the greatest lady. * He was a soldier, and a brave one; and by his conduct in bloody wars against the Turks⑪, had risen to the rank of general in the Venetian⑫ service, and was esteemed and trusted by the state.[ii]

He had been a traveller, and * Desdemona (as is the manner of ladies) loved to hear him tell the story of his adventures, which he would run through from his earliest recollection⑬; the battles, sieges, and encounters⑭, which he had passed through; the perils he had been exposed to by land and by water; his hair-breadth escapes⑮, when he had entered a breach⑯, or marched up

---

① senator [ˈsenətə] *n*. 参议员 lawmaker
② divers [ˈdaɪvəz] *adj*. 各种各样的 diverse, diversified, various
③ clime [klaɪm] *n*. 气候 climate, weather
④ complexion [kəmˈplekʃn] *n*. 肤色 skin tone, hue
⑤ affect [əˈfekt] *v*. 喜欢 like, love, adore, delight, be fond of
⑥ regard [rɪˈgɑːd] *v*. 看重 consider, value, account, esteem
⑦ singularity [ˌsɪŋgjuˈlærəti] *n*. 奇特 oddity, peculiarity
⑧ imitate [ˈɪmɪteɪt] *v*. 模仿 copy
⑨ Moor [mɔː(r)] *n*. 摩尔人
⑩ bating [ˈbeɪtɪŋ] *prep*. 除……之外 except, apart/aside from
⑪ Turk [tɜːk] *n*. 土耳其人
⑫ Venetian [vəˈniːʃn] *adj*. 威尼斯的
⑬ recollection [ˌrekəˈlekʃn] *n*. 回忆 recall, memory
⑭ encounter [ɪnˈkaʊntə(r)] *n*. 冲突,交锋 battle, fight, conflict, combat
⑮ hair-breadth escape 死里逃生 narrow escape
⑯ breach [briːtʃ] *n*. 突破口 opening

to the mouth of a cannon①;[iii] and * how he had been taken prisoner by the insolent② enemy, and sold to slavery; how he demeaned③ himself in that state, and how he escaped—all these accounts, added to the narration④ of the strange things he had seen in foreign countries; the vast wilderness⑤ and romantic caverns⑥, the quarries⑦, the rocks and mountains, whose heads are in the clouds; of the savage⑧ nations, the cannibals⑨ who are man-eaters, and a race of people in Africa whose heads do grow beneath their shoulders[iv] — * these travellers' stories would so enchain⑩ the attention of Desdemona, that if she were called off at any time by household affairs, she would despatch⑪ with all haste that business, and return, and with a greedy ear devour⑫ Othello's discourse⑬.[v] And * once he took advantage of a pliant⑭ hour, and drew from her a prayer⑮, that he would tell her the whole story of his life at large, of which she had heard so much, but only by parts—to which he consented, and beguiled⑯ her of many a tear, when he spoke of some distressful⑰ stroke⑱ which his youth had suffered.[vi]

* His story being done, she gave him for his pains a world of sighs—she swore a pretty oath, that it was all passing⑲ strange, and pitiful, wondrous⑳ pitiful—she wished (she said) she had not heard it, yet she wished that heaven had made her such a man;[vii] and then she thanked him, and told him, * if he had a friend who loved her, he had only to teach him how to tell his story, and that would woo her.[viii] * Upon this hint, delivered not with more frankness than modesty, accompanied with certain bewitching㉑ prettiness, and blushes, which Othello could not but understand, he spoke more openly of his love, and in this golden opportunity gained the consent of the generous lady Desdemona privately to marry him.[ix]

Neither Othello's colour nor his fortune were such that it could be hoped Brabantio would accept him for a son-in-law. He had left his daughter free; but he did expect that, as the manner of noble Venetian ladies was, she would choose ere long㉒ a husband of senatorial㉓ rank or

---

① cannon ['kænən] *n*. 大炮 artillery
② insolent ['ɪnsələnt] *adj*. 无礼的 rude, cheeky, insulting
③ demean [dɪ'mi:n] *v*. 降低身份
④ narration [nə'reɪʃn] *n*. 讲述 relation, description, account
⑤ wilderness ['wɪldənəs] *n*. 荒野 desert, wasteland
⑥ cavern ['kævən] *n*. 洞穴 cave, hollow, grotto, pothole
⑦ quarry ['kwɒri] *n*. 采石场 stone pit
⑧ savage ['sævɪdʒ] *adj*. 野蛮的 wild, beastly, barbarous
⑨ cannibal ['kænɪbl] *n*. 食人肉者 man-eater, anthropophagus
⑩ enchain [ɪn'tʃeɪn] *v*. 吸引住,束缚 bind, capture, enslave, hold fast
⑪ despatch [dɪ'spætʃ] *v*. 迅速处理
⑫ devour [dɪ'vaʊə(r)] *v*. 吞食;热切地看、听、读
⑬ discourse ['dɪskɔ:s] *n*. 话语 talk, speech, conversation
⑭ pliant ['plaɪənt] *adj*. 易受影响的 impressionable, susceptible
⑮ prayer [preə(r)] *n*. 恳求 plea, appeal, request, entreaty
⑯ beguile [bɪ'gaɪl] *v*. 骗取 fool, trick, cheat, deceive, take in
⑰ distressful [dɪ'stresfl] *adj*. 苦恼的 worrying, troublesome
⑱ stroke [strəʊk] *n*. 打击 hit, blow, knock, attack, raid
⑲ passing ['pɑ:sɪŋ] *adv*. 极其 extremely, exceedingly
⑳ wondrous ['wʌndrəs] *adv*. 非常
㉑ bewitching [bɪ'wɪtʃɪŋ] *adj*. 迷人的 attractive, fascinating
㉒ ere long (=erelong) 不久 soon, shortly, before long
㉓ senatorial [ˌsenə'tɔ:riəl] *adj*. 参议院的,参议员的

expectations; but in this he was deceived①; Desdemona loved the Moor, though he was black, and devoted her heart and fortunes to his valiant② parts and qualities; * so was her heart subdued③ to an implicit④ devotion to the man she had selected for a husband, that his very colour, which to all but this discerning⑤ lady would have proved an insurmountable⑥ objection, was by her esteemed above all the white skins and clear complexions of the young Venetian nobility⑦, her suitors.[x]

* Their marriage, which, though privately carried, could not long be kept a secret, came to the ears of the old man, Brabantio, who appeared in a solemn⑧ council⑨ of the senate, as an accuser of the Moor Othello, who by spells⑩ and witchcraft⑪(he maintained⑫) had seduced⑬ the affections of the fair Desdemona to marry him, without the consent of her father, and against the obligations⑭ of hospitality⑮.[xi]

At this juncture⑯ of time it happened that the state of Venice had immediate need of the services of Othello, * news having arrived that the Turks with mighty preparation had fitted out⑰ a fleet⑱, which was bending⑲ its course to the island of Cyprus, with intent to regain that strong post⑳ from the Venetians, who then held it;[xii] in this emergency the state turned its eyes upon Othello, who alone was deemed㉑ adequate to conduct the defence of Cyprus against the Turks. * So that Othello, now summoned㉒ before the senate, stood in their presence at once as a candidate for a great state employment, and as a culprit㉓, charged with offences㉔ which by the laws of Venice were made capital㉕.[xiii]

* The age and senatorial character of old Brabantio, commanded a most patient hearing㉖ from that grave assembly; but the incensed㉗ father conducted his accusation with so much

---

① deceived [dɪ'siːvd] *adj*. 失望的 disappointed
② valiant ['væliənt] *adj*. 英勇的 brave, heroic, courageous
③ subdue [səb'djuː] *v*. 征服 defeat, conquer, triumph over
④ implicit [ɪm'plɪsɪt] *adj*. 完全的,无保留的 total, entire, complete
⑤ discerning [dɪ'sɜːnɪŋ] *adj*. 有洞察力的 sharp, sensitive
⑥ insurmountable [ˌɪnsə'maʊntəbl] *adj*. 无法克服的 impassable
⑦ nobility [nəʊ'bɪləti] *n*. 贵族 noble, aristocracy, high society
⑧ solemn ['sɒləm] *adj*. 严肃的 serious, earnest, grave
⑨ council ['kaʊnsl] *n*. 地方议会 committee, parliament
⑩ spell [spel] *n*. 咒语,魔法 charm, sorcery, conjuration
⑪ witchcraft ['wɪtʃkrɑːft] *n*. 巫术 magic, witchery
⑫ maintain [meɪn'teɪn] *v*. 断言 assert, state, claim
⑬ seduce [sɪ'djuːs] *v*. 引诱 attract, tempt, lure, entice, trap
⑭ obligation [ˌɒblɪ'geɪʃn] *n*. 义务 duty, mission, responsibility
⑮ hospitality [ˌhɒspɪ'tæləti] *n*. 款待 welcome, cordiality
⑯ juncture ['dʒʌŋktʃə(r)] *n*. 关头 moment, crisis
⑰ fit out 装备 equip, outfit
⑱ fleet [fliːt] *n*. 舰队 navy, warship
⑲ bend [bend] *v*. 拐弯 wind, turn, twist, swerve
⑳ post [pəʊst] *n*. 岗位,哨所
㉑ deem [diːm] *v*. 认为 consider, believe, hold, regard, reckon
㉒ summon ['sʌmən] *v*. 召唤 call, send for
㉓ culprit ['kʌlprɪt] *n*. 肇事者,过失者 offender, wrongdoer, malefactor
㉔ offence [ə'fens] *n*. 罪行 crime, wrong, sin, misdeed
㉕ capital ['kæpɪtl] *adj*. 可处死刑的
㉖ hearing ['hɪərɪŋ] *n*. 审讯,听证会 inquiry, trial, investigation
㉗ incensed [ɪn'senst] *adj*. 激怒的 mad, furious, fuming, enraged

intemperance①, producing likelihoods② and allegations③ for proofs④, that, when Othello was called upon for his defence, he had only to relate a plain tale of the course of his love; which he did with such an artless⑤ eloquence⑥, recounting⑦ the whole story of his wooing, as we have related it above, and delivered his speech with so noble a plainness⑧(the evidence of truth), that the duke, who sat as chief judge, could not help confessing that a tale so told would have won his daughter too[xiv] —and * the spells and conjurations⑨ which Othello had used in his courtship, plainly appeared to have been no more than the honest arts of men in love; and the only witchcraft which he had used, the faculty⑩ of telling a soft tale to win a lady's ear.[xv]

This statement⑪ of Othello was confirmed⑫ by the testimony⑬ of the lady Desdemona herself, who appeared in court, and * professing a duty to her father for life and education, challenged leave of him to profess a yet higher duty to her lord and husband, even so much as her mother had shown in preferring him (Brabantio) above her father.[xvi]

The old senator, unable to maintain his plea, called the Moor to him with many expressions of sorrow, and, as an act of necessity, bestowed upon him his daughter, whom, if he had been free to withhold⑭ her (he told him), he would with all his heart have kept from him; adding, that * he was glad at soul that he had no other child, for this behaviour of Desdemona would have taught him to be a tyrant, and hang clogs⑮ on them for her desertion⑯.[xvii]

* This difficulty being got over, Othello, to whom custom had rendered⑰ the hardships of a military life as natural as food and rest are to other men, readily undertook the management of the wars in Cyprus[xviii] —and * Desdemona, preferring the honour of her lord (though with danger)

---

① intemperance [ɪn'tempərəns] *n*. 无节制 excess, immoderation
② likelihood ['laɪklihʊd] *n*. 可能性 probability, possibility
③ allegation [ˌælə'geɪʃn] *n*. 指控 claim, charge, accusation
④ proof [pruːf] *n*. 证据 evidence, testimony
⑤ artless ['ɑːtləs] *adj*. 单纯自然的 natural, simple, unaffected
⑥ eloquence ['eləkwəns] *n*. 流利的口才,雄辩 fluency
⑦ recount [rɪ'kaʊnt] *v*. 叙述 tell, relate, give an account of
⑧ plainness ['pleɪnnəs] *n*. 朴素,简单 simplicity
⑨ conjuration [ˌkɒndʒʊ'reɪʃn] *n*. 魔法 witchery, enchantment
⑩ faculty ['fæklti] *n*. 才能 talent, aptitude, ability, capability
⑪ statement ['steɪtmənt] *n*. 陈述 account, report, narration
⑫ confirm [kən'fɜːm] *v*. 证实 prove, affirm
⑬ testimony ['testɪməni] *n*. 证词 proof, evidence
⑭ withhold [wɪð'həʊld] *v*. 保留 keep, reserve, hold back
⑮ clog [klɒg] *n*. 木底鞋,木屐
⑯ desertion [dɪ'zɜːʃn] *n*. 逃跑
⑰ render ['rendə(r)] *v*. 使成为 make, turn

before the indulgence① of those idle② delights in which new-married people usually waste their time, cheerfully consented to his going.[xix]

* No sooner were Othello and his lady landed in Cyprus, than news arrived, that a desperate③ tempest had dispersed④ the Turkish fleet, and thus the island was secure from any immediate apprehension⑤ of an attack.[xx] * But the war, which Othello was to suffer, was now beginning; and the enemies, which malice stirred up against his innocent lady, proved in their nature more deadly than strangers or infidels⑥.[xxi]

Among all the general's friends no one possessed the confidence of Othello more entirely than Cassio. Michael Cassio was a young soldier, a Florentine⑦, gay⑧, amorous⑨, and of pleasing address⑩, favourite qualities with women; * he was handsome and eloquent⑪, and exactly such a person as might alarm the jealousy⑫ of a man advanced in years (as Othello in some measure⑬ was), who had married a young and beautiful wife;[xxii] but * Othello was as free from jealousy as he was noble, and as incapable⑭ of suspecting as of doing a base⑮ action.[xxiii] He had employed this Cassio in his love affair with Desdemona, and Cassio had been a sort of go-between⑯ in his suit—for * Othello, fearing that himself had not those soft parts of conversation which please ladies, and finding these qualities in his friend, would often depute⑰ Cassio to go (as he phrased⑱ it) a courting for him—such innocent simplicity being rather an honour than a blemish⑲ to the character of the valiant Moor.[xxiv] * So that no wonder, if next to Othello himself (but at far distance, as beseems⑳ a virtuous wife) the gentle Desdemona loved and trusted Cassio.[xxv] Nor had the marriage of this couple made any difference in their behaviour to Michael Cassio. * He frequented㉑ their house, and his free and rattling㉒ talk was no unpleasing㉓ variety to Othello, who was himself of a more serious temper—for such tempers are observed often to delight in their

---

① indulgence [ɪn'dʌldʒəns] *n*. 放纵 spoiling, permissiveness
② idle ['aɪdl] *adj*. 无聊的 empty
③ desperate ['despərət] *adj*. 极严重的,极危险的
④ disperse [dɪ'spɜːs] *v*. 驱散,分散 scatter, break up
⑤ apprehension [ˌæprɪ'henʃn] *n*. 忧虑,恐惧 fear, anxiety, misgiving
⑥ infidel ['ɪnfɪdəl] *n*. 异教徒 heretic, pagan
⑦ Florentine ['flɒrəntaɪn] *n*. 佛罗伦萨人
⑧ gay [geɪ] *adj*. 快乐的 joyful, happy, carefree, light-hearted
⑨ amorous ['æmərəs] *adj*. 多情的 affectionate
⑩ of pleasing address 举止文雅 of elegant manners
⑪ eloquent ['eləkwənt] *adj*. 善辩的,口才流利的 fluent, expressive, silver-tongued
⑫ jealousy ['dʒeləsi] *n*. 忌妒 envy
⑬ in some measure 在某种程度上 to a certain degree/extent
⑭ incapable [ɪn'keɪpəbl] *adj*. 不能的,无能为力的 unable, incompetent
⑮ base [beɪs] *adj*. 卑鄙的 wicked, infamous, shameful, immoral
⑯ go-between ['gəʊbɪˌtwiːn] *n*. 中间人 intermediary, mediator, middleman
⑰ depute [dɪ'pjuːt] *v*. 委派 appoint, assign, commission
⑱ phrase [freɪz] *v*. 表达 express, convey
⑲ blemish ['blemɪʃ] *n*. 缺点 fault, weakness, shortcoming
⑳ beseem [bɪ'siːm] *v*. 适合 fit, suit, match, go/agree with
㉑ frequent [fri'kwənt] *v*. 常去,常出入于 visit, haunt
㉒ rattle ['rætl] *v*. 喋喋不休 chatter, babble
㉓ unpleasing [ʌn'pliːzɪŋ] *adj*. 使人不快的 undesirable, disagreeable

contraries, as a relief from the oppressive① excess② of their own[xxvi] —and Desdemona and Cassio would talk and laugh together, as in the days when he went a courting for his friend.

Othello had lately promoted Cassio to be the lieutenant③, a place of trust, and nearest to the general's person. This promotion gave great offence④ to Iago, an older officer who thought he had a better claim⑤ than Cassio, and would often ridicule⑥ Cassio as a fellow fit only for the company of ladies, and one that knew no more of the art of war or how to set an army in array⑦ for battle, than a girl. * Iago hated Cassio, and he hated Othello, as well for favouring Cassio, as for an unjust suspicion, which he had lightly taken up against Othello, that the Moor was too fond of Iago's wife Emilia.[xxvii] From these imaginary provocations⑧, the plotting⑨ mind of Iago conceived a horrid scheme⑩ of revenge, which should involve both Cassio, the Moor, and Desdemona, in one common ruin.

* Iago was artful⑪, and had studied human nature deeply, and he knew that of all the torments⑫ which afflict the mind of man (and far beyond bodily torture⑬), the pains of jealousy were the most intolerable⑭, and had the sorest sting.[xxviii] If he could succeed in making Othello jealous⑮ of Cassio, he thought it would be an exquisite plot of revenge, and might end in the death of Cassio or Othello, or both; he cared not.

The arrival of the general and his lady, in Cyprus, meeting with the news of the dispersion⑯ of the enemy's fleet, made a sort of holiday in the island. Everybody gave themselves up to feasting and making merry. * Wine flowed in abundance, and cups went round to the health of the black Othello, and his lady the fair Desdemona.[xxix]

Cassio had the direction of the guard that night, with

---

① oppressive [ə'presɪv] *adj*. 压迫的 repressive, stifling
② excess [ɪk'ses] *n*. 过度 surfeit, surplus, overflow, superfluity
③ lieutenant [lef'tenənt] *n*. 中尉
④ offence [ə'fens] *n*. 冒犯 insult, rudeness, slight, affront
⑤ claim [kleɪm] *n*. 权利 right, entitlement
⑥ ridicule ['rɪdɪkjuːl] *v*. 嘲笑 mock, taunt, laugh at, make fun of
⑦ array [ə'reɪ] *n*. 队形,队列 line-up, formation
⑧ provocation [ˌprɒvə'keɪʃn] *n*. 挑衅 offence, insult, affront
⑨ plotting ['plɒtɪŋ] *adj*. 阴险的 snaky, viperish, sly, crafty
⑩ scheme [skiːm] *n*. 诡计 plot, trick, intrigue, contrivance
⑪ artful ['ɑːtfl] *adj*. 狡猾的 foxy, tricky, cunning
⑫ torment ['tɔːment] *n*. 痛苦 pain, suffering, agony, anguish
⑬ torture ['tɔːtʃə(r)] *n*. 折磨 torment, persecution, ill-treatment
⑭ intolerable [ɪn'tɒlərəbl] *adj*. 无法忍受的 unbearable, insufferable
⑮ jealous ['dʒeləs] *adj*. 妒忌的 envious, green-eyed
⑯ dispersion [dɪ'spɜːʃn] *n*. 驱散,分散 dispersal, diffusion, scattering

a charge from Othello to keep the soldiers from excess[1] in drinking, that no brawl[2] might arise, to fright the inhabitants, or disgust[3] them with the new-landed forces. * That night Iago began his deep-laid[4] plans of mischief—under colour of loyalty and love to the general, he enticed[5] Cassio to make rather too free with the bottle (a great fault in an officer upon guard).[xxx]

Cassio for a time resisted, but he could not long hold out against[6] the honest freedom which Iago knew how to put on[7], but kept swallowing glass after glass (as Iago still plied[8] him with drink and encouraging songs), and * Cassio's tongue ran over in praise of the lady Desdemona, whom he again and again toasted[9], affirming[10] that she was a most exquisite lady—until at last the enemy which he put into his mouth stole away his brains;[xxxi] and upon some provocation given him by a fellow whom Iago had set on, swords were drawn, and Montano, a worth officer, who interfered[11] to appease[12] the dispute[13], was wounded in the scuffle. The riot[14] now began to be general, and Iago, who had set on foot the mischief, was foremost[15] in spreading[16] the alarm, causing the castle-bell to be rung (as if some dangerous mutiny[17] instead of a slight drunken quarrel had arisen)—the alarm-bell ringing awakened Othello, who, dressing in a hurry, and coming to the scene of action, questioned Cassio of the cause. * Cassio was now come to himself, the effect of the wine having a little gone off, but was too much ashamed to reply; and Iago, pretending a great reluctance[18] to accuse Cassio, but, as it were[19], forced into it by Othello, who insisted to know the truth, gave an account of the whole matter (leaving out his own share in it, which Cassio was too far gone to remember) in such a manner, as while he seemed to make Cassio's offence less, did indeed make it appear greater than it was.[xxxii] The result was, that Othello, who was a strict observer of discipline[20], was compelled[21] to take away Cassio's place of lieutenant from him.

* Thus did Iago's first artifice[22] succeed completely; he had now undermined[23] his hated

---

① excess [ɪk'ses] *n*. 过度 surfeit, surplus, overflow, superfluity
② brawl [brɔːl] *n*. 争吵 fight, battle, row, clash, fray, squabble
③ disgust [dɪs'gʌst] *v*. 使反感 sicken, offend, repel, put off
④ deep-laid ['diːp'leɪd] *adj*. 秘密策划的
⑤ entice [ɪn'taɪs] *v*. 引诱 allure, attract, invite, tempt, seduce
⑥ hold out against 抵抗,抵挡 withstand, stand up to
⑦ put on 假装 feign, affect, assume, pretend, imitate, simulate
⑧ ply [plaɪ] *v*. 不断供应 provide, supply, shower, lavish
⑨ toast [təʊst] *v*. 祝酒 drink to, propose a toast to
⑩ affirm [ə'fɜːm] *v*. 断言 declare, state, maintain, assert, avow
⑪ interfere [ˌɪntə'fɪə(r)] *v*. 干预 meddle, intervene, intercede, step in
⑫ appease [ə'piːz] *v*. 平息,安抚 pacify, calm, soothe, placate, conciliate
⑬ dispute [dɪ'spjuːt] *n*. 争端,争论 quarreling, conflict, controversy
⑭ riot ['raɪət] *n*. 骚乱 disturbance, row, disorder
⑮ foremost ['fɔːməʊst] *adj*. 最前的 first, front, top, leading, headmost
⑯ spread [spred] *v*. 传播 distribute, transmit
⑰ mutiny ['mjuːtəni] *n*. 叛乱 rebellion, revolt, uprising, insurrection
⑱ reluctance [rɪ'lʌktəns] *n*. 不情愿 unwillingness, hesitancy
⑲ as it were 可以说是 in a way, to some extent, so to say/speak
⑳ discipline ['dɪsəplɪn] *n*. 纪律 rule, strictness, self-mastery
㉑ compel [kəm'pel] *v*. 强迫 force, drive, oblige, impel, necessitate
㉒ artifice ['ɑːtɪfɪs] *n*. 诡计 scheme, trick, craft, tactic, stratagem
㉓ undermine [ˌʌndə'maɪn] *v*. 暗中破坏,逐渐削弱 weaken, disable, impair

rival[1], and thrust[2] him out of his place—but a further use was hereafter to be made of the adventure of this disastrous night.[xxxiii]

Cassio, whom this misfortune had entirely sobered[3], now lamented to his seeming friend Iago that he should have been such a fool as to transform himself into a beast. He was undone[4], for how could he ask the general for his place again? He would tell him he was a drunkard. He despised himself. * Iago, affecting to make light of[5] it, said, that he, or any man living, might be drunk upon occasion[6]; it remained now to make the best of a bad bargain[7];[xxxiv] the general's wife was now the general, and could do anything with Othello; that he were best to apply[8] to the lady Desdemona to mediate[9] for him with her lord; that she was of a frank, obliging[10] disposition, and would readily undertake a good office[11] of this sort, and set Cassio right again in the general's favour; and then this crack[12] in their love would be made stronger than ever. * A good advice of Iago, if it had not been given for wicked purposes, which will after appear.[xxxv]

Cassio did as Iago advised him, and made application[13] to the lady Desdemona, who was easy to be won over in any honest suit[14]; and she promised Cassio that she should be his solicitor[15] with her lord, and rather die than give up his cause. * This she immediately set about[16] in so earnest and pretty a manner, that Othello, who was mortally[17] offended with Cassio, could not put her off[18].[xxxvi] When he pleaded[19] delay, and that it was too soon to pardon such an offender[20], she would not be beat back, but insisted that it should be the next night, or the morning after, or the next morning to that at farthest. Then she showed how penitent[21] and humbled[22] poor Cassio was,

---

① rival [ˈraɪvl] *n*. 竞争对手 opponent, competitor, contender
② thrust [θrʌst] *v*. 猛推 push, force, shove, propel
③ sober [ˈsəʊbə(r)] *v*. 使清醒
④ undone [ʌnˈdʌn] *adj*. 完蛋的,毁掉了的 ruined, destroyed, wretched
⑤ make light of 轻视 minimize, play down, set no store by
⑥ upon occasion 偶尔 occasionally, at times, now and then
⑦ bargain [ˈbɑːgən] *n*. 交易 deal, settlement, transaction
⑧ apply [əˈplaɪ] *v*. 请求,申请 request, petition, solicit
⑨ mediate [ˈmiːdieɪt] *v*. 调解 intervene, reconcile
⑩ obliging [əˈblaɪdʒɪŋ] *adj*. 乐于助人的 helpful, good-natured
⑪ good office 调解
⑫ crack [kræk] *n*. 裂纹,裂缝 break, chink, fracture
⑬ application [ˌæplɪˈkeɪʃn] *n*. 请求,申请 request, appeal, plea, petition
⑭ suit [suːt] *n*. 请求 appeal, request, entreaty, imploration
⑮ solicitor [səˈlɪsɪtə(r)] *n*. 支持者 advocate, supporter, defender
⑯ set about 开始,着手 begin, start, get down to, make a start on
⑰ mortally [ˈmɔːtəli] *adv*. 极端地 extremely
⑱ put sb. off 搪塞,打发
⑲ plead [pliːd] *v*. 恳求 beg, appeal, petition, solicit, implore
⑳ offender [əˈfendə(r)] *n*. 违法者 wrongdoer, lawbreaker, malefactor
㉑ penitent [ˈpenɪtənt] *adj*. 忏悔的 sorry, regretful, repentant
㉒ humbled [ˈhʌmbld] *adj*. 谦逊的 humble, modest, unassuming

and that his offence did not deserve so sharp a check①. And when Othello still hung back②—"* What! My lord," said she, "that I should have so much to do to plead for Cassio, Michael Cassio, that came a courting for you, and oftentimes③, when I have spoken in dispraise④ of you, has taken your part! [xxxvii] * I count this but a little thing to ask of you. When I mean to try your love indeed, I shall ask a weighty matter. [xxxviii]" Othello could deny nothing to such a pleader, and only requesting that Desdemona would leave the time to him, promised to receive Michael Cassio again in favour.

It happened that Othello and Iago had entered into the room where Desdemona was, just as Cassio, who had been imploring⑤ her intercession⑥, was departing at the opposite door—and Iago, who was full of art⑦, said in a low voice, as if to himself: "I like not that." Othello took no great notice of what he said; indeed, the conference which immediately took place with his lady put it out of his head; but he remembered it afterwards. For when Desdemona was gone, Iago, as if for mere satisfaction of his thought, questioned Othello whether Michael Cassio, when Othello was courting his lady, knew of his love. * To this the general answering in the affirmative⑧ and adding, that he had gone between them very often during the courtship, Iago knitted his brow, as if he had got fresh light on some terrible matter, and cried: "Indeed!" [xxxix] This brought into Othello's mind the words which Iago had let fall⑨ upon entering the room, and seeing Cassio with Desdemona; and he began to think there was some meaning in all this—for he deemed⑩ Iago to be a just man, and full of love and honesty, and * what in a false knave⑪ would be tricks, in him seemed to be the natural workings of an honest mind, big with something too great for utterance [xl]—and Othello prayed Iago to speak what he knew, and to give his worst thoughts words.

"* And what," said Iago, "if some thoughts very vile should have intruded⑫ into my breast, as where is the palace into which foul things do not enter? [xli]" * Then Iago went on to say, what a pity it were, if any trouble should arise to Othello out of his imperfect observations; that it would not be for Othello's peace to know his thoughts; that people's good names were not to be taken away for slight suspicions; [xlii] and * when Othello's curiosity was raised almost to distraction with these hints

① check [tʃek] *n*. 惩戒 punishment, discipline
② hang back 犹豫,迟疑 hesitate, hold back
③ oftentimes [ˈɒfntaɪmz] *adv*. 时常 often, ofttimes, frequently
④ dispraise [dɪsˈpreɪz] *n*. 指责 blame, reproach
⑤ implore [ɪmˈplɔː(r)] *v*. 恳求 beg, beseech, entreat, solicit
⑥ intercession [ˌɪntəˈseʃn] *n*. 求情 pleading, intervention, mediation
⑦ art [ɑːt] *n*. 诡计 trickery, deceit, cunning, guile, artifice
⑧ affirmative [əˈfɜːmətɪv] *n*. 肯定
⑨ let fall 泄露,无意中吐露
⑩ deem [diːm] *v*. 认为 consider, regard, hold, judge, suppose
⑪ knave [neɪv] *n*. 无赖 rogue, villain, rascal, scoundrel, blackguard
⑫ intrude [ɪnˈtruːd] *v*. 闯入 encroach, obtrude

and scattered① words, Iago, as if in earnest care for Othello's peace of mind, besought him to beware② of jealousy—with such art did this villain raise suspicions in the unguarded③ Othello, by the very caution④ which he pretended to give him against suspicion.[xliii] "* I know," said Othello, "that my wife is fair, loves company and feasting, is free of speech, sings, plays, and dances well—but where virtue is, these qualities are virtuous.[xliv] I must have proof before I think her dishonest."* Then Iago, as if glad that Othello was slow to believe ill of his lady, frankly declared that he had no proof, but begged Othello to observe her behaviour well, when Cassio was by; not to be jealous nor too secure neither, for that he (Iago) knew the dispositions of the Italian ladies, his countrywomen, better than Othello could do; and that in Venice the wives let heaven see many pranks they dared not show their husbands.[xlv] * Then he artfully insinuated⑤ that Desdemona deceived her father in marrying with Othello, and carried it so closely, that the poor old man thought that witchcraft⑥ had been used.[xlvi] * Othello was much moved with this argument, which brought the matter home to him, for if she had deceived her father, why might she not deceive her husband?[xlvii]

Iago begged pardon for having moved him; but Othello, assuming an indifference⑦, while he was really shaken with inward grief at Iago's words, begged him to go on, which Iago did with many apologies, as if unwilling to produce anything against Cassio, whom he called his friend—* he then came strongly to the point, and reminded Othello how Desdemona had refused many suitable matches of her own clime and complexion, and had married him, a Moor, which showed unnatural in her, and proved her to have a head-strong⑧ will; and when her better judgement returned, how probable it was she should fall upon comparing Othello with the fine forms and clear white complexions of the young Italians her countrymen.[xlviii] * He concluded with advising Othello to put off his reconcilement⑨ with Cassio a little longer, and in the meanwhile to note with what earnestness Desdemona should intercede⑩ in his behalf; for that much would be seen in that.[xlix] * So mischievously⑪ did this artful villain lay his plots to turn the gentle qualities of this innocent lady into her destruction, and make a net for her out of her own goodness to entrap⑫ her—first setting Cassio on to entreat her mediation, and then out of that very mediation contriving stratagems⑬ for her ruin.[l]

The conference ended with Iago's begging Othello to account his wife innocent, until he had more decisive proof; and Othello promised to be patient; but from that moment the deceived

---

① scattered [ˈskætəd] *adj*. 分散的 separated, dispersed, distributed
② beware [bɪˈweə(r)] *v*. 小心，当心 watch out
③ unguarded [ʌnˈɡɑːdɪd] *adj*. 无防备的，大意的 undefended, unwary
④ caution [ˈkɔːʃn] *n*. 提醒，告诫 warning
⑤ insinuate [ɪnˈsɪnjueɪt] *v*. 暗示 imply, suggest, hint, allude
⑥ witchcraft [ˈwɪtʃkrɑːft] *n*. 巫术，魔法 magic, witchery, sorcery
⑦ indifference [ɪnˈdɪfrəns] *n*. 漠不关心 coldness, unconcern
⑧ head-strong [ˈhedstrɒŋ] *adj*. 固执的，顽固的 stubborn, willful
⑨ reconcilement [ˈrekənsaɪlmənt] *n*. 和解，调停
⑩ intercede [ˌɪntəˈsiːd] *v*. 说情，调停 mediate, intervene, arbitrate
⑪ mischievously [ˈmɪstʃɪvəsli] *adv*. 恶意地 viciously, maliciously, spitefully
⑫ entrap [ɪnˈtræp] *v*. 诱骗 trick, lure, seduce, entice, ensnare
⑬ stratagem [ˈstrætədʒəm] *n*. 计谋 trick, plot, device, scheme

Othello never tasted content of mind. * Poppy①, nor the juice of mandragora②, nor all the sleeping potions③ in the world, could ever again restore to him that sweet rest, which he had enjoyed but yesterday.[li] His occupation④ sickened upon him. He no longer took delight in arms. * His heart, that used to be roused⑤ at the sight of troops, and banners⑥, and battle-array, and would stir and leap at the sound of a drum, or a trumpet⑦, or a neighing⑧ war-horse, seemed to have lost all that pride and ambition which are a soldier's virtue; and his military ardour⑨ and all his old joys forsook⑩ him.[lii] Sometimes he thought his wife honest, and at times he thought her not so; sometimes he thought Iago just, and at times he thought him not so; then he would wish that he had never known of it; * he was not the worse for her loving Cassio, so long as he knew it not—torn to pieces with these distracting⑪ thoughts, he once laid hold on⑫ Iago's throat, and demanded proof of Desdemona's guilt, or threatened instant death for his having belied⑬ her.[liii] Iago, feigning indignation⑭ that his honesty should be taken for a vice⑮, asked Othello, if he had not sometimes seen a handkerchief spotted with strawberries in his wife's hand. Othello answered, that he had given her such a one, and that it was his first gift. "That same handkerchief," said Iago, "did I see Michael Cassio this day wipe his face with." "If it be as you say," said Othello, "I will not rest till a wide revenge swallow them up—and first, for a token of your fidelity, I expect that Cassio shall be put to death within three days; and for that fair devil (meaning his lady), I will withdraw and devise⑯ some swift means of death for her."

* Trifles⑰ light as air are to the jealous proofs as strong as holy⑱ writ⑲.[liv] A handkerchief of his wife's seen in Cassio's hand, was motive⑳ enough to the deluded㉑ Othello to pass sentence of

---

① poppy [ˈpɒpi] *n*. 罂粟(鸦片的主要原料,有镇静麻醉的作用)
② mandragora [mænˈdræɡərə] *n*. 曼陀罗草(可以用于麻醉)
③ potion [ˈpəʊʃn] *n*. 药水 tonic
④ occupation [ˌɒkjuˈpeɪʃn] *n*. 消遣 hobby, pastime
⑤ rouse [raʊz] *v*. 激起 excite, arouse, stir, incite, stimulate, fire up
⑥ banner [ˈbænə(r)] *n*. 旗帜 flag, colours, pennant, ensign, streamer
⑦ trumpet [ˈtrʌmpɪt] *n*. 小号;喇叭 horn, clarion, bugle
⑧ neigh [neɪ] *v*. (马)嘶鸣
⑨ ardour [ˈɑːdə(r)] *n*. 激情 passion, fervour, enthusiasm, zeal
⑩ forsake [fəˈseɪk] *v*. (forsook, forsaken) 抛弃 desert, abandon, cast off
⑪ distracting [dɪˈstræktɪŋ] *adj*. 令人分心的 disturbing, bothering
⑫ lay hold on 抓住 catch, grip, grab, grasp, seize, take hold of
⑬ belie [bɪˈlaɪ] *v*. 诬陷,表明……不正确
⑭ indignation [ˌɪndɪɡˈneɪʃn] *n*. 愤怒 anger, rage, fury, wrath
⑮ vice [vaɪs] *n*. 罪行 fault, evil, wickedness
⑯ devise [dɪˈvaɪz] *v*. 策划 plot, design, work out, think up
⑰ trifle [ˈtraɪfl] *n*. 琐事 trivia, minutiae
⑱ holy [ˈhəʊli] *adj*. 神圣的 sacred, blessed, hallowed, consecrated
⑲ writ [rɪt] *n*. 令状 document, decree, indictment
⑳ motive [ˈməʊtɪv] *adj*. 使有动机的,推动的
㉑ deluded [dɪˈluːdɪd] *adj*. 受骗的 tricked, cheated, fooled, deceived

death upon them both, without once inquiring how Cassio came by① it. * Desdemona had never given such a present to Cassio, nor would this constant lady have wronged her lord with doing so naughty a thing as giving his presents to another man; both Cassio and Desdemona were innocent of any offence against Othello[lv] —but * the wicked Iago, whose spirits never slept in contrivance of villainy②, had made his wife (a good, but a weak woman) steal this handkerchief from Desdemona, under pretence③ of getting the work copied, but in reality to drop it in Cassio's way, where he might find it, and give a handle to Iago's suggestion that it was Desdemona's present.[lvi]

* Othello, soon after meeting his wife, pretended that he had a headache (as he might indeed with truth), and desired her to lend him her handkerchief to hold to his temples④.[lvii] She did so. "Not this," said Othello. "but that handkerchief I gave you." Desdemona had it not about her (for indeed it was stolen, as we have related). "How?" said Othello. "This is a fault indeed. That handkerchief an Egyptian woman gave to my mother; the woman was a witch and could read people's thoughts—she told my mother, while she kept it, it would make her amiable⑤, and my father would love her; but, if she lost it, or gave it away, my father's fancy would turn, and he would loathe⑥ her as much as he had loved her. She dying gave it to me, and bade me, if I ever married, to give it to my wife. I did so; take heed of⑦ it. Make it a darling as precious as your eye." "It is possible?" said the frighted⑧ lady. "* 'Tis true," continued Othello, "it is a magical handkerchief; a sibyl⑨ that had lived in the world two hundred years, in a fit of prophetic⑩ fury worked it; the silkworms that furnished the silk were hallowed⑪, and it was dyed⑫ in a mummy of maidens' hearts conserved⑬.[lviii]"

Desdemona, hearing the wondrous virtues of the handkerchief, was ready to die with fear, for she plainly perceived she had lost it, and with it, she feared, the affections of her husband. Then Othello started, and looked as if he were going to do some rash⑭ thing, and still he demanded the handkerchief, which when she could not produce, she tried to divert⑮ her husband from too serious thoughts, and cheerfully told him she saw all his talk about the handkerchief was only to put her off from her suit about Michael

---

① come by 得到 get hold of
② villainy [ˈvɪləni] *n*. 邪恶,罪行 vice, sin, iniquity, devilry, wickedness
③ pretence [prɪˈtens] *n*. 托词 excuse, pretext
④ temple [ˈtempl] *n*. 太阳穴
⑤ amiable [ˈeɪmiəbl] *adj*. 令人愉悦的,和蔼可亲的 pleasant, pleasing
⑥ loathe [ləʊð] *v*. 厌恶 hate, dislike, despise, detest, abominate
⑦ take heed of 留心 pay attention to, attend to
⑧ frighted [ˈfraɪtɪd] *adj*. 〈古〉恐惧的 frightened, terrified
⑨ sibyl [ˈsɪbl] *n*. 女巫 witch, sorceress, enchantress
⑩ prophetic [prəˈfetɪk] *adj*. 预言的 predictive, divinatory
⑪ hallowed [ˈhæləʊd] *adj*. 神圣的 holy, blessed, sacred, sanctified
⑫ dye [daɪ] *v*. 染色 colour, tint, pigment
⑬ conserve [kənˈsɜːv] *v*. 保存 save, preserve, hoard, store up
⑭ rash [ræʃ] *adj*. 鲁莽的 hasty, reckless, hot-headed, ill-advised
⑮ divert [daɪˈvɜːt] *v*. 转移,分散 avert, deflect, distract

Cassio, whom she went on to praise (as Iago had foretold), till Othello in perfect distraction burst out of the room, and then Desdemona, though unwillingly, began to suspect that her lord was jealous.

* What cause she could have ministered to him she knew not, and then she accused herself for accusing the noble Othello, and thought to be sure that some untoward① news from Venice, or some state troubles had muddled② his spirits, and made his temper not so sweet as formerly.[lix] And she said: "* Men are not gods, and we must not look for that observance from them when they are married, which they show us on the bridal day.[lx]" And * she beshrewed③ herself for so unkindly judging of his unkindness.[lxi]

Again Othello and Desdemona met, and he accused her more plainly of being unfaithful④, and of loving another man, but he did not name whom—and Othello wept, and Desdemona said: "Alas! The heavy day! Why do you weep?" And Othello told her, he could have borne all sorts of evils with fortitude⑤—poverty, and disease, and disgrace; but her infidelity⑥ had broken his heart—and * he called her a weed, that looked so fair, and smelled so sweet, that the sense ached at it;[lxii] and wished she had never been born. And when he had left her, this innocent lady was so stupefied⑦ with wonder at her lord's untrue suspicion of her, that a weight-like sleep came over her, and she only desired her attendant to make her bed, and to lay her wedding-sheets upon it, saying, that * when people teach their babes, they do it by gentle means and easy tasks, and Othello might have chid⑧ her so; for in good faith she was but a child when she was chidden.[lxiii] And this was all the complaint which this gentle lady made.

Desdemona being retired⑨ to bed expecting her lord would follow her, soon fell into a slumber⑩, the effect of her troubled spirits, when Othello entered the chamber, full of the black purpose which he had meditated of putting his lady to death. But when he saw her asleep, he thought he would not shed⑪ her blood, nor scar⑫ that white skin of hers, more white than alabaster⑬. But he was resolved⑭ she should die; else (as he said) she would live to betray⑮ more

---

① untoward [ˌʌntəˈwɔːd] *adj*. 不幸的 unfortunate, unfavourable
② muddle [ˈmʌdl] *v*. 使糊涂 confuse, confound, perplex, mix up
③ beshrew [bɪˈʃruː] *v*. 责备,咒骂 blame, scold, reproach
④ unfaithful [ʌnˈfeɪθfl] *adj*. 不忠贞的 faithless, disloyal, inconstant
⑤ fortitude [ˈfɔːtɪtjuːd] *n*. 刚毅,不屈不挠 resolution, determination
⑥ infidelity [ˌɪnfɪˈdeləti] *n*. 不忠 faithlessness, disloyalty
⑦ stupefied [ˈstjuːpɪfaɪd] *adj*. 惊讶的 astonished, astounded
⑧ chide [tʃaɪd] (chid/chided, chid/chided/chidden) *v*. 责骂 scold, blame, reproach
⑨ retire [rɪˈtaɪə(r)] *v*. 离去 depart, withdraw
⑩ slumber [ˈslʌmbə(r)] *n*. 睡眠 sleep, nap, doze, rest, snooze
⑪ shed [ʃed] *v*. 使流(血) drop, spill
⑫ scar [skɑː(r)] *v*. 使留下伤痕 mark, blemish, disfigure, deface
⑬ alabaster [ˈæləbɑːstə(r)] *n*. 雪花石膏 compact gypsum
⑭ resolved [rɪˈzɒlvd] *adj*. 下定决心的,坚决的 determined, resolute, bent on
⑮ betray [bɪˈtreɪ] *v*. 背叛 desert, forsake, sell out

men, as she had done him. * Then he kissed her for the last time (as he said), and that kiss was so sweet, that he must needs kiss her again—and he wept, but he said they were cruel tears.[lxiv]

Desdemona was awakened with his kisses, and she looked upon Othello, and she saw him gnaw① his under lip, and roll his eyes, and she knew he was always fatal② when he looked so—and he bade her prepare for death, and to say her prayers, for he would not kill her soul. And this innocent wife, as she lay at his mercy③, begged for compassion④, and to know her fault, and then he named Cassio, and the handkerchief which (he said) she had given him; and as the guiltless lady was proceeding to clear herself he suddenly would hear no more, but covering her up in the bed-clothes, stifled⑤ her till she died.

In this instant of time was brought into the house Cassio, wounded and bleeding, whom Iago had set one of his creatures⑥ on to assassinate⑦; but * the fellow not succeeding in his attempt to kill Cassio (whom he wounded, but not mortally⑧), and being himself killed by Iago to prevent discovery, in his pockets were found certain letters, which made the guilt of Iago, and the innocence⑨ of Cassio, clear beyond all doubt;[lxv] and Cassio now came to beg pardon of Othello, and to ask wherein⑩ he had offended him, that he had employed Iago to murder him.

This discovery was as a thunderstroke to Othello, who now plainly saw that he was no better than a murderer, and that his wife (poor innocent lady) had been ever faithful⑪ to him; the extreme anguish⑫ of which discovery making life insupportable⑬, he fell upon his sword, and throwing himself upon the body of his dear injured⑭ lady, expired⑮.

* These rash acts raised much passion of horror and amazement in the bystanders, for Othello had borne a fair reputation, and till he was wrought upon⑯ by the arts of a villain, which his own noble nature never gave him leave to suspect, he was a loving and a doting⑰ husband.[lxvi] * He had

---

① gnaw [nɔː] v. 咬,啃,啮 bite, chew, nibble, munch
② fatal [ˈfeɪtl] adj. 致命的 deadly
③ at sb.'s mercy 任某人摆布
④ compassion [kəmˈpæʃn] n. 怜悯 pity, mercy, sympathy
⑤ stifle [ˈstaɪfl] v. 使窒息 choke, smother, suffocate
⑥ creature [ˈkriːtʃə(r)] n. 人 man, person, fellow, individual
⑦ assassinate [əˈsæsɪneɪt] v. 刺杀,暗杀 kill, slay, murder, eliminate
⑧ mortally [ˈmɔːtəli] adv. 致命地 fatally
⑨ innocence [ˈɪnəsns] n. 清白 sinlessness, guiltlessness, blamelessness
⑩ wherein [weərˈɪn] adv. 在何处 where, at which point
⑪ faithful [ˈfeɪθfl] adj. 忠贞的 loyal, truthful, devoted, reliable
⑫ anguish [ˈæŋgwɪʃ] n. 极度痛苦 suffering, agony, torment
⑬ insupportable [ˌɪnsəˈpɔːtəbl] adj. 无法忍受的 unbearable
⑭ injure [ˈɪndʒə(r)] v. 伤害 hurt, harm, wound, damage, impair
⑮ expire [ɪkˈspaɪə(r)] v. 断气,死亡 die, decease, perish, pass away
⑯ work upon 影响 affect, influence
⑰ doting [ˈdəʊtɪŋ] adj. 溺爱的,偏爱的 loving, indulgent, affectionate

loved not wisely, but too well; and his manly eyes (when he learned his mistake), though not used to weep on every small occasion, dropped tears as fast as the Arabian trees their gum.[lxvii] And when he was dead all his former merits① and his valiant acts were remembered. Nothing now remained for his successor② but to put the utmost censure③ of the law in force against Iago, who was executed with strict tortures; and to send word to the state of Venice of the lamentable④ death of their renowned⑤ general.

① merit ['merɪt] *n*. 优点 advantage, strength
② successor [sək'sesə(r)] *n*. 继任者 inheritor, next-in-line
③ censure ['senʃə(r)] *n*. 谴责 blame, criticism, condemnation
④ lamentable [lə'mentəbl] *adj*. 可悲的 tragic, regrettable, mournful
⑤ renowned [rɪ'naʊnd] *adj*. 有名的 famous, notable, distinguished

i This noble lady, who regarded the mind more than the features of men, with a singularity rather to be admired than imitated, had chosen for the object of her affections, a Moor, a black, whom her father loved, and often invited to his house. 这位高贵的姑娘把人的心灵看得比相貌更重要,她用一种只可羡慕而不可仿效的非凡眼光,看中了一个摩尔人——一个黑人;她的父亲非常喜欢这个人,经常请他到家里来。(who..., whom...:双重定语从句)

ii He was a soldier, and a brave one; and by his conduct in bloody wars against the Turks, had risen to the rank of general in the Venetian service, and was esteemed and trusted by the state. 他是军人,而且是一位骁勇的军人。由于多次在与土耳其人的血腥战争中指挥有功,他被提拔为威尼斯军队里的将军,受到国家的尊敬和信任。

iii Desdemona (as is the manner of ladies) loved to hear him tell the story of his adventures, which he would run through from his earliest recollection; the battles, sieges, and encounters, which he had passed through; the perils he had been exposed to by land and by water; his hair-breadth escapes, when he had entered a breach, or marched up to the mouth of a cannon. 苔丝狄蒙娜(正像所有的姑娘一样)喜欢听他讲他的冒险故事。他从早年的事情回忆起,谈到他经历的战役、围攻和会战,谈到他在水上和陆地上遇到的种种凶险,谈到他进入突破口或者炮眼并在千钧一发之际脱险的情况。(which..., which...; ...perils (that)...:三重定语从句)

iv How he had been taken prisoner by the insolent enemy, and sold to slavery; how he demeaned himself in that state, and how he escaped—all these accounts, added to the narration of the strange things he had seen in foreign countries; the vast wilderness and romantic caverns, the quarries, the rocks and mountains, whose heads are in the clouds; of the savage nations, the cannibals who are man-eaters, and a race of people in Africa whose heads do grow beneath their shoulders.（他谈起）他怎样被粗野的敌人俘虏后当作奴隶卖掉，他又怎样忍气吞声而得以逃脱。在讲这些经历的时候，他还附带讲了他在外国看到的一些新奇事物：一望无际的荒野、瑰丽动人的洞穴、石坑、岩石和插入云霄的山峰；也讲到一些野蛮的国家和吃人的部落，还谈到非洲有一个民族，他们的脑袋长在肩膀底下。（how…; how…, and how…：排比修辞；…things (that)…; …whose…; …who…, …whose…：四重定语从句）

v These travellers' stories would so enchain the attention of Desdemona, that if she were called off at any time by household affairs, she would despatch with all haste that business, and return, and with a greedy ear devour Othello's discourse. 这些旅行故事深深吸引了苔丝狄蒙娜的注意，要是她正听的时候因为家务事被叫走了，她总会赶快把那件事料理完，然后马上回来，用永远也听不够的耳朵去听奥瑟罗的叙述。

vi Once he took advantage of a pliant hour, and drew from her a prayer, that he would tell her the whole story of his life at large, of which she had heard so much, but only by parts—to which he consented, and beguiled her of many a tear, when he spoke of some distressful stroke which his youth had suffered. 有一次，奥瑟罗趁着一个很好的时机，引得苔丝狄蒙娜向他提出一个请求：要求他把一生的经历完整地讲给她听。尽管过去她已经听了很多，但都只是零零碎碎的。奥瑟罗答应了这个请求，他讲到自己少年时代遭受的艰难困苦，勾出了她不少的眼泪。（prayer, that…, of which…：同位语从句中嵌套定语从句；pliant hour：适当的时间；at large＝at length, in detail：详尽地）

vii His story being done, she gave him for his pains a world of sighs—she swore a pretty oath, that it was all passing strange, and pitiful, wondrous pitiful—she wished (she said) she had not heard it, yet she wished that heaven had made her such a man. 他的故事讲完了，苔丝狄蒙娜因为他遭受的痛苦不知叹了多少气。她发了一个很巧妙的誓说，这一切都是奇异而且悲惨的，悲惨极了，她希望（她说）她没有听到这些就好了，然而她又希望上天给她造出这样一位男子。（being…：独立主格结构；oath, that…：同位语从句；wish…had not heard…：与过去事实相反的虚拟语气）

viii If he had a friend who loved her, he had only to teach him how to tell his story, and that would woo her. 假如他有一位朋友爱上了她，他只要教给那个人如何讲他的故事，那个人就可以得到她的爱了。

ix Upon this hint, delivered not with more frankness than modesty, accompanied with certain bewitching prettiness, and blushes, which Othello could not but understand, he spoke more openly of his love, and in this golden opportunity gained the consent of the generous lady Desdemona privately to marry him. 这个暗示虽然坦率，但也不失含蓄，而且还伴随着苔丝狄蒙娜迷人的妩媚和羞涩，奥瑟罗自然明白她的意思，于是就更明白地向她表达了爱意，趁这个宝贵的时机得到了落落大方的苔丝狄蒙娜的同意，她预备私下跟他结婚。（could not but…：只能……，不得不……）

x So was her heart subdued to an implicit devotion to the man she had selected for a husband, that his very colour, which to all but this discerning lady would have proved an insurmountable objection, was by her esteemed above all the white skins and clear complexions of the young Venetian nobility, her suitors. 她全心全意地爱着她挑选来做丈夫的这个人。除了颇有眼力的她,对其他所有女人来说,他的肤色都是无法逾越的障碍,而她却把他的肤色看得比向她求过婚的威尼斯年轻贵族的白净肤色还要高贵。(so...man (that)..., that..., which...:部分倒装的结果状语从句中嵌套双重定语从句;would have proved...: 与过去事实相反的虚拟语气)

xi Their marriage, which, though privately carried, could not long be kept a secret, came to the ears of the old man, Brabantio, who appeared in a solemn council of the senate, as an accuser of the Moor Othello, who by spells and witchcraft (he maintained) had seduced the affections of the fair Desdemona to marry him, without the consent of her father, and against the obligations of hospitality. 他们的婚礼虽然是私下里举行的,但瞒了没多久就传到老人家勃拉班修的耳朵里了。勃拉班修到庄严的元老院会议上去控告摩尔人奥瑟罗,说奥瑟罗用符咒和巫术(他坚持说)骗得美丽的苔丝狄蒙娜爱上他,让她没有得到父亲的同意就跟他结了婚,奥瑟罗这样做违反了主客之间的道义。(...which, though (it was)...:定语从句中嵌套省略的让步状语从句; who..., who...: 定语从句的嵌套)

xii News having arrived that the Turks with mighty preparation had fitted out a fleet, which was bending its course to the island of Cyprus, with intent to regain that strong post from the Venetians, who then held it. 有消息传来说,土耳其人调集了强大的舰队,正向塞浦路斯岛进发,想把这个军事据点从当时的占领者威尼斯人手里夺回来。(news having arrived that..., which..., who...:独立主格结构、同位语从句和双重定语从句的嵌套;塞浦路斯岛:地中海东部的一个大岛,历史上曾短暂属于威尼斯,1571 年又被土耳其夺去,1960 年独立成为共和国。)

xiii So that Othello, now summoned before the senate, stood in their presence at once as a candidate for a great state employment, and as a culprit, charged with offences which by the laws of Venice were made capital. 所以这时候奥瑟罗就被元老院召去,他站在元老跟前,一方面是国家重大职位的候选人,一方面又是个犯人——根据威尼斯法律,他被指控犯有死罪。

xiv The age and senatorial character of old Brabantio, commanded a most patient hearing from that grave assembly; but the incensed father conducted his accusation with so much intemperance, producing likelihoods and allegations for proofs, that, when Othello was called upon for his defence, he had only to relate a plain tale of the course of his love; which he did with such an artless eloquence, recounting the whole story of his wooing, as we have related it above, and delivered his speech with so noble a plainness (the evidence of truth), that the duke, who sat as chief judge, could not help confessing that a tale so told would have won his daughter too. 勃拉班修年事已高,又是元老,大家在庄严的会场上都不得不非常耐心地去听他的控诉。可是这位气鼓鼓的父亲在控诉的时候过于激动,一点儿也不冷静,只举出一些迹象和疑点作为证据。因此,奥瑟罗站出来替自己辩护的时候,只要把他跟苔丝狄蒙娜恋爱的经过平铺直叙地讲一遍就够了。他朴实而娓娓动听地把他向苔丝狄蒙娜求爱的全部经过讲了出来,像上边叙述的那样。他的话讲得那么光明磊落(这就证明他说的是实情),连当审判官的公爵也不得不承认,要是他自己的女儿听了这样的故事,也会爱上奥瑟罗的。(结果状语从句、时间状语从句、定语从句、方式状语从句和宾语从句的嵌套)

xv The spells and conjurations which Othello had used in his courtship, plainly appeared to have been no more than the honest arts of men in love; and the only witchcraft which he had used, the faculty of telling a soft tale to win a lady's ear. 奥瑟罗在求爱时所用的符咒和魔法,看来只不过是男人在恋爱时用的正大光明的方法,他唯一用过的巫术,就是讲一个柔情的故事来赢得姑娘的芳心。(no more than...:仅仅,只不过……)

xvi Professing a duty to her father for life and education, challenged leave of him to profess a yet higher duty to her lord and husband, even so much as her mother had shown in preferring him (Brabantio) above her father. (苔丝狄蒙娜)首先承认她父亲的养育之恩和自己应尽的本分,然后要求父亲准许她承认一种更高的本分——对她的主人和丈夫应尽的本分,就像她母亲爱他(勃拉班修)胜过爱自己的父亲一样。(challenged leave of him: 要求他准许她)

xvii He was glad at soul that he had no other child, for this behaviour of Desdemona would have taught him to be a tyrant, and hang clogs on them for her desertion. 他很高兴自己没有其他儿女,因为苔丝狄蒙娜的这种行为会把他变成一个暴君。由于她的私奔,他会让其他的儿女都戴上脚镣。

xviii This difficulty being got over, Othello, to whom custom had rendered the hardships of a military life as natural as food and rest are to other men, readily undertook the management of the wars in Cyprus. 这个纠纷解决之后,奥瑟罗马上就去指挥塞浦路斯的战事了。艰苦的军队生活对于他,就像吃饭和休息对于其他人那样自然。

xix Desdemona, preferring the honour of her lord (though with danger) before the indulgence of those idle delights in which new-married people usually waste their time, cheerfully consented to his going. 苔丝狄蒙娜更愿意她的丈夫去建立功绩(尽管很危险),而不是像一般新婚夫妇那样整天逍遥闲荡、荒废时光,于是欣然同意他去出征。

xx No sooner were Othello and his lady landed in Cyprus, than news arrived, that a desperate tempest had dispersed the Turkish fleet, and thus the island was secure from any immediate apprehension of an attack. 奥瑟罗和他的妻子刚在塞浦路斯上岸,就接到报告说土耳其舰队被一场剧烈的暴风给刮散了。这样一来,塞浦路斯岛一时没有受到攻击的危险了。(no sooner...than...: 刚一……就……,倒装结构)

xxi But the war, which Othello was to suffer, was now beginning; and the enemies, which malice stirred up against his innocent lady, proved in their nature more deadly than strangers or infidels. 但是,奥瑟罗将要遭遇的战争已然开始了。他的敌人对他清白无辜的妻子生出恶意,他们的本性比外国人或是异教徒更加致命。

xxii He was handsome and eloquent, and exactly such a person as might alarm the jealousy of a man advanced in years (as Othello in some measure was), who had married a young and beautiful wife. 他长得漂亮,而且很会说话,恰好是这样一种人最能引起年纪大一些(奥瑟罗的年纪也不算小了)并且娶了年轻美貌的妻子的人的嫉妒。(alarm=excite)

xxiii Othello was as free from jealousy as he was noble, and as incapable of suspecting as of doing a base action. 奥瑟罗具有高贵的品质,从来不嫉妒别人,也从来不会怀疑别人,正如他不会做出卑鄙的事来一样。

xxiv Othello, fearing that himself had not those soft parts of conversation which please ladies, and finding these qualities in his friend, would often depute Cassio to go (as he phrased it) a courting for him—such innocent simplicity being rather an honour than a blemish to the character of the valiant Moor. 奥瑟罗担心自己不善于跟女人温柔地谈话，没法叫她们高兴，而他觉得他的朋友很有这种本领，就时常请凯西奥（奥瑟罗是这么说的）代表他去求爱。这种对人毫不猜忌的单纯性格正是这个勇敢的摩尔人性格上的亮点，而不是他的缺陷。

xxv So that no wonder, if next to Othello himself (but at far distance, as beseems a virtuous wife) the gentle Desdemona loved and trusted Cassio. 这样一来，难怪温柔的苔丝狄蒙娜除了奥瑟罗本人，最喜欢和最信任的人就是凯西奥了（但是正像一切贤惠的妻子一样，她对凯西奥总是保持着很远的距离）。（no wonder：难怪……）

xxvi He frequented their house, and his free and rattling talk was no unpleasing variety to Othello, who was himself of a more serious temper—for such tempers are observed often to delight in their contraries, as a relief from the oppressive excess of their own. 凯西奥时常到他们家去，奥瑟罗自己的性格比较严肃，但他并不讨厌凯西奥的东拉西扯。正如人们经常看到的那样，这种性格的人往往喜欢与相反性格的人在一起，这样可以缓解他们自己性格造成的过度压抑。

xxvii Iago hated Cassio, and he hated Othello, as well for favouring Cassio, as for an unjust suspicion, which he had lightly taken up against Othello, that the Moor was too fond of Iago's wife Emilia. 伊阿古恨凯西奥，他也恨奥瑟罗，一半是因为奥瑟罗偏爱凯西奥，一半是由于毫无根据的猜忌——他轻率地认为这个摩尔人看上了他的妻子爱米莉娅。（…suspicion, which…, that…：同位语从句和定语从句的嵌套）

xxviii Iago was artful, and had studied human nature deeply, and he knew that of all the torments which afflict the mind of man (and far beyond bodily torture), the pains of jealousy were the most intolerable, and had the sorest sting. 伊阿古诡计多端，他很仔细地研究过人的天性，晓得在一切折磨人心的痛苦（远比肉体折磨更痛苦）中，再没有比嫉妒更难忍受、更能刺痛人的了。

xxix Wine flowed in abundance, and cups went round to the health of the black Othello, and his lady the fair Desdemona. 推杯换盏之间，人们为黑人奥瑟罗和他的夫人——美丽的苔丝狄蒙娜的健康干杯。

xxx That night Iago began his deep-laid plans of mischief—under colour of loyalty and love to the general, he enticed Cassio to make rather too free with the bottle (a great fault in an officer upon guard). 伊阿古当天晚上就开始了他那处心积虑的阴谋。他借口向将军表示忠诚和爱戴，怂恿凯西奥拼命喝酒（对一个担任警卫的军官来说，纵酒是很严重的错误）。

xxxi Cassio's tongue ran over in praise of the lady Desdemona, whom he again and again toasted, affirming that she was a most exquisite lady—until at last the enemy which he put into his mouth stole away his brains. 凯西奥嘴里不断地称赞苔丝狄蒙娜，一遍遍地为她干杯，满口夸着她是一位最了不起的夫人。最后，他咽到肚子里去的那个敌人迷住了他的心窍。（the enemy which he put into his mouth：指酒）

xxxii Cassio was now come to himself, the effect of the wine having a little gone off, but was too much ashamed to reply; and Iago, pretending a great reluctance to accuse Cassio, but, as it were, forced into it by Othello, who insisted to know the truth, gave an account of the whole matter (leaving out his own share in it, which Cassio was too far gone to remember) in such a manner, as while he seemed to make Cassio's offence less, did indeed make it appear greater than it was. 凯西奥这时清醒过来,酒劲儿也过去一些了,可是他惭愧得答不出话来。伊阿古假装不愿意告凯西奥的状,似乎是因为奥瑟罗坚持要问个水落石出,他被逼得没有办法,才将整件事情说了出来(略去了他自己参与的那部分,而凯西奥醉得太厉害,根本不记得)。伊阿古讲的话听起来好像是在为凯西奥开脱,而实际上却大大地加重了凯西奥的罪过。(was come＝had come;as it were:可以说,在某种程度上)

xxxiii Thus did Iago's first artifice succeed completely; he had now undermined his hated rival, and thrust him out of his place—but a further use was hereafter to be made of the adventure of this disastrous night. 这样一来,伊阿古的第一个阴谋就完全成功了。他已经暗中陷害了他所恨的对头,把凯西奥的副官职位搞掉了。可是他还要进一步利用在这个灾难之夜发生的事情。

xxxiv Iago, affecting to make light of it, said, that he, or any man living, might be drunk upon occasion; it remained now to make the best of a bad bargain. 伊阿古假装把事情看得没什么了不起,说他自己或是任何活着的人,都难免偶尔喝醉,当前只能去想办法挽救这个倒霉的局面。(make the best of a bad bargain:善处逆境)

xxxv A good advice of Iago, if it had not been given for wicked purposes, which will after appear. 假如不是伊阿古别有用心(这一点大家后面会看到),他提出的这个主意还算不错。

xxxvi This she immediately set about in so earnest and pretty a manner, that Othello, who was mortally offended with Cassio, could not put her off. 苔丝狄蒙娜立刻就去求情了,她说得那么诚恳又那么灵巧,奥瑟罗虽然很生凯西奥的气,但也不能拒绝她。(this:宾语前置)

xxxvii What! My lord, that I should have so much to do to plead for Cassio, Michael Cassio, that came a courting for you, and oftentimes, when I have spoken in dispraise of you, has taken your part! 怎么,我替凯西奥求情要费这么大事吗? 当初迈克尔·凯西奥来替你追我,我说过好多次不满意你的话,他总是替你辩护呢!(take your part:为你辩护)

xxxviii I count this but a little thing to ask of you. When I mean to try your love indeed, I shall ask a weighty matter. 我认为我请你做的只是一件小事,要是我真的想试探你的爱情的话,我会要求你做一件大事的。

xxxix To this the general answering in the affirmative and adding, that he had gone between them very often during the courtship, Iago knitted his brow, as if he had got fresh light on some terrible matter, and cried: "Indeed!" 将军告诉他凯西奥知道,并且说自己追求苔丝狄蒙娜的时候凯西奥还时常替他们撮合呢。伊阿古听了皱起眉头,好像在一件可怕的事情上又找到新的线索,只嚷了一声:"真的吗?"

xl What in a false knave would be tricks, in him seemed to be the natural workings of an honest mind, big with something too great for utterance. 如果一个奸诈的恶棍这样吞吞吐吐,那就是心怀鬼胎了,可是伊阿古这样做,就像是一个正直的人的自然之举,他表现得好像一件很严重的事情堵在心里,说不出口。(big with＝filled with)

xli And what if some thoughts very vile should have intruded into my breast, as where is the palace into which foul things do not enter? 哪座宫殿能免得了有脏东西进去呢? 要是有什么非常污秽的思想闯进了我的心里,可该怎么办呢?(What if...?:要是……该怎么办?)

xlii Then Iago went on to say, what a pity it were, if any trouble should arise to Othello out of his imperfect observations; that it would not be for Othello's peace to know his thoughts; that people's good names were not to be taken away for slight suspicions. 伊阿古接着又说,

如果他这些不完整的观察竟给奥瑟罗带来麻烦，那就太可惜了。他说要是把他脑子里想的事情说出来，就会叫奥瑟罗心神不安，不该为了轻微的猜疑就毁掉人家的名誉。

xliii When Othello's curiosity was raised almost to distraction with these hints and scattered words, Iago, as if in earnest care for Othello's peace of mind, besought him to beware of jealousy—with such art did this villain raise suspicions in the unguarded Othello, by the very caution which he pretended to give him against suspicion. 当这些旁敲侧击的一言半语把奥瑟罗弄得疑神疑鬼快要发疯，伊阿古又装得十分关心奥瑟罗的精神安宁，劝他不要吃醋。这个坏人就是这样巧妙地通过假装劝他不要猜忌，而在奥瑟罗毫无戒备的心上引起了猜忌。

xliv I know that my wife is fair, loves company and feasting, is free of speech, sings, plays, and dances well—but where virtue is, these qualities are virtuous. 我知道我的妻子长得美，她喜欢交际和宴会，爱谈天，会唱歌、弹琴和跳舞，但只要她贞洁，这些都是美德。

xlv Then Iago, as if glad that Othello was slow to believe ill of his lady, frankly declared that he had no proof, but begged Othello to observe her behaviour well, when Cassio was by; not to be jealous nor too secure neither, for that he (Iago) knew the dispositions of the Italian ladies, his countrywomen, better than Othello could do; and that in Venice the wives let heaven see many pranks they dared not show their husbands. 伊阿古又装作很高兴奥瑟罗不轻易怀疑他的夫人，坦率地说他并没拿到什么证据，只叫奥瑟罗仔细留意凯西奥在场时苔丝狄蒙娜的举止神情。他劝奥瑟罗不要嫉妒，也不要认为安然无事，因为他（伊阿古）比奥瑟罗更了解意大利妇女（他本国的女人）的性格，说威尼斯的女人背着她们丈夫玩的鬼把戏是瞒不过上天的。

xlvi Then he artfully insinuated that Desdemona deceived her father in marrying with Othello, and carried it so closely, that the poor old man thought that witchcraft had been used. 然后他又狡猾地暗示说，苔丝狄蒙娜跟奥瑟罗结婚的时候就骗过了她的父亲，而且做得非常巧妙，可怜那位老人家竟以为奥瑟罗用了巫术呢。（carried it so closely：做得非常隐秘）

xlvii Othello was much moved with this argument, which brought the matter home to him, for if she had deceived her father, why might she not deceive her husband? 奥瑟罗觉得这番话很有道理，想到苔丝狄蒙娜既然能欺骗她的父亲，为什么就不能欺骗她的丈夫呢？

xlviii He then came strongly to the point, and reminded Othello how Desdemona had refused many suitable matches of her own clime and complexion, and had married him, a Moor, which showed unnatural in her, and proved her to have a head-strong will; and when her better judgement returned, how probable it was she should fall upon comparing Othello with the fine forms and clear white complexions of the young Italians her countrymen. 然后他就狠狠地说到要害了。他提醒奥瑟罗说，曾经有许多跟苔丝狄蒙娜同国家、同肤色、门当户对的人向她求过婚，然而她全都拒绝了，嫁给了他，一个摩尔人，这对她来说很不正常，足见她很任性。等她清醒过来，她很有可能拿奥瑟罗跟那些相貌清秀、皮肤白净的意大利青年（她的本国人）做比较。

xlix He concluded with advising Othello to put off his reconcilement with Cassio a little longer, and in the meanwhile to note with what earnestness Desdemona should intercede in his behalf; for that much would be seen in that. 最后，他劝奥瑟罗把跟凯西奥和解的事再缓一缓，同时留意苔丝狄蒙娜会多么殷切地替他求情，从那上头可以看出很多东西。（much would be seen in that：从那上面可以看出不少名堂来）

l So mischievously did this artful villain lay his plots to turn the gentle qualities of this innocent lady into her destruction, and make a net for her out of her own goodness to entrap her—first setting Cassio on to entreat her mediation, and then out of that very mediation contriving stratagems for her ruin. 这个奸诈的坏蛋就这样布置下了阴谋。他利用清白无辜的苔丝狄蒙娜那种温柔的性情来毁灭她，用她自己的善良编织套住她的罗网：他先怂恿凯西奥向她求情，然后又通过这个求情来布置叫她毁灭的诡计。(so...did...：部分倒装结构)

li Poppy, nor the juice of mandragora, nor all the sleeping potions in the world, could ever again restore to him that sweet rest, which he had enjoyed but yesterday. 不论是罂粟花、曼陀罗汁还是世界上所有的安眠药，都不能叫他重新享受他昨天还享受过的酣睡。

lii His heart, that used to be roused at the sight of troops, and banners, and battle-array, and would stir and leap at the sound of a drum, or a trumpet, or a neighing war-horse, seemed to have lost all that pride and ambition which are a soldier's virtue; and his military ardour and all his old joys forsook him. 他的心，过去一看到队伍、旗帜、阵形就会被唤醒，一听到鼓声、号角声或者战马的嘶叫就激动雀跃，但如今，他似乎失去了军人所有的骄傲。他失去了对军事的热情，也没有了他一向保持着的愉快心情。

liii He was not the worse for her loving Cassio, so long as he knew it not—torn to pieces with these distracting thoughts, he once laid hold on Iago's throat, and demanded proof of Desdemona's guilt, or threatened instant death for his having belied her. 只要他不知道这件事，哪怕她爱上凯西奥对他也没有害处。这些纷乱的思绪把他的心撕得粉碎。有一次奥瑟罗掐住伊阿古的脖子，要他一定拿出苔丝狄蒙娜有罪的证据，不然就要立刻处死他，因为他诬陷了她。

liv Trifles light as air are to the jealous proofs as strong as holy writ. 即使像空气那样轻飘飘的东西，对于善妒的人来说，也会成为像《圣经》那样确凿的铁证。(比喻修辞)

lv Desdemona had never given such a present to Cassio, nor would this constant lady have wronged her lord with doing so naughty a thing as giving his presents to another man; both Cassio and Desdemona were innocent of any offence against Othello. 苔丝狄蒙娜从来没给过凯西奥这样一件礼物，这位忠实的夫人也做不出如此不端之事，把丈夫送她的礼物送给别的男人。凯西奥和苔丝狄蒙娜都没有冒犯过奥瑟罗。

lvi The wicked Iago, whose spirits never slept in contrivance of villainy, had made his wife (a good, but a weak woman) steal this handkerchief from Desdemona, under pretence of getting the work copied, but in reality to drop it in Cassio's way, where he might find it, and give a handle to Iago's suggestion that it was Desdemona's present. 这个邪恶的伊阿古无时无刻不在想方设法陷害别人，手绢是他叫他的妻子(一个善良但软弱的女人)从苔丝狄蒙娜那里偷来的。伊阿古装作要把手绢上的花样描下来，其实是为了把它丢到凯西奥可以捡着的地方，这样就可以给伊阿古一个口实，暗示说手绢是苔丝狄蒙娜送他的。(夸张修辞；give a handle to Iago's suggestion：给伊阿古的暗示一个由头)

lvii Othello, soon after meeting his wife, pretended that he had a headache (as he might indeed with truth), and desired her to lend him her handkerchief to hold to his temples. 奥瑟罗见到他的妻子没多久，就假装头痛(老实说，这也可能是真的)，要借她的手绢来按住他的太阳穴。

lviii 'Tis true, it is a magical handkerchief; a sibyl that had lived in the world two hundred years, in a fit of prophetic fury worked it; the silkworms that furnished the silk were hallowed, and it was dyed in a mummy of maidens' hearts conserved. 确实是这样，那块手绢有魔法。它是一个活了两百岁的巫婆在一阵狂热的神通到来的时候编织的，吐丝的蚕也是神蚕，然后用保存着处女之心的木乃伊来染色。

lix What cause she could have ministered to him she knew not, and then she accused herself for accusing the noble Othello, and thought to be sure that some untoward news from Venice, or some state troubles had muddled his spirits, and made his temper not so sweet as formerly. 苔丝狄蒙娜不清楚她究竟做了什么事情使他吃起醋来，她又为责怪高贵的奥瑟罗而自责起来。她认为一定是威尼斯来了什么不好的消息，或是一些国家大事使他烦心，弄得他的脾气没有以前那样温和了。

lx Men are not gods, and we must not look for that observance from them when they are married, which they show us on the bridal day. 男人不是神仙，不能指望他们在结婚以后仍然跟婚礼那天一样体贴。

lxi She beshrewed herself for so unkindly judging of his unkindness. 她责备自己不应该往坏处去想他的不近人情。(unkindly...unkindness...：同源并列修辞)

lxii He called her a weed, that looked so fair, and smelled so sweet, that the sense ached at it. 他把她叫作毒草，颜色是那样娇艳，香气是那样芬芳，让人看到、嗅到就会心疼。(比喻修辞)

lxiii When people teach their babes, they do it by gentle means and easy tasks, and Othello might have chid her so; for in good faith she was but a child when she was chidden. 当大人教育小孩子的时候，他们总是用温柔的方法，从容易的任务开始；奥瑟罗本可以那样温和地责备她，因为老实说，当她被责备的时候，她也只是个孩子。

lxiv Then he kissed her for the last time (as he said), and that kiss was so sweet, that he must needs kiss her again—and he wept, but he said they were cruel tears. 奥瑟罗最后一次吻了她(他是这么说的)。那个吻真甜啊，他不由得再吻了一次。然后他哭了，可是他说他流的是无情的眼泪。(must needs＝needs must：必须，不得不)

lxv The fellow not succeeding in his attempt to kill Cassio (whom he wounded, but not mortally), and being himself killed by Iago to prevent discovery, in his pockets were found certain letters, which made the guilt of Iago, and the innocence of Cassio, clear beyond all doubt. 那家伙并没能杀死凯西奥。他把凯西奥刺伤了，可是并没伤着致命的地方。伊阿古为了避免别人发觉这件事情是他主使的，把刺客本人杀死了。可是从刺客口袋里翻出来的一些信清清楚楚地证实了伊阿古的奸计，也证实了凯西奥的清白。

lxvi These rash acts raised much passion of horror and amazement in the bystanders, for Othello had borne a fair reputation, and till he was wrought upon by the arts of a villain, which his own noble nature never gave him leave to suspect, he was a loving and a doting husband. 这些鲁莽的行为使在场的人都感到极大的恐怖和惊愕，因为奥瑟罗一向名声很好，在他没有被那个坏蛋的阴谋欺骗以前(他自己高贵的性格使他从不曾对那个坏蛋起疑心)，他本是个深情又宠溺妻子的丈夫。(wrought：旧时 work 的过去式和过去分词)

lxvii He had loved not wisely, but too well; and his manly eyes (when he learned his mistake), though not used to weep on every small occasion, dropped tears as fast as the Arabian trees their gum. 他爱得不明智，却爱得很深沉。他那双刚毅的眼睛虽然不是在每一件小事上都会流泪，可是(当他发觉他的错误时)他的眼泪就像阿拉伯橡树的树胶那样流个不停。(比喻和夸张修辞)

罗密欧与朱丽叶
Romeo and Juliet

These violent delights have violent ends
And in their triumph die, like fire and powder,
Which, as they kiss, consume. The sweetest honey
Is loathsome in his own deliciousness
And in the taste confounds the appetite.
Therefore love moderately. Long love doth so.
Too swift arrives as tardy as too slow.

这种狂暴的快乐将会产生狂暴的结局，
正像火和火药的亲吻，
就在最得意的一刹那烟消云散。
最甜的蜜糖
可以使味觉麻木；
不太热烈的爱情才会维持久远；
太快和太慢，结果都不会圆满。

莎士比亚是精神上的太阳，这个太阳以最绚丽的光彩、以大慈大悲的光辉普照着那片国土。那里的一切都使我们记起莎士比亚，在我们眼里，即使是最平凡的事物也因此显得容光焕发。

——海涅

罗密欧就是恋爱中的哈姆莱特。

——威廉·黑兹利特

罗密欧与朱丽叶的爱，既是诗的爱，也是爱的诗。莎士比亚让诗的爱情在他们第一次见面的第一吻中开始，又让爱的诗篇在他们情殇的最后一吻中结束。

——傅光明

主要人物

Capulet　凯普莱特　维洛纳城大家族
Montague　蒙太古　维洛纳城大家族
Romeo　罗密欧　蒙太古之子
Juliet　朱丽叶　凯普莱特之女
Benvolio　班伏里奥　蒙太古之侄，罗密欧的朋友
Mercutio　茂丘西奥　亲王的亲戚，罗密欧的朋友
Tybalt　提伯尔特　凯普莱特夫人之内侄
Escalus　爱斯卡勒斯　维洛那亲王
Paris　帕里斯　少年贵族，亲王的亲戚
Friar Lawrence　劳伦斯神父　法兰西斯派教士

地点　维洛那；曼多亚

Romeo and Juliet

The two chief families in Verona were the rich Capulets and the Montagues. * There had been an old quarrel between these families, which was grown to such a height, and so deadly was the enmity[1] between them, that it extended to the remotest kindred[2], to the followers and retainers[3] of both sides, insomuch that a servant of the house of Montague could not meet a servant of the house of Capulet, nor a Capulet encounter with a Montague by chance, but fierce words and sometimes bloodshed ensued; and frequent were the brawls[4] from such accidental meetings, which disturbed the happy quiet of Verona's streets.[i]

Old lord Capulet made a great supper, to which many fair ladies and many noble guests were invited. All the admired beauties of Verona were present, and all comers were made welcome if they were not of the house of Montague. At this feast of Capulets, Rosaline, beloved of Romeo, son to the old lord Montague, was present; and though it was dangerous for a Montague to be seen in this assembly, yet * Benvolio, a friend of Romeo, persuaded the young lord to go to this assembly in the disguise of a mask, that he might see his Rosaline, and seeing her compare her with some choice beauties of Verona, who (he said) would make him think his swan a crow.[ii] Romeo had small faith in Benvolio's words; nevertheless, for the love of Rosaline, he was persuaded to go. For Romeo was a sincere and passionate lover, and one that lost his sleep for love, and fled society to be alone, thinking on Rosaline, who disdained[5] him, and never

---

① enmity ['enməti] n. 仇恨 hate, hatred, hostility, resentment

② kindred ['kɪndrəd] n. 亲属 relation, relative, kin, kinsmen

③ retainer [rɪ'teɪnə(r)] n. 家臣 servant, attendant, footman, vassal

④ brawl [brɔːl] n. 争吵 fight, row, quarrel, fray, altercation

⑤ disdain [dɪs'deɪn] v. 鄙视 scorn, despise, slight, look down on

requited[1] his love, with the least show of courtesy[2] or affection; and Benvolio wished to cure his friend of this love by showing him diversity of ladies and company. To this feast of Capulets then young Romeo with Benvolio and their friend Mercutio went masked[3]. * Old Capulet bid them welcome, and told them that ladies who had their toes unplagued[4] with corns[5] would dance with them.[iii] And the old man was light-hearted and merry, and said that he had worn a mask when he was young, and could have told a whispering tale in a fair lady's ear. And they fell to dancing[6], and * Romeo was suddenly struck[7] with the exceeding[8] beauty of a lady who danced there, who seemed to him to teach the torches to burn bright, and her beauty to show by night like a rich jewel worn by a blackamoor[9];[iv] * beauty too rich for use, too dear for earth! like a snowy dove trooping with crows (he said), so richly did her beauty and perfections shine above the ladies her companions.[v] While he uttered[10] these praises, he was overheard by Tybalt, a nephew of lord Capulet, who knew him by his voice to be Romeo. And this Tybalt, being of a fiery[11] and passionate temper, could not endure[12] that a Montague should come under cover of a mask, to fleer[13] and scorn[14] (as he said) at their solemnities[15]. And he stormed[16] and raged[17] exceedingly[18], and would have struck young Romeo dead. But his uncle, the old lord Capulet, would not suffer him to do any injury at that time, both out of respect to his guests, and because Romeo had borne himself[19] like a gentleman, and all tongues in Verona bragged[20] of him to be a virtuous and well-governed[21] youth. * Tybalt, forced to be patient against his will, restrained[22] himself, but swore that this vile Montague should at another time dearly[23] pay for his intrusion[24].[vi]

The dancing being done, Romeo watched the place where the lady stood; and * under favour

---

① requite [rɪ'kwaɪt] *v*. 回报 return, reward, repay, compensate
② courtesy ['kɜːtəsi] *n*. 礼貌 politeness, civility, good manners
③ masked [mɑːskt] *adj*. 戴面具的
④ unplagued [ʌn'pleɪgd] *adj*. 未受困扰的
⑤ corn [kɔːn] *n*. 鸡眼 clavus
⑥ fall to doing sth. 开始做某事
⑦ strike [straɪk] *v*. (struck) 迷住
⑧ exceeding [ɪk'siːdɪŋ] *adj*. 极其的,非常的 unusual, extreme, exceptional
⑨ blackamoor ['blækəmɔː(r)] *n*. 黑人
⑩ utter ['ʌtə(r)] *v*. 说出 say, speak, state, articulate, enunciate
⑪ fiery ['faɪəri] *adj*. 暴躁的 excitable, violent, irritable, hot-headed
⑫ endure [ɪn'djʊə(r)] *v*. 忍受 stand, bear, tolerate, put up with
⑬ fleer [flɪə(r)] *v*. 嘲笑 laugh, mock, scoff, taunt, make fun of
⑭ scorn [skɔːn] *v*. 鄙视 despise, disdain, slight, look down on
⑮ solemnity [sə'lemnəti] *n*. 仪式 rite, ritual, ceremony
⑯ storm [stɔːm] *v*. 怒吼 rage, rave, thunder, fly off the handle
⑰ rage [reɪdʒ] *v*. 发怒 rave, rant, fume, lose one's temper
⑱ exceedingly [ɪk'siːdɪŋli] *adv*. 极度地,非常 extremely, exceptionally
⑲ bear oneself 举止,表现 behave oneself
⑳ brag [bræg] *v*. 夸耀 boast, flaunt, vaunt, show off
㉑ well-governed ['wel'gʌvənd] *adj*. 有教养的 polite, well-bred, well-mannered
㉒ restrain [rɪ'streɪn] *v*. 抑制 check, control, contain, hold back
㉓ dearly ['dɪəli] *adv*. 代价极大地,深深地 at great cost, at a high price
㉔ intrusion [ɪn'truːʒn] *n*. 侵犯 invasion, infringement, encroachment

of① his masking habit②, which might seem to excuse in part the liberty③, he presumed④ in the gentlest manner to take her by the hand, calling it a shrine⑤, which if he profaned⑥ by touching it, he was a blushing pilgrim⑦, and would kiss it for atonement⑧.[vii] "* Good pilgrim," answered the lady, "your devotion shows by far too mannerly⑨ and too courtly⑩—saints⑪ have hands, which pilgrims may touch, but kiss not.[viii]" "Have not saints lips, and pilgrims too?" said Romeo. "Ay," said the lady, "lips which they must use in prayer." "* O then, my dear saint," said Romeo, "hear my prayer, and grant⑫ it, lest I despair.[ix]"

In such like allusions⑬ and loving conceits⑭ they were engaged⑮, when the lady was called away to her mother. And * Romeo inquiring⑯ who her mother was, discovered that the lady whose peerless⑰ beauty he was so much struck with, was young Juliet, daughter and heir to the lord Capulet, the great enemy of the Montagues; and that he had unknowingly engaged his heart to his foe⑱.[x] This troubled him, but it could not dissuade⑲ him from loving. * As little rest had Juliet, when she found that the gentleman that she had been talking with was Romeo and a Montague, for she had been suddenly smit⑳ with the same hasty㉑ and inconsiderate㉒ passion for Romeo, which he had conceived for her; and a prodigious㉓ birth of love it seemed to her, that she must love her enemy, and that her affections should settle there, where family considerations should induce㉔ her chiefly to hate.[xi]

It being midnight, Romeo with his companions departed; but they soon missed him, for,

---

① under favour of 在……庇护下
② habit [ˈhæbɪt] *n*. 服装 clothes, costume, attire, garment
③ liberty [ˈlɪbəti] *n*. 冒失
④ presume [prɪˈzjuːm] *v*. 擅自,冒昧
⑤ shrine [ʃraɪn] *n*. 圣祠 altar, sanctuary, holy place
⑥ profane [prəˈfeɪn] *v*. 亵渎 abuse, violate, pollute
⑦ pilgrim [ˈpɪlgrɪm] *n*. 朝圣者 devotee
⑧ atonement [əˈtəʊnmənt] *n*. 赎罪 payment, compensation
⑨ mannerly [ˈmænəli] *adj*. 彬彬有礼的,客气的 polite, gracious
⑩ courtly [ˈkɔːtli] *adj*. 温文尔雅的 civil, elegant, refined, dignified
⑪ saint [seɪnt] *n*. 圣人 holy being
⑫ grant [grɑːnt] *v*. 同意 accept, allow, acknowledge
⑬ allusion [əˈluːʒn] *n*. 暗示 hint, suggestion, implication
⑭ conceit [kənˈsiːt] *n*. 幻想
⑮ engage [ɪnˈgeɪdʒ] *v*. 与……建立密切关系
⑯ inquire [ɪnˈkwaɪə(r)] *v*. 询问 ask, question, interrogate
⑰ peerless [ˈpɪələs] *adj*. 无与伦比的 unmatched, unequalled
⑱ foe [fəʊ] *n*. 仇敌 enemy, opponent, adversary, antagonist
⑲ dissuade [dɪˈsweɪd] *v*. 劝阻 discourage
⑳ smite [smaɪt] *v*. (smote/smit, smitten/smit) 重击 hit, strike
㉑ hasty [ˈheɪsti] *adj*. 仓促的,草率的 rapid, swift; rash, incautious
㉒ inconsiderate [ˌɪnkənˈsɪdərət] *adj*. 欠考虑的 unconsidered
㉓ prodigious [prəˈdɪdʒəs] *adj*. 奇异的 unusual, amazing, fantastic
㉔ induce [ɪnˈdjuːs] *v*. 引起 cause, bring about, give rise to

unable to stay away from the house where he had left his heart, he leaped the wall of an orchard which was at the back of Juliet's house. * Here he had not been long, ruminating① on his new love, when Juliet appeared above at a window, through which her exceeding beauty seemed to break like the light of the sun in the east; and the moon, which shone in the orchard with a faint light, appeared to Romeo as if sick and pale with grief at the superior lustre② of this new sun.[xii] And * she, leaning her cheek upon her hand, he passionately wished himself a glove upon that hand, that he might touch her cheek.[xiii] She all this while thinking herself alone, fetched a deep sigh, and exclaimed: "Ah me!" Romeo, enraptured③ to hear her speak, said softly, and unheard by her: "* O speak again, bright angel, for such you appear, being over my head, like a winged messenger from heaven whom mortals fall back to gaze upon.[xiv]"

She, unconscious of being overheard, and full of the new passion which that night's adventure had given birth to, called upon her lover by name (whom she supposed absent): "O Romeo, Romeo!" said she. "* Wherefore art thou Romeo? Deny thy father, and refuse thy name, for my sake; or if thou wilt not, be but my sworn love, and I no longer will be a Capulet.[xv]" Romeo, having this encouragement, would fain④ have spoken, but he was desirous⑤ of hearing more; and * the lady continued her passionate discourse with herself (as she thought), still chiding Romeo for being Romeo and a Montague, and wishing him some other name, or that he would put away that hated name, and for that name which was no part of himself, he should take all herself.[xvi] * At this loving word Romeo could no longer refrain⑥, but taking up the dialogue as if her words had been addressed to him personally, and not merely in fancy, he bade her call him Love, or by whatever other name she pleased, for he was no longer Romeo, if that name was displeasing to her.[xvii] * Juliet, alarmed to hear a man's voice in the garden, did not at first know who it was, that by favour of the night and darkness had thus stumbled upon⑦ the discovery of her secret; but when he spoke again, though her ears had not yet drunk a hundred words of that tongue's uttering, yet so nice is a lover's hearing, that she immediately knew him to be young Romeo, and she expostulated⑧ with him on the danger to which he had exposed himself by climbing the orchard walls, for if any of her kinsmen⑨ should find him there, it would be death to him, being a Montague.[xviii] "* Alack⑩," said Romeo, "there

---

① ruminate ['ruːmɪneɪt] *v*. 沉思 consider, reflect
② lustre ['lʌstə(r)] *n*. 光彩 sparkle, shine, glow, glitter, brightness
③ enraptured [ɪn'ræptʃəd] *adj*. 狂喜的 delighted, charmed, enchanted
④ fain [feɪn] *adv*. 欣然地 gladly, willingly, cheerfully
⑤ desirous [dɪ'zaɪərəs] *adj*. 渴望的 wishing, wanting, longing for
⑥ refrain [rɪ'freɪn] *v*. 克制
⑦ stumble upon 偶然发现 come/run across, run into
⑧ expostulate [ɪk'spɒstʃuleɪt] *v*. 告诫 remonstrate
⑨ kinsman ['kɪnzmən] *n*. 亲属 relative, relation, kin
⑩ alack [ə'læk] *int*. (表示悲伤或遗憾)唉,哎呀,呜呼

is more peril in your eye, than in twenty of their swords. Do you but look kind upon me, lady, and I am proof① against their enmity. Better my life should be ended by their hate, than that hated life should be prolonged, to live without your love.[xix]" "How came you into this place," said Juliet, "and by whose direction?" "Love directed me," answered Romeo. "* I am no pilot, yet wert thou as far apart from me, as that vast② shore which is washed with the farthest sea, I should venture for such merchandise③.[xx]" * A crimson④ blush came over Juliet's face, yet unseen by Romeo by reason of the night, when she reflected upon the discovery which she had made, yet not meaning to make it, of her love to Romeo.[xxi] She would fain have recalled her words, but that was impossible—* fain would she have stood upon form, and have kept her lover at a distance, as the custom of discreet⑤ ladies is, to frown and be perverse⑥, and give their suitors harsh denials at first; to stand off, and affect a coyness⑦ or indifference, where they most love, that their lovers may not think them too lightly or too easily won; for the difficulty of attainment⑧ increases the value of the object.[xxii] But there was no room in her case for denials, or any of the customary⑨ arts of delay and protracted⑩ courtship. Romeo had heard from her own tongue, when she did not dream that he was near her, a confession of her love. * So with an honest frankness, which the novelty⑪ of her situation excused, she confirmed the truth of what he had before heard, and addressing him by the name of fair Montague (love can sweeten a sour name), she begged him not to impute⑫ her easy yielding⑬ to levity⑭ or an unworthy mind, but that he must lay the fault of it (if it were a fault) upon the accident of the night which had so strangely discovered her thoughts.[xxiii] *And she added, that though her behaviour to him might not be sufficiently prudent⑮, measured by the custom of her sex, yet that she would prove more true than many whose prudence⑯ was dissembling⑰, and their modesty artificial⑱ cunning.[xxiv]

* Romeo was beginning to call the heavens to witness, that nothing was farther from his thoughts than to impute a shadow of dishonour to such an honoured lady, when she stopped him, begging him not to swear; for although she joyed in him, yet she had no joy of that night's

---

① proof [pruːf] *adj*. 防……的,耐……的 resistant
② vast [vɑːst] *adj*. 巨大的 huge, massive, enormous, immense
③ merchandise [ˈmɜːtʃəndaɪs] *n*. 货物 goods, commodity
④ crimson [ˈkrɪmzn] *adj*. 通红的 red, reddish, scarlet, blood-red
⑤ discreet [dɪˈskriːt] *adj*. 谨慎的 careful, cautious, wary, prudent
⑥ perverse [pəˈvɜːs] *adj*. 执拗的 stubborn, obstinate, headstrong
⑦ coyness [ˈkɔɪnəs] *n*. 羞怯 shyness, bashfulness, timidity
⑧ attainment [əˈteɪnmənt] *n*. 获得 achievement, acquisition
⑨ customary [ˈkʌstəməri] *adj*. 通常的 usual, regular, traditional
⑩ protracted [prəˈtræktɪd] *adj*. 拖延的 extended, prolonged
⑪ novelty [ˈnɒvlti] *n*. 新奇 newness, uniqueness, originality
⑫ impute [ɪmˈpjuːt] *v*. 归咎于
⑬ yield [jiːld] *v*. 屈服 surrender, give up/in, concede
⑭ levity [ˈlevəti] *n*. 轻浮 frivolity, fickleness
⑮ prudent [ˈpruːdnt] *adj*. 谨慎的 careful, cautious, wary, discreet
⑯ prudence [ˈpruːdns] *n*. 审慎 caution, wariness, discretion
⑰ dissemble [dɪˈsembl] *v*. 假装 feign, affect, simulate, falsify
⑱ artificial [ˌɑːtɪˈfɪʃl] *adj*. 假的 false, pretended, feigned, affected

contract[1]—it was too rash, too unadvised[2], too sudden.[xxv] * But he being urgent with her to exchange a vow of love with him that night, she said that she already had given him hers before he requested it; meaning, when he overheard her confession; but she would retract what she then bestowed, for the pleasure of giving it again, for her bounty[3] was as infinite[4] as the sea, and her love as deep.[xxvi] From this loving conference[5] she was called away by her nurse, who slept with her, and thought it time for her to be in bed, for it was near to daybreak; but hastily returning, she said three or four words more to Romeo, the purport[6] of which was, that if his love was indeed honourable, and his purpose marriage, she would send a messenger to him to-morrow, to appoint a time for their marriage, when * she would lay all her fortunes at his feet, and follow him as her lord through the world.[xxvii] While they were settling this point, Juliet was repeatedly called for by her nurse, and went in and returned, and went and returned again, for * she seemed as jealous of Romeo going from her, as a young girl of her bird, which she will let hop[7] a little from her hand, and pluck[8] it back with a silken thread[9]; and Romeo was as loath[10] to part as she; for the sweetest music to lovers is the sound of each other's tongues at night.[xxviii] But at last they parted, wishing mutually[11] sweet sleep and rest for that night.

The day was breaking when they parted, and Romeo, who was too full of thoughts of his mistress and that blessed meeting to allow him to sleep, instead of going home, bent his course to a monastery[12] hard by, to find friar[13] Lawrence. The good friar was already up at his devotions, but seeing young Romeo abroad so early, he conjectured rightly that he had not been abed that night, but that some distemper[14] of youthful affection had kept him waking. He was right in imputing the cause of Romeo's wakefulness to love, but he made a wrong guess at the object, for he thought that his love for Rosaline had kept him waking. * But when Romeo revealed his new passion for Juliet, and requested the assistance of the friar to marry them that day, the holy man lifted up his eyes and hands in a sort of wonder at the sudden change in Romeo's affections, for he had been privy to all Romeo's love for Rosaline,

---

① contract ['kɒntrækt] *n*. 合约 agreement, settlement, engagement
② unadvised [ˌʌnəd'vaɪzd] *adj*. 鲁莽的 rash, imprudent, indiscreet
③ bounty ['baʊnti] *n*. 慷慨 generosity, charity, liberality
④ infinite ['ɪnfɪnət] *adj*. 无限的 countless, numberless, innumerable
⑤ conference ['kɒnfərəns] *n*. 交谈 talk, chat, conversation
⑥ purport [pə'pɔːt] *n*. 要旨,主旨 gist, drift
⑦ hop [hɒp] *v*. 跳跃 jump, spring, bound, leap, skip
⑧ pluck [plʌk] *v*. 猛拉 draw, tug, snatch, jerk, yank, pull at
⑨ thread [θred] *n*. 线 strand, yarn, filament, line, string
⑩ loath [ləʊθ] *adj*. 不情愿的 unwilling, reluctant
⑪ mutually ['mjuːtʃuəli] *adv*. 相互地 jointly, commonly, reciprocally
⑫ monastery ['mɒnəstri] *n*. 修道院 abbey, convent, cloister
⑬ friar ['fraɪə(r)] *n*. 男修道士 monk, abbot
⑭ distemper [dɪ'stempə(r)] *n*. 坏脾气

and his many complaints① of her disdain②—and he said, that young men's love lay not truly in their hearts, but in their eyes.[xxix] But Romeo replying, that he himself had often chidden him for doting on Rosaline, who could not love him again, whereas③ Juliet both loved and was beloved by him, the friar assented④ in some measure⑤ to his reasons; and * thinking that a matrimonial⑥ alliance⑦ between young Juliet and Romeo might happily be the means of making up the long breach⑧ between the Capulets and the Montagues; which no one more lamented than this good friar, who was a friend to both the families and had often interposed⑨ his mediation to make up the quarrel without effect; partly moved by policy, and partly by his fondness for young Romeo, to whom he could deny nothing, the old man consented to join their hands in marriage.[xxx]

* Now was Romeo blessed indeed, and Juliet, who knew his intent from a messenger which she had despatched according to promise, did not fail to be early at the cell of friar Lawrence, where their hands were joined in holy marriage;[xxxi] the good friar praying the heavens to smile upon that act, and in the union of this young Montague and young Capulet to bury the old strife⑩ and long dissensions⑪ of their families.

The ceremony being over, Juliet hastened⑫ home, where she stayed impatient⑬ for the coming of night, at which time Romeo promised to come and meet her in the orchard, where they had met the night before; and * the time between seemed as tedious⑭ to her, as the night before some great festival seems to an impatient child, that has got new finery⑮ which it may not put on till the morning.[xxxii]

That same day, about noon, Romeo's friends, Benvolio and Mercutio, walking through the streets of Verona, were met by a party of the Capulets with the impetuous⑯ Tybalt at their head. This was the same angry Tybalt who would have fought with Romeo at old lord Capulet's feast. He, seeing Mercutio, accused him bluntly of associating⑰ with Romeo, a Montague. Mercutio, who had as much fire and youthful blood in him as Tybalt, replied to this accusation with some sharpness; and in spite of all Benvolio could say

① complaint [kəm'pleɪnt] *n*. 抱怨，投诉 accusation, charge
② disdain [dɪs'deɪn] *n*. 鄙视 contempt, scorn
③ whereas [ˌweər'æz] *conj*. 然而 yet, but, while, however
④ assent [ə'sent] *v*. 同意 approve, agree, consent
⑤ in some measure 在某种程度上 to some degree/extent
⑥ matrimonial [ˌmætrɪ'məʊniəl] *adj*. 婚姻的 marital, wedding
⑦ alliance [ə'laɪəns] *n*. 联盟 union, league
⑧ breach [briːtʃ] *n*. 决裂
⑨ interpose [ˌɪntə'pəʊz] *v*. 介入 interfere, intervene, step in
⑩ strife [straɪf] *n*. 冲突 conflict, battle, clash, combat, discord
⑪ dissension [dɪ'senʃn] *n*. 纷争 disagreement, dissent, dispute
⑫ hasten ['heɪsn] *v*. 赶往 rush, race, hurry up
⑬ impatient [ɪm'peɪʃnt] *adj*. 不耐烦的 fretful
⑭ tedious ['tiːdiəs] *adj*. 乏味的 boring, dull, drab, dreary, wearisome
⑮ finery ['faɪnəri] *n*. 鲜艳服饰
⑯ impetuous [ɪm'petʃuəs] *adj*. 鲁莽的 rash, impulsive, headlong
⑰ associate [ə'səʊsieɪt] *v*. 交往 mix, socialize

to moderate① their wrath, a quarrel was beginning, when Romeo himself passing that way, the fierce Tybalt turned from Mercutio to Romeo, and gave him the disgraceful appellation② of villain. Romeo wished to avoid a quarrel with Tybalt above all men, because he was the kinsman of Juliet, and much beloved by her; besides, this young Montague had never thoroughly③ entered into the family quarrel, being by nature wise and gentle, and * the name of a Capulet, which was his dear lady's name, was now rather a charm to allay④ resentment⑤, than a watchword⑥ to excite fury.[xxxiii]

So he tried to reason with Tybalt, whom he saluted⑦ mildly by the name of good Capulet, as if he, though a Montague, had some secret pleasure in uttering that name—but Tybalt, who hated all Montagues as he hated hell, would hear no reason, but drew his weapon; and * Mercutio, who knew not of Romeo's secret motive for desiring peace with Tybalt, but looked upon his present forbearance⑧ as a sort of calm dishonourable submission, with many disdainful words provoked⑨ Tybalt to the prosecution⑩ of his first quarrel with him;[xxxiv] and Tybalt and Mercutio fought, till Mercutio fell, receiving his death's wound while Romeo and Benvolio were vainly endeavouring to part the combatants⑪. Mercutio being dead, Romeo kept his temper no longer, but returned the scornful appellation of villain which Tybalt had given him; and they fought till Tybalt was slain by Romeo. This deadly broil⑫ falling out in the midst of Verona at noonday, the news of it quickly brought a crowd of citizens to the spot, and among them the old lords Capulet and Montague, with their wives; and * soon after arrived the prince himself, who being related to Mercutio, whom Tybalt had slain, and having had the peace of his government often disturbed by these brawls of Montagues and Capulets, came determined to put the law in strictest force against those who should be found to be offenders.[xxxv]

Benvolio, who had been eyewitness to the fray⑬, was commanded by the prince to relate the origin of it; which he did, keeping as near the truth as he could without injury to Romeo, softening and excusing the part which his friends took in it. Lady Capulet, whose extreme grief for the loss of her kinsman Tybalt made her keep no bounds in her revenge, exhorted⑭ the prince to do strict justice upon his murderer, and to pay no attention to Benvolio's representation⑮, who, being Romeo's friend and a Montague, spoke partially⑯. Thus she pleaded against her new son-in-

---

① moderate [ˈmɒdəreɪt] *v*. 缓和 soften, lessen
② appellation [ˌæpəˈleɪʃn] *n*. 称呼 name, term, title, address
③ thoroughly [ˈθʌrəli] *adv*. 完全地 fully, completely, entirely
④ allay [əˈleɪ] *v*. 减轻 reduce, lessen, relieve, diminish, soften
⑤ resentment [rɪˈzentmənt] *n*. 怨恨 bitterness, grudge, malice
⑥ watchword [ˈwɒtʃwɜːd] *n*. 口号 motto, slogan, catchword
⑦ salute [səˈluːt] *v*. 问候 greet
⑧ forbearance [fɔːˈbeərəns] *n*. 忍耐 patience, tolerance
⑨ provoke [prəˈvəʊk] *v*. 激起 rouse, inspire, stimulate, motivate
⑩ prosecution [ˌprɒsɪˈkjuːʃn] *n*. 实施 execution
⑪ combatant [ˈkɒmbətənt] *n*. 争斗者 fighter, warrior, contender
⑫ broil [brɔɪl] *n*. 争辩 argument, quarrel, brawl, dispute, clash
⑬ fray [freɪ] *n*. 争斗,打架 fight, battle, row, conflict, clash, brawl
⑭ exhort [ɪɡˈzɔːt] *v*. 敦促,劝诫 urge, encourage, press, call upon
⑮ representation [ˌreprɪzenˈteɪʃn] *n*. 陈述 statement, account
⑯ partially [ˈpɑːʃəli] *adv*. 不完全地,部分地 biasedly, prejudicedly, unfairly, one-sidedly

law, but she knew not yet that he was her son-in-law and Juliet's husband. On the other hand was to be seen Lady Montague pleading for her child's life, and arguing with some justice that Romeo had done nothing worthy of punishment in taking the life of Tybalt, which was already forfeited[1] to the law by his having slain Mercutio. The prince, unmoved by the passionate exclamations[2] of these women, on a careful examination of the facts, pronounced his sentence, and by that sentence Romeo was banished from Verona.

Heavy news to young Juliet, who had been but a few hours a bride, and now by this decree[3] seemed everlastingly[4] divorced[5]! When the tidings reached her, she at first gave way to rage against Romeo, who had slain her dear cousin—* she called him a beautiful tyrant, a fiend[6] angelical, a ravenous[7] dove[8], a lamb with a wolf's nature, a serpent-heart hid with a flowering face, and other like contradictory[9] names, which denoted[10] the struggles in her mind between her love and her resentment[xxxvi] —but in the end love got the mastery[11], and the tears which she shed for grief that Romeo had slain her cousin, turned to drops of joy that her husband lived whom Tybalt would have slain. Then came fresh tears, and they were altogether of grief for Romeo's banishment. That word was more terrible to her than the death of many Tybalts.

Romeo, after the fray, had taken refuge[12] in friar Lawrence's cell, where he was first made acquainted[13] with the prince's sentence, which seemed to him far more terrible than death. * To him it appeared there was no world out of Verona's walls, no living out of the sight of Juliet. Heaven was there where Juliet lived, and all beyond was purgatory[14], torture, hell. The good friar would have applied the consolation[15] of philosophy to his griefs—but this frantic young man would hear of none, but like a madman he tore his hair, and threw himself all along upon the ground, as he said, to take the measure of his grave.[xxxvii]

From this unseemly[16] state he was roused[17] by a message from his dear lady, which a little revived[18] him; and then the friar took the advantage to expostulate with him on the unmanly weakness which he had shown. * He had slain Tybalt, but would he also slay himself, slay his dear lady, who lived but in his life?[xxxviii] * The noble form of man, he said, was but a shape of wax,

---

① forfeit [ˈfɔːfɪt] *v*. 丧失 lose, relinquish, give up, be deprived of
② exclamation [ˌekskləˈmeɪʃn] *n*. 叫嚷 cry, call, shout, yell
③ decree [dɪˈkriː] *n*. 判决,法令 judgment, decision, conclusion
④ everlastingly [ˌevərˈlæstɪŋli] *adv*. 永久地 forever, permanently
⑤ divorced [dɪˈvɔːst] *adj*. 分离的 separated, deserted
⑥ fiend [fiːnd] *n*. 魔鬼 demon, devil, evil spirit
⑦ ravenous [ˈrævənəs] *adj*. 贪婪的 greedy, insatiable, avaricious
⑧ dove [dəʊv] *n*. 鸽子
⑨ contradictory [ˌkɒntrəˈdɪktəri] *adj*. 矛盾的 contrary, opposite
⑩ denote [dɪˈnəʊt] *v*. 意指,表示 mean, indicate, imply, suggest, refer to
⑪ mastery [ˈmɑːstəri] *n*. 控制 control, command
⑫ take refuge 避难
⑬ acquainted [əˈkweɪntɪd] *adj*. 知晓的 familiar, aware, informed
⑭ purgatory [ˈpɜːgətri] *n*. 炼狱;折磨 torment, torture
⑮ consolation [ˌkɒnsəˈleɪʃn] *n*. 安慰 comfort, relief, solace
⑯ unseemly [ʌnˈsiːmli] *adj*. 不得体的 improper, inappropriate
⑰ rouse [raʊz] *v*. 唤醒 awaken, excite, arouse
⑱ revive [rɪˈvaɪv] *v*. 使恢复精神 revitalize, restore, renew

when it wanted the courage which should keep it firm.[xxxix] The law had been lenient① to him, that instead of death, which he had incurred②, had pronounced by the prince's mouth only banishment. He had slain Tybalt, but Tybalt would have slain him—there was a sort of happiness③ in that. Juliet was alive, and (beyond all hope④) had become his dear wife; therein⑤ he was most happy. * All these blessings, as the friar made them out to be, did Romeo put from him like a sullen⑥ misbehaved⑦ wench⑧.[xl] * And the friar bade him beware, for such as despaired, (he said) died miserable.[xli] * Then when Romeo was a little calmed, he counselled⑨ him that he should go that night and secretly take his leave of⑩ Juliet, and thence⑪ proceed⑫ straightway⑬ to Mantua, at which place he should sojourn⑭, till the friar found fit occasion to publish his marriage, which might be a joyful means of reconciling their families; and then he did not doubt but the prince would be moved to pardon him, and he would return with twenty times more joy than he went forth⑮ with grief.[xlii] Romeo was convinced by these wise counsels of the friar, and took his leave to go and seek his lady, proposing to stay with her that night, and by daybreak pursue⑯ his journey alone to Mantua; to which place the good friar promised to send him letters from time to time, acquainting⑰ him with the state of affairs at home.

That night Romeo passed with his dear wife, gaining secret admission to her chamber, from the orchard in which he had heard her confession of love the night before. That had been a night of unmixed joy and rapture⑱; but the pleasures of this night, and the delight which these lovers took in each other's society, were sadly allayed with the prospect⑲ of parting, and the fatal adventures of the past day. * The unwelcome daybreak seemed to come too soon, and when Juliet heard the

---

① lenient ['liːniənt] *adj*. 宽容的,仁慈的 merciful, forgiving, tolerant
② incur [ɪn'kɜː(r)] *v*. 招致 induce
③ happiness ['hæpinəs] *n*. 运气 luck, fortune, chance
④ beyond all hope 出乎意料 beyond all expectations
⑤ therein [ˌðeər'ɪn] *adv*. 在其中,在那里 there, within, in there
⑥ sullen ['sʌlən] *adj*. 愠怒的 cross, moody, sulky
⑦ misbehave [ˌmɪsbɪ'heɪv] *v*. 行为不端
⑧ wench [wentʃ] *n*. 少女;乡下姑娘 lass, maiden, damsel
⑨ counsel ['kaʊnsl] *v*. 建议,忠告 advise, recommend
⑩ take leave of 告别
⑪ thence [ðens] *adv*. 从那里 from there, from that place
⑫ proceed [prə'siːd] *v*. 继续前进 continue, advance, go ahead
⑬ straightway [ˌstreɪt'weɪ] *adv*. 立刻 straightaway, immediately
⑭ sojourn ['sɒdʒən] *v*. 暂住,逗留 stop, stay, rest, lodge, dwell, abide
⑮ forth [fɔːθ] *adv*. 向前 forward, ahead, onward
⑯ pursue [pə'sjuː] *v*. 执行 take up, carry on, engage in
⑰ acquaint [ə'kweɪnt] *v*. 使了解 inform, familiarize, notify
⑱ rapture ['ræptʃə(r)] *n*. 狂喜 joy, delight, happiness, ecstasy
⑲ prospect ['prɒspekt] *n*. 前景 possibility

morning song of the lark①, she would have persuaded herself that it was the nightingale②, which sings by night; but it was too truly the lark which sang, and a discordant③ and unpleasing note it seemed to her; and the streaks④ of day in the east too certainly pointed out that it was time for these lovers to part.[xliii] Romeo took his leave of his dear wife with a heavy heart, promising to write to her from Mantua every hour in the day—and *when he had descended⑤ from her chamber-window, as he stood below her on the ground, in that sad foreboding⑥ state of mind in which she was, he appeared to her eyes as one dead in the bottom of a tomb.[xliv] Romeo's mind misgave⑦ him in like manner—but now he was forced hastily⑧ to depart, for it was death for him to be found within the walls of Verona after daybreak.

This was but the beginning of the tragedy of this pair of star-crossed⑨ lovers. Romeo had not been gone many days, before the old lord Capulet proposed a match for Juliet. The husband he had chosen for her, not dreaming that she was married already, was count⑩ Paris, a gallant⑪, young, and noble gentleman, no unworthy suitor to the young Juliet, if she had never seen Romeo.

The terrified Juliet was in a sad perplexity⑫ at her father's offer. She pleaded her youth unsuitable to marriage, the recent death of Tybalt, which had left her spirits too weak to meet a husband with any face of joy, and how indecorous⑬ it would show for the family of the Capulets to be celebrating a nuptial⑭ feast, when his funeral solemnities⑮ were hardly over—she pleaded every reason against the match, but the true one, namely, that she was married already. But lord Capulet was deaf to⑯ all her excuses, and in a peremptory⑰ manner ordered her to get ready, for by the following Thursday she should be married to Paris—and *having found her a husband, rich, young, and noble, such as the proudest maid in Verona might joyfully accept, he could not bear that out of an affected coyness⑱, as he construed⑲ her denial, she should oppose obstacles⑳ to her own good fortune.[xlv]

*In this extremity㉑ Juliet applied to the friendly friar, always her counsellor in distress, and

---

① lark [lɑːk] n. 百灵鸟，云雀
② nightingale [ˈnaɪtɪŋgeɪl] n. 夜莺
③ discordant [dɪsˈkɔːdənt] adj. 不协调的，不和谐的 conflicting, inharmonious
④ streak [striːk] n. 条纹 band, strip, stripe
⑤ descend [dɪˈsend] v. 下去 alight, dismount, go down, get off
⑥ foreboding [fɔːˈbəʊdɪŋ] adj. 不祥之兆的 ominous, threatening
⑦ misgive [mɪsˈgɪv] v. (misgave, misgiven) 使担心 upset, bother, unsettle, disquiet
⑧ hastily [ˈheɪstɪli] adv. 匆忙地 quickly, rapidly, speedily, hurriedly
⑨ star-crossed [ˈstɑːkrɒst] adj. 不幸的 unlucky, doomed, ill-fated
⑩ count [kaʊnt] n. 伯爵(欧洲国家的贵族头衔)
⑪ gallant [ˈgælənt] adj. 勇敢的 brave, heroic, courageous, valiant
⑫ perplexity [pəˈpleksəti] n. 困惑 puzzlement, confusion
⑬ indecorous [ɪnˈdekərəs] adj. 失礼的，不合礼节的 rude, impolite, indecent
⑭ nuptial [ˈnʌpʃl] adj. 婚姻的 marital, wedding, matrimonial, bridal
⑮ solemnity [səˈlemnəti] n. 仪式 rite, ritual, ceremony
⑯ be deaf to 对……充耳不闻
⑰ peremptory [pəˈremptəri] adj. 专横的 bossy, commanding
⑱ coyness [ˈkɔɪnəs] n. 羞怯 shyness, modesty, timidity
⑲ construe [kənˈstruː] v. 理解 understand, comprehend
⑳ obstacle [ˈɒbstəkl] n. 障碍 obstruction, block, barrier, hurdle
㉑ extremity [ɪkˈstreməti] n. 绝境 crisis, trouble, emergency

he asking her if she had resolution to undertake a desperate remedy①, and she answering that she would go into the grave alive rather than marry Paris, her own dear husband living;[xlvi] * he directed her to go home, and appear merry, and give her consent to marry Paris, according to her father's desire, and on the next night, which was the night before the marriage, to drink off the contents of a phial② which he then gave her, the effect of which would be that for two-and-forty hours after drinking it she should appear cold and lifeless;[xlvii] and when the bridegroom came to fetch her in the morning, he would find her to appearance dead; that * then she would be borne, as the manner in that country was, uncovered on a bier③, to be buried in the family vault④; that if she could put off womanish fear, and consent to this terrible trial, in forty-two hours after swallowing⑤ the liquid (such was its certain operation) she would be sure to awake, as from a dream;[xlviii] and before she should awake, he would let her husband know their drift⑥, and he should come in the night, and bear her thence to Mantua. Love, and the dread⑦ of marrying Paris, gave young Juliet strength to undertake this horrible adventure; and she took the phial of the friar, promising to observe his directions.

Going from the monastery, she met the young count Paris, and modestly dissembling, promised to become his bride. This was joyful news to the lord Capulet and his wife. It seemed to put youth into the old man; and Juliet, who had displeased him exceedingly, by her refusal of the count, was his darling again, now she promised to be obedient. * All things in the house were in a bustle⑧ against the approaching nuptials⑨. No cost was spared to prepare such festival rejoicings as Verona had never before witnessed.[xlix]

On the Wednesday night Juliet drank off the potion. * She had many misgivings⑩ lest the friar, to avoid the blame which might be imputed to him for marrying her to Romeo, had given her poison; but then he was always known for a holy man—then lest she should awake before the time that Romeo was to come for her; whether the terror of the place, a vault of dead Capulets' bones, and where Tybalt, all bloody, lay festering⑪ in his shroud⑫, would not be enough to drive her distracted—again she thought of all the stories she had heard of spirits haunting the places where their bodies were bestowed.[l] But then her love for Romeo, and her aversion⑬ for Paris

① remedy ['remədi] n. 处理方法,解决方法 solution, cure
② phial ['faɪəl] n. 小药瓶 vial
③ bier [bɪə(r)] n. 停尸架,棺材架
④ vault [vɔːlt] n. 地下墓室 crypt, tomb, catacomb, mausoleum
⑤ swallow ['swɒləʊ] v. 吞下,咽下 consume, devour, gulp
⑥ drift [drɪft] n. 主旨 point, gist
⑦ dread [dred] n. 恐惧 fear, horror, terror, fright, apprehension
⑧ bustle ['bʌsl] n. 忙乱
⑨ nuptial ['nʌpʃəl] n. 婚礼 wedding, marriage ceremony
⑩ misgiving [ˌmɪs'gɪvɪŋ] n. 疑虑,担忧 worry, anxiety, doubt, distrust
⑪ fester ['festə(r)] v. 溃烂 rot, decay
⑫ shroud [ʃraʊd] n. 裹尸布 cerecloth, winding sheet
⑬ aversion [ə'vɜːʃn] n. 憎恶 hate, hatred, dislike, disgust

returned, and she desperately swallowed the draught①, and became insensible②.

When young Paris came early in the morning with music to awaken his bride, instead of a living Juliet, her chamber presented the dreary③ spectacle④ of a lifeless corpse⑤. What death to his hopes! What confusion then reigned⑥ through the whole house! * Poor Paris lamenting his bride, whom most detestable⑦ death had beguiled him of, had divorced⑧ from him even before their hands were joined.[li] * But still more piteous⑨ it was to hear the mournings⑩ of the old lord and lady Capulet, who having but this one, one poor living child to rejoice⑪ and solace⑫ in, cruel death had snatched⑬ her from their sight, just as these careful parents were on the point of seeing her advanced (as they thought) by a promising and advantageous match.[lii] * Now all things that were ordained⑭ for the festival were turned from their properties to do the office of a black funeral.[liii] * The wedding cheer served for a sad burial feast, the bridal⑮ hymns⑯ were changed for sullen⑰ dirges⑱, the sprightly⑲ instruments⑳ to melancholy bells, and the flowers that should have been strewed㉑ in the bride's path, now served but to strew her corse㉒.[liv] Now, instead of a priest to marry her, a priest was needed to bury her; and she was borne to church indeed, not to augment㉓ the cheerful hopes of the living, but to swell㉔ the dreary numbers of the dead.

Bad news, which always travels faster than good, now brought the dismal㉕ story of his Juliet's death to Romeo, at Mantua, before the messenger could arrive, who was sent from friar Lawrence to apprise㉖ him that these were mock funerals only, and but the shadow and representation of death, and that his dear lady lay in the tomb but for a short while, expecting when Romeo would come to release her from that dreary mansion㉗. Just before, Romeo had been

---

① draught [drɑːft] *n.* 一饮(的量) drink, swallow, gulp, mouthful
② insensible [ɪnˈsensəbl] *adj.* 失去知觉的,昏迷的 insensate, benumbed
③ dreary [ˈdrɪəri] *adj.* 令人沮丧的 sorrowful, gloomy, melancholy
④ spectacle [ˈspektəkl] *n.* 景象 sight, scene, phenomenon
⑤ corpse [kɔːps] *n.* 尸体 body, remains, carcass, cadaver, corse
⑥ reign [reɪn] *v.* 盛行 prevail, predominate, rule, hold sway
⑦ detestable [dɪˈtestəbl] *adj.* 可憎的 hateful, disgusting
⑧ divorce [dɪˈvɔːs] *v.* 使分离 separate, disunite, set apart
⑨ piteous [ˈpɪtiəs] *adj.* 可怜的 pitiable, sorrowful, heartbreaking
⑩ mourning [ˈmɔːnɪŋ] *n.* 哀悼 grieving, grief, weeping
⑪ rejoice [rɪˈdʒɔɪs] *v.* 高兴 joy, delight, be happy/overjoyed
⑫ solace [ˈsɒləs] *v.* 安慰 comfort, console, relieve
⑬ snatch [snætʃ] *v.* 夺取 grab, grip, grasp, seize, take hold of
⑭ ordain [ɔːˈdeɪn] *v.* 规定,命令 appoint, commission, lay down
⑮ bridal [ˈbraɪdl] *adj.* 婚礼的 marriage, wedding, matrimonial
⑯ hymn [hɪm] *n.* 圣歌 carol, chant, anthem
⑰ sullen [ˈsʌlən] *adj.* 闷闷不乐的 cross, moody, out of humour
⑱ dirge [dɜːdʒ] *n.* 哀歌,挽歌 elegy, funeral song
⑲ sprightly [ˈspraɪtli] *adj.* 轻快的 lively, spirited, active, brisk, airy
⑳ instrument [ˈɪnstrəmənt] *n.* 乐器 tool
㉑ strew [struː] *v.* 散播 scatter, spread, sprinkle, disperse
㉒ corse [kɔːs] *n.* 〈古〉尸体 corpse, carcass, cadaver, dead body
㉓ augment [ɔːgˈment] *v.* 增加 increase, heighten, raise, build up
㉔ swell [swel] *v.* 使膨胀 expand, surge, multiply, grow larger
㉕ dismal [ˈdɪzməl] *adj.* 忧郁的 sad, gloomy, dreary, melancholy
㉖ apprise [əˈpraɪz] *v.* 告知 tell, inform, notify, make aware
㉗ mansion [ˈmænʃn] *n.* 宅邸 residence, manor, hall, villa, abode

unusually joyful and light-hearted①. * He had dreamed in the night that he was dead (a strange dream, that gave a dead man leave to think), and that his lady came and found him dead, and breathed such life with kisses in his lips, that he revived, and was an emperor![lv] And now that a messenger came from Verona, he thought surely it was to confirm some good news which his dreams had presaged②. * But when the contrary to this flattering③ vision④ appeared, and that it was his lady who was dead in truth, whom he could not revive by any kisses, he ordered horses to be got ready, for he determined that night to visit Verona, and to see his lady in her tomb.[lvi] And as mischief is swift to enter into the thoughts of desperate men, he called to mind a poor apothecary⑤, whose shop in Mantua he had lately passed, and from the beggarly appearance of the man, who seemed famished⑥, and the wretched show in his shop of empty boxes ranged⑦ on dirty shelves, and other tokens of extreme wretchedness, he had said at the time (* perhaps having some misgivings that his own disastrous⑧ life might haply⑨ meet with a conclusion so desperate[lvii]), "If a man were to need poison, which by the law of Mantua it is death to sell, here lives a poor wretch who would sell it him." These words of his now came into his mind, and he sought out the apothecary, who after some pretended scruples, Romeo offering him gold, which his poverty could not resist, sold him a poison, which, if he swallowed, he told him, if he had the strength of twenty men, would quickly despatch him.

With this poison he set out for Verona, to have a sight of his dear lady in her tomb, meaning, when he had satisfied his sight, to swallow the poison, and be buried by her side. He reached Verona at midnight, and found the churchyard, in the midst of which was situated the ancient tomb of the Capulets. He had provided a light, and a spade, and wrenching iron, and was proceeding to break open the monument, when he was interrupted by a voice, which by the name of vile Montague, bade him desist from his unlawful business. It was the young count Paris, who had come to the tomb of Juliet at that unseasonable⑩ time of night, to strew flowers and to weep over the grave of her that should have been his bride. * He knew not what an interest Romeo had in the dead, but knowing him to be a Montague, and (as he supposed) a sworn⑪ foe to all the Capulets, he judged

① light-hearted ['laɪt'hɑːtɪd] *adj*. 轻松愉快的 carefree, happy, cheerful, joyful
② presage ['presɪdʒ] *v*. 预兆，预示 predict, foretell, portend, betoken
③ flattering ['flætərɪŋ] *adj*. 令人愉快的 pleasing, favorable, satisfying
④ vision ['vɪʒn] *n*. 幻象 fancy, fantasy, delusion, illusion
⑤ apothecary [ə'pɒθəkəri] *n*. 药剂师，药商 pharmacist, druggist
⑥ famished ['fæmɪʃt] *adj*. 极饿的 starving
⑦ range [reɪndʒ] *v*. 排列 rank, arrange
⑧ disastrous [dɪ'zɑːstrəs] *adj*. 灾难性的 destructive, catastrophic
⑨ haply ['hæpli] *adv*. 偶然 accidentally, by luck/chance/accident
⑩ unseasonable [ʌn'siːznəbl] *adj*. 不合时宜的 untimely, unsuitable
⑪ sworn [swɔːn] *adj*. 不共戴天的

that he was come by night to do some villainous① shame to the dead bodies; therefore in an angry tone he bade him desist; and as a criminal, condemned by the laws of Verona to die if he were found within the walls of the city, he would have apprehended② him. Romeo urged Paris to leave him, and warned him by the fate of Tybalt, who lay buried there, not to provoke③ his anger, or draw down another sin upon his head, by forcing him to kill him.[lviii] But the count in scorn refused his warning, and laid hands on him as a felon④, which Romeo resisting, they fought, and Paris fell. * When Romeo, by the help of a light, came to see who it was that he had slain, that it was Paris, who (he learned in his way from Mantua) should have married Juliet, he took the dead youth by the hand, as one whom misfortune had made a companion, and said that he would bury him in a triumphal⑤ grave, meaning in Juliet's grave, which he now opened[lix] —and * there lay his lady, as one whom death had no power upon to change a feature or complexion, in her matchless beauty; or as if death were amorous⑥, and the lean⑦ abhorred⑧ monster kept her there for his delight;[lx] for she lay yet fresh and blooming⑨, as she had fallen to sleep when she swallowed that benumbing⑩ potion; and * near her lay Tybalt in his bloody shroud, whom Romeo seeing, begged pardon of his lifeless corpse, and for Juliet's sake called him cousin, and said that he was about to do him a favour by putting his enemy to death.[lxi] Here Romeo took his last leave of his lady's lips, kissing them; and * here he shook the burden of his cross stars from his weary body, swallowing that poison which the apothecary had sold him, whose operation was fatal and real, not like that dissembling potion which Juliet had swallowed, the effect of which was now nearly expiring, and she about to awake to complain that Romeo had not kept his time, or that he had come too soon.[lxii]

For now the hour was arrived at which the friar had promised that she should awake; and he, having learned that his letters which he had sent to Mantua, by some unlucky detention⑪ of the messenger, had never reached Romeo, came himself, provided with the pickaxe⑫ and lantern, to deliver the lady from her confinement⑬; but he was surprised to find a light already burning in the Capulets' monument, and to see swords and blood near it, and Romeo and Paris lying breathless by the monument.

---

① villainous ['vɪlənəs] *adj*. 邪恶的 bad, evil, vile, wicked, vicious
② apprehend [ˌæprɪ'hend] *v*. 逮捕 catch, capture, arrest
③ provoke [prə'vəʊk] *v*. 激起 rouse, excite, inspire, stimulate
④ felon ['felən] *n*. 重罪犯 criminal, convict, offender, evildoer
⑤ triumphal [traɪ'ʌmfl] *adj*. 凯旋的,胜利的 triumphant, victorious
⑥ amorous ['æmərəs] *adj*. 多情的 loving, affectionate
⑦ lean [liːn] *adj*. 瘦的 thin, skinny, bony, slim, slender, lanky
⑧ abhor [əb'hɔː(r)] *v*. 憎恨 hate, loathe, detest, abominate
⑨ blooming ['bluːmɪŋ] *adj*. 盛开的 flowering, blossoming, budding
⑩ benumb [bɪ'nʌm] *v*. 使麻木 paralyse, freeze, make numb
⑪ detention [dɪ'tenʃn] *n*. 延迟 delay, hold-up, interruption
⑫ pickaxe ['pɪkæks] *n*. 镐,鹤嘴锄
⑬ confinement [kən'faɪnmənt] *n*. 拘禁 imprisonment, custody

* Before he could entertain[1] a conjecture[2], to imagine how these fatal accidents had fallen out[3], Juliet awoke out of her trance[4], and seeing the friar near her, she remembered the place where she was, and the occasion of her being there, and asked for Romeo, but the friar, hearing a noise, bade her come out of that place of death, and of unnatural sleep, for a greater power than they could contradict[5] had thwarted[6] their intents[7];[lxiii] and being frightened by the noise of people coming, he fled—but when Juliet saw the cup closed in her true love's hand, she guessed that poison had been the cause of his end, and she would have swallowed the dregs[8] if any had been left, and she kissed his still warm lips to try if any poison yet did hang upon them; then hearing a nearer noise of people coming, she quickly unsheathed[9] a dagger[10] which she wore, and stabbing[11] herself, died by her true Romeo's side.

The watch by this time had come up to the place. A page belonging to count Paris, who had witnessed the fight between his master and Romeo, had given the alarm, which had spread among the citizens, who went up and down the streets of Verona confusedly exclaiming, *A Paris! a Romeo! a Juliet!* As the rumour had imperfectly reached them, till the uproar[12] brought lord Montague and lord Capulet out of their beds, with the prince, to inquire into the causes of the disturbance[13]. The friar had been apprehended by some of the watch, coming from the churchyard, trembling[14], sighing, and weeping, in a suspicious manner. A great multitude[15] being assembled[16] at the Capulets' monument, the friar was demanded by the prince to deliver what he knew of these strange and disastrous accidents.

And there, in the presence of the old lords Montague and Capulet, he faithfully related the story of their children's fatal love, the part he took in promoting their marriage, in the hope in that union to end the long quarrels between their families—how Romeo, there dead, was husband to Juliet; and Juliet, there dead, was Romeo's faithful wife; how before he could find a fit opportunity to divulge[17] their marriage, another match was projected[18] for Juliet, who, to avoid the crime of a second marriage, swallowed the sleeping draught (as he advised), and all thought

---

① entertain [ˌentəˈteɪn] *v*. 心存，怀有 consider, imagine

② conjecture [kənˈdʒektʃə(r)] *n*. 猜测 guess, speculation, assumption

③ fall out 发生 happen, occur, take place, come to pass

④ trance [trɑːns] *n*. 恍惚，出神 daze, stupor, unconsciousness

⑤ contradict [ˌkɒntrəˈdɪkt] *v*. 抵触 challenge, oppose, counter

⑥ thwart [θwɔːt] *v*. 挫败 frustrate, stop, foil, check

⑦ intent [ɪnˈtent] *n*. 意图 intention, aim, purpose, objective

⑧ dreg [dreg] *n*. 残渣 sediment, residue, scum

⑨ unsheathe [ʌnˈʃiːð] *v*. 拔出鞘

⑩ dagger [ˈdægə(r)] *n*. 匕首，短剑 knife, blade, bayonet, poniard

⑪ stab [stæb] *v*. 刺 pierce, jab, puncture

⑫ uproar [ˈʌprɔː(r)] *n*. 喧嚣 commotion, noise, riot, confusion

⑬ disturbance [dɪˈstɜːbəns] *n*. 骚动，干扰 disorder, uproar, tumult

⑭ tremble [ˈtrembl] *v*. 颤抖 shake, shiver, quake, shudder, quiver

⑮ multitude [ˈmʌltɪtjuːd] *n*. 人群，民众 crowd, throng, congregation

⑯ assemble [əˈsembl] *v*. 聚集 gather, congregate

⑰ divulge [daɪˈvʌldʒ] *v*. 透露，泄露 reveal, disclose, declare

⑱ project [prəˈdʒekt] *v*. 规划 plan, design, scheme, map out

her dead; how meantime① he wrote to Romeo, to come and take her thence② when the force of the potion should cease, and by what unfortunate miscarriage③ of the messenger the letters never reached Romeo; * further than this the friar could not follow the story, nor knew more than that coming himself, to deliver Juliet from that place of death, he found the count Paris and Romeo slain.[lxiv] * The remainder of the transactions④ was supplied by the narration of the page who had seen Paris and Romeo fight, and by the servant who came with Romeo from Verona, to whom this faithful lover had given letters to be delivered to his father in the event of⑤ his death, which made good the friar's words, confessing his marriage with Juliet, imploring the forgiveness of his parents, acknowledging the buying of the poison of the poor apothecary, and his intent in coming to the monument, to die, and lie with Juliet.[lxv] * All these circumstances⑥ agreed together to clear the friar from any hand he could be supposed to have in these complicated slaughters, further than as the unintended consequences of his own well meant, yet too artificial and subtle contrivances.[lxvi]

* And the prince, turning to these old lords, Montague and Capulet, rebuked⑦ them for their brutal and irrational⑧ enmities, and showed them what a scourge⑨ Heaven had laid upon such offences, that it had found means even through the love of their children to punish their unnatural hate.[lxvii] And these old rivals⑩, no longer enemies, agreed to bury their long strife in their children's graves; and lord Capulet requested lord Montague to give him his hand, calling him by the name of brother, as if in acknowledgement of the union of their families, by the marriage of the young Capulet and Montague; and saying that lord Montague's hand (in token of reconcilement) was all he demanded for his daughter's jointure⑪— * but lord Montague said he would give him more, for he would raise her a statue of pure gold, that while Verona kept its name, no figure should be so esteemed for its richness and workmanship⑫ as that of the true and faithful Juliet.[lxviii] And lord Capulet in return said that he would raise another statue to Romeo. * So did these poor old lords, when it was too late, strive to outdo⑬ each other in mutual courtesies—while so deadly had been their rage and enmity in past times, that nothing but the fearful overthrow⑭ of their children (poor sacrifices to their quarrels and dissensions⑮) could remove the rooted hates and jealousies⑯ of the noble families. [lxix]

---

① meantime [ˈmiːntaɪm] *adv*. 与此同时 in the meanwhile
② thence [ðens] *adv*. 从那里;从那时起
③ miscarriage [ˈmɪskærɪdʒ] *n*. 失败 failure
④ transaction [trænˈzækʃn] *n*. 事务 deal, matter, affair
⑤ in the event of 万一,倘若 in the eventuality/situation of
⑥ circumstance [ˈsɜːkəmstəns] *n*. 状况,情况 condition, situation
⑦ rebuke [rɪˈbjuːk] *v*. 斥责 scold, reproach, blame
⑧ irrational [ɪˈræʃənl] *adj*. 不合逻辑的,非理性的 illogical, unreasonable
⑨ scourge [skɜːdʒ] *n*. 祸害,灾祸 affliction, plague
⑩ rival [ˈraɪvl] *n*. 竞争对手 opponent, adversary, antagonist
⑪ jointure [ˈdʒɔɪntʃə] *n*. 寡妇所得遗产
⑫ workmanship [ˈwɜːkmənʃɪp] *n*. 技艺 skill, craftsmanship
⑬ outdo [ˌaʊtˈduː] *v*. 胜过 beat, triumph over
⑭ overthrow [ˈəʊvəθrəʊ] *n*. 毁灭 destruction, downfall, ruin
⑮ dissension [dɪˈsenʃn] *n*. 纷争 conflict, dissent, dispute, discord
⑯ jealousy [ˈdʒeləsi] *n*. 猜忌,嫉妒 envy

Juliet. O Heaven, she comes!
Act II. Scene V.

There had been an old quarrel between these families, which was grown to such a height, and so deadly was the enmity between them, that it extended to the remotest kindred, to the followers and retainers of both sides, insomuch that a servant of the house of Montague could not meet a servant of the house of Capulet, nor a Capulet encounter with a Montague by chance, but fierce words and sometimes bloodshed ensued; and frequent were the brawls from such accidental meetings, which disturbed the happy quiet of Verona's streets. 两家之间旧日发生过一场争吵,后来越吵越厉害,仇恨结得非常深,连两方最远的亲戚,甚至侍从和仆役都牵连上了,弄得只要蒙太古家的仆人一碰到凯普莱特家的仆人,或是凯普莱特家的人偶然碰到蒙太古家的人,他们就会对骂起来,有时候还会闹出流血事件。他们偶然碰到就吵

起来的事情时常发生，把维洛那街巷可喜的清静都扰乱了。（which…such…，and so…was..，that…：非限制性定语从句中嵌套 so…that…部分倒装的结果状语从句；but：强调一贯事实；happy＝pleasant）

ii Benvolio，a friend of Romeo，persuaded the young lord to go to this assembly in the disguise of a mask，that he might see his Rosaline，and seeing her compare her with some choice beauties of Verona，who（he said）would make him think his swan a crow. 罗密欧的朋友班伏里奥怂恿这个少爷戴上面具去参加宴会，好让他看到他的罗瑟琳。（班伏里奥说）等罗密欧看到她后，再把她跟维洛那出色的美人比一比，就会觉得他心目中的天鹅不过是一只乌鸦罢了。（that＝so that：目的状语从句）

iii Old Capulet bid them welcome，and told them that ladies who had their toes unplagued with corns would dance with them. 凯普莱特老爷向他们表示欢迎，并且告诉他们说，只要姑娘们脚上没长鸡眼，都可以和他们跳舞。

iv Romeo was suddenly struck with the exceeding beauty of a lady who danced there，who seemed to him to teach the torches to burn bright，and her beauty to show by night like a rich jewel worn by a blackamoor. 罗密欧突然被一位正在跳舞的姑娘的美貌打动了，他觉得灯火好像因为她而燃得更亮了，她的美貌宛如黑人戴的一颗贵重的宝石，在夜晚显得格外灿烂。（lady who…，who…：并列的定语从句；比喻修辞）

v Beauty too rich for use，too dear for earth！like a snowy dove trooping with crows（he said），so richly did her beauty and perfections shine above the ladies her companions. 这样的美在人间太贵重了，简直舍不得碰！她的美貌和才艺大大超出了和她在一起的姑娘们，（他说）就像一只雪白的鸽子跟乌鸦结群一样。（so…did…：部分倒装结构；比喻修辞）

vi Tybalt，forced to be patient against his will，restrained himself，but swore that this vile Montague should at another time dearly pay for his intrusion. 提伯尔特不得已，只好按捺住性子，可是他发誓说，改天一定要让这个卑鄙的蒙太古家的人为他的擅自闯入付出惨重的代价。

vii Under favour of his masking habit，which might seem to excuse in part the liberty，he presumed in the gentlest manner to take her by the hand，calling it a shrine，which if he profaned by touching it，he was a blushing pilgrim，and would kiss it for atonement. 幸亏有面具遮着，他的放肆好像有了一些借口。他壮起胆子来，温柔地握了一下她的手，管她的手叫神龛；既然他亵渎地触碰了它，作为一个羞怯的朝圣者，他想吻它一下来赎罪。（under favour of his masking habit：幸亏有面具遮掩）

viii Good pilgrim，your devotion shows by far too mannerly and too courtly—saints have hands，which pilgrims may touch，but kiss not. 好个朝圣者，你朝拜得太殷勤、太隆重了吧——圣人有手，可是朝圣者只许摸，不许吻。（罗密欧是朝圣者，朱丽叶是圣人）

ix O then，my dear saint，hear my prayer，and grant it，lest I despair. 哦，那么我亲爱的圣人，听听我的祈祷，许了我吧，不然我会绝望的。

x Romeo inquiring who her mother was，discovered that the lady whose peerless beauty he was so much struck with，was young Juliet，daughter and heir to the lord Capulet，the great enemy of the Montagues；and that he had unknowingly engaged his heart to his foe. 罗密欧询问她的母亲是谁，才知道打动了他的心的这位顶标致的姑娘名叫朱丽叶，是蒙太古家大仇人凯普莱特老爷的女儿和继承人，他这才知道他无意中爱上了他的仇人。（discovered that…whose…：宾语从句中嵌套定语从句）

xi As little rest had Juliet, when she found that the gentleman that she had been talking with was Romeo and a Montague, for she had been suddenly smit with the same hasty and inconsiderate passion for Romeo, which he had conceived for her; and a prodigious birth of love it seemed to her, that she must love her enemy, and that her affections should settle there, where family considerations should induce her chiefly to hate. 当朱丽叶发觉跟她谈话的那个人是蒙太古家的罗密欧时，她也同样感到不安，因为她也轻率、冲动地爱上了罗密欧，正像他爱上她一样。朱丽叶觉得这爱情产生得真是奇怪，她得去爱她的仇人，她的心得属于出于家庭因素她更应该憎恨的地方。(when...that...that...：时间状语从句、宾语从句和定语从句的嵌套)

xii Here he had not been long, ruminating on his new love, when Juliet appeared above at a window, through which her exceeding beauty seemed to break like the light of the sun in the east; and the moon, which shone in the orchard with a faint light, appeared to Romeo as if sick and pale with grief at the superior lustre of this new sun. 他在那里默默地想着刚刚发生的恋爱，想了没多久，朱丽叶就从上面的窗口出现了。她卓绝的美貌就像东方的太阳那样放出光彩。在罗密欧看来，映在果园上空的月亮似乎因为这轮旭日的灿烂光辉而显得苍白无力，满怀忧伤。(比喻、拟人和对比修辞)

xiii She, leaning her cheek upon her hand, he passionately wished himself a glove upon that hand, that he might touch her cheek. 朱丽叶用手托着腮，罗密欧热切地希望自己是她手上的一只手套，这样他就可以触摸她的面颊。(she, leaning...：独立主格结构)

xiv O speak again, bright angel, for such you appear, being over my head, like a winged messenger from heaven whom mortals fall back to gaze upon. 啊，光明的天使，再说点儿什么吧！因为你在我上面出现，正像一个从天上降下来的有翅膀的使者，凡人只能仰起头来瞻望。(比喻修辞)

xv Wherefore art thou Romeo? Deny thy father, and refuse thy name, for my sake; or if thou wilt not, be but my sworn love, and I no longer will be a Capulet. 你为什么是罗密欧？为了我，否认你的父亲，抛弃你的姓氏吧！要是你不愿意的话，只要你发誓永远爱我，我就不再姓凯普莱特了。(wherefore =why, for what reason; art=are; thou=you; thy=your; wilt=will)

xvi The lady continued her passionate discourse with herself (as she thought), still chiding Romeo for being Romeo and a Montague, and wishing him some other name, or that he would put away that hated name, and for that name which was no part of himself, he should take all herself. 那位姑娘继续热情地独自说着(她以为是这样)，仍然怪罗密欧不该叫罗密欧，不该是蒙太古家的人；但愿他姓别的姓，或者把那可恨的姓丢掉；那个姓并不是他本身的任何一部分，丢掉它，他就可以得到她的一切了。(正如朱丽叶在剧中所言：That which we call a rose / By any other name would smell as sweet. 玫瑰若不叫玫瑰，亦无损其芬芳)

xvii At this loving word Romeo could no longer refrain, but taking up the dialogue as if her words had been addressed to him personally, and not merely in fancy, he bade her call him Love, or by whatever other name she pleased, for he was no longer Romeo, if that name was displeasing to her. 罗密欧听到这样缠绵的话，再也按捺不住了，他接着往下说了，仿佛她刚才是直接和他对话，而不是想象着和他对话。他要她管他叫"爱人"，或者随便什么她喜欢的名字；如果她不喜欢罗密欧这个名字，他就不再叫罗密欧了。

xviii Juliet, alarmed to hear a man's voice in the garden, did not at first know who it was, that by favour of the night and darkness had thus stumbled upon the discovery of her secret; but when he spoke again, though her ears had not yet drunk a hundred words of that tongue's uttering, yet so nice is a lover's hearing, that she immediately knew him to be young Romeo, and she expostulated with him on the danger to which he had exposed himself by climbing the orchard walls, for if any of her kinsmen should find him there, it would be death to him, being a Montague. 朱丽叶听到花园里有男人讲话的声音,大吃一惊。最初她不晓得是谁借着黑夜偷听了她的秘密。可是一个情人的耳朵尖得很,罗密欧再一开口,还没说到一百个字,她就马上认出了那正是年轻的罗密欧。她说爬果园的墙很危险,万一她家里人发现了他这个蒙太古家的人,他必死无疑。(so...is..., that...: 部分倒装结构;though her ears had not yet drunk a hundred words of that tongue's uttering: 尽管她的耳朵里还没有灌进从那嘴里吐出来的一百个字)

xix Alack, there is more peril in your eye, than in twenty of their swords. Do you but look kind upon me, lady, and I am proof against their enmity. Better my life should be ended by their hate, than that hated life should be prolonged, to live without your love. 唉,你的眼睛比他们二十把剑还要厉害。只要你对我温存地望一眼,我就不怕他们的仇恨了。我宁可死在他们的仇恨下面,也不愿意延长这可恨的生命而得不到你的爱。(twenty: 泛指数量多,夸张修辞)

xx I am no pilot, yet wert thou as far apart from me, as that vast shore which is washed with the farthest sea, I should venture for such merchandise. 我不是领航员,可是无论你离我多远,哪怕是在天涯海角,我也会冒着风险去找寻你这颗珍宝。(wert = were; thou = you; wert thou... = if you were...)

xxi A crimson blush came over Juliet's face, yet unseen by Romeo by reason of the night, when she reflected upon the discovery which she had made, yet not meaning to make it, of her love to Romeo. 朱丽叶想到自己无意中让罗密欧知道了她对他的爱,脸上就泛起一阵红晕;可是因为夜色昏暗,罗密欧没有看见。

xxii Fain would she have stood upon form, and have kept her lover at a distance, as the custom of discreet ladies is, to frown and be perverse, and give their suitors harsh denials at first; to stand off, and affect a coyness or indifference, where they most love, that their lovers may not think them too lightly or too easily won; for the difficulty of attainment increases the value of the object. 她本想守着礼法,和她的情人保持一定的距离,正如谨慎的闺秀们所习惯的那样:皱着眉头,要耍脾气,先狠狠地拒绝她们的求婚者;显得满不在乎,装作很羞怯、很冷淡,而心里明明很爱。这样,她们的情人才觉得她们不是轻易能得到的。因为一件东西追求起来越是吃力,它的身价就越高。(would she have... = she would have...: 部分倒装)

xxiii So with an honest frankness, which the novelty of her situation excused, she confirmed the truth of what he had before heard, and addressing him by the name of fair Montague (love can sweeten a sour name), she begged him not to impute her easy yielding to levity or an unworthy mind, but that he must lay the fault of it (if it were a fault) upon the accident of the night which had so strangely discovered her thoughts. 由于朱丽叶身处的形势跟一般人的不一样,她就只好坦率地承认他刚才听到的都是她的真心话,并且称呼他为俊秀的蒙太古(爱情可以把一个刺耳的姓变得甜蜜)。她请求他不要把她的轻易让步归因于轻佻或是不端庄,请他务必把这过错(如果这是个过错的话)归咎于夜晚的巧遇,让他意外地发现了她的心思。(...begged..., but that...which...: 宾语从句中嵌套定语从句)

xxiv And she added, that though her behaviour to him might not be sufficiently prudent, measured by the custom of her sex, yet that she would prove more true than many whose prudence was dissembling, and their modesty artificial cunning. 她还说，尽管用女性的礼法来衡量，她对他的举止可能不够端庄，但和那些假装出来的端庄和矫揉造作的腼腆比起来，她要真实多了。(that though…, yet that…whose…：并列的宾语从句中分别嵌套让步状语从句和定语从句)

xxv Romeo was beginning to call the heavens to witness, that nothing was farther from his thoughts than to impute a shadow of dishonour to such an honoured lady, when she stopped him, begging him not to swear; for although she joyed in him, yet she had no joy of that night's contract—it was too rash, too unadvised, too sudden. 罗密欧刚要开口对苍天起誓，说他绝对没想过要怪这样可敬的姑娘有一丝一毫不体面的地方，朱丽叶赶快拦住他，求他不要起誓，因为尽管她很喜欢罗密欧，可是她不喜欢当天晚上就交换誓言，那样做未免太仓促、太轻率、太突兀了。

xxvi But he being urgent with her to exchange a vow of love with him that night, she said that she already had given him hers before he requested it; meaning, when he overheard her confession; but she would retract what she then bestowed, for the pleasure of giving it again, for her bounty was as infinite as the sea, and her love as deep. 但是罗密欧急着要在当天晚上就和她交换爱情的誓言。朱丽叶说，在他没有要求她之前，她就已经对他发过了——意思是他已经偷听到她的告白了。但是她要把已经发过的誓言再收回来，为了享受重新对他发誓的快乐，因为她的慷慨像大海那样没有边际，她的爱也像大海那样深沉。(比喻和夸张修辞)

xxvii She would lay all her fortunes at his feet, and follow him as her lord through the world. 她要把自己的整个命运委托给他，把他当作主人，跟他走到天涯海角。

xxviii She seemed as jealous of Romeo going from her, as a young girl of her bird, which she will let hop a little from her hand, and pluck it back with a silken thread; and Romeo was as loath to part as she; for the sweetest music to lovers is the sound of each other's tongues at night. 她舍不得让罗密欧离开她，就好像一个年轻的姑娘舍不得放走她的鸟儿一样：她会让它从手掌上跳出去一会儿，再用丝线把它拽回来。罗密欧也同样舍不得离开她，因为在情人的耳朵里，最甜蜜的音乐就是他们在深夜里互相倾吐的话语。(比喻修辞；jealous of＝worried about)

xxix But when Romeo revealed his new passion for Juliet, and requested the assistance of the friar to marry them that day, the holy man lifted up his eyes and hands in a sort of wonder at the sudden change in Romeo's affections, for he had been privy to all Romeo's love for Rosaline, and his many complaints of her disdain—and he said, that young men's love lay not truly in their hearts, but in their eyes. 可是当罗密欧告诉劳伦斯神父他最近爱上了朱丽叶，并且请神父帮忙当天就替他们主持婚礼的时候，那位圣洁的人抬起眼睛，举起手来，对罗密欧感情的忽然变化感到惊奇，因为神父一直都知道罗密欧对罗瑟琳的爱，知道他屡次埋怨罗瑟琳看不起自己。他说年轻人的爱不是真的放在心里，只是放在眼里。

xxx Thinking that a matrimonial alliance between young Juliet and Romeo might happily be the means of making up the long breach between the Capulets and the Montagues; which no one more lamented than this good friar, who was a friend to both the families and had often interposed his mediation to make up the quarrel without effect; partly moved by policy, and partly by his fondness for young Romeo, to whom he could deny nothing, the old man consented to join their hands in marriage.（他）想，也许可以借着年轻的朱丽叶跟罗密欧的亲事把凯普莱特跟蒙太古两家多年的冤仇好好消解了呢。这位好神父跟这两家都很要好，他时常想替他们调解，但总没成功，没有人比他更惋惜这种冤仇的了。一半为了达到这个目的，一半也为了他对年轻的罗密欧的喜欢——神父难以拒绝罗密欧的任何要求，神父答应了替他们主持婚礼。

xxxi Now was Romeo blessed indeed, and Juliet, who knew his intent from a messenger which she had despatched according to promise, did not fail to be early at the cell of friar Lawrence, where their hands were joined in holy marriage. 这时候的罗密欧真是幸福极了。朱丽叶照约好的派人来，她通过那人知晓了罗密欧的心意以后，就尽早赶到劳伦斯神父修道的密室，他们在那里举行了神圣的婚礼。（who...which...：定语从句的嵌套，这里的 which 指代人，而在现代英语中只能用 who/whom/that 指代人）

xxxii The time between seemed as tedious to her, as the night before some great festival seems to an impatient child, that has got new finery which it may not put on till the morning. 当中的一段时间对她来说真是难熬啊，就像重大节日的前夜对一个急切的孩子那样，他得到了新衣裳，却要等到第二天早晨才能穿。

xxxiii The name of a Capulet, which was his dear lady's name, was now rather a charm to allay resentment, than a watchword to excite fury. 凯普莱特这个姓氏，也是他心爱的姑娘的姓氏，如今与其说是引起愤怒的暗号，不如说是消解仇恨的灵符。

xxxiv Mercutio, who knew not of Romeo's secret motive for desiring peace with Tybalt, but looked upon his present forbearance as a sort of calm dishonourable submission, with many disdainful words provoked Tybalt to the prosecution of his first quarrel with him. 茂丘西奥不晓得罗密欧想跟提伯尔特讲和的秘密原因，就把当前罗密欧的容忍看作怕事的、不体面的屈服，于是就用许多轻蔑的话来激怒提伯尔特，叫他继续刚才跟自己的争吵。

xxxv Soon after arrived the prince himself, who being related to Mercutio, whom Tybalt had slain, and having had the peace of his government often disturbed by these brawls of Montagues and Capulets, came determined to put the law in strictest force against those who should be found to be offenders. 不久，亲王自己也来了。亲王跟提伯尔特杀死的茂丘西奥是亲戚，而且凯普莱特和蒙太古两家的争吵时常扰乱由他治理的这个地方的安宁，他决定要查出犯法的人来，严加惩办。（...arrived the prince：完全倒装结构；who..., whom...：定语从句的嵌套）

xxxvi She called him a beautiful tyrant, a fiend angelical, a ravenous dove, a lamb with a wolf's nature, a serpent-heart hid with a flowering face, and other like contradictory names, which denoted the struggles in her mind between her love and her resentment. 她管他叫"俊秀的暴君""天使般的魔鬼""像乌鸦的鸽子""性情像豺狼的羊""花容月貌的蛇蝎心肠"，以及其他诸如此类的矛盾的名字，表明她的心在爱与恨之间挣扎着。（矛盾修辞）

xxxvii To him it appeared there was no world out of Verona's walls, no living out of the sight of Juliet. Heaven was there where Juliet lived, and all beyond was purgatory, torture, hell. The good friar would have applied the consolation of philosophy to his griefs—but this frantic young man would hear of none, but like a madman he tore his hair, and threw himself all along upon the ground, as he said, to take the measure of his grave. 对他来说,维洛那的城墙外头就再没有了世界,他看不见朱丽叶就活不下去。朱丽叶所在的地方就是天堂,这以外都是炼狱、酷刑和地狱。那位好神父本想用哲理来安慰他,可是这个疯狂的青年什么也听不进去。他像疯子一样揪自己的头发,整个身子挺在地上,说是要量一量他的墓穴的尺寸。

xxxviii He had slain Tybalt, but would he also slay himself, slay his dear lady, who lived but in his life? 他已经把提伯尔特杀了,难道他还要杀了自己,杀了因他而活的亲爱的妻子吗?(lived but in his life: 因他活着而活着)

xxxix The noble form of man, he said, was but a shape of wax, when it wanted the courage which should keep it firm. 他说,人要是外表上高贵,而内里没有坚定的勇气,那就不过是蜡人而已。(比喻修辞)

xl All these blessings, as the friar made them out to be, did Romeo put from him like a sullen misbehaved wench. 神父指出这种种幸福来,可罗密欧却像一个乖张的、不懂规矩的小姑娘一样,理都不理。(部分倒装;比喻修辞;put from him: 置之不理)

xli And the friar bade him beware, for such as despaired, (he said) died miserable. 神父要他当心,(他说)自暴自弃的人会不得好死。

xlii Then when Romeo was a little calmed, he counselled him that he should go that night and secretly take his leave of Juliet, and thence proceed straightway to Mantua, at which place he should sojourn, till the friar found fit occasion to publish his marriage, which might be a joyful means of reconciling their families; and then he did not doubt but the prince would be moved to pardon him, and he would return with twenty times more joy than he went forth with grief. 等罗密欧平静了一些,神父劝他当天晚上偷偷去跟朱丽叶告别,然后马上就到曼多亚去,在那里住下来,等神父找到适当的机会来公布他跟朱丽叶的婚姻。这个喜讯也许可以使两家和解,神父相信那时候一定可以说动亲王赦免他。罗密欧现在是伤着心走的,到那时候他就可以无比欢欣地回到维洛那来了。(twenty times: 莎士比亚原剧中为 twenty hundred thousand times,更为夸大)

xliii The unwelcome daybreak seemed to come too soon, and when Juliet heard the morning song of the lark, she would have persuaded herself that it was the nightingale, which sings by night; but it was too truly the lark which sang, and a discordant and unpleasing note it seemed to her; and the streaks of day in the east too certainly pointed out that it was time for these lovers to part. 不受欢迎的天明好像来得太快。朱丽叶听到云雀早晨的歌声,她还竭力想叫自己相信那是晚上唱歌的夜莺呢。然而那的确是云雀在唱,而且那歌声在她听来很不和谐、很不悦耳。同时,东方的曙光也清楚地表明,这对恋人分别的时候到了。

xliv When he had descended from her chamber-window, as he stood below her on the ground, in that sad foreboding state of mind in which she was, he appeared to her eyes as one dead in the bottom of a tomb. 罗密欧从她房间的窗口爬下来,站在地上抬头望她,朱丽叶心中充满了悲怆和不祥的感觉,在她看来,他仿佛坟坑底部的一具尸首。

xlv Having found her a husband, rich, young, and noble, such as the proudest maid in Verona might joyfully accept, he could not bear that out of an affected coyness, as he construed her denial, she should oppose obstacles to her own good fortune. 他既然给朱丽叶找到这样一位年轻、富有又高贵的丈夫,一位维洛那城里最骄傲的姑娘也会欣然接受的人物,他就无法忍受她

因为故作矜持(在他看来她的拒绝就是这样)而阻碍自己的好姻缘。(out of…:出于……)

xlvi In this extremity Juliet applied to the friendly friar, always her counsellor in distress, and he asking her if she had resolution to undertake a desperate remedy, and she answering that she would go into the grave alive rather than marry Paris, her own dear husband living. 在这种极端的情况下,朱丽叶就去求助于那位友善的神父了,他一向是她在困境中的顾问。他问她是否有决心采取一个铤而走险的办法,她回答说,她宁愿活着进坟墓,也不愿在自己亲爱的丈夫活着的时候嫁给帕里斯。(he asking…, and she answering that…, …husband living:独立主格结构的并列,宾语从句中嵌套独立主格结构)

xlvii He directed her to go home, and appear merry, and give her consent to marry Paris, according to her father's desire, and on the next night, which was the night before the marriage, to drink off the contents of a phial which he then gave her, the effect of which would be that for two-and-forty hours after drinking it she should appear cold and lifeless. 神父叫她先回家去,装作很高兴地答应照她父亲的意思跟帕里斯结婚。他交给她一小瓶药,叫她第二天晚上,也就是婚礼的前一天晚上,把它喝下去;喝下药以后的四十二小时内,她都会变得僵冷、毫无知觉。

xlviii Then she would be borne, as the manner in that country was, uncovered on a bier, to be buried in the family vault; that if she could put off womanish fear, and consent to this terrible trial, in forty-two hours after swallowing the liquid (such was its certain operation) she would be sure to awake, as from a dream. 然后,人们就会照当地的风俗,把她脸也不蒙地放在柩车上运走,好葬到本族的墓穴里。如果她能够克服女人的胆怯,同意这个可怕的尝试,那么喝下那瓶药四十二小时以后她就一定会醒过来(这是一准灵验的),像做了一场梦似的。(as引导非限制性定语从句)

xlix All things in the house were in a bustle against the approaching nuptials. No cost was spared to prepare such festival rejoicings as Verona had never before witnessed. 全家都在为就要举行的婚礼奔忙着,为了准备这场维洛那前所未见的盛大庆典,凯普莱特家不计成本。(such…as…:定语从句;against=in preparation for)

l She had many misgivings lest the friar, to avoid the blame which might be imputed to him for marrying her to Romeo, had given her poison; but then he was always known for a holy man—then lest she should awake before the time that Romeo was to come for her; whether the terror of the place, a vault of dead Capulets' bones, and where Tybalt, all bloody, lay festering in his shroud, would not be enough to drive her distracted—again she thought of all the stories she had heard of spirits haunting the places where their bodies were bestowed. 她有很多顾虑。她怕神父为了逃避为她和罗密欧证婚的责任,给了她毒药,然而大家一向知道他是个圣洁的人。她又怕没等罗密欧来接,她就先醒过来了。那个可怕的地方堆满了凯普莱特家的人的尸骨,又躺着满身是血、在尸衣里腐烂着的提伯尔特,会不会把她吓得神经错乱呢?她又想起以前听过的一些鬼魂在停着它们尸体的地方转的故事。

li Poor Paris lamenting his bride, whom most detestable death had beguiled him of, had divorced from him even before their hands were joined. 可怜的帕里斯为他的新娘哀悼,最可恨的死神从他手里把她骗了去,甚至没等他们牵手就把他们拆散了。

lii But still more piteous it was to hear the mournings of the old lord and lady Capulet, who having but this one, one poor living child to rejoice and solace in, cruel death had snatched her from their sight, just as these careful parents were on the point of seeing her advanced (as they thought) by a promising and advantageous match. 但听到卡普莱特老爷和夫人的哀哭声就更令人悲伤了。他们只有这么一个孩子，唯一一个活着的孩子，可以带给他们喜悦和安慰。而就在这对尽心的父母即将看到她与一位有前途、门第好的女婿结婚，从此地位提升(他们这样认为)的时候，残酷的死亡却在他们眼前将她夺走。

liii Now all things that were ordained for the festival were turned from their properties to do the office of a black funeral. 这么一来，本来为喜事预备好的一切都改了用场，被拿来办丧事了。

liv The wedding cheer served for a sad burial feast, the bridal hymns were changed for sullen dirges, the sprightly instruments to melancholy bells, and the flowers that should have been strewed in the bride's path, now served but to strew her corse. 婚宴改成悲伤的丧席，婚礼上的颂诗改成了沉痛的挽歌，轻快的乐器改成了忧郁的丧钟，本来准备撒在新娘走的花路上的鲜花只能拿来撒在她的尸身上了。(cheer：酒食)

lv He had dreamed in the night that he was dead (a strange dream, that gave a dead man leave to think), and that his lady came and found him dead, and breathed such life with kisses in his lips, that he revived, and was an emperor! 他夜里梦见自己死了(这真是个奇怪的梦，在梦里死人还能思考)，他的妻子赶来了，发现他死了就亲吻他，把生命吐进他的嘴唇里，他又活了过来，并且成了一个皇帝！

lvi But when the contrary to this flattering vision appeared, and that it was his lady who was dead in truth, whom he could not revive by any kisses, he ordered horses to be got ready, for he determined that night to visit Verona, and to see his lady in her tomb. 可是他听到发生的事跟他梦见的如意情景正相反，原来死了的是他的妻子，而且他怎样吻也吻不活了。于是，他吩咐人替他备马，决定当天晚上去维洛那，到他妻子的坟墓上看她。

lvii Perhaps having some misgivings that his own disastrous life might haply meet with a conclusion so desperate. (他)可能有一些预感，觉得他自己多灾多难的生活也许会落到这样不可挽回的地步。

lviii He knew not what an interest Romeo had in the dead, but knowing him to be a Montague, and (as he supposed) a sworn foe to all the Capulets, he judged that he was come by night to do some villainous shame to the dead bodies; therefore in an angry tone he bade him desist; and as a criminal, condemned by the laws of Verona to die if he were found within the walls of the city, he would have apprehended him. Romeo urged Paris to leave him, and warned him by the fate of Tybalt, who lay buried there, not to provoke his anger, or draw down another sin upon his head, by forcing him to kill him. 他不知道罗密欧跟死者的关系，但知道他是蒙太古家的，跟凯普莱特家所有的人都是死敌(他这样认为)。他猜测罗密欧这样深更半夜跑来，一定是存心来侮辱尸体的。因此，他愤怒地叫他住手，并且说罗密欧是被维洛那的法律判了刑的罪犯，如果被发现出现在城里，就要处死刑。帕里斯要逮住罗密欧，但罗密欧劝帕里斯走开，不然的话，他的下场会跟埋葬在那里的提伯尔特一个样。他警告帕里斯不要惹他发火，不要逼着他把帕里斯也杀死，叫他再犯一次罪。(interest＝concern；was come＝had come)

lix When Romeo, by the help of a light, came to see who it was that he had slain, that it was Paris, who (he learned in his way from Mantua) should have married Juliet, he took the dead youth by the hand, as one whom misfortune had made a companion, and said that he would bury him in a triumphal grave, meaning in Juliet's grave, which he now opened. 罗密

欧借着灯光去看他杀死的是谁，等到看出是本来预备娶朱丽叶的帕里斯（这是他从曼多亚来的路上知道的），就握住那死了的青年的手，像是厄运使帕里斯跟他成了伙伴一样，说要把帕里斯葬在胜利的坟墓里，也就是他现在打开的朱丽叶的坟墓。（in his way＝on his way）

lx There lay his lady，as one whom death had no power upon to change a feature or complexion，in her matchless beauty；or as if death were amorous，and the lean abhorred monster kept her there for his delight. 那儿躺着他的妻子，仿佛死神也无法改变她的容貌和肤色，她仍然无比美丽；又好像死神也爱上了她，所以这个消瘦和讨厌的魔鬼故意把她留下供自己欣赏。

lxi Near her lay Tybalt in his bloody shroud，whom Romeo seeing，begged pardon of his lifeless corpse，and for Juliet's sake called him cousin，and said that he was about to do him a favour by putting his enemy to death. 她旁边躺着裹了血淋淋的尸衣的提伯尔特。罗密欧看见后就对着他的死尸道歉，并且因朱丽叶的缘故，管他叫“堂兄”，说他马上就要替他做一件事：把他的仇人（指罗密欧自己）杀死。

lxii Here he shook the burden of his cross stars from his weary body，swallowing that poison which the apothecary had sold him，whose operation was fatal and real，not like that dissembling potion which Juliet had swallowed，the effect of which was now nearly expiring，and she about to awake to complain that Romeo had not kept his time，or that he had come too soon. 在这里，他从疲惫的身躯上卸去厄运的负担，一口吞下药剂师卖给他的毒药。罗密欧服用的毒药是真的会送命的，和朱丽叶服用的假毒药可不一样。那药的药效快过了，她不久就要苏醒过来，抱怨罗密欧不守时，或者应该说他来得太早了。（cross stars：厄运）

lxiii Before he could entertain a conjecture，to imagine how these fatal accidents had fallen out，Juliet awoke out of her trance，and seeing the friar near her，she remembered the place where she was，and the occasion of her being there，and asked for Romeo，but the friar，hearing a noise，bade her come out of that place of death，and of unnatural sleep，for a greater power than they could contradict had thwarted their intents. 没等神父猜出这起不幸的意外是怎样发生的，朱丽叶就从昏迷状态里醒过来了。她看到神父在旁边，才恍然想起她身在何处和为什么到了这里。她问起罗密欧，可是神父听到有声音传来，就叫她离开这个死亡之地，离开不自然的睡眠，因为一种超乎人力的力量已经挫败了他们的计划。

lxiv Further than this the friar could not follow the story，nor knew more than that coming himself，to deliver Juliet from that place of death，he found the count Paris and Romeo slain. 这以后的事情，神父就说不上来了。他只知道他亲自跑来，打算把朱丽叶从这个死亡之地救出去，结果看到帕里斯和罗密欧都死了。

lxv The remainder of the transactions was supplied by the narration of the page who had seen Paris and Romeo fight，and by the servant who came with Romeo from Verona，to whom this faithful lover had given letters to be delivered to his father in the event of his death，which made good the friar's words，confessing his marriage with Juliet，imploring the forgiveness of his parents，acknowledging the buying of the poison of the poor apothecary，and his intent in coming to the monument，to die，and lie with Juliet. 剩下的情节就由那个看到帕里斯跟罗密欧交手的侍从和随着罗密欧到维洛那来的那个仆人来补充。忠实的情人罗密欧曾经把写给他父亲的信交给这个仆人，嘱咐仆人说如果他死了就替他送去。罗密欧的信证实了神父说的话。他承认跟朱丽叶结了婚，要求他父母饶恕他，也提到从那个可怜的

药剂师手里买到了毒药，他到这灵堂来就是为了寻死，好跟朱丽叶永眠在一起。

lxvi All these circumstances agreed together to clear the friar from any hand he could be supposed to have in these complicated slaughters, further than as the unintended consequences of his own well meant, yet too artificial and subtle contrivances. 所有这些情节都吻合，证明了神父与这起复杂的凶杀案无关。他本是一番好意，然而他的计谋过于巧妙和精细，无意间导致了这后果。

lxvii And the prince, turning to these old lords, Montague and Capulet, rebuked them for their brutal and irrational enmities, and showed them what a scourge Heaven had laid upon such offences, that it had found means even through the love of their children to punish their unnatural hate. 然后亲王转过身来，责备蒙太古老爷和凯普莱特老爷彼此不该怀着这种又野蛮又没理性的仇恨，指出他们已经触犯天怒，上天甚至借着他们子女的恋爱来惩罚他们这种不正常的冤仇。

lxviii But lord Montague said he would give him more, for he would raise her a statue of pure gold, that while Verona kept its name, no figure should be so esteemed for its richness and workmanship as that of the true and faithful Juliet. 可是蒙太古老爷说他要给他更多，他要用纯金替朱丽叶铸一座像，只要维洛那的名字存在一天，就不会有任何一座塑像比真挚、忠诚的朱丽叶的塑像更辉煌、更精致。（that＝the figure）

lxix So did these poor old lords, when it was too late, strive to outdo each other in mutual courtesies—while so deadly had been their rage and enmity in past times, that nothing but the fearful overthrow of their children (poor sacrifices to their quarrels and dissensions) could remove the rooted hates and jealousies of the noble families. 两个可怜的老人家就这样到了无可挽救的时候才争着对彼此示好。过去他们的愤怒和仇恨是那样深，只有他们儿女的悲惨牺牲（他们这些争执、纠纷的可怜的牺牲品），才能消除这两个贵族家庭之间根深蒂固的仇恨和嫉妒。

Juliet. This is thy sheath; there rest, and let me die.
Act V. Scene III.

Romance 传奇剧

暴风雨
The Tempest

Oh，wonder!	神奇啊！
How many goodly creatures are there here!	这里有多少好看的人！
How beauteous mankind is! O brave new world，	人类是多么美丽！啊，辉煌的新世界，
That has such people in 't!	有这么出色的人物！

如果说，有一个人使我心里浮现出这样一个庄严的画面："高高地坐在一块岩石顶上！他脚下风暴雷雨交加，海在咆哮；但他的头部却被明朗的天光照耀着！"那么，莎士比亚就是这样！

——赫尔德

莎士比亚的幻想的对象是多么奇妙地迷人，多么无限地美好！……单是米兰达就是一个充满诗意的美的完整世界。

——别林斯基

这《暴风雨》是何等的一出戏！莎士比亚终于看出了他自己的本色，是一位没有国土的帝王；他是一位很"有力的魔术"的专家，一位大魔术师，以想象为随身的侍从的精灵，能点化沉舟，能奴役敌人，能任意捏合情人；所有的力量都用在温柔仁厚上面。

——弗兰克·哈里斯

他创造的思想和美如此广受传播而俯拾即是，令人出于本能与之亲近。

——简·奥斯汀

莎士比亚这种天才的降临，使得艺术、科学、哲学或者整个社会焕然一新。他的光辉照耀着全人类，从时代的这一个尽头到那一个尽头。

——雨果

主要人物

Prospero　普洛斯彼罗　旧米兰公爵
Miranda　米兰达　普洛斯彼罗的女儿
Ariel　爱丽儿　一个活泼的精灵
Caliban　凯列班　一个野蛮而丑怪的奴隶
Antonio　安东尼奥　普洛斯彼罗的弟弟，米兰的篡位公爵
Gonzalo　贡柴罗　正直的老枢密大臣
Ferdinand　腓迪南　那不勒斯王子
Alonso　阿隆佐　那不勒斯王
Sebastian　西巴斯辛　阿隆佐之弟
Sycorax　西考拉克斯　女巫

地点　海船上；岛上

The Tempest

There was a certain island in the sea, the only inhabitants① of which were an old man, whose name was Prospero, and his daughter Miranda, a very beautiful young lady. She came to this island so young, that she had no memory of having seen any other human face than her father's.

They lived in a cave or cell, made out of a rock; it was divided into several apartments, one of which Prospero called his study; there he kept his books, which chiefly treated of② magic, a study at that time much affected by all learned men—and the knowledge of this art he found very useful to him; for * being thrown by a strange chance upon this island, which had been enchanted by a witch called Sycorax, who died there a short time before his arrival, Prospero, by virtue of③ his art, released many good spirits that Sycorax had imprisoned in the bodies of large trees, because they had refused to execute④ her wicked commands.[i] These gentle spirits were ever after obedient to the will of Prospero. Of these Ariel was the chief⑤.

* The lively little sprite Ariel had nothing mischievous⑥ in his nature, except that he took rather too much pleasure in tormenting⑦ an ugly monster called Caliban, for he owed⑧ him a grudge because he was the son of his old enemy Sycorax.[ii] This Caliban, Prospero found in the woods, a strange misshapen thing, far less human in form than an ape—he took him home to his cell, and taught him to speak; and Prospero would have been very kind to him, but the bad nature which Caliban inherited from his mother Sycorax, would not let him learn anything good or useful—therefore he was employed like a slave, to fetch wood, and do the most laborious⑨

---

① inhabitant [ɪn'hæbɪtənt] *n*. 居民 resident, dweller
② treat of 探讨 discuss, deal with
③ by virtue of 凭借,由于 due to, on account of
④ execute ['eksɪkjuːt] *v*. 执行 enact, perform, carry out
⑤ chief [tʃiːf] *n*. 首领 head, leader, director, commander
⑥ mischievous ['mɪstʃɪvəs] *adj*. 恶意的 harmful, evil
⑦ torment [tɔː'ment] *v*. 折磨 torture, afflict, agonize
⑧ owe [əʊ] *v*. 欠 be in debt, be indebted
⑨ laborious [lə'bɔːriəs] *adj*. 艰苦的 exhausting, backbreaking

offices①; and Ariel had the charge of compelling him to these services.

When Caliban was lazy and neglected his work, Ariel (who was invisible to all eyes but Prospero's) would come slyly② and pinch③ him, and sometimes tumble④ him down in the mire⑤; and then Ariel, in the likeness of an ape, would make mouths at him. Then swiftly changing his shape, in the likeness of a hedgehog⑥, he would lie tumbling in Caliban's way, who feared the hedgehog's sharp quills⑦ would prick⑧ his bare feet. With a variety of such-like vexatious⑨ tricks Ariel would often torment him, whenever Caliban neglected the work which Prospero commanded him to do.

Having these powerful spirits obedient to his will, Prospero could by their means command the winds, and the waves of the sea. * By his orders they raised a violent storm, in the midst of which, and struggling with the wild sea-waves that every moment threatened to swallow it up, he showed his daughter a fine large ship, which he told her was full of living beings like themselves.[iii] "O my dear father," said she, "if by your art you have raised this dreadful storm, have pity on their sad distress. See! The vessel will be dashed⑩ to pieces. Poor souls! They will all perish⑪. * If I had power, I would sink the sea beneath the earth, rather than the good ship should be destroyed, with all the precious souls within her.[iv]"

"Be not so amazed, daughter Miranda," said Prospero, "there is no harm done. I have so ordered it, that no person in the ship shall receive any hurt. What I have done has been in care of you⑫, my dear child. You are ignorant⑬ who you are, or where you came from, and you know no more of me, but that I am your father, and live in this poor cave. Can you remember a time before you came to this cell? I think you cannot for you were not then three years of age."

"Certainly I can, sir," replied Miranda.

"By what?" asked Prospero. "By any other house or person? Tell me what you can remember, my child."

Miranda said: "It seems to me like the recollection of a dream. But had I not once four or five

---

① office ['ɒfɪs] *n*. 职务 duty
② slyly ['slaɪli] *adv*. 狡猾地 trickily, artfully, foxily
③ pinch [pɪntʃ] *v*. 拧,捏 squeeze
④ tumble ['tʌmbl] *v*. 使跌倒 fall, topple, stumble
⑤ mire ['maɪə(r)] *n*. 泥潭 bog, marsh, swamp
⑥ hedgehog ['hedʒhɒg] *n*. 刺猬
⑦ quill [kwɪl] *n*. (刺猬的)刺
⑧ prick [prɪk] *v*. 刺,戳 pierce, stab, puncture, impale
⑨ vexatious [vek'seɪʃəs] *adj*. 令人烦恼的 annoying, bothersome
⑩ dash [dæʃ] *v*. 猛撞 break, crash, smash, shatter, splinter
⑪ perish ['perɪʃ] *v*. 死亡 die, expire, decease, pass away
⑫ in care of you 为你打算 for your benefit, in your interest
⑬ ignorant ['ɪgnərənt] *adj*. 无知的 uninformed

women who attended upon[①] me?"

Prospero answered: "You had, and more. How is it that this still[②] lives in your mind? Do you remember how you came here?"

"No, sir," said Miranda, "I remember nothing more."

"Twelve years ago, Miranda," continued Prospero, "I was duke of Milan, and you were a princess, and my only heir. I had a younger brother, whose name was Antonio, to whom I trusted everything—and as I was fond of retirement[③] and deep study, I commonly left the management of my state affairs to your uncle, my false brother (for so indeed he proved)—I, neglecting all worldly ends[④], buried among my books, did dedicate[⑤] my whole time to the bettering of my mind. My brother Antonio being thus in possession of my power, began to think himself the duke indeed. * The opportunity I gave him of making himself popular among my subjects[⑥] awakened in his bad nature a proud ambition to deprive me of my dukedom ∨ —this he soon effected with the aid of the king of Naples, a powerful prince, who was my enemy."

"Wherefore[⑦]," said Miranda, "did they not that hour destroy us?"

"My child," answered her father, "they durst[⑧] not, so dear was the love that my people bore me. Antonio carried us on board a ship, and when we were some leagues out at sea, he forced us into a small boat, without either tackle[⑨], sail[⑩], or mast[⑪] there he left us, as he thought, to perish. But a kind lord of my court, one Gonzalo, who loved me, had privately placed in the boat, water, provisions[⑫], apparel, and some books which I prize above my dukedom."

"O my father," said Miranda, "what a trouble must I have been to you then!"

"No, my love," said Prospero, "you were a little cherub[⑬] that did preserve me. Your innocent smiles made me bear up against[⑭] my misfortunes. Our food lasted till we landed on this

---

① attend upon 照料 look after, care for, take care of
② still [stɪl] *adv*. 一直,总是 always, for ever, at all times
③ retirement [rɪˈtaɪəmənt] *n*. 独处,退隐 retreat, solitude
④ worldly ends 世俗的事务 temporal/secular affairs
⑤ dedicate [ˈdedɪkeɪt] *v*. 奉献 devote, commit
⑥ subject [ˈsʌbdʒɪkt] *n*. 臣民 citizen, resident, inhabitant
⑦ wherefore [ˈweəfɔː(r)] *adv*. 为什么 why, for what reason
⑧ durst [dɜːst] (= dared) *v*. 〈古〉敢于(dare 的过去式)
⑨ tackle [ˈtækl] *n*. 索具
⑩ sail [seɪl] *n*. 帆
⑪ mast [mɑːst] *n*. 桅杆
⑫ provision [prəˈvɪʒn] *n*. 供给 supply
⑬ cherub [ˈtʃerəb] *n*. 小天使 angel
⑭ bear up against 在……面前不颓丧,鼓起勇气对付

desert① island, since when my chief delight has been in teaching you, Miranda, and well have you profited② by my instructions."

"Heaven thank you, my dear father," said Miranda. "Now pray③ tell me, sir, your reason for raising this sea-storm?"

"Know then," said her father, "that by means of this storm, my enemies, the king of Naples, and my cruel brother, are cast ashore④ upon this island."

Having so said, Prospero gently touched his daughter with his magic wand, and she fell fast asleep; for the spirit Ariel just then presented himself before his master, to give an account of the tempest, and how he had disposed of⑤ the ship's company, and though the spirits were always invisible to Miranda, Prospero did not choose⑥ she should hear him holding converse⑦ (as would seem to her) with the empty air.

"Well, my brave⑧ spirit," said Prospero to Ariel, "how have you performed your task?"

Ariel gave a lively description of the storm, and of the terrors of the mariners⑨; and how the king's son, Ferdinand, was the first who leaped into the sea; and his father thought he saw his dear son swallowed up by the waves and lost. "But he is safe," said Ariel, "in a corner of the isle, sitting with his arms folded, sadly lamenting the loss of the king, his father, whom he concludes drowned. Not a hair of his head is injured, and his princely garments, though drenched⑩ in the sea-waves, look fresher than before."

"That's my delicate⑪ Ariel," said Prospero. "Bring him hither—my daughter must see this young prince. Where is the king, and my brother?"

"I left them," answered Ariel, "searching for Ferdinand, whom they have little hopes of finding, thinking they saw him perish. Of the ship's crew not one is missing; though each one thinks himself the only one saved—and the ship, though invisible to them, is safe in the harbour."

"Ariel," said Prospero, "thy charge is faithfully performed—but there is more work yet."

"Is there more work?" said Ariel. "Let me remind you, master, you have promised me my liberty. I pray, remember, I have done you worthy service, told you no lies, made no mistakes, served you without grudge or grumbling⑫."

"How now!" said Prospero. "You do not recollect what a torment I freed you from. * Have you forgot the wicked witch Sycorax, who with age and envy was almost bent double?[vi] Where was she born? Speak; tell me."

"Sir, in Algiers," said Ariel.

① desert [ˈdezət] *adj*. 荒凉的 wild, bare, barren, desolate
② profit [ˈprɒfɪt] *v*. 获益 benefit, gain, turn to sb's advantage
③ pray [preɪ] (=please) *adv*. 请
④ ashore [əˈʃɔː(r)] *adv*. 在岸上 aground, on land, on the shore
⑤ dispose of 处理 handle, deal with
⑥ choose [tʃuːz] *v*. 情愿 wish, desire
⑦ converse [ˈkɒnvɜːs] *n*. 〈古〉谈话 talk, conversation
⑧ brave [breɪv] *adj*. 机灵的 clever, bright, brilliant
⑨ mariner [ˈmærɪnə(r)] *n*. 水手 sailor, seaman, sea dog
⑩ drench [drentʃ] *v*. 使湿透 wet, soak, saturate
⑪ delicate [ˈdelɪkət] *adj*. 敏锐的 sensitive, thoughtful, considerate
⑫ grumble [ˈgrʌmbl] *v*. 抱怨 complain, gripe, grouse, grouch

"O was she so?" said Prospero. "I must recount① what you have been, which I find you do not remember. * This bad witch, Sycorax, for her witchcrafts②, too terrible to enter human hearing, was banished from Algiers, and here left by the sailors; and because you were a spirit too delicate to execute her wicked commands, she shut you up in a tree, where I found you howling③.[vii] This torment, remember, I did free you from."

"Pardon me, dear master," said Ariel, ashamed to seem ungrateful. "I will obey your commands."

"Do so," said Prospero, "and I will set you free." He then gave orders what further he would have him do; and away went Ariel, first to where he had left Ferdinand, and found him still sitting on the grass in the same melancholy posture.

"O my young gentleman," said Ariel, when he saw him, "I will soon move you. You must be brought, I find, for the Lady Miranda to have a sight of your pretty person. Come, sir, follow me." He then began singing—

"* Full fathom five thy father lies—
Of his bones are coral made;
Those are pearls that were his eyes—
Nothing of him that doth fade,
But doth suffer a sea-change
Into something rich and strange.
Sea-nymphs hourly ring his knell—
Hark! now I hear them, —Ding-dong, bell.[viii]"

This strange news of his lost father soon roused the prince from the stupid fit④ into which he had fallen. He followed in amazement the sound of Ariel's voice, till it led him to Prospero and Miranda, who were sitting under the shade of a large tree. Now Miranda had never seen a man before, except her own father.

"Miranda," said Prospero, "tell me what you are looking at yonder⑤."

"O father," said Miranda, in a strange surprise, "surely that is a spirit. Lord! How it looks about! Believe me, sir, it is a beautiful creature. Is it not a spirit?"

"No, girl," answered her father, "it eats, and sleeps, and has senses such as we have. This young man you see was in the ship. He is somewhat altered by grief, or you might call him a handsome person. He has lost his companions, and is wandering about to find them."

Miranda, who thought all men had grave faces and grey beards like her father, was delighted with the appearance of this beautiful young prince; and Ferdinand, seeing such a lovely lady in this desert place, and from the strange sounds he had heard, expecting nothing but wonders, thought

---

① recount [rɪˈkaʊnt] *v*. 叙述 relate, narrate, give an account of
② witchcraft [ˈwɪtʃkrɑːft] *n*. 巫术 magic, sorcery
③ howl [haʊl] *v*. 大声叫喊 cry, shout, roar, yell, scream
④ stupid fit 昏沉状态 mindless/senseless state
⑤ yonder [ˈjɒndə(r)] *adv*. 在那边

he was upon an enchanted① island, and that Miranda was the goddess of the place, and as such he began to address her.

She timidly answered, she was no goddess, but a simple maid, and was going to give him an account of herself, when Prospero interrupted her. He was well pleased to find they admired each other, for he plainly perceived they had (as we say) fallen in love at first sight—but * to try Ferdinand's constancy②, he resolved to throw some difficulties in their way—therefore advancing forward, he addressed the prince with a stern③ air, telling him, he came to the island as a spy, to take it from him who was the lord of it.[ix] "Follow me," said he, "I will tie your neck and feet together. You shall drink sea-water; shell-fish, withered④ roots, and husks of acorns shall be your food." "No," said Ferdinand, "I will resist such entertainment, till I see a more powerful enemy," and drew his sword; but Prospero, waving his magic wand, fixed him to the spot where he stood, so that he had no power to move.

Miranda hung upon her father, saying: "Why are you so ungentle? Have pity, sir; I will be his surety⑤. This is the second man I ever saw, and to me he seems a true one."

"Silence," said the father, "one word more will make me chide you, girl! What! An advocate⑥ for an impostor⑦! You think there are no more such fine men, having seen only him and Caliban. * I tell you, foolish girl, most men as far excel⑧ this, as he does Caliban.[x]" This he said to prove his daughter's constancy; and she replied: "* My affections are most humble. I have no wish to see a goodlier⑨ man.[xi]"

"Come on, young man," said Prospero to the prince. "You have no power to disobey⑩ me."

"I have not indeed," answered Ferdinand; and * not knowing that it was by magic he was deprived of all power of resistance, he was astonished to find himself so strangely compelled to follow Prospero[xii] —looking back on Miranda as long as he could see her, he said, as he went after Prospero into the cave, "* My spirits are all bound up as if I were in a dream; but this man's threats, and the weakness which I feel, would seem light to me if from my prison I might once a day behold this fair maid.[xiii]"

Prospero kept Ferdinand not long confined⑪ within the cell—he soon brought out his prisoner, and set him a severe task to perform, taking care to let his daughter know the hard labour he had imposed⑫ on him, and then pretending to go into his study, he secretly watched them both.

Prospero had commanded Ferdinand to pile up some heavy logs of wood. Kings' sons not being

---

① enchanted [ɪn'tʃɑːntɪd] *adj*. 中魔法的 bewitched, under a spell
② constancy ['kɒnstənsi] *n*. 坚定 firmness, steadfastness
③ stern [stɜːn] *adj*. 严厉的 strict, hard, harsh, rigorous
④ wither ['wɪðə(r)] *v*. 枯萎 wilt, dry
⑤ surety ['ʃʊərəti] *n*. 担保；保证人 guarantee, guarantor
⑥ advocate ['ædvəkət] *n*. 拥护者 backer, supporter, defender
⑦ impostor [ɪm'pɒstə(r)] *n*. 骗子 fraud, cheat, deceiver
⑧ excel [ɪk'sel] *v*. 胜过 beat, outdo, surpass, be superior to
⑨ goodly ['gʊdli] *adj*. 好看的 good-looking, handsome, attractive
⑩ disobey [ˌdɪsə'beɪ] *v*. 不服从 defy, ignore, rebel, resist
⑪ confine [kən'faɪn] *v*. 监禁 imprison, enclose, cage
⑫ impose [ɪm'pəʊz] *v*. 强加 force, enforce, press

much used to laborious work, Miranda soon after found her lover almost dying with fatigue. "Alas!" said she, "do not work so hard; * my father is at his studies, he is safe for these three hours; pray rest yourself.[xiv]"

"O my dear lady," said Ferdinand, "I dare not. I must finish my task before I take my rest."

"If you will sit down," said Miranda, "I will carry your logs the while." But this Ferdinand would by no means① agree to. Instead of a help Miranda became a hindrance②, for they began a long conversation, so that the business of log-carrying went on very slowly.

Prospero, who had enjoined③ Ferdinand this task merely as a trial④ of his love, was not at his books, as his daughter supposed, but was standing by them invisible, to overhear⑤ what they said.

Ferdinand inquired her name, which she told, saying it was against her father's express⑥ command she did so.

* Prospero only smiled at this first instance of his daughter's disobedience⑦, for having by his magic art caused his daughter to fall in love so suddenly, he was not angry that she showed her love by forgetting to obey his commands.[xv] And he listened well pleased to a long speech of Ferdinand's, in which he professed to love her above all the ladies he ever saw.

In answer to his praises of her beauty, which he said exceeded⑧ all the women in the world, she replied: "I do not remember the face of any woman, nor have I seen any more men than you, my good friend, and my dear father. * How features are abroad, I know not; but, believe me, sir, I would not wish any companion in the world but you, nor can my imagination form any shape but yours that I could like.[xvi] But, sir, I fear I talk to you too freely, and my father's precepts⑨ I forget."

At this Prospero smiled, and nodded his head, as much as to say, "This goes on exactly as I could wish; my girl will be queen of Naples."

And then Ferdinand, in another fine long speech (for young princes speak in courtly⑩ phrases), told the innocent Miranda he was heir to the crown of Naples, and that she should be his queen.

"Ah! sir," said she, "I am a fool to weep at what I am glad of. I will answer you in plain and holy innocence. I am your wife if you will marry me."

---

① by no means 绝不 in no way, at no time, on no account
② hindrance[ˈhɪndrəns] *n*. 妨碍 barrier, block, obstacle
③ enjoin [ɪnˈdʒɔɪn] *v*. 吩咐,命令 order, command
④ trial [ˈtraɪəl] *n*. 考验 test, experiment, proof, try-out
⑤ overhear [əʊvəˈhɪə(r)] *v*. 偷听 eavesdrop, listen in
⑥ express [ɪkˈspres] *adj*. 明确的 clear, direct, particular, distinct
⑦ disobedience [dɪsəˈbiːdiəns] *n*. 不服从 revolt, defiance
⑧ exceed [ɪkˈsiːd] *v*. 超过 excel, outdo, surpass, be superior to
⑨ precept [ˈpriːsept] *n*. 戒律,规则 rule, order, principle, regulation
⑩ courtly [ˈkɔːtli] *adj*. 温文尔雅的 civil, refined, polite, dignified, elegant

Prospero prevented Ferdinand's thanks by appearing visible before them.

"Fear nothing, my child," said he. "I have overheard, and approve of[1] all you have said. And, Ferdinand, if I have too severely used you, I will make you rich amend, by giving you my daughter. All your vexations[2] were but trials of your love, and you have nobly stood the test[3]. Then as my gift, which your true love has worthily purchased, take my daughter, and do not smile that I boast she is above all praise." He then, telling them that he had business which required his presence, desired they would sit down and talk together till he returned; and this command Miranda seemed not at all disposed[4] to disobey.

When Prospero left them, he called his spirit Ariel, who quickly appeared before him, eager to relate what he had done with Prospero's brother and the king of Naples. Ariel said he had left them almost out of their senses[5] with fear, at the strange things he had caused them to see and hear. When fatigued[6] with wandering about, and famished for want of food, he had suddenly set before them a delicious banquet, and then, just as they were going to eat, he appeared visible before them in the shape of a harpy[7], a voracious[8] monster with wings, and the feast[9] vanished away. Then, to their utter[10] amazement, this seeming harpy spoke to them, reminding them of their cruelty in driving Prospero from his dukedom, and leaving him and his infant daughter to perish in the sea; saying, that for this cause these terrors were suffered[11] to afflict them.

The king of Naples, and Antonio the false brother, repented[12] the injustice they had done to Prospero; and Ariel told his master he was certain their penitence was sincere, and that he, though a spirit, could not but pity them.

"Then bring them hither, Ariel," said Prospero, "if you, who are but a spirit, feel for[13] their distress, shall not I, who am a human being like themselves, have compassion[14] on them? Bring them, quickly, my dainty[15] Ariel."

Ariel soon returned with the king, Antonio, and old Gonzalo in their train, who had followed him, wondering at the wild music he played in the air to draw them on to his master's presence. This Gonzalo was the same who had so kindly provided Prospero formerly with books and provisions, when his wicked brother left him, as he thought, to perish in

① approve of 赞成 favour, support, agree with
② vexation [vek'seɪʃn] n. 恼火 annoyance, irritation
③ stand the test 经受住考验
④ disposed [dɪ'spəʊzd] adj. 有……倾向的 tending, inclined, prone
⑤ out of one's senses 某人失去理智
⑥ fatigued [fə'ti:gd] adj. 精疲力竭的 tired, weary, exhausted
⑦ harpy ['hɑ:pi] n. 鸟身女妖;残酷贪婪的人
⑧ voracious [və'reɪʃəs] adj. 贪吃的 greedy, gluttonous, devouring
⑨ feast [fi:st] n. 盛宴 banquet, meal, dinner
⑩ utter ['ʌtə(r)] adj. 完全的,彻底的 absolute, complete, total, thorough
⑪ suffer ['sʌfə(r)] v. 听任,容许 allow, bear, stand, tolerate, put up with
⑫ repent [rɪ'pent] v. 后悔 regret, feel remorse
⑬ feel for 同情 pity, feel sorry for, sympathize with
⑭ compassion [kəm'pæʃn] n. 怜悯,同情 pity, sympathy
⑮ dainty ['deɪnti] adj. 美丽的,秀丽的 delicate, charming

an open boat in the sea.

Grief and terror had so stupefied[①] their senses, that they did not know Prospero. He first discovered himself[②] to the good old Gonzalo, calling him the preserver of his life; and then his brother and the king knew that he was the injured Prospero.

Antonio with tears, and sad words of sorrow and true repentance, implored his brother's forgiveness, and the king expressed his sincere remorse[③] for having assisted Antonio to depose his brother—and Prospero forgave them; and, upon their engaging[④] to restore his dukedom, he said to the king of Naples: "I have a gift in store[⑤] for you too"; and opening a door, showed him his son Ferdinand playing at chess with Miranda.

Nothing could exceed the joy of the father and the son at this unexpected meeting, for they each thought the other drowned in the storm.

"O wonder!" said Miranda, "what noble creatures these are! It must surely be a brave[⑥] world that has such people in it."

The king of Naples was almost as much astonished at the beauty and excellent graces of the young Miranda, as his son had been. "Who is this maid?" said he, "she seems the goddess that has parted us, and brought us thus together." "No, sir," answered Ferdinand, smiling to find his father had fallen into the same mistake that he had done when he first saw Miranda, "she is a mortal[⑦] but by immortal Providence[⑧] she is mine; I chose her when I could not ask you, my father, for your consent, not thinking you were alive. She is the daughter to this Prospero, who is the famous duke of Milan, of whose renown[⑨] I have heard so much, but never saw him till now—of him I have received a new life—he has made himself to me a second father, giving me this dear lady."

"Then I must be her father," said the king, "but oh! how oddly[⑩] will it sound, that I must ask my child forgiveness."

"No more of that," said Prospero, "let us not remember our troubles past, since they so happily have ended." And then Prospero embraced his brother, and again assured him of his forgiveness; and said that a wise overruling[⑪] Providence had permitted that he should be driven from his poor dukedom of Milan, that his daughter might inherit the crown of Naples, for that[⑫] by their meeting in this desert island, it had happened that the king's son had loved Miranda.

These kind words which Prospero spoke, meaning to comfort his brother, so filled Antonio with shame and remorse, that he wept and was unable to speak; and the kind old Gonzalo wept to

---

① stupefy ['stjuːpɪfaɪ] *v*. 使惊讶;使昏迷 surprise, shock, astonish
② discover oneself 表明自己身份
③ remorse [rɪ'mɔːs] *n*. 懊悔 regret, contrition, self-reproach
④ engage [ɪn'geɪdʒ] *v*. 承诺,允诺 promise, guarantee, pledge
⑤ in store 准备着,预备着 ready, prepared, in readiness
⑥ brave [breɪv] *adj*. 美丽的 pretty, lovely, beautiful
⑦ mortal ['mɔːtl] *n*. 凡人 human, human being, earthling
⑧ Providence ['prɒvɪdəns] *n*. 天命,上帝,苍天 fate, destiny, God's will
⑨ renown [rɪ'naʊn] *n*. 声望,名誉 fame, repute, reputation
⑩ oddly ['ɒdli] *adv*. 怪异地 strangely, bizarrely, singularly
⑪ overruling [ˌəʊvə'ruːlɪŋ] *adj*. 统治的 controlling, governing
⑫ for that 因为 as, since, in that, because

see this joyful reconciliation, and prayed for blessings on the young couple.

Prospero now told them that their ship was safe in the harbour, and the sailors all on board her, and that he and his daughter would accompany them home the next morning. "* In the meantime," says he, "partake of① such refreshments② as my poor cave affords; and for your evening's entertainment I will relate the history of my life from my first landing in this desert island.[xvii]" He then called for Caliban to prepare some food, and set the cave in order; and the company were astonished at the uncouth③ form and savage appearance of this ugly monster, who (Prospero said) was the only attendant he had to wait upon him.

Before Prospero left the island, he dismissed Ariel from his service, to the great joy of that lively little spirit; who, though he had been a faithful servant to his master, was always longing to enjoy his free liberty, to wander uncontrolled in the air, like a wild bird, under green trees, among pleasant fruits, and sweet-smelling flowers. "My quaint④ Ariel," said Prospero to the little sprite when he made him free, "I shall miss you; yet you shall have your freedom." "Thank you, my dear master," said Ariel, "* but give me leave⑤ to attend your ship home with prosperous⑥ gales⑦, before you bid farewell to⑧ the assistance of your faithful spirit;[xviii] and then, master, when I am free, how merrily I shall live!" Here Ariel sung this pretty song:

"* Where the bee sucks, there suck I;
In a cowslip's bell I lie;
There I crouch when owls do cry.
On the bat's back I do fly
After summer merrily.
Merrily, merrily shall I live now
Under the blossom that hangs on the bough.[xix]"

Prospero then buried deep in the earth his magical books and wand, for he was resolved never more to make use of the magic art. And having thus overcome his enemies, and being reconciled to his brother and the king of Naples, nothing now remained to complete his happiness, but to revisit his native land, to take possession of his dukedom, and to witness the happy nuptials of his daughter and Prince Ferdinand, which the king said should be instantly celebrated with great

---

① partake of 享用 eat, drink, consume
② refreshment [rɪˈfreʃmənts] *n*. 茶点 dimsum
③ uncouth [ʌnˈkuːθ] *adj*. 粗野的,笨拙的 rough, coarse, awkward, clumsy
④ quaint [kweɪnt] *adj*. 机灵的,古怪的 clever, smart, shrewd, quick-witted
⑤ leave [liːv] *n*. 准许,许可 permission, consent, sanction
⑥ prosperous [ˈprɒspərəs] *adj*. 繁荣的,富足的
⑦ gale [geɪl] *n*. 大风 hurricane, whirlwind
⑧ bid farewell to 向……告别 say goodbye to

splendour on their return to Naples. At which place, under the safe convoy[①] of the spirit Ariel, they, after a pleasant voyage, soon arrived.

i Being thrown by a strange chance upon this island, which had been enchanted by a witch called Sycorax, who died there a short time before his arrival, Prospero, by virtue of his art, released many good spirits that Sycorax had imprisoned in the bodies of large trees, because they had refused to execute her wicked commands. 普洛斯彼罗是由于一个奇怪的机缘漂到这座岛上的。这座岛曾经被一个名叫西考拉克斯的女巫施过法术，在普洛斯彼罗到达之前不久她死了。普洛斯彼罗凭着自己的魔法，解放了许多善良的精灵。这些精灵因为不肯照西考拉克斯的邪恶命令办事，曾经被她囚禁在一些大树干里。(being thrown...：现在分词被动式作状语；which..., who...that...：三重定语从句)

ii The lively little sprite Ariel had nothing mischievous in his nature, except that he took rather too much pleasure in tormenting an ugly monster called Caliban, for he owed him a grudge because he was the son of his old enemy Sycorax. 这个活泼的小精灵爱丽儿本性不坏，他只是喜欢捉弄一个名叫凯列班的丑妖怪。他恨凯列班，因为凯列班是他以前的仇人西考拉克斯的儿子。(owed him a grudge：与他有宿怨)

iii By his orders they raised a violent storm, in the midst of which, and struggling with the wild sea-waves that every moment threatened to swallow it up, he showed his daughter a fine large ship, which he told her was full of living beings like themselves. 按照他的吩咐，他们兴起一阵猛烈的风浪，一艘精美的大船正在狂暴的波涛中挣扎着，随时都会被波涛吞没。普洛斯彼罗指着船对女儿说，船里载满了和他们一样的生灵。(struggling...：分词修饰 ship)

iv If I had power, I would sink the sea beneath the earth, rather than the good ship should be destroyed, with all the precious souls within her. 我要是有力量的话，宁可叫大海沉到地底下，也不愿让这么好的一艘船和船上所载的宝贵的生灵毁灭。(If I had..., I would...：与现在事实相反的虚拟语气；power＝magical power)

v The opportunity I gave him of making himself popular among my subjects awakened in his bad nature a proud ambition to deprive me of my dukedom. 我给他机会让他在我的臣民中建立起威望，却激起了他邪恶本性里的狂妄野心，他竟想夺取我的爵位。

vi Have you forgot the wicked witch Sycorax, who with age and envy was almost bent double? 你难道忘记那个凶恶的女巫西考拉克斯了吗？她因为年老和善妒，身体几乎弓成了一个圈。

---

① convoy [ˈkɒnvɔɪ] *n*. 护送 guard, protection

(forgot＝forgotten：莎士比亚常用动词过去式代替过去分词，属过时用法；almost bent double：身子几乎是弓着的)

vii This bad witch，Sycorax，for her witchcrafts，too terrible to enter human hearing，was banished from Algiers，and here left by the sailors；and because you were a spirit too delicate to execute her wicked commands，she shut you up in a tree，where I found you howling. 没有人听到这个坏女巫西考拉克斯的法术能不害怕，所以她被驱逐出了阿尔及尔，水手们把她丢在这里。你心太软，不能照着她的邪恶命令办事，她就把你囚在大树里，是我发现你在那儿哇哇哭着呢。

viii

Full fathom five thy father lies—	五寻的水深处躺着你的父亲，
Of his bones are coral made；	他的骨骼已化成珊瑚；
Those are pearls that were his eyes—	他眼睛是耀眼的明珠；
Nothing of him that doth fade，	他消失的全身没有一处不曾
But doth suffer a sea-change	受到海水神奇的变幻，
Into something rich and strange.	化成瑰宝，富丽的珍怪。
Sea-nymphs hourly ring his knell—	海的女神时时摇起他的丧钟，
Hark! now I hear them，—Ding-dong，bell.	听！我现在听到了叮咚的丧钟。

ix To try Ferdinand's constancy，he resolved to throw some difficulties in their way—therefore advancing forward，he addressed the prince with a stern air，telling him，he came to the island as a spy，to take it from him who was the lord of it. 为了试试腓迪南的爱情究竟靠不靠得住，他决定故意为难他们一下。于是他走过去，正言厉色地说王子是个奸细，到岛上来是想从他这个岛主手里把岛夺走。

x I tell you，foolish girl，most men as far excel this，as he does Caliban. 我告诉你，愚蠢的姑娘，大多数男人都比他好多了，就像他比凯列班好一样。(as：引导方式状语从句；does＝excels)

xi My affections are most humble. I have no wish to see a goodlier man. 我对爱情的所求并不多，我也不奢望看到一个比他更漂亮的男人。

xii Not knowing that it was by magic he was deprived of all power of resistance，he was astonished to find himself so strangely compelled to follow Prospero. 他还不知道是魔法叫他失掉了所有抵抗的力量，他吃惊地发现自己不得不莫名其妙地跟着普洛斯彼罗走。(not knowing…：现在分词否定形式作状语)

xiii My spirits are all bound up as if I were in a dream；but this man's threats，and the weakness which I feel，would seem light to me if from my prison I might once a day behold this fair maid. 我的精神全都被束缚住了，好像在梦里一样；可是只要我能每天从牢房里看一眼这位美丽的姑娘，这个人的威胁恐吓和我浑身感觉到的虚弱，对我来说都算不了什么。(as if I were…：非真实条件句)

xiv My father is at his studies，he is safe for these three hours；pray rest yourself. 我父亲正读书呢，这三个钟头以内他不会来的，请你歇歇吧。(he is safe：指对米兰达和腓迪南来说是安全的，因为她的父亲不会来；pray＝please)

xv Prospero only smiled at this first instance of his daughter's disobedience，for having by his magic art caused his daughter to fall in love so suddenly，he was not angry that she showed her love by forgetting to obey his commands. 普洛斯彼罗对他女儿头一回的违抗命令只是微

微笑了笑，因为是他用魔法叫他女儿这么快就陷进情网的，所以对于她女儿为了示爱而忘记服从他的命令这件事，他并不生气。

xvi How features are abroad, I know not; but, believe me, sir, I would not wish any companion in the world but you, nor can my imagination form any shape but yours that I could like. 外面的人长什么样，我不知道；但是相信我，先生，除了您，在这个世界上我不愿有别的伴侣；除了您，我再也想象不出一个让我喜欢的容貌。（how…：宾语从句前置；know not＝do not know：中世纪英语否定形式常直接在动词后加 not；nor…：否定部分倒装；but＝except：除……之外，只有）

xvii In the meantime, partake of such refreshments as my poor cave affords; and for your evening's entertainment I will relate the history of my life from my first landing in this desert island. 这会儿，请来享用我这破洞窟所能招待的吃食吧。晚上，我要把我在这个荒岛上度过的生活讲给你们听，给你们解解闷。

xviii But give me leave to attend your ship home with prosperous gales, before you bid farewell to the assistance of your faithful spirit. 可是，先让我用和风把你们的船吹送到家，然后你再跟帮助过你的这个忠实仆人告别吧。

xix Where the bee sucks, there suck I;	蜂儿吮啜的地方，我也在那儿吮啜；
In a cowslip's bell I lie;	在一朵莲香花的冠中我躺着休息；
There I crouch when owls do cry.	我安然睡去，当夜枭开始它的鸣咽。
On the bat's back I do fly	骑在蝙蝠背上我快活地飞舞翩翩，
After summer merrily.	快活地快活地追随着逝去的夏天；
Merrily, merrily shall I live now	快活地快活地我要如今
Under the blossom that hangs on the bough.	向垂在枝头的花底安身。